Microsoft

Microsoft®
Commerce
Server 2000

W9-AGQ-589

Resource Kit

PUBLISHED BY
Microsoft Press
A Division of Microsoft Corporation
One Microsoft Way
Redmond, Washington 98052-6399

Library of Congress Cataloging-in-Publication Data
Microsoft Commerce Server 2000 Resource Kit / Microsoft Corporation.
     p. cm.
  Includes index.
  ISBN 0-7356-1128-9
    1. Microsoft Commerce Server.   2. Electronic commerce.   I. Microsoft Corporation.
  HF5548.32 .M53 2001
  005.7'13769--dc21   00-051954

Printed and bound in the United States of America.

1 2 3 4 5 6 7 8 9   MLML   6 5 4 3 2 1

Distributed in Canada by Penguin Books Canada Limited.

A CIP catalogue record for this book is available from the British Library.

Microsoft Press books are available through booksellers and distributors worldwide. For further information about international editions, contact your local Microsoft Corporation office or contact Microsoft Press International directly at fax (425) 936-7329. Visit our Web site at mspress.microsoft.com. Send comments to *rkinput@microsoft.com.*

Acquisitions Editor: Juliana Aldous
Project Editor: Maureen Williams Zimmerman

Principal Writer: Carolyn Bryce

Contributing Writers:

Diane Faigel, Grant Fjermedal, Charles Freeman, Liza Leif,
John MacKenzie, Robin Van Steenburgh, Jamie Westover

Project Manager: Robin Van Steenburgh

Resource Kit CD Release Manager: Alex Shogren

Documentation Manager: Charles Freeman

Lead Technical Writer: Diane Faigel

Production Lead: Scott Dines

Desktop Publisher: Cheryl Howlett

Lead Editor: Renee Wesberry

Editors: Laurie Grendahl, Susan Woodside

Indexer: Carolyn Bryce

Graphic Arts Lead: Curtis Christman

Graphic Artist: Scott Perrine

Technical Contributors:

Mukesh Agarwal, Aamer Ali, Eric Askilsrud, Anthony Baron, Jason Bender, Mary Blake,
Mike Blumenthal, Ron Bokleman, D.P. Brightful, Steve Busby, Simone Cannon,
Thomas Chan, Calvin Clarke, Rick Davis, Louis de Klerk, Roy Dictus, Kelley DuBois,
Laurie Dunham, Joe Eldridge, Craig Fisher, Tom Fuchs, Mona Guentzel, David Guimbellot,
Laura Hargrave, Paul Harvey, Alex Hernandez, Harlan Husmann, John Inman, Tim Jarvis,
Nikki Jerome, Mark Kapczynski, Arminder Kaur, Ken Knight, Thyagi Lakshmanan,
Johanna Lynn, Atsushi Maekawa, Doug Martin, Neil McGarry, Scott McMahon,
David Messner, Constantin Mihai, Jayaram Mulupuru, Joe Murray, Peter Musgrave,
Rajivendra Nath, Sonia Pande, Travis Plunk, Bob Rapp, Biraj Rath, Jim Reynolds,
Arianto Ridwan, Reed Robison, Dave Rothenberg, Joseph Ruedlinger, Caesar Samsi,
Rob Sanfilippo, Michael Shea, Don Smith, Donovan Smith, James B. Speer, Jr.,
Jean Summers, Paul Thomsen, Peter Van Niman, Christine Waresak, Richard R. Wolfe,
Billy Woo, Barry Wright

Preface

This book is designed for Information Technology (IT) professionals engaged in all phases of implementing e-commerce sites: planners, developers, testers, system administrators, and consultants. This audience includes Web developers, as well as traditional software developers and testers, system and network administrators, consultants hired to develop and deploy e-commerce sites, and business decision makers who evaluate the product as part of the planning process.

About This Book

The *Microsoft Commerce Server 2000 Resource Kit* consists of one book and a single compact disc (CD) containing tools, additional reference materials, and a fully searchable online version of the book.

Resource Kit Support Policy

The software supplied in the *Commerce Server 2000 Resource Kit* is not supported. Microsoft does not guarantee the performance of the tools, response times for answering questions, or bug fixes for the tools. However, Microsoft does provide a way for customers who purchase the *Commerce Server 2000 Resource Kit* to report bugs and to receive possible fixes for their issues. You can do this by sending e-mail to rkinput@microsoft.com. This e-mail address is only for issues related to the *Commerce Server 2000 Resource Kit*. For issues related to the Microsoft Commerce Server 2000 product, see the support information included with the product. For more information about support for Microsoft products, see http://support.microsoft.com.

Additional Information Online

Updates and information about deploying sites with Commerce Server 2000 are available at http://www.microsoft.com/commerceserver on an ongoing basis.

Additional information and resources, including white papers and hosted online chats, are available at http://www.microsoft.com/technet/comm.

Contents

Part One: Overview and Scenarios **1**

CHAPTER 1   Overview and Scenarios **3**

    Introduction to Commerce Server 2000 3

    Commerce Server and .NET Enterprise Servers 5

        COM+ Services 5

        Application Center 5

        BizTalk Server 6

        Host Integration Server 6

        SQL Server 6

    Solution Sites 6

    Introduction to the Resource Kit 8

    Introduction to the Resource Kit Scenarios 9

CHAPTER 2   A Retail Scenario **11**

    Putting Together the Contoso Team 11

    Planning 13

        Commerce Server Installation Planning 13

        Administration and Management Tools 14

        Business Analytics System 15

        Business Process Pipelines 17

        Product Catalog System 18

        Profiling System 19

        Targeting System 20

    Capacity and Performance 23

    Security 25

    Completing the Planning Process 26

Development 27

    Importing the Catalog 27

    Acquiring New Pipeline Components 27

    Modifying Site Look and Feel 28

    Adjusting Settings in the App Default Config Resource 29

    Setting Up the Development Environment 29

Deployment 30

    Performing Final Testing 32

    Preparing for Business 32

    Verifying Security 33

    Going Live 33

    Closing the Loop 34

        Collecting and Storing Customer Data 34

        Analyzing Customer Data 35

        Implementing the Site Management Cycle 35

CHAPTER 3   A Supplier Scenario **37**

Planning 37

    Organization Profiles 38

    Authentication 38

    Active Directory Integration 39

    Integration with BizTalk Server 40

    Partner Service 41

    Capacity, Performance, and Growth Requirements 42

    Integration with Existing Systems 43

    Completing the Planning Process 43

Development 44

    Converting and Importing the Catalog 44

    Developing COM Components 45

    Modifying Site Look and Feel 45

    Modifying the _Recvpo.asp File 46

    Adjusting Settings in the App Default Config Resource 47

Deployment 48

    Testing Business Processes 49

    Verifying Security 50

    Going Live 50

Configuring a Sample Supplier Solution Site 50

    Configuring Active Directory and DNS (Computer 1) 51

    Configuring SQL Server 2000 and Commerce Server (Computer 2) 54

Configuring IIS and Unpacking the Supplier Site (Computer 3) 55

Configuring the Business Desk Client (Computer 4) 56

Verifying the Configuration 56

Configuring the Computers for Trusted Delegation 57

Verifying Business Desk and the Supplier Site 57

Closing the Loop 58

Analyzing Customer Data 58

Implementing the Site Management Cycle 58

Part Two: Planning **59**

CHAPTER 4   Defining Project Goals and Requirements **61**

Creating a Project Goals and Requirements Document 64

Vision 64

Scope 65

Constraints 66

Assumptions 66

Risks 67

Developing a Conceptual Design 68

Defining Requirements 68

Business Requirements 69

System Integration Requirements 69

Security Requirements 70

Single-Firewall Solution 72

Two-Firewall Solution 74

Three-Firewall Solution 75

Site Architecture Requirements 78

Performance and Capacity Requirements 79

Performance 79

Capacity 80

Performance and Capacity Considerations for Site Architecture 82

System Administration Requirements 86

International Requirements 87

Selecting Commerce Server Features 88

Administration and Management Tools 88

Business Analytics System 89

Business Process Pipelines System 90

Product Catalog System 91

Profiling System 92

Targeting System 93

    Content Selection Framework 93

    Direct Mailer 94

    Expressions 95

    Predictor Resource 95

Planning for Migration 96

CHAPTER 5 Planning for Scalability **97**

Scaling Hardware Vertically 99

Scaling Hardware Horizontally 101

Optimizing Site Architecture to Improve Scalability 102

    Disabling IIS Session Management and Removing Session Variables 105

    Separating Static Content from Other Types of Content 106

    Caching Static Content 107

    Caching Static Lookup Data 107

    Using the Caching Technology Provided by Commerce Server 108

    Consolidating Business Rules on Dedicated Servers 108

    Using Message Queuing or E-mail to Update Systems 109

    Processing Requests in Batches 109

CHAPTER 6 Planning for Reliability and High Availability **111**

    Availability Checklist 111

Designing a Highly Available E-Commerce Site 114

    Operational Procedures 116

    Site Capacity 118

    Preventing Failures 119

A Highly Available Commerce Server Architecture 126

    Small Commerce Server Configuration 126

    Large Commerce Server Configuration 127

    Commerce Server Component Design Considerations 131

        Administration Database 132

        Profiling System 132

        Product Catalog System 136

        Targeting System 137

        Direct Mailer 138

        Business Process Pipelines 140

        Data Warehouse 142

Operating System Availability 143

    Network Load Balancing 143

    Web Farm/Active Directory Authentication 144

Active Directory Availability 145

    Replication Between Sites 146

    Disaster Recovery 147

    Backup Strategies 147

    Restoration strategies 147

    Active Directory Monitoring Tools 148

SQL Server Availability 148

    Clustering 148

    Replication 150

    Warm Backup 152

    Retry Code Logic 154

Additional Resources 155

CHAPTER 7   Building the Project Plan **157**

Creating a Functional Specification 158

    Summary 158

    Design Goals and Justification 158

    Design 159

        Data 159

        Security 159

    Compatibility and Platform Requirements 160

    Third-Party Involvement 161

    Localization 161

    Migration 161

    Issues and Risks 161

Identifying the Project Team 161

Building the Project Schedule 164

Part Three: Developing **165**

CHAPTER 8   Developing Your Site **167**

Development Checklist 169

    Completing the Development Phase 170

Selecting a Development Methodology 172

    Jump-Starting Development with the Solution Sites 172

Managing Site Configurations 174

   Configuration Items 175

   Configuration Management Database 176

   Core Configuration Management Processes 178

      Identification 178

      Status Accounting 179

      Verification and Auditing 179

Managing Change 180

   Change Requests 180

   Change Database 181

   Change Advisory Board 181

   Change Process 181

Development Tools and Resources 183

   Commerce Server 2000 Help 184

   Commerce Server SDK 184

   Commerce Server Management Tools 188

   Other Microsoft Tools 189

   Configuration Management Tools 190

   Other Resources 190

   Related Web Sites 191

CHAPTER 9   Developer Notes **193**

Gift Certificate Feature 193

   Business Desk Modifications 195

   Site Resource Modifications 198

   Site Page Modifications 198

   Checkout Pipeline Modifications 199

   COM Object Development 199

   Profile Modifications 199

   Report Modifications 200

   Site Term Modifications 200

   Campaign Modifications 200

   Deployment Summary 201

Profiling System Utilities 201
    Profiles Schema Mover 202
        Installation 203
        Operation 203
        Exporting a Catalog 204
        Importing a Catalog 209
        Deployment Scenarios 212
    Site Terms Viewer 213
Profiling System: Operational Considerations 215
    Profile Definition Keys 216
        Unique Key 216
        Primary Key 216
        Join Key 216
        Hashing Key 217
    Profiling System Design Considerations 218
        Keys 218
        Recommended Data Type Mappings 219
        Other Considerations 220
    Profiling System Run-Time Considerations 221
        CSOLEDB Handles 221
        Accessing Properties 221
        Transaction Support 221
        Data Size Validation 223
    Managing Pre-Existing Accounts in Active Directory Stores 223
        Starting Container for Directory Operations 223
        Search Scope 226
    User Profile Import DTS Task 226
        Importing New Profile Types 226
        Profile Mappings 226
Advertising Scoring and Selection 228
    Campaign Goals and Item Goals 228
    Initial Scoring 229
    Scoring (Targeting) 230
    Selection 231
    Troubleshooting Ad Scoring and Selection 232

CHAPTER 10 Integrating Third-Party ERP Systems with Commerce Server Applications **233**

Integration Techniques 235
    Batch Downloads 235
    Real-Time Connectors 240
    Queued Connectors 244
    Mirrored Updates 247
General Considerations and Best Practices 249
    ERP Systems and Commerce Server Business Rules 249
    Pricing and Promotions 250
    Shipping, Taxation, and Credit Card Authorization 251
    Product Catalog 251
    Replication 252
    Physical Architecture 252
Integrating with SAP 254
    SAP DCOM Connector 256
    Product Catalog 258
        Batch Download Product Catalog Data 259
        Batch Download Incremental Catalog Changes 260
        Mirrored Updates 260
    Item Pricing 262
        Batch Download Item Prices 262
        ALE-Triggered Price Change Download 263
        Real-Time Pricing Integration 264
    Inventory Data 266
        Batch Download Inventory Data 266
        Batch Download Incremental Inventory Changes 268
        Mirrored Updates Using ALE 268
        Real-Time Connections 269
    Orders 270
        Batch Integration Using IDOC 271
        Real-Time Integration Using the DCOM Connector 272
        Integration Using Queued Components 273
        Mirrored Updates Using Message Queuing 275
        Mirrored Updates Using BizTalk Server 277
        Real-Time Integration Using Custom COM Objects and DCOM Connector Objects 279

Integrating with J.D. Edwards OneWorld 281

   OneWorld GenCom Component Wrapper 283

   Product Catalog and Pricing 285

      Batch Download Data from OneWorld 285

      Mirrored Updates 287

      Real-Time Integration 289

   Orders 290

      Batch Download Using the Z-Table 291

      Real-Time Integration Using OneWorld COM Objects in the Purchase Pipeline 291

      Integration Using Queued Connectors 293

      Mirrored Updates Using Message Queuing 295

      Mirrored Updates Using BizTalk Server 297

CHAPTER 11   Migrating from Site Server to Commerce Server 2000 . . . . **299**

Planning the Migration 302

   Feature Analysis 304

   Migration Strategies and Scenarios 306

      Phase 1: Set Up Commerce Server in Your Test Environment 306

      Phase 2: Migrate Site Code and Content 310

      Phase 3: Move Your New Commerce Server 2000 Site into Production 313

      Phase 4: Convert P1 to Commerce Server 314

      Phase 5: Decommission the N1 Environment 316

   Fallback Plan 316

Developing 317

   Migrating Site Server 3.0 Features 318

      Analysis 319

      Content Management 320

      Knowledge Management 321

      Personalization & Membership 323

      Membership Migration Tool (Directory Migration Toolbox) 327

   Migrating SSCE Features 330

      Ad Server 330

      Online Store 330

      Pipelines 331

      Predictor 332

      Promotions 333

      Transaction Data 333

Deploying 334

CHAPTER 12   Developing an International Site **335**

Using Multiple Languages 335

Language-Dependent Strings 335

Product Information 336

Site Information 336

Caching 337

Choosing the Language 337

Changing Languages 338

Using a Client-Side Cookie with Language Codes 338

Encoding the Language Code in the URL 338

Storing the Language Preference in the User Profile 339

Using Pre-Generated Pages 339

Using Multiple Currencies 340

Product Pricing 340

Different Prices for Different Locales 341

Different Discounts for Different Locales 341

Changing Currency 341

Configuring International Locale Settings 342

CHAPTER 13   Integrating Commerce Server with BizTalk Server **345**

BizTalk Server Overview 345

BizTalk Messaging Services 346

Receive Functions 346

Transport Services 347

Data Parsers 347

Data Validation Services 347

Document Delivery Services 347

Security 348

BizTalk Orchestration Services 348

XLANG Language 348

XLANG Schedules 348

Common Business-to-Business Requirements 349

Catalog Exchange and Management 349

Catalog Mapping Tools 351

Mapping from a Commerce Server Catalog to a Flat Schema 353

Mapping from a Flat Schema to a Commerce Server Catalog 354

Generating Catalogs in the Commerce Server XML Format 355

Catalog Import, Export, and Exchange Tools 356

Application Integration Components 358

Order Management 358

Order Routing Manager 358

Order Form Integration 361

Integrating Commerce Server and BizTalk Server 365

Configuring Commerce Server and BizTalk Server to Send and Receive a Catalog 366

Setting Up the Environment 367

Configuring the Site Options on the Wholesaler Site 367

Copying CatalogXmlSchema.xml to the BizTalkServerRepository 367

Creating the Catalog Document Definition 368

Configuring Receivestandard.asp to Receive the Catalog 368

Modifying the Home Organization 368

Creating the Retailer Organization 369

Creating the Catalog Application for the Wholesaler Organization 369

Creating the Wholesaler Messaging Port to the Retailer Organization 370

Creating the CatalogImportChannel and Retailer Receive Port 371

Testing Your Configuration 372

Processing a Commerce Server Purchase Order Through BizTalk Server 373

Configuring the Site Options for the Retailer Site 373

Copying POSchema.xml to the WebDAV Repository 374

Configuring the PurchaseOrder Document Definition 374

Adding the Identifier to the Retailer Organization 374

Configuring a Vendor for the Imported Catalog 375

Creating a WholesalerPO Application for the Wholesaler Organization 375

Creating a New Messaging Port to an Application 375

Creating a New Channel that Uses the WholesalerPO as the Messaging Port 376

Testing Your Configuration 377

Part Four: Deploying **379**

CHAPTER 14   Deploying Your Site **381**

Deployment Checklists 384

Site Architecture Checklist 385

Availability Checklist 385

Site Development and Testing Checklist 386

Business Process Checklist 387

Platform Security Checklist 387

Commerce Server Security Checklist 391

Implementing Your Contingency Plan 392
   Technical Solutions for Risk Reduction 392
      Network Load Balancing 393
      Application Load Balancing 393
      Windows Clustering 394
Deploying Your Commerce Server Site 395
   Deploying Your Site Architecture 395
      Installing Hardware and Software 397
   Deploying Site Platform Software 398
      Application Center 398
      Active Directory 398
   Deploying Commerce Server Software 398
      Installing Commerce Server 399
      Packaging Your Application 400
      Unpacking Your Application 402
      Site Packager 403
   Deploying Commerce Server Features 404
      Product Catalog System 404
      Direct Mailer 406
      Profiling System 406
      Data Warehouse 408
Securing Your Site 408
   General Security Elements 408
      Authentication 409
      Access Control 409
      Certificates 410
      Encryption 410
      Auditing 411
   Platform Security 411
      Separating Users from Internal Domains 411
      Securing Cookies 412
      Using Scripts to Set Permissions on Folders 412
      Limiting Access to Your Site 412
      Using Windows Authentication with Active Directory in a Web Farm 413
      Securing an Intranet (Supplier) Site 414
      Hosting Sites for External Customers 414

Network Security 414

   DMZ 414

   Firewalls 415

   Network Segregation 416

   Data Encryption Using SSL 416

   Credit Card Information Security 417

   Intrusion Detection 417

Database Security 418

   Active Directory Security 418

   SQL Server Security 419

   Using Active Directory and SQL Server 419

Web Server Security 420

Commerce Server Security 421

   Using AuthFilter and AuthManager 421

   Authenticating Users in a Web Farm 422

   Using Commerce Server Authentication Modes 423

   Using Commerce Server Authentication Features 427

   Securing Business Desk 430

   Securing Commerce Server Databases 433

   Limiting Access to Commerce Server Services 435

   Providing Access to Commerce Server Resources 435

   Commerce Server and Outlook Web Access (OWA) Integration 435

   Active Directory and Anonymous Users on the Supplier Site 436

   Adding Products to a Basket Without an Account 436

Security and Authentication Scenarios 437

   Protecting Static Content 437

   Protecting Dynamic Content 437

Site Security Deployment Notes 437

   Auditing Site Deletions 437

   Using Windows Authentication against Windows NT 4.0 Domain Accounts 438

Testing Your Environment 438

Implementing Initial Operational Procedures 439

Final Steps Before Production 439

After Your Site Is in Production 439

Backing Up Your Site 440

   Gathering Server Configuration Data 440

   System State Backup 441

   File System Backup 442

   Application Data Backup 443

   Network Configuration Backup 443

CHAPTER 15   Deploying Content **445**

Deployment Tools 451

   Application Center 451

   Content Replication Service 452

   Custom SQL Server DTS Tasks and Packages 453

   Custom Scripts 454

   Third-Party Deployment Tools 454

Deployment Scenarios 455

   Small-to-Medium Site 455

   Medium-to-Large Site 457

   Global Site 459

Deployment Examples 461

   Campaigns, Campaign Items, and Expressions 461

   COM+ Applications 462

   Databases 464

CHAPTER 16   Testing Your Site **467**

Testing Methodology 467

   Types of Tests 467

   Types of Test Documents 468

      Test Plan 468

      Test Cases 470

      Test Error Reports 471

Testing a Commerce Server Site 472

   User Interface Layer (Top Tier) 472

      Visual Appearance and Usability 473

      Links 474

      Browser Compatibility 475

      Business Logic Layer (Middle Tier) 475

   Database Layer (Bottom Tier) 476

   Security 478

      Networks 479

      Payment Transactions 479

Part Five: Managing **481**

CHAPTER 17   Managing Your Site **483**

Performing a Site Checkup 484

Monitoring and Analyzing Log Data 487

   Analyzing Log Data 487

   Reports 490

Setting Up and Performing Operational Procedures 491

   Creating a Site Administration Plan 492

      Creating and Performing Operational Procedures 493

      Managing Security 495

      Managing Changes 495

   Backing Up and Restoring Site Data 495

CHAPTER 18   Problem Management **497**

Incident Control 497

Problem Control 500

   Isolating the Problem 500

   Using Historical Performance Data 501

System Health 502

   Response Failures 502

   Errors and Access Violations 503

   Memory and Resource Leaks 503

   Security Failures 503

   Queuing 503

   CPU Saturation 504

   Corruption 504

Troubleshooting Your Commerce Server System 505

CHAPTER 19   Maximizing Performance **507**

Transaction Cost Analysis 509

   Documenting Your Site 510

   Analyzing Traffic 512

   Creating a Site Usage Profile 512

   Defining Acceptable Operating Parameters 513

      Calculating Cost per User 515

      Calculating Cost per User for CPUs 518

      Calculating Memory Cost per User 526

      Calculating Cost per User for Disks 528

      Calculating Cost per User for Networks 531

Managing Performance 534
   Identifying Site Constraints 535
   Defining Load 536
   Setting Performance Goals 536
   Measuring Performance 537
      Memory 539
      Processor Capacity 539
      Networks 539
      Disk Access 540
      Database 541
      Security 541
      Bottlenecks 542
      Optimizations 544
Case Study: MSNBC 546
   Load Monitoring Tools 549
   Planning for the Future 549
   Best Practices 550
Tools 551
   Microsoft Web Application Stress Tool 551
   Microsoft Network Monitor 552
   SQL Profiler 552
   System Monitor 552
   Visual Studio Analyzer 553

Part Six: Appendices **555**

APPENDIX A   Commerce Server 2000 Resource Kit CD Contents **557**

Additional Resources **563**
   Microsoft Products and Tools 563
   Design Tips and Code Samples 565
   White Papers, Case Studies, and Technical Information 566
   Third-Party References 567
   Miscellaneous 568

Glossary **569**

Index **587**

Part One: Overview and Scenarios

Microsoft
**Commerce
Server** 2000

Overview and Scenarios

Welcome to the *Microsoft Commerce Server 2000 Resource Kit*. This kit consists of one book and a single compact disc (CD) containing tools, additional reference materials, and an online version of the book. In addition, updates and information about deploying sites with Commerce Server 2000 are available at http://www.microsoft.com/commerceserver on an ongoing basis.

The *Commerce Server 2000 Resource Kit* supplements Microsoft Commerce Server 2000 product software and documentation in the same way that a good tour guide supplements a set of detailed street maps. Commerce Server 2000 Help contains step-by-step descriptions for using the software. It is procedural information—a guide to the features of the product and instructions for using them. The *Commerce Server 2000 Resource Kit* expands on this information by providing real-world scenarios and guidelines for setting up e-commerce Web sites with Commerce Server.

Introduction to Commerce Server 2000

Commerce Server 2000 delivers a scalable e-commerce platform that provides ready-to-use features for developing, deploying, and upgrading effective e-commerce applications for the Web. This extensible platform enables customers, Independent Software Vendors (ISVs), and Internet Service Providers (ISPs) to build solutions that scale with business needs and integrate with existing systems and data. Using Commerce Server scalable server architecture with Microsoft Windows 2000, you can meet the increasing performance demands of growing e-commerce infrastructures.

Commerce Server is comprised of five systems: the Business Analytics System, the Product Catalog System, the Targeting System, the Profiling System, and the Business Process Pipelines System. Each system is designed so that you can easily customize it to meet your business needs.

Business managers use Commerce Server Business Desk to work with the five Commerce Server systems. For example, they can use Business Desk to update catalogs, target content to users, profile users and organizations, and analyze site usage and productivity. System administrators use Commerce Server Manager to configure system resources and manage the applications, databases, and Web servers.

The Commerce Server systems, Business Desk, Commerce Server Manager, and the Commerce Server databases are pre-configured and packaged in the Solution Sites, which you can use as a starting point for building a custom site and integrating third-party applications.

Figure 1.1 illustrates the Commerce Server architecture.

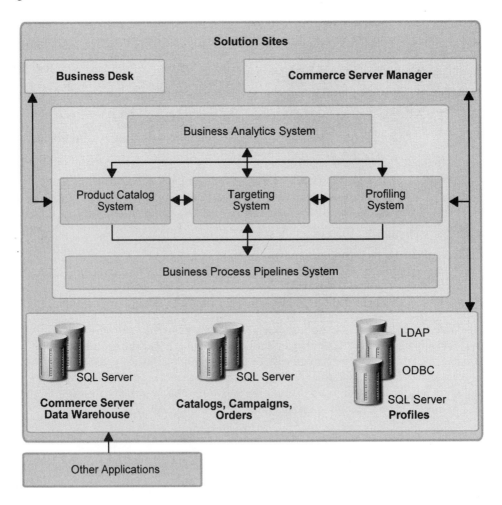

Figure 1.1 Commerce Server architecture

Commerce Server and .NET Enterprise Servers

Although Commerce Server is a stand-alone product, it is designed to operate seamlessly with other Microsoft .NET Enterprise Servers. The .NET Enterprise Servers are Microsoft's comprehensive family of server applications for building, deploying, and managing scalable, integrated Web solutions with fast time to market. You can use .NET Enterprise Servers to build systems that integrate Commerce Server sites with the rest of your management information system. If you need this level of integration, you can implement one or more of the other .NET technologies in conjunction with Commerce Server.

Some of the .NET technologies that typically are used with Commerce Server include:

- COM+ Services (an extension to the Component Object Model)
- Microsoft Application Center 2000
- Microsoft BizTalk Server 2000
- Microsoft Host Integration Server 2000
- Microsoft SQL Server 2000

COM+ Services

COM+ Services (Component Services, including MTS) is a unified programming model that you can use to build component-based, three-tier distributed applications. COM+ builds on the Microsoft Component Object Model (COM) by combining COM with the transactional features of Microsoft Transaction Server (MTS). It extends the programming environment by adding a rich set of features to make it easier to develop, deploy, and administer highly scalable, distributed, component-based solutions.

Application Center

Application Center is a high-availability deployment and management tool for Web applications built on Windows 2000. It extends the core set of Web application services found in Windows 2000 (Internet Information Services (IIS) 5.0, Active Server Pages (ASP), COM+, Message Queuing), and provides a suite of monitoring, testing, and diagnostic tools not available in the core operating system. Application Center is designed for customers with high-end requirements for scalability and availability.

You can use Application Center with Commerce Server to deploy content and make incremental updates to your Web site. For more information about using Application Center with Commerce Server, see "Deploying Your Site" in Commerce Server 2000 Help and Chapter 15, "Deploying Content," in the *Commerce Server 2000 Resource Kit.*

BizTalk Server

BizTalk Server provides a comprehensive solution for business-to-business electronic document exchange and business process integration. BizTalk Server acts as a business document gateway between trading partners and manages the data translation, encryption, digital signatures, and document tracking services for many different transport mechanisms.

You can integrate Commerce Server with BizTalk Server, for example, to exchange catalogs of products that you post on your Web site, and to send orders entered on your Web site to suppliers for fulfillment. For more information about integrating Commerce Server with BizTalk Server, see Chapter 13, "Integrating Commerce Server with BizTalk Server," as well as the topics "Integrating with BizTalk Server" and "Using BizTalk Server and Commerce Server" in Commerce Server 2000 Help.

Host Integration Server

Host Integration Server is a comprehensive integration platform that provides support for Internet, intranet, and client/server technologies, while preserving investments in existing systems. By recognizing that accessing existing data is only the first step in leveraging enterprise computing resources, Host Integration Server enables you to create distributed applications that make the most of either client/server or Web computing and host information.

SQL Server

SQL Server provides a scalable database that combines ease of use with complex analysis and data warehousing tools. SQL Server includes a rich graphical user interface (GUI) and a complete development environment for creating data-driven applications. Commerce Server takes advantage of SQL Server data warehousing and analysis capabilities. The Commerce Server Data Warehouse, for example, uses SQL Server Data Transformation Services (DTS) to transform data stored in SQL Server databases to the format used by Commerce Server resources.

Solution Sites

The Commerce Server Solution Sites are development reference sites that provide an integrated set of Commerce Server features for building comprehensive e-commerce sites. You can use the Solution Sites as a starting point for developing your own Web site, and, when you are ready, add functionality that is specific to your business.

Commerce Server includes the following Solution Sites:

- **Blank**. You can use the Blank Solution Site as a starting point for building your own custom site. It includes all of the Commerce Server resources. The Blank site is included in the Commerce Server box.

- **Retail**. You can use the Retail Solution Site as a starting point for building a business-to-consumer site. It includes functionality for personalization, merchandising, catalog search, customer service, and business analytics. It also includes the Customer Service, which enables users to manage their own profile information and to view their order status. The Retail site is available from http://www.microsoft.com/commerceserver/solutionsites.

- **Supplier**. You can use the Supplier Solution Site as a starting point for building a business-to-business site. It uses Microsoft Active Directory in Windows 2000 to provide secure user authentication and group access permissions. It provides purchase order and requisition handling, Extensible Markup Language-based (XML-based) catalog updates and exchange, and trading partner self-service. It also includes the Partner Service, which enables a delegated administrator (a contact at a supplier company) to manage organizational information, purchase orders, and order status for the supplier company. The Supplier site is available from http://www.microsoft.com/commerceserver/solutionsites.

The Solution Sites provide the following capabilities:

- **Merchandising**. You can create targeted advertisements and discounts and personalized direct mail campaigns to increase sales and enhance the user experience.

- **Catalog display**. You can display catalogs that users can easily search by:

  - Browsing categories.

  - Specifying full or partial names of products or their attributes.

  - Narrowing their search until they find what they need.

  - Searching for multiple attributes at once (for example, price less than ten dollars and color equal to "red").

- **Customer service**. Users visiting your site can change their logon and password, view their order status and history, and change their profile information.

- **Order capture and receipt**. After ordering products, users can receive a receipt with a final total and order tracking number.

Because the Solution Sites provide comprehensive e-commerce functionality, you can use them as a starting point for developing your own Web site. Beginning with a Solution Site will free you to spend more time adding functionalities specific to your business.

Introduction to the Resource Kit

The *Commerce Server 2000 Resource Kit* can help you work with Commerce Server in two ways: by helping you understand common e-business scenarios and by explaining in detail each phase of the development of an e-commerce site.

The *Commerce Server 2000 Resource Kit* provides a detailed description of the following two common types of e-business scenarios:

- Business-to-consumer (B2C), or retail site scenario, which resembles a storefront for consumer-oriented direct sales
- Business-to-business (B2B), or supplier site scenario, such as a supply-chain or value chain site that facilitates purchasing, order processing, and account management for business trading partners

You can use Commerce Server to implement both types of sites.

In addition, the *Commerce Server 2000 Resource Kit* provides detailed information about using Commerce Server during each of the four phases in the life cycle of an e-commerce site: Plan, Develop, Deploy, and Manage. Building and maintaining a successful e-commerce Web site is a continuous process, in which you develop a vision of your site and then:

- Plan how to implement that vision.
- Develop the plan and code all the elements of the site, including Web site pages.
- Deploy the site and perform system validation.
- Manage the site in production and analyze the Web logs to plan for future upgrades.

Chapter 11, "Migrating from Site Server to Commerce Server 2000," describes how to migrate a site developed with Microsoft Site Server 3.0 or Site Server 3.0 Commerce Edition (SSCE) to take advantage of Commerce Server features. Chapter 11 includes a feature-by-feature analysis and comparison of those products, plus instructions for using the migration tools included with Commerce Server.

Some other *Commerce Server 2000 Resource Kit* highlights include the following:

- Planning for scalability and high availability (Chapters 5 and 6)
- Integrating Commerce Server with ERP systems (Chapter 10)
- Designing your site to serve an international audience (Chapter 12)
- Maximizing site performance (Chapter 19)

This book is designed for Information Technology (IT) professionals engaged in all phases of implementing e-commerce sites: planners, developers, testers, system administrators, and consultants. This audience includes Web developers, as well as traditional software developers and testers, system and network administrators, consultants hired to develop and deploy e-commerce sites, and business decision makers who evaluate the product as part of the planning process.

Introduction to the Resource Kit Scenarios

E-commerce sites can be characterized in different ways, including the following:

- Size (small-to-medium, medium-to-large, or global)

- Availability (weekdays only, limited use, or close to 100 percent availability)

- End-user or audience description (retail consumers, corporate customers, or trading partners)

- Commerce Server features used (catalog display only, order pipeline, inventory management, site usage analysis, direct mailings, and advertising)

The *Commerce Server 2000 Resource Kit* focuses on the retail and supplier site scenarios. These case studies can help you plan and build your site by sharing lessons learned from specific Commerce Server implementations. They can provide a frame of reference for you to use as you plan, develop, deploy, and manage your own site using Commerce Server.

The *Commerce Server 2000 Resource Kit* scenarios present information about business goals, site architecture, planning methodologies and considerations, development best practices, deployment procedures, and system administration for typical retail and supplier sites.

For the Planning phase, the scenarios describe the following:

- Business description

- Business objectives

- Scope (including existing systems, technical issues, and staffing issues)

- Project time constraints

- Hardware and software

- Planning for disaster recovery

For the Development phase, the scenarios describe the following:

- Development using the Solution Sites

- Change management

- Source control

- Product catalog design

- Development best practices

For the Deployment phase, the scenarios describe the following:

- Network architecture
- Testing
- Performance tuning

For the Management phase, the scenarios describe the following:

- System administration (including regular system backups)
- Performance management
- Site usage data assembly, reporting, and analysis

CHAPTER 2

A Retail Scenario

Planning, developing, and deploying a retail Web site is an exciting, yet substantial, undertaking. In this chapter, you can look over the shoulders of the team members of a fictitious company – Contoso, Ltd.– as they plan, develop, and deploy their retail Web site. The content for this chapter is drawn from real deployments of Microsoft Commerce Server 2000. For detailed information about these deployments, see http://www.microsoft.com/commerceserver.

The purpose of this scenario is to help you understand the planning and development required to deploy a Commerce Server retail (business-to-consumer) site, and to familiarize you with the extensive resources found in Commerce Server 2000 Help and in this *Commerce Server 2000 Resource Kit.*

Although every company has its own specific needs and objectives and no two commercial Web sites are exactly the same, there are many common areas that most retail sites need to address. For an example of a supplier (business-to-business) Web site, see Chapter 3, "A Supplier Scenario."

Putting Together the Contoso Team

Contoso, Ltd. is a healthy international catalog business that generates significant revenues from mail order and toll-free telephone business. When mail order and telephone customers began asking why the company didn't have a Web site, Contoso decided that it was risking the loss of a significant sector of its market if it didn't make the move to the Web.

To begin the project, a group of Contoso senior executives put together a cross-discipline team to plan, develop, and deploy a Web site that would enable customers to browse an online version of their existing catalog, make credit card purchases, and specify types of shipments. The senior executives wanted their team to create a site that would easily scale for growth and from which they could gather data that would enable them to anticipate and plan to meet their customers' needs.

Contoso created a cross-functional team to ensure that the Web site would integrate with their company's existing infrastructure, that it could be scaled to handle growth, and that it would integrate successfully with the rest of their company's business. The team was comprised of the following members:

- **System administrator**. Responsible for making sure the new Web site integrates well with existing enterprise systems and for planning operational procedures to support the new site.

- **Site designers**. Responsible for designing an attractive site that maintains the existing Contoso look, feel, and branding.

- **Interface designers**. Responsible for creating an intuitive, easy-to-navigate environment in which customers can find what they need without becoming overwhelmed, frustrated, or lost.

- **Site developers**. Responsible for maximizing the benefits of Commerce Server and its supporting infrastructure, and for creating custom code where needed.

- **Testers**. Responsible for working with the site developers to ensure that the site is stable and robust before final deployment.

- **Marketing staff**. Responsible for maximizing the benefits of the Commerce Server Business Analytics and Targeting Systems.

- **Technical writers**. Responsible for writing and editing on-screen content to simplify and enhance the customer experience.

- **Accounting staff**. Responsible for working with site developers to modify the Business Process Pipelines System so that it integrates with existing systems.

- **Security staff**. Responsible for designing security for the Web site and working with the site developers to implement security.

- **Third-party systems integrator**. Responsible for integrating third-party software solutions with Commerce Server functionality.

Planning

The Contoso team had two main goals: to deploy their retail Web site as soon as possible, and to deploy a site that was well designed, thoroughly tested, and seamlessly integrated with the company's existing infrastructure.

Planning was essential to meet these goals. Planning facilitated development by clearly delineating what needed to be done and helping to ensure that the site integrated well with the existing infrastructure.

The Contoso team divided into the following planning groups:

- **Commerce Server Installation Planning**. Chose which Commerce Server features to use.

- **Site Architecture and Security Planning**. Planned how to integrate with existing systems and identified the custom code, including Active Server Pages (ASP) pages, that had to be written.

- **Deployment Planning**. Developed checklists to make sure that all systems were ready for deployment.

The members of each group researched their area, and then reported back to the full team. The full team then worked together to create a comprehensive Project Plan and to ensure that all the parts would come together for final deployment.

Commerce Server Installation Planning

The Contoso Commerce Server Installation Planning group used Commerce Server 2000 Help to research the following features:

- Administration and Management Tools

- Business Analytics System

- Business Process Pipelines

- Product Catalog System

- Profiling System

- Targeting System

Administration and Management Tools

Commerce Server 2000 provides two tools for managing and administering the Contoso Web site: Commerce Server Business Desk and Commerce Server Manager.

Business Desk is a site management tool that hosts business management modules for managing day-to-day operations and analyzing site activity. The following table summarizes how Contoso decided to use the Business Desk to manage its site.

Business Desk category	Implementation
Analysis	• The Contoso team decided to use Commerce Server standard reports.
	• They don't plan to integrate a third-party reporting solution in the initial deployment of the site, but will re-evaluate this decision after running the site for six months. The specific requirements for Analysis are explained in "Planning the Business Analytics System" later in this chapter.
Campaigns	• Contoso will sell advertisements and offer house ads to suppliers.
	• The team will create direct-mail campaigns to send sales announcements to regular customers.
Catalog	• Contoso must convert its existing catalog structure into the appropriate Extensible Markup Language (XML) format and then import it, using the Catalog Editor module.
	• The team established a process for keeping the two catalog systems synchronized.
	For more information about updating catalog data, see Chapter 15, "Deploying Content."
Orders	• Contoso has a contract with a shipping company, so it simply added the appropriate billing information using the Shipping Methods module.
	• The team entered tax information required by a third-party tax component using the Tax Rates module.
Users	• The Contoso team defined additional **User** properties for analyzing its customer base and targeting content.

Contoso used Commerce Server Manager to manage and configure the Commerce Server resources, sites, applications, and Web servers it would need to administer its site. The following table describes the site resources Contoso implemented.

Resource	Implementation
App Default Config	Contoso used the App Default Config resource to set up site functionality, such as currency and billing options. For more details, see "Adjusting Settings in the App Default Config Resource" later in this chapter.
Commerce Server Data Warehouse	Contoso decided to use Microsoft SQL Server 2000 for its Data Warehouse. It installed the Data Warehouse on a dedicated computer. For more details, see "Deployment" later in this chapter.
Commerce Server Direct Mailer	Contoso set up a direct-mail campaign to send mail about special offerings to customers who signed up for this service.
CS Authentication	Contoso based its site on the Retail Solution Site, using the default authentication scheme provided. The Retail Solution Site enables customers to shop without accepting cookies. This was a significant factor for Contoso; it didn't want to force customers to accept cookies.
Predictor	Contoso chose not to use the Predictor resource in its initial deployment, but plans to incorporate it later, when there is sufficient information in the Data Warehouse.
Profiles	Contoso extended the User profile to track customers who have signed up to be notified about special offerings.

Business Analytics System

The Business Desk Analysis modules and the Data Warehouse provide the foundation for a powerful Business Analytics System. Business analytics provides you with a way to analyze the performance of your Web site. You can use the information provided by the Commerce Server Business Analytics System to improve your customer service and to target content to users.

The Data Warehouse is a combination of a SQL Server database, an online analytical processing (OLAP) database, and a set of processes that a system administrator uses to import and maintain large amounts of data from multiple data sources. This data is gathered from Web server logs, the Commerce Server databases (Profiles, Catalogs, Campaigns, and Transactions) and other data sources that you can specify. You can use the Data Warehouse to manage, query, and analyze the data in the SQL Server and OLAP databases. The Analysis modules use Data Warehouse information to identify user trends, analyze the effectiveness of a campaign, and monitor user click patterns and a host of other information.

You can use the standard reports provided by the Reports module to answer the following types of questions:

- What Uniform Resource Locator (URL) did the customer visit before arriving at our site (referring URL)?

- What type of advertising works?

- What pages on our site are the most popular?

- Which products sell the best?

- Which customers buy the most?

You can use this information to increase sales and retain customers. For example, after displaying an advertisement to promote a new product for a week, you might decide to run a report to determine whether the ad increased sales. If it didn't, you might decide to add a 10-percent discount and then, after a week, once again analyze sales results.

The data that populates the Data Warehouse can come from multiple data sources: Web server logs, Commerce Server databases, and other data sources that you specify. Because the Data Warehouse isn't part of your run-time environment, you must decide how frequently to import operational data into the Data Warehouse. For example, you can set up the Data Warehouse so that it automatically imports new data every day or every week, depending on the amount of new data you collect every day. Commerce Server provides custom Data Transformation Services (DTS) tasks to simplify the data importing process.

The Contoso Commerce Server Installation Planning group interviewed the members of the executive committee to determine success criteria for the site. The success criteria were then used to establish reporting requirements. The Installation Planning group read the "Business Desk Analysis" section of Commerce Server 2000 Help to evaluate the standard reports provided by Commerce Server. As a result of their research and interviews, they decided to provide the reports listed in the following table to upper management on a monthly basis.

Report	Success criteria
Product Sales	Minimum average monthly revenue of $250,000
Buyer Browse to Purchase	30 percent of browsers make a purchase
User Visit Trends	20 percent increase per month in number of site visits

The team also identified other reports, such as those listed in the following table, to help them monitor and maintain the site.

Report	Purpose
Registered Users by Date Registered	Monitor capacity requirements for the back-end data store
User Visit Trends	Determine whether customers are returning to the site
Usage Summary Reports	Determine best days and times to perform maintenance operations
Entry Path Analysis	Identify site pages that receive the most traffic

The Installation Planning group also reviewed the extensions to the Commerce Server reporting capabilities offered by third parties (located at http://www.microsoft.com/commerceserver/partners). Although the group felt that these third-party reports might add greater depth to their analysis, they decided to use only the standard reports during the initial phase of the project.

Business Process Pipelines

The Contoso team was pleased with the Commerce Server Business Process Pipelines System. They saw many opportunities for bundling their business processes into pipelines. They planned to use the pipelines to define and link together the stages of their business processes, and then run them in sequence to complete each task.

A pipeline is a way of stacking up tasks into a list for processing. For example, the Order Processing pipeline (OPP) contains the sequence of steps necessary to process orders. For example, in the first stage in the OPP, you retrieve product information from the Catalogs database. In the next stage, you add the customer's address to the order. Each stage in the pipeline represents a task. The sequence of the stages determines the sequence in which the tasks are done.

Commerce Server provides a set of pipelines that perform much of the standard processing required by a Commerce Server site. You can tailor the pipelines to meet your specific needs. For example, you can add new stages to the pipeline, integrate pipeline components with your existing system, or replace pipeline components with other components supplied by third parties.

The Installation Planning group studied the pipelines provided by Commerce Server very carefully. They downloaded the Retail Solution Site from http://www.microsoft.com/commerceserver/solutionsites and used Commerce Server Site Packager to unpack it on their development Web server. After examining the way in which the pipelines were implemented in the Retail site, they decided to use the pipelines in the following table.

Pipeline	Purpose
Product	Retrieve product information from the product catalog (OPP)
Basket	Manage the customer's shopping basket (OPP)
Checkout	Complete a purchase (OPP)
Advertising	Display appropriate advertisements (Content Selection pipeline (CSP))
Discounts	Apply appropriate discounts to an order (CSP)
Direct Mailer	Send e-mail messages announcing special discounts to registered customers who have signed up for this service (Direct Mailer pipeline)

The Installation Planning group also discovered that the Retail Solution Site provided template files for all of the pipelines they had selected except the Direct Mailer pipeline. They used the DMLPipe.pcf file (provided by Commerce Server Setup) to create their Direct Mailer pipeline. The team also examined the list of pipeline component vendors at http://www.microsoft.com/commerceserver/thirdparty/partners.htm to find the pipeline components they needed for their tax and credit card processing requirements.

Product Catalog System

The Contoso team was especially interested in the Commerce Server Product Catalog System, because the product catalog is the mainstay of their business. One assignment was to bring their existing catalog online and to make sure that the online and offline versions were always the same. They had to be sure that customers were always presented with the same products and product numbers, whether shopping online or from the mail order catalog.

The team used the Catalog Editor module from the Product Catalog System to import catalogs and to create, modify, and delete categories and catalogs. They used an XML file to import their existing catalog information. The following code fragment, taken from their XML file, illustrates how they imported catalog information:

```
<?xml version="1.0" ?>
<MSCommerceCatalogCollection>
 <CatalogSchema>
  <AttributeDefinition name="RequiredProperty" dataType="string" />
    <PropertiesDefinition>
      <Property name="Artist" dataType="string" IsFreeTextSearchable="1"
       IncludeInSpecSearch="0" MinValue="0" MaxValue="100"
       DisplayOnSite="0" DisplayName="Artist" AssignAll="0" ExportToDW="0"
       DisplayInProductsList="0" id="CatalogProperty0" />
 ...
    </PropertiesDefinition>
  </AttributeDefinition>
 </CatalogSchema>
</MSCommerceCatalogCollection>
```

Contoso purchases books for resale in its catalog from ten different book and software distributors and eight hardware suppliers. Their primary supplier for books is Ferguson and Bardell Book Distributors. Contoso currently receives catalog information from Ferguson and Bardell by an e-mail update sent once a week. Contoso incorporates the information from the Ferguson and Bardell e-mail into the mail-order catalogs they publish quarterly. Prior to publishing their catalog, Contoso contacts all of their suppliers by phone or e-mail to verify product availability.

The following table summarizes the structure and product property requirements for the Contoso online catalog.

Feature	Implementation
Catalog schema	Contoso's catalog schema was already well established, so they simply had to recreate that schema in the XML file they imported. The schema includes three high-level product categories, with variant properties for each: Books, Hardware, and Software.
Custom catalogs	Contoso has decided to provide custom catalogs for registered users, based on user preferences. The custom catalogs will provide discounted prices.
Pricing rules	Prices are set at both the category and individual-product level.

Profiling System

The marketing members of the Installation Planning group were very interested in the Commerce Server Profiling System because they felt that it was extremely important to gather additional information about the company's customer base.

You can use Commerce Server profiles to collect and store information about the customers who visit your Web site. A *profile* is a set of characteristics that define any business-related item, such as a user, a company, or a context (date and time). For example, a user profile can include characteristics such as first name, last name, city, and e-mail address. A context profile can include characteristics such as the date and time when a page is displayed, and the path a customer takes to get to that page. The data that forms a profile comes from multiple sources, such as Web log files and Commerce Server databases. You can import profile data into the Data Warehouse for analysis, and then use the results to target content to groups of users.

The Installation Planning group realized that they had to be sure that the data entities they used to construct the profiles were consistent with entities that already existed in the database. They decided to add some properties to the user object to make targeting advertisements and discounts to their customers easier. For example, they added a **Preferences** property for targeting music and book advertisements. They made this a multi-value property because they knew they would want to allow multiple entries for user preferences.

The following table summarizes the property requirements for the user profile.

Property	Attributes, values, and usage
Preference	**Preferences** are multi-valued strings used to target ads and discounts to customers.
Custom catalog	**Custom catalog** is a string. There are eight different custom catalogs. Customers specify a custom catalog preference when they register.

Targeting System

Targeting and personalization are the processes used to deliver personalized content to one or more customers, or any other business entity that has a profile. Contoso decided to deliver advertisements and announcements about special discounts that were targeted to customer preferences.

The Targeting System has four sub-systems:

- Content Selection Framework (CSF)

- Direct Mailer

- Expression Evaluator

- Predictor resource

Content Selection Framework

The Content Selection Framework (CSF), based on the Commerce Server pipeline architecture, is a platform-level framework that contains the components and pipelines you use to specify the content you want to deliver for advertising and discount campaigns. You use CSF primarily to manage campaigns (the delivery of advertisements and promotions), but you can also use it to rank, select, and schedule any type of content.

The CSF architecture supports an open scoring system that enables you to change the algorithm you use to determine which piece of content to deliver. In addition, CSF supports a trace mode so that you can see exactly how the content has been scored and that enables you to adjust the algorithms accordingly.

Business Desk Campaigns modules provide a user interface that you can use to create campaign items such as advertisements, discounts, and direct mail. You can use the Expression Builder to build expressions for targeting an ad or discount to a specific group. The campaign items and expressions you create with Business Desk are then stored in the Campaigns database.

Contoso decided to provide house advertisements for partners and for discounted items, and to sell advertisements. They also decided to target these ads to registered customers. They defined the requirements listed in the following table for targeting these advertisements.

Content	Target
House ads	None. House ads aren't targeted; they are shown when there aren't sufficient paid advertisements to display.
Discounts	Registered customers, based on their preferences. For example, registered customers who prefer mystery books will be offered discounts on the mystery titles they add to their baskets. In addition, they will be shown advertisements for these discounts when they visit the site.
Paid ads	Customers, based on properties requested by advertisers. Advertisers can select three profile properties to which their ads will be targeted.

Direct Mailer

You use Direct Mailer to manage user mailing lists and to coordinate the sending of direct e-mail to list members. The e-mail you create can be personalized using ASP or it can be sent from a static file. The List Manager service can import e-mail addresses from either a flat file or a SQL Server database into a mailing database.

Direct Mailer is a Microsoft Windows 2000 service that can be installed with Commerce Server as part of a Complete or a Custom installation. There can be only one instance of Direct Mailer per server. However, you can include more than one Direct Mailer resource in your Commerce Server implementation by defining multiple instances at the Global Resource level. (Global resources are available for use by all sites. Global resources expose an object at the global level in Commerce Server Manager, and at the site level for those sites that are using the global resource.)

Direct Mailer performs the following tasks:

- Manages Direct Mailer jobs

- Constructs personalized and non-personalized messages

- Formats e-mail message headers

- Sets the code-page value (language) and converts messages to the correct type (MIME Encapsulation of Aggregate HTML Documents (MHTML), Multipurpose Internet Mail Extensions (MIME), or text)

- Sends e-mail messages to recipients

You can supply a list of recipients to Direct Mailer by using the List Manager module in Business Desk or you can run Direct Mailer in stand-alone mode from the command line and specify a list by file name or SQL Server query. You can use Direct Mailer to send personalized e-mail messages from a Web page or non-personalized mailings from a flat text file to large groups of recipients.

Contoso's marketing team decided to create the direct mail campaigns described in the following table.

Direct Mailer feature	Implementation
Target group	Contoso identified target groups for each of their three catalog categories: Books, Hardware, and Software. They might expand this list in the future.
Custom content	Contoso decided to provide custom e-mail content for registered users. The Custom content feature selects monthly discounts based on the preferences stored in the user's profile and sends them to users through e-mail.

Expression Evaluator

You can use expression-based targeting (also known as *explicit targeting*) when you know the profile properties of the users to whom you are delivering content, or you know the context and the content that is to be delivered. You use the Expression Evaluator to create business rules for personalized ad targeting, promotions, direct mail campaigns, and content targeting, based on the evaluations of conditional expressions.

You use the Campaigns modules in Business Desk to define expressions and deliver the content to the user. For example, if the Contoso site has a sale on books about snowstorm survival, they could use expression-based targeting to notify customers in North Dakota, but not send notifications to customers in Florida. If Contoso were trying to move their golf manuals, they could target customers who listed golf as a hobby.

Contoso's marketing team decided to create expressions to target the preferences they collect from customers at registration. For example, they created the expression *Preference Contains "Mystery"* to display discount information about mystery novels to registered customers who are mystery fans.

Predictor Resource

You use prediction, also known as *implicit targeting*, when you don't know all of the necessary profile properties to use to target a group of customers, or you don't have specific content to deliver. You can use the Commerce Server Predictor resource to extrapolate this information from existing data so that you can deliver content specific to each customer. For example, you can use the Predictor resource to discover what type of content, ads, and cross sells might interest your customers.

The Predictor resource is a Windows 2000 service that you can install with Commerce Server as part of a Complete or a Custom installation. Commerce Server supports multiple instances of the Predictor resource per commerce site, but only one instance per computer. You can install the Predictor resource on each computer that contains your Data Warehouse, or you can install it on separate computers, to save system memory.

Both expression-based targeting and prediction make it easier for you to deliver content to your customers. Customers are more likely to return to your site when they expect to receive a personalized experience.

Contoso decided not to implement the Predictor resource in its initial deployment, but the team realizes that they should plan to use it in the near future. Before Contoso can successfully implement the Predictor resource, they need to gather sufficient data in the Data Warehouse to build the required analysis models. The following table describes the models that the Contoso marketing team plans to build and the data those models require.

Model	Description	Data required
User preference	A Prediction model to determine which products to recommend on the Basket page.	<ul><li>Click history</li><li>Transactions</li><li>User preferences</li></ul>
User demographics	A Segment model for ongoing analysis of the site's audience.	The following properties from registered users:<ul><li>Country and postal code</li><li>Age bracket</li><li>Gender</li></ul>The team added age bracket and gender to the user profile, and added fields to capture these properties to the user registration form.

Capacity and Performance

It is difficult to predict how variables in site design, coding practices, user behavior, and site architecture will combine to affect site performance, so it is important to plan and test the capacity and performance of your site before deploying to a live production environment.

Performance planning and capacity planning go hand in hand; however, each addresses site usage from a different perspective. Performance planning addresses the technical aspects of the site, focusing on performance metrics, such as ASP page throughput and ASP latency. Capacity planning addresses both the technical aspects and the business perspective, focusing on maximizing the number of users that the site can handle.

Of the two, performance planning is the more straightforward. It is relatively easy to measure the number of checkout transactions per second and make comparisons to other commerce sites.

Analyzing user capacity is a little more complex. Before you can predict maximum user capacity, you first need to profile user behavior, and then use the user profile information in conjunction with your performance metrics to calculate capacity. User behavior varies from site to site, depending on the richness of the shopping experience (page design, site design, and response time), as well as the types of products being sold and the extent of the product line. One site may support 1,000 users, while another site installed on an identical platform may support only 200 users because of differences in user behavior. For more information about planning for capacity and performance, see Chapter 19, "Maximizing Performance."

The following table lists Contoso architecture and performance requirements.

Area	Description
Customer experience	Contoso realized that their biggest asset is their extensive catalog. They believe that providing fast access to catalog items is critical to their success. They agreed that the maximum time for returning an item from a free-text catalog search should be one second when the site is running at full capacity.
Usage profile	The Contoso team created a usage profile for measuring site performance, which includes the following factors: • Total user base = 1,000,000 • Concurrent user % = 1% (10,000) • Average length of a session = 10 minutes • Average number of operations per session = 10 The team also developed detailed usage profiles for each page on the site.

Web server configuration	They decided to begin with two front-end Web servers, based on the following calculation:
	
	`Number of concurrent users/server capacity`
	`10,000/5,000 = 2`
	
	Note The complete hardware configuration is summarized in "Deployment" later in this chapter.

Growth forecast	Contoso used the growth in their mail-order business to project the growth of their Web site. Their customer base is currently growing at a 20 percent annual rate. They project that they will reach a base of 1,000,000 customers by the end of the first year and maintain a 20 percent growth rate from that point on.
Integration with existing systems	The team decided to integrate the Web business with their existing systems in a series of stages. In the first stage, they integrated the product catalog. In subsequent stages, they plan to integrate their accounting system and their order-fulfillment system.
Availability	To provide for failover capabilities for the Contoso database, the team set up their two database servers using Windows 2000 Cluster service and SQL Server 2000 replication features.

Security

When you plan for Commerce Server security, you begin by deciding how to defeat security threats for each feature you deploy and by selecting the policies and tools necessary to achieve the level of security you want. To build a secure site, you need to configure Secure Sockets Layer (SSL) so that certain pages (such as pages that request credit card information) are served through SSL. To set this up, you need to get a server certificate and configure Internet Information Services (IIS) 5.0 to use SSL.

You should also specify a Secure Host Name for each Commerce Server application in the Microsoft Management Console (MMC). The **AuthManager** object uses the Secure Host Name to create links to secure pages. The links could lead to a different Commerce Server application or to a secure section of the same application.

To minimize the likelihood of a security breach, you must be able to:

- Lock down the site (control access to files, pages, and applications with access control lists (ACLs) on files that use the NTFS file system (NTFS)).

- Control access to reading or running scripts, and write access on various folders defined in your site for IIS security.

- Authenticate site visitors.

The Contoso team agreed that they must be able to guarantee the integrity of transactions conducted through their site. To accomplish this, they planned methods of locking down the site and creating a secure environment. They also decided to support a variety of authentication schemes. The following table describes the security decisions the Contoso team made.

Security issue	Description
Authentication	The team decided to allow customers to shop without registering, so the authentication system had to support both registered and anonymous users. The team determined that the authentication system built into the Retail Solution Site does exactly what they wanted.
Identification	Contoso elected to use cookies to identify users if a user's browser is configured to support cookies or to append an identification ticket to the **QueryString** data member if cookie support has been disabled. The Retail Solution Site also provides this functionality.
Firewall placement	The team consulted with a network expert to design the appropriate firewall configuration. Their configuration included two firewalls, one to isolate the data center from the Internet, and another one to isolate the database layer from the Web servers.

Completing the Planning Process

The Commerce Server Installation Planning group met regularly to describe what they had learned and to make a case for the features and functionalities they wanted to include in their site. The group had a reserved project room where they charted their plans and hung them on the wall, and then converted the charts into a project specification. Their project specification included the Commerce Server features described in the following table.

Feature	To be used to
Business Desk	Host business management modules for configuring site options and for managing the day-to-day marketing and analysis of site activity.
Commerce Server Manager	Manage and configure Commerce Server resources, sites, applications, and Web servers.
Data Warehouse	Import and maintain data in a combination of a SQL Server database and an OLAP database.
Business Process Pipelines	Define and link together the stages of their business processes, and then run them in sequence to complete each task.
Product Catalog System	Import their existing catalog and then manage the catalog online.
Profiling System	Collect and store information about the customers who visit their site.
Targeting System	Deliver personalized content to one or more customers.
CSF	Determine the content to be delivered for advertising and discount campaigns.
Direct Mailer	Manage mailing lists and coordinate the sending of direct mail to customers on the mailing lists.
Expression Evaluator	Target ads, promotions, and other campaigns.
Predictor resource	Extrapolate targeting information from the user data collected in the Data Warehouse. (This feature won't be implemented until the Contoso team determines that they have sufficient data in the Data Warehouse.)

The Installation Planning group also identified architectural and security requirements:

- High capacity and performance
- Ability to grow
- Integration with existing systems
- High availability
- Security
- Microsoft Active Directory integration

With these areas identified, the next step was to begin development.

Development

The Contoso development team began developing the new site by downloading the Retail Solution Site (from http://www.microsoft.com/commerceserver/solutionsites) and experimenting with the built-in and extendable functionality. They also reviewed the Blank Solution Site which, when unpacked, provides a Web site which is essentially empty. The Blank site contains Business Desk and the set of empty databases upon which the site ultimately depends. They decided that the Retail Solution Site provided the most appropriate foundation for their site.

Using the Retail Solution Site as a starting point, the Contoso team identified the following areas in which they wanted to take advantage of the extensible design provided by Commerce Server:

- Importing the catalog

- Acquiring new pipeline components

- Modifying site look and feel

- Adjusting settings in the App Default Config resource

Importing the Catalog

Before the Contoso development team could import their catalog, they had to create an XML file that matched the Commerce Server Catalog XML structure. The development team examined the structure specified in the "Programmer's Reference" section of Commerce Server 2000 Help and the sample XML files provided as part of the Business Desk tutorial. They based their XML file on these two sources. When they were satisfied that they had structured their XML file appropriately, they used the Business Desk Catalog Editor module to import it.

Acquiring New Pipeline Components

A pipeline component is a Component Object Model (COM) object that supports a standard set of interfaces that you can invoke in a uniform fashion during the execution of the pipeline. The pipeline architecture enables you to create new pipeline components and "plug" them into existing pipelines. When you do this, you often replace an existing pipeline component and alter the processing that pipeline is performing.

A common example of this type of pipeline component replacement is the pipeline that is executed when a customer decides to check out, and the basket is processed to complete the transaction. The Retail Solution Site provides a complete pipeline for calculating the order total when a customer clicks the **Check out** button on the Basket page. This pipeline includes the **SampleRegionalTax** component to demonstrate the tax stage of the Purchase pipeline. Contoso acquired a tax component from ProseWare Corporation to replace this demonstration component. They also replaced the **Scriptor – Payment Info** component included in the Checkout pipeline with one of the payment components offered by a third-party.

Modifying Site Look and Feel

The development team studied the documentation for the Retail Solution Site to determine the best way to customize it. They decided to do the following to customize the site:

- Modify the site name

- Create new site styles by modifying the dictionary of styles in the Global_ui_lib.asp file

- Change the layout for the standard page by modifying the HTML in the Layout1.asp file.

- Change strings as necessary in the Rc.xml file

Figure 2.1 shows the Contoso home page after the team finished modifying the Retail Solution Site.

Figure 2.1 The new Contoso home page

Adjusting Settings in the App Default Config Resource

The App Default Config resource is a Commerce Server resource with site-level properties that you manage through Commerce Server Manager. You can use App Default Config to set properties that determine site functionality in areas such as currency options, billing options, and Microsoft BizTalk Server 2000 integration.

The Contoso development team found that they didn't need to adjust many of the settings in the App Default Config resource. The majority of the values set by unpacking the Retail Solution Site package, Retail.pup, met their requirements. The following table describes the settings they decided to adjust.

Setting	Description
BizTalk Catalog Doc Type	The document definition name that BizTalk Server requires for catalogs.
BizTalk options	Options that determine whether or not a site can integrate with BizTalk Server. In the Retail Solution Site, the default value is 0 to disable integration. The development team set it to 1.
Add item redirect options	Options that determine whether or not a browser is redirected to the Basket page after a customer adds an item to the basket. In the Retail Solution Site, the default value is 1, which means that the product page will continue to be displayed. The development team set the value to 0 to enable them to redirect the customer to a different page.
Site privacy options	Options that determine whether or not to track profile information. The team consulted with the executive committee, and then decided that they didn't need this information. In the Retail Solution Site, the default value is 1, which means that anonymous users are tracked. The development team set this value to 0 to disable this feature.

Setting Up the Development Environment

The Contoso team created a development environment centered on Microsoft Windows.Net technology, Microsoft Visual Studio and other development tools, and the Commerce Server 2000 Software Development Kit (SDK). The team also created a three-tiered testbed with IIS running on the user interface layer (top tier), Commerce Server 2000 and COM/COM+ objects providing the business logic (middle tier), and SQL Server on the database layer (bottom tier). Although the application architecture continues to be three-tiered, the developers decided to combine Web servers and application servers on the same computer, to prevent invoking objects over-the-wire in a separate application server scenario. That is, Commerce Server and other objects reside directly on the Web servers.

Deployment

By the end of the development and testing process, the Contoso team had created a system in their test environment that exactly duplicated the system they had decided to use for production. The test site consisted of the items listed in the following table.

Servers	Software
Two Web servers	• Windows 2000 Advanced Server with Network Load Balancing
	• IIS 5.0
	• Microsoft Internet Explorer 5.5
	• Commerce Server 2000
	• Windows 2000 Terminal Services (to support remote access to Business Desk)
	Note Both servers use Active Directory and serve as replicated domain controllers.
Two database servers	• Windows 2000 Advanced Server with Windows Cluster service
	• Microsoft SQL Server 7.0 Enterprise Edition and Microsoft SQL Server Analysis Services (OLAP)
	Notes The Contoso team used SQL Server replication to synchronize their database servers.
	They used Open Database Connectivity (ODBC) communication for retrieving information, such as order status, from their IBM AS/400 system.
	They replicated their catalog data, which the AS/400 also stores and manages, to the Commerce Server catalog schema residing in a SQL Server database.
One server for firewall and proxy services	• Windows 2000 Advanced Server using proxy and firewall services.

Figure 2.2 shows the site architecture for the deployed site.

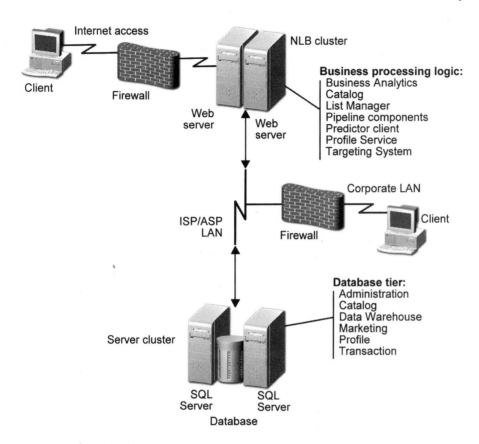

Figure 2.2 Contoso's site architecture

Performing Final Testing

The Contoso test team tested the site continually as part of the development process, but when the tested site was completed and ready to move into production, they did final site testing, verifying the following:

- Content
- Browser compatibility
- Performance
- Server load
- Databases
- Search options
- Query response time
- Data validity and integrity
- System recovery
- Visual consistency
- Links
- Routers
- Stress testing (using the Microsoft Web Application Stress (WAS) tool)

Preparing for Business

The Contoso team ensured that all team members were prepared for the site to go live by reviewing with them the processes described in the following table.

Team members	Description
Business managers	- Reviewed and tested workflows - Completed the Business Desk tutorial
System administrators	- Received training on how to administer the site
Entire team	- Reviewed operational procedures (change requests, change control logs, maintenance schedules, problem escalation procedures, and so on)

Verifying Security

The Contoso team verified security in the following areas prior to placing their tested site into production:

- **Securing Business Desk sessions**. When Site Packager unpacks a Business Desk application, it is configured to use Integrated Windows authentication. Although this secures client authentication, the Business Desk session itself passes data in clear text. To provide security for their Business Desk sessions, Contoso set up their Business Desk client computers inside their firewall.

- **Setting up Data Warehouse permissions**. One way to give Business Desk users the ability to read and modify objects in the Data Warehouse is to give them a Windows Administrator account. However, Contoso wanted some Business Desk users to be able only to read reports. They accomplished this by assigning the following SQL Server database roles to each of their system users:

    - **Db_datareader role**. User can see all data from all tables in a database.

    - **Db_datawriter role**. User can add, change, or delete data from tables in the database.

- **Securing cookies**. By default, cookies travel in clear text. It is possible for hackers to intercept information contained in cookies and use that information to impersonate users. Cookies can be encrypted. Commerce Server uses encrypted authentication and anonymous cookies to enhance security. To help secure cookies, Contoso used encryption and embedded the Internet Protocol (IP) address of the client in the cookies so that the Web server could verify that the correct user actually sent the cookies.

- **Setting permissions on folders that contain the site**. Site Packager doesn't package or unpack any NTFS folder or file permissions (ACLs). Contoso secured the files and folders that contain their site.

Going Live

When the development site was completely tested and ready for production, the Contoso team used Site Packager to prepare their site for deployment in the production environment. The production environment was an exact duplicate of their test environment.

In addition to site resources, applications, and the IIS settings needed to recreate the Web server configurations, Site Packager also includes the property values from the Administration database. For example, when you package the App Default Config resource, all of the current property values are also packaged. When you unpack the App Default Config resource, the property values are unpacked onto the Administration database. The package includes global resource pointers but not the global resources themselves. Connection strings are packaged without the user name and password fields.

During the application packaging process, Site Packager searches the IIS metabase on your local computer, and finds the physical directory that is the root for that application. It then starts at that root directory and packages all the subdirectories below into a new file with a .pup file name extension. Site Packager preserves certain settings in IIS, such as authorizations and access permissions. Site Packager doesn't package properties that are specific to the computer you are working on. For example, Web server properties and some application properties set in Commerce Server Manager aren't packaged.

Closing the Loop

The Contoso team realized from the beginning of the project that an e-commerce Web site is a corporate asset that business managers must continuously manage, analyze, and enhance in order to keep their Web site competitive. Business managers need to quickly analyze customer activity to measure the effectiveness of their sites, and then use the results to fine-tune the sites. By analyzing customer data, the business manager can make decisions about how to improve the site and meet business goals. Post-deployment responsibilities fall into the following three basic areas:

- Collecting and storing customer data

- Analyzing customer data

- Implementing the site management cycle

Collecting and Storing Customer Data

Contoso is collecting three types of data, listed in the following table, about the customers who visit their site.

Data type	Description
Explicit profile data	Obtained when customers provide information about themselves by completing online forms, surveys, and polls.
Click history	Obtained when customers visit the site and click links to site pages. The click history includes the length of time spent visiting the site, referring URLs, ad clicks, ad reach, click frequency, and the path of the user through the site (including entry and exit pages). For example, Contoso recorded the following information for a typical user session: - Time on the site = 17 minutes - Catalog product descriptions viewed = 3 - Item selected = special promotion
Transaction history	Products a customer purchased. The transaction history records baskets and orders. The transaction history Contoso is tracking includes customer name, shipping address, date and time of purchase, product purchased, and order total.

This data is collected in the Web server log files and the Commerce Server databases. On a regular basis Contoso's system administration team imports the data from the Web server log files and Commerce Server databases into their Data Warehouse.

Analyzing Customer Data

Contoso's site administration team analyzes customer data from the Data Warehouse, then provides this information to the management team. They use the data to identify the types of customers who visit the site, what is selling well, and which advertising campaigns are successful.

Implementing the Site Management Cycle

To effectively implement the site management cycle, the business management, site development, and system administration teams agreed to inform each other about the updates they make to the site. They established a process to facilitate this communication. For example, to update a large set of user profiles in bulk, the business management team contacts the system administration team, who then performs this task. To add new functionality to Business Desk, such as a module for selling gift certificates, the business management team sends their requirements to the site development team.

The teams have a process for requesting changes. (For more information about designing a process for requesting changes, see Chapter 8, "Developing Your Site.") They also established a regular meeting schedule to resolve any communication issues that might arise as they continue to refine their site.

A Supplier Scenario

Chapter 2, "A Retail Scenario," introduced the fictitious Contoso, Ltd. company and described how Contoso implemented a retail Web site using Microsoft Commerce Server 2000 and the Retail Solution Site. This chapter describes how one of Contoso's suppliers, the fictitious company called Ferguson and Bardell, implemented a supplier integration (business-to-business) site. Like the Contoso example, this scenario information is drawn from real deployments of Commerce Server. For detailed information about these deployments, see http://www.microsoft.com/commerceserver. At the end of this chapter, there is also a step-by-step example that describes how to configure a sample supplier site.

Ferguson and Bardell are book distributors. They serve as an intermediary between publishing houses and retail book outlets. Their customers include large retail chains as well as independent bookstores throughout the United States and Canada. They decided to create a Web site on which their customers could place orders and manage account information. One of the primary reasons for putting together the site was that Contoso had approached Ferguson and Bardell about using Commerce Server 2000 and Microsoft BizTalk Server 2000 to exchange catalogs and purchase orders. Ferguson and Bardell plan to offer this service to other customers after they have tested the exchange with Contoso.

Planning

The Ferguson and Bardell development effort followed the same general processes described in Chapter 2, "A Retail Scenario." They created a development and implementation team and reviewed the product documentation to decide which Commerce Server and BizTalk Server features would best meet their business needs. They decided to implement the following features:

- Organization profile tracking (from the Commerce Server Business Desk Organizations module)
- Integrated Windows authentication
- Microsoft Active Directory integration
- Product catalog and purchase-order transmission (using BizTalk Server)
- Partner Service

In addition, this section explains how the Ferguson and Bardell team planned site capacity, performance, and growth, as well as how to integrate with their existing systems. The Ferguson and Bardell team decided to base their new site on the Supplier Solution Site, which provides all of these features.

Organization Profiles

You use the Organizations module in the Users category of Business Desk to manage organization profiles. The organization profile included with the Supplier Solution Site provides the following properties:

- Organization ID
- Name
- Trading partner number
- Administrative contact
- Receiver
- Organization catalog set
- Purchasing Manager

The database administrator for Ferguson and Bardell provided the necessary information for the Contoso organization profile. The team appointed a site manager to update the organizational information when necessary. In the initial phase of the project, they added the organization profile only for Contoso, Ltd.

Authentication

Ferguson and Bardell have a Microsoft Windows 2000 network and security infrastructure in place. They planned to use the existing network account structure to authenticate organizational contacts when they log into the site. They realized that this would mean adding network accounts for each of their trading partners. Because Ferguson and Bardell work with a relatively small number of high-volume customers, they did not anticipate any difficulties in setting up the new network accounts.

The development team assembled the requirements described in the following table for their authentication system.

Requirement	Description
Identify users	Identification is the process of tracking customers between visits and during a single session. Because Ferguson and Bardell had well-established relationships with their customers, they believed they could ask customers to enable cookie support in their Internet browsers. They decided to use the AuthFilter in Autocookie mode with the authentication scheme set to Windows Authentication.
Delegate administration	Ferguson and Bardell created a delegated administration account for each customer organization. When a user logs on to the Ferguson and Bardell site using this account, they can create and manage accounts for other members of their organization.
Customize the login page	Because Ferguson and Bardell are using the Supplier Solution Site as the foundation for building their site, they need to modify the login page to work with the AuthFilter. (This is described in more detail in the "Development" section later in this chapter.)

Active Directory Integration

Ferguson and Bardell already use Active Directory to store information about internal users. These users are arranged in groups that match the company's organizational structure. When the development team read that the Supplier Solution Site supports Active Directory as a back-end data store for user profile information, they knew they needed to determine whether they could incorporate the user information from their Web site into their current Active Directory implementation. They decided to store the information listed in the following table.

Profile	Description
Organization	The development team decided to store the trading partner profile information in Active Directory.
Users	The development team researched the scaling capabilities of Active Directory and decided that Active Directory could accommodate their requirements for storing user information. They decided to store the complete user profile in Active Directory.
Purchase orders	Ferguson and Bardell handle approximately 100,000 purchase orders per month. Because this is highly volatile data, the development team decided to store purchase orders in their Microsoft SQL Server 2000 database.

Integration with BizTalk Server

Ferguson and Bardell's long-term plan is to migrate their product catalog to Commerce Server. Their current catalog is stored on an IBM AS/400 mainframe computer. Because the goal for the first phase of their project was to integrate with Contoso, Ltd., the planning team decided to keep their existing catalog system, store a copy of the product catalog in a Commerce Server database, and run the two systems in parallel.

The team decided to use the BizTalk Mapper tool to convert their catalog to the Commerce Server catalog Extensible Markup Language (XML) format. They also established a schedule for updating the Contoso online catalog with new data from the AS/400 mainframe. The following table summarizes the tasks the development team performed to coordinate their BizTalk Server implementation with Contoso.

Task	Description
Establish catalog update schedule	Because Ferguson and Bardell are planning to maintain their existing catalog on the AS/400, they needed to establish a regular schedule for updating the Commerce Server catalog and sending it to Contoso. They updated the catalog by running a script that uses a BizTalk Server functoid to convert the catalog from the AS/400 format into the Commerce Server XML format.
Coordinate with Contoso to configure BizTalk Server	Because Ferguson and Bardell planned to exchange catalog information with Contoso, they informed Contoso of the appropriate Commerce Server and BizTalk Server configuration settings.
Configure BizTalk Server to receive purchase orders from Contoso	Ferguson and Bardell had to set several configuration settings using both Commerce Server Manager and the BizTalk Messaging Manager. (For information about specific configuration settings, see Chapter 13, "Integrating Commerce Server with BizTalk Server.")
Modify the Supplier Solution Site to work with the order management system	The Supplier Solution Site provides starter files for integrating with a Commerce Server retail site. For example, the _Recvpo.asp file described in the "Development" section later in this chapter is a starter file for integrating purchase order processing with an order fulfillment system.

Partner Service

Ferguson and Bardell found that the Partner Service area of the Supplier Solution Site was one of the most compelling reasons to use it as the basis for developing their site. They found that the Partner Service enabled them to quickly develop a site in which trading partners could manage their own accounts remotely. This delegated administration feature was important to them. The following table summarizes Ferguson and Bardell's requirements for the Partner Service.

Requirement	Description
Create delegated administration accounts	Ferguson and Bardell's site administrator created a single administrative account for Contoso and sent the login name and initial password to the Contoso system administrator. Contoso could then use this account to log on to the site and access the Partner Service.
Create user accounts	Although partner account management is limited to a single account, the team decided to enable partners to create multiple user accounts for making purchases. Partners logging in to user accounts could also make purchases, view order information, and view information about their account.

Capacity, Performance, and Growth Requirements

The development team defined their architecture and described their performance requirements in the areas listed in the following table.

Area	Description and performance requirements
User experience	The development team believed that because the users on the site will be professional book buyers, they generally know what they want. Two factors critical to their success were the ability to provide users with an interface that facilitated locating books from their extensive collection, and fast access time. They set a performance goal for the maximum time for returning an item from a free-text catalog search as one second when the site is running at full capacity.
Usage profile	The usage profile for Ferguson and Bardell was somewhat different from the profile the Contoso team developed. Ferguson and Bardell projected a significantly smaller number of users, but they expected a higher percentage of purchases. They also expected users to have shorter sessions, because they would be less likely to simply browse the catalog.
	Their site usage profile includes the following factors:
	• Total user base = 100,000
	• Concurrent user % = 10% (10,000)
	• Average length of a session = 5 minutes
	• Average number of operations per session = 10
	The team also developed detailed usage profiles for each of the site pages.
Web server configuration	They decided to begin with two front-end Web servers, based on the following calculation:
| | ```
Number of concurrent users/server capacity
10,000/5,000 = 2
``` |
	Note The complete hardware configuration is summarized in "Deployment" later in this chapter.
Growth forecast	Although this project is being rolled out with Contoso as a test, Ferguson and Bardell intend to bring their other partners online in the future. The estimated total user base of 100,000 is based on the assumption that most of their corporate customers will change to making their purchases from their Web site.
Integration with existing systems	Ferguson and Bardell's order processing and account management system is implemented using J. D. Edwards OneWorld®, running on an IBM AS/400 platform. This system serves as an integration point for all of their sales channels. The new site had to integrate seamlessly with existing systems.
Availability	The team decided that two Web servers would provide sufficient capacity for serving Web pages; however, they also wanted to provide failover capacity in the database layer. They set up their two database servers using Windows 2000 Cluster service and SQL Server 2000 replication features.
```

Integration with Existing Systems

The development team realized that integrating their Web-based order entry and management system with their existing system was going to be a major challenge. They decided to use Microsoft Host Integration Server 2000 to integrate the two. The following table summarizes their requirements for this integration.

Requirement	Description
Retrieve catalog information	Because Ferguson and Bardell decided to maintain their existing catalog system in parallel with their Web catalog system, the development team decided to use Host Integration Server to retrieve catalog information. For more information, see "Development" later in this chapter.
Update order information	Ferguson and Bardell are storing the orders that Contoso places on their Web site in a SQL Server 2000 database. They want to pass order data through the Host Integration Server implementation to the order fulfillment system on their AS/400 mainframe.

Completing the Planning Process

At the end of the planning process, the Ferguson and Bardell development team presented their complete project specification to the executive committee and to the Contoso development team. Their proposal included the following set of Microsoft .NET Enterprise Server features:

- Catalog and purchase order exchange

- Profile aggregation from Active Directory and SQL Server 2000

- Integration with existing systems

- Delegated administration

  Note   The Ferguson and Bardell team also planned for other aspects of their Web site, such as their use of the Targeting and Business Analytics Systems. They used the same procedures to plan for these systems as Contoso did. The planning process is described in detail in Chapter 2, "A Retail Scenario."

The next step was to begin development.

Development

The Ferguson and Bardell development team began by downloading the Supplier Solution Site (from http://www.microsoft.com/commerceserver/solutionsites) and analyzing the built-in, extendable functionality. They decided that the Supplier Solution Site provided the best foundation on which to build their site.

The Supplier Solution Site is a development reference site that provides an integrated set of features for building a site to manage partner relationships. In addition to the business-to-business functionality for personalization, merchandising, catalog search, customer service, and business analytics, the Supplier Solution Site also contains the delegated administration features that Ferguson and Bardell required. For example, it includes the Partner Service, which enables corporate customers to manage accounts for their organizational representatives.

Using the Supplier Solution Site as a starting point, the Ferguson and Bardell development team identified key areas in which they wanted to take advantage of the extensible design of Commerce Server:

- Converting and importing the catalog

- Developing Component Object Model (COM) components

- Modifying site look and feel

- Modifying the _Recvpo.asp file

- Adjust settings in the App Default Config resource

Converting and Importing the Catalog

The development team read the product documentation for both Commerce Server and BizTalk Server to determine how to use the BizTalk Server mapper tool to convert their catalog into the appropriate format. They discovered that they could use the BizTalk Server Looping functoid to convert their catalog.

They performed an initial mapping of their catalog data, and then arranged for the Contoso team to confirm that they could successfully import the mapped catalog data. When Contoso had successfully imported the catalog, Ferguson and Bardell used the **CatalogUpdate** component (described in the table in the following section) to automate the process.

Developing COM Components

The development team created the COM components listed in the following table to integrate with their existing catalog system.

Component	Description
CatalogUpdate	BizTalk Server application integration component that retrieves catalog data from the IBM AS/400 using Host Integration Server. It also implements the **IFunctoid** interface to convert catalog data to the Commerce Server catalog format. The development team also created a script to update the Contoso catalog that is run according to their schedule for updating the catalog.
OrderUpdate	Component that passes an order through the Host Integration Server implementation to the existing order-fulfillment system. When partners place an order on the Web site, it is stored in a SQL Server 2000 database.

Modifying Site Look and Feel

The Ferguson and Bardell development team took the same basic steps to modify the Supplier Solution Site as the Contoso development team took to modify the Retail Solution Site:

- Modify the site name

- Create new site styles by modifying the dictionary of styles in the Global_ui_lib.asp file

- Change the layout for the standard page by modifying the Hypertext Markup Language (HTML) in the Layout1.asp file

- Change strings as necessary in the Rc.xml file

Figure 3.1 shows the Ferguson and Bardell home page after they finished modifying the Supplier Solution site.

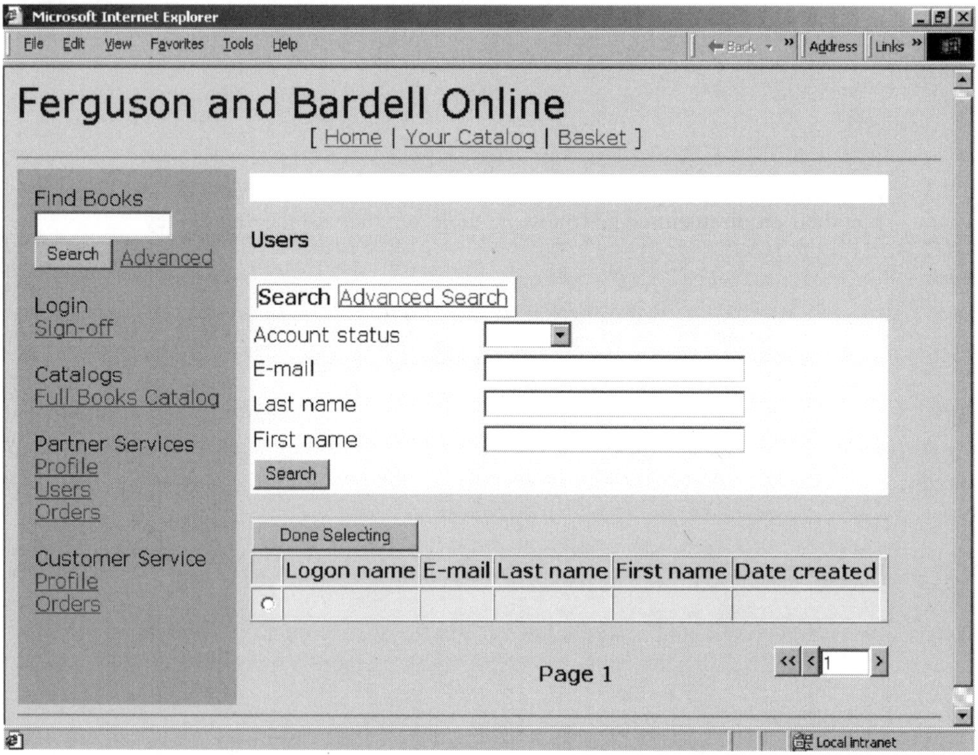

Figure 3.1 Ferguson and Bardell home page

Modifying the _Recvpo.asp File

The Supplier Solution Site contains the _Recvpo.asp file, which you can use to facilitate setting up a vendor's Commerce Server installation. (The Default installation location for the _Recvpo.asp file is the \SupplierAd folder.)

When _Recvpo.asp receives an XML document, it starts the XMLTransforms process and converts the XML document back to an order form. Commerce Server then runs a pipeline on the order form. After the pipeline processes the order form, the order is saved in the Commerce Server database. To implement _Recvpo.asp, the Ferguson and Bardell development team added a pipeline component that updates their back-end order processing system with the order information to the Recvpo.pcf pipeline template.

Adjusting Settings in the App Default Config Resource

The development team found that they did not need to adjust most of the settings in the App Default Config resource. The majority of the default values set in the Supplier Solution Site (SupplierAD.pup) met their requirements. The following table summarizes the values they adjusted.

Setting	Description
BizTalk Catalog Doc Type	The document definition name required by BizTalk Server for catalogs.
BizTalk Source Org Qualifier	An alias used to identify the organization that is sending the catalog. Because Ferguson and Bardell are generating their catalog internally, they set this alias to "Internal."
BizTalk Source Org Qualifier Value	The role of the source organization. The development team set this value to "CatalogSender."

Deployment

By the end of the development and testing process, the Ferguson and Bardell team had created an exact duplicate of the system that they wanted to use for production in their test environment. The production site consisted of the servers and software listed in the following table.

Servers	Software
Two Web servers	<ul><li>Windows 2000 Advanced Server with Network Load Balancing</li><li>Internet Information Services (IIS) 5.0</li><li>Microsoft Internet Explorer 5.5</li><li>Commerce Server</li><li>Windows 2000 Terminal Services (to support remote access to Business Desk)</li></ul>**Note** Both servers handle Active Directory and serve as replicated domain controllers.
One server	<ul><li>BizTalk Server</li></ul>
Two database servers	<ul><li>Windows 2000 Advanced Server with Windows Clustering service</li><li>Microsoft SQL Server 2000 Enterprise Edition and Microsoft SQL Server Analysis Services (OLAP)</li></ul>**Notes** Ferguson and Bardell used SQL Server replication to synchronize their database servers. They used Open Database Connectivity (ODBC) communication for retrieving information, such as order status, from their IBM AS/400 system. They replicated their catalog data, which the AS/400 also stores and manages, on the Commerce Server catalog schema residing in a SQL Server database.
One server for firewall and proxy services	<ul><li>Windows 2000 Advanced Server using proxy and firewall services.</li></ul>
One domain controller	<ul><li>Active Directory store used by the Profile Service. The domain controller is part of the Ferguson and Bardell forest and is replicated on a second clustered server.</li></ul>
One IBM AS/400	<ul><li>J.D. Edwards OneWorld.</li></ul>

Figure 3.2 shows the site architecture for the deployed site.

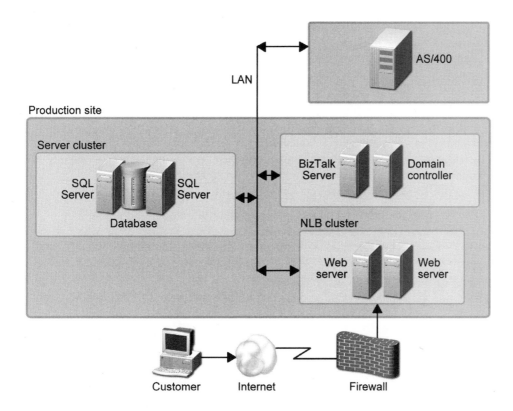

Figure 3.2 Ferguson and Bardell production site

Testing Business Processes

The Ferguson and Bardell team tested the system thoroughly to assure that all software operated correctly. In addition, they ensured that all team members were prepared for the site to go live by reviewing with them the processes described in the following table.

Team members	Description
Business managers	• Reviewed and tested workflows
	• Completed the Business Desk tutorial
System administrators	• Received training on how to administer the site
Entire team	• Reviewed operational procedures (change requests, change control logs, maintenance schedules, problem escalation procedures, and so on)

Verifying Security

Ferguson and Bardell performed all of the security verifications that Contoso performed (described in Chapter 2, "A Retail Scenario"). In addition, they verified that only delegated administrators could create new user accounts.

Going Live

When the development site was completely tested and ready for production, the Ferguson and Bardell team used Commerce Server Site Packager to prepare their site for deployment in the production environment. After they successfully unpacked the site, they did final site acceptance testing with the Contoso team before going live on the production site.

The Ferguson and Bardell team realized from the beginning of the project that this was just the first step towards migrating to full partner integration over the Internet. They planned to explore further integration after evaluating their experience integrating with Contoso.

Configuring a Sample Supplier Solution Site

This section describes how to configure four computers for a Supplier Solution Site that uses both Active Directory and SQL Server 2000. You can perform these steps to build a supplier site for evaluation and testing purposes. There are several other ways to set up a supplier site, including Windows 2000, Domain Name System (DNS) servers, and local intranets, depending on your company's requirements. This section provides a step-by-step example to highlight the points you must consider for a supplier implementation. Figure 3.3 shows the sample configuration.

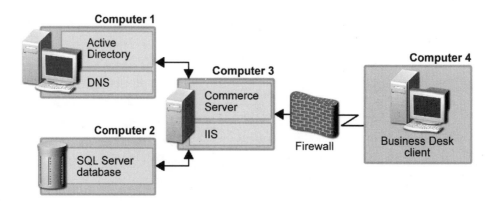

Figure 3.3 Sample supplier site

To set up the sample configuration, perform the following steps:

1. Configure Active Directory and DNS on Computer 1, and then promote it to an Active Directory domain controller.

2. Configure SQL Server 2000 and Commerce Server on Computer 2.

3. Configure IIS and unpack the Supplier Solution Site on Computer 3.

4. Configure the Business Desk client on Computer 4.

5. Verify software configuration on the four computers.

6. Configure all four computers for trusted delegation.

7. Verify Business Desk and the Supplier Solution Site.

The previous steps are described in detail in the following sections.

These steps assume that:

- You have experience installing Windows 2000 Advanced Server, Windows 2000 Server, Commerce Server 2000, and SQL Server 2000.

- You are creating a new domain (Active Directory) for the first time.

- You are creating a new DNS server.

- You are using mixed mode authentication for your SQL Server, and Basic authentication for your Web server. If you want to use this configuration in an Internet scenario, you should also enable Hypertext Transfer Protocol Secure (HTTPS) for your Web server.

Configuring Active Directory and DNS (Computer 1)

You configure the first computer for Active Directory and DNS, and then promote it to an Active Directory domain controller. Active Directory will store the profile data for Commerce Server.

To configure the first computer, perform the following steps:

1. Install Windows 2000 Advanced Server, using the **Default** installation.

2. Install Windows 2000 Service Pack 1 (SP1) and the required hotfixes specified at http://support.microsoft.com/support/commerceserver/2000/install/default.asp.

3. Open the **Control Panel**, and then use **Network and Dial-up Connections** to configure the static Internet Protocol (IP) address.

4. Promote the server to an Active Directory domain controller. For detailed steps, see "Promoting an Active Directory Domain Controller" later in this chapter.

5. Use **Network and Dial-up Connections** to configure the server's DNS entries to point to your domain controller, and configure Windows Internet Name Service (WINS) to point

to itself. For detailed instructions, see "Configure TCP/IP to use DNS" and "Configure TCP/IP to use WINS" in Windows 2000 Server Help.

For additional networking information, see the *Microsoft Windows 2000 Server Resource Kit*.

6. Optionally, if the computer has more than two gigabytes (GB) of physical RAM, add a "/3GB" switch to the Boot.ini file after /fastdetect. By adding this switch, the address space for the user mode processes is increased.

   For more information about this step, see the following Microsoft Knowledge Base articles:

   - Q171793 - Information on Application Use of 4GT RAM Tuning, available at http://support.microsoft.com/support/kb/articles/Q171/7/93.ASP.

   - Q189293 - XADM: Enabling 4GT Switch When Using Windows NT/Enterprise, available at http://support.microsoft.com/support/kb/articles/Q189/2/93.ASP.

7. In the Registry, go to HKEY_LOCAL_MACHINE\SYSTEM\CurrentControlSet\Services\Tcpip\Parameters, and do the following:

   - Add (or set if the key is already there) the **DWORD** value **MaxUserPort = 0000fffe**.

   - Add (or set if the key is already there) the **DWORD** value **TcpWindowSize = 0000ffff**.

   Any site using Active Directory requires these Transmission Control Protocol/Internet Protocol (TCP/IP) keys. They improve performance on high-speed networks.

8. Optionally, open **Administrative Tools**, click **Domain Controllers Security Policies**, and then set the "logon locally policy" if you want to permit domain users to have that privilege.

You have successfully configured the software on the first computer.

To promote Computer 1 to an Active Directory domain controller, you must use the Active Directory Installation Wizard to specify that this computer is the domain controller.

To promote Computer 1 to a domain controller, perform the following steps:

1. Click **Start**, and then click **Run**.

2. In the **Run** dialog box, in the **Open** box, type **dcpromo**, and then click **OK**.

3. In the **Active Directory Installation Wizard**, click **Next**.

4. In the **Domain Controller Type** dialog box, select **Domain controller for a new domain**, and then click **Next**.

5. In the **Create Tree or Child Domain** dialog box, select the **Create a new domain tree** option, and then click **Next**.

6. In the **Create or Join Forest** dialog box, do the following:

Use this	To do this
Create a new forest of domain trees	Select this option if this is the first domain in your organization, or if you want the new domain tree you are creating to be completely independent of your current forest.
Place this new domain tree in an existing forest	Select this option if you want the users in the new domain tree to have access to resources in existing domain trees, and vice versa.

7. If you selected the **Create a new forest of domain trees** option, in the **New Domain Name** dialog box, in the **Full DNS name for new domain** box, type the full DNS name for the new domain.

8. In the **NetBIOS Domain Name** dialog box, in the **Domain NetBIOS name** box, type the name that users of earlier versions of Windows will use to identify the domain. It is recommended that you accept the default, which is a shortened version of the full DNS name. Click **Next**.

9. In the **Database and Log Locations** dialog box, accept the default settings, unless you have a specific reason to change them.

10. In the **Shared System Volume** dialog box, accept the defaults settings, unless you have a specific reason to change them.

11. If DNS is not installed on your computer, you will be prompted to install it. Select **Yes, install and configure DNS on this computer**, and then click **Next**.

12. In the **Permissions** dialog box, select the **Permissions compatible only with Windows 2000 servers** option, and then click **Next**.

    Caution   Allowing backward compatibility can lead to security problems with Commerce Server.

13. In the **Directory Services Restore Mode Administrator Password** dialog box, do the following:

Use this	To do this
Password	Type the password you want to assign to the Administrator account for the server.
Confirm password	Type the password again to confirm it.

14. In the **Summary** dialog box, review the options you selected to ensure your Active Directory configuration is correct. If it is, click **Next**, or to reconfigure your selections, click **Back**.

15. The **Configuring Active Directory** dialog box appears, notifying you that the Active Directory you configured is being installed on your computer.

16. In the **Completing the Active Directory Installation Wizard** dialog box, click **Finish**.

You have successfully promoted the first computer to the domain controller.

Configuring SQL Server 2000 and Commerce Server (Computer 2)

The second computer hosts your Commerce Server databases, such as the Administration database, the Direct Mailer database, and the Commerce Server Data Warehouse database. On this computer you install SQL Server 2000, and then install Commerce Server, creating the databases on this computer.

To install SQL Server and Commerce Server

1. Install Windows 2000 Advanced Server, using the **Default** installation.

2. Install Windows 2000 SP1 and the required hotfixes specified at http://support:microsoft.com/support/commerceserver/2000/install/default.asp.

3. Open **Control Panel**, and then use **Network and Dial-up Connections** to configure the static IP address on the same subnet and add it to the domain that was created. For detailed instructions, see "Configure TCP/IP for static addressing" in Windows 2000 Server Help.

4. Use **Network and Dial-up Connections** to configure the preferred DNS servers list to point to the Active Directory server (Computer 1, which in turn is hosting the DNS server) for DNS lookups. Configure the WINS servers list to point to the Active Directory server. For detailed instructions, see "Configure TCP/IP to use DNS" and "Configure TCP/IP to use WINS" in Windows 2000 Server Help.

   For additional networking information, see the *Microsoft Windows Server 2000 Resource Kit*.

5. Open **Control Panel**, and then use **System** to join the Active Directory domain.

6. Install SQL Server 2000 and Analysis Services as specified at http://support.microsoft.com/support/commerceserver/2000/install/default.asp.

7. Install Commerce Server as specified at http://support.microsoft.com/support/commerceserver/2000/install/default.asp. Note the following:

   - In the **Setup Type** screen, select **Complete**.
   - In the **Administration Database Configuration** screen, select the current computer as the SQL Server server.
   - In the **Direct Mailer Configuration** screen, select the current computer as the SQL Server server.

You have successfully configured the software on the second computer.

Configuring IIS and Unpacking the Supplier Site (Computer 3)

The third computer hosts IIS 5.0, Commerce Server core objects, the Supplier Solution Site, and the Business Desk application for the Supplier Solution Site. To configure IIS and unpack the Supplier Solution Site, perform the following steps:

1. Install Windows 2000 Server, using the **Default** installation.

2. Install Windows 2000 SP1 and the required hotfixes specified at http://support.microsoft.com/support/commerceserver/2000/install/default.asp.

3. Open the **Control Panel**, and then use **Network and Dial-up Connections** to configure the static IP address on the same subnet and add to the domain that was created.

4. Use **Network and Dial-up Connections** to configure the preferred DNS servers list to point to the Active Directory server (Computer 1, which is hosting the DNS server) for DNS lookups. Configure the WINS servers list to point to the Active Directory server. For detailed instructions, see "Configure TCP/IP to use DNS" and "Configure TCP/IP to use WINS" in Windows 2000 Server Help.

   For additional networking information, see the *Microsoft Windows Server 2000 Resource Kit*, available at http://mspress.microsoft.com/books/1394.htm.

5. Open **Control Panel**, and then use **System** to join the Active Directory domain.

6. Install SQL Server 2000 and Analysis Services as specified at http://support.microsoft.com/support/commerceserver/2000/install/default.asp.

7. Install Commerce Server. Note the following:

   - In the **Setup Type** screen, select **Web Server**.

   - In the **Administration Database Configuration** screen, select the remote SQL Server server for use as the primary SQL Server server. This will cause the Web server to use the remote Administration database in the SQL Server server.

8. Download the Supplier Solution Site from http://www.microsoft.com/commerceserver/solutionsites.

9. Use Site Packager to unpack the Supplier site (SupplierAD.pup) package using the **Quick Unpack** mode. Accept the default options. For detailed instructions, see "Using Site Packager" in Commerce Server 2000 Help.

You have successfully configured the software on the third computer.

Configuring the Business Desk Client (Computer 4)

On the fourth computer you install the Business Desk client. This computer can be on the outside of a firewall.

To install the Business Desk client, perform the following steps:

1. Install Windows 2000 Server, using the **Default** installation.

2. Install Windows 2000 SP1 and the required hotfixes specified at http://support.microsoft.com/support/commerceserver/2000/install/default.asp.

3. Open **Control Panel**, and then use **System** to join the Active Directory domain.

4. Use **Network and Dial-up Connections** to configure DNS to point to the Active Directory server (Computer 1).

5. Install Internet Explorer 5.5, which is available on the Commerce Server 2000 CD.

6. Use Internet Explorer 5.5 to access the /supplieradbizdesk site. The Business Desk client will be downloaded and installed on your computer.

You have successfully configured the software on the fourth computer.

Verifying the Configuration

To verify that you have configured the software correctly on each computer, perform the following steps:

1. On each computer, in the **Run** menu, type **nltest /dsgetdc:<Domain-DNS-Name>**, and then click **OK**. This operation must succeed. If it does not, then the configuration is not correct.

    The Nltest.exe utility is provided in the *Microsoft Windows 2000 Server Resource Kit*.

2. On the Active Directory server, point to **Administrative Tools**, and then click **DNS**. The domain information should appear under the **Forward Zones** node. If it does not appear, then the configuration is not correct.

Configuring the Computers for Trusted Delegation

You can configure the computer for trusted delegation.

To configure the computers for trusted delegation

1. On the Active Directory server (Computer 1), open **Active Directory Users and Computers Manager**.

2. For each of the three computers in the domain (the domain controller is not listed), right-click on the computer name, and in the *<computer name>* **Properties** dialog box, select the **Trust computer for delegation** option, and then click **OK**.

Verifying Business Desk and the Supplier Site

In this verification procedure, you use Business Desk to create a new user who is an administrator, and then you create a delegated administrator at the Supplier site.

To verify Business Desk and the Supplier Solution Site

1. On the client computer, log on as a user of the domain. Do not log on using an account local to the client computer.

2. Double-click the **Business Desk** icon on your desktop or click **Start**, and then click the **Business Desk** shortcut.

3. In **Business Desk**, in **Users**, click **Organizations**, and then add an organization. For instructions for adding an organization, see "Adding an Organization" in Commerce Server 2000 Help.

4. Click **Users**, and then add a new user, for example, Joe User. Assign the user to the organization you created, and set the user's **Partner service role flag** to **Administrator**. For instructions for adding a user, see "Adding a User" in Commerce Server 2000 Help.

5. Do a search on that user, and then update an attribute of the user, for example, the password. If you can change the password, then the user is set up correctly.

6. On the Active Directory computer, use **Active Directory Users and Computers Manager** to give the user you just added (for example, Joe User) sufficient permissions to access the Business Desk application.

7. On the client computer, log on to the Supplier site as the administrator you just created (for example, Joe User).

To create a delegated administrator

1. In the left pane, under **Partner Service**, click **Users**, and then above the user information, click **New**.

2. In the **Account Info** section, from the **Account status** drop-down list, select **Active**.

3. In the **Business Desk** section, from the **Partner service role flags** drop-down list, select **Delegated Admin**.

4. In the **General information** section, type the logon name and password for the delegated administrator.

After you create the delegated administrator, the delegated administrator can log in to the client computer and create users for the administrator's specific organization.

Closing the Loop

The Ferguson and Bardell team realized from the beginning of the project that an e-commerce Web site is a corporate asset that business managers must continuously manage, analyze, and enhance in order to keep their Web site competitive. Business managers need to quickly analyze customer activity to measure the effectiveness of their sites, and then use the results to fine-tune the sites. By analyzing customer data, the business manager can make decisions about how to improve the site and meet business goals. Post-deployment responsibilities fall into the following two basic areas:

- Analyzing customer data

- Implementing the site management cycle

Analyzing Customer Data

Ferguson and Bardell's site administration team analyzes customer data from the Data Warehouse, then provides this information to the management team. They use the data to identify the types of customers who visit the site, what is selling well, and which advertising campaigns are successful.

Implementing the Site Management Cycle

To effectively implement the site management cycle, the business management, site development, and system administration teams agreed to inform each other about the updates they make to the site. They established a process to facilitate this communication. For example, to update a large set of user profiles in bulk, the business management team contacts the system administration team, who then performs this task. To add new functionality to Business Desk, such as a module for selling gift certificates, the business management team sends their requirements to the site development team.

The teams have a process for requesting changes. (For more information about designing a process for requesting changes, see Chapter 8, "Developing Your Site.") They also established a regular meeting schedule to resolve any communication issues that might arise as they continue to refine their site.

Part Two: Planning

Microsoft
Commerce Server 2000

Defining Project Goals and Requirements

This chapter describes how to plan your Microsoft Commerce Server 2000 implementation to accomplish your business goals. A successful Commerce Server implementation requires a clearly defined vision of what you want to accomplish. By thoroughly examining and planning your e-commerce site before installation, you can significantly increase the efficiency and availability of the services your site provides, ensure the general success of your site, and make sure that your goals are accurately reflected in future phases of the project.

Planning is the first phase in the Plan-Develop-Deploy-Manage cycle. The following table shows the two documents you create during the Planning phase.

Document	Activities
Project Goals and Requirements	• Define project goals and scope.
	• Develop a conceptual design.
	• Define your requirements for the new e-commerce site: What do you want to accomplish?
	• Plan for migration.
Project Plan	• Create a functional specification to define the new e-commerce site.
	• Identify the project team.
	• Develop a project schedule.
	• Develop a project budget.

For more information about the Project Goals and Requirements document and the Project Plan document, see Chapter 5, "Planning for Scalability," Chapter 6, "Planning for Reliability and High Availability," and Chapter 7, "Building the Project Plan."

The Planning phase is critical to the success of your project. To ensure that you have all the essential information you need during the planning process, you should include the team members listed in the following table.

Team members	Tasks
Company executives	• Define project goals and scope (with other team members)
	• Approve the conceptual design
	• Define project requirements (with other team members)
	• Approve the functional specification
	• Approve the project schedule
	• Approve the project budget
	• Allocate resources for development, deployment, and management
Marketing and sales personnel	• Define project goals and scope (with other team members)
	• Approve the conceptual design
	• Define project requirements (with other team members)
	• Approve the functional specification
	• Approve the project schedule
Site developers and system administrators	• Create the conceptual design
	• Define project requirements (with other team members)
	• Plan for migration
	• Create the functional specification
	• Create a project schedule
	• Propose a project budget
	• Propose a list of project team members

Figure 4.1 illustrates the tasks that you need to complete during the Planning phase.

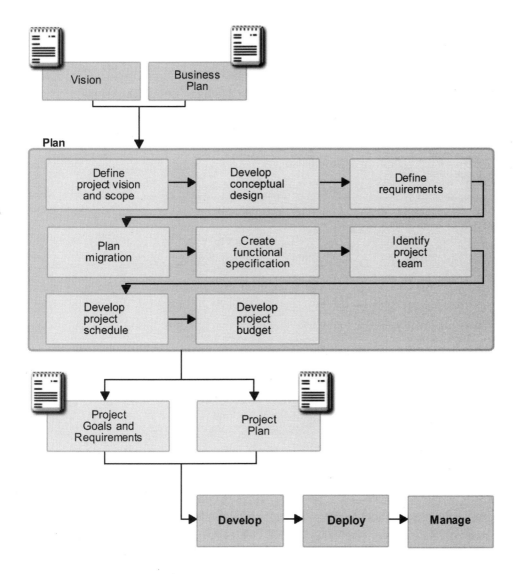

Figure 4.1 Planning phase

The following sections provide detailed information about how to plan your Commerce Server implementation. The Planning phase is complete when your company accepts a finished Project Plan. The Project Plan is then used by project team members to develop and deploy the site.

Creating a Project Goals and Requirements Document

The Project Goals and Requirements document contains the following information:

- Project vision and scope (including project constraints, assumptions, and risks)
- Conceptual design
- Requirement definitions
- Commerce Server features
- Migration plan

This document is used as the basis for creating the Project Plan. Begin the planning process by defining project vision and scope (given the schedule and constraints). Asking the questions listed in this section, among others, will help you to define these elements.

Vision

A comprehensive vision statement is a tool that empowers the entire organization to work together to build a successful e-commerce site. The following table describes the elements of a comprehensive vision statement.

Element	Description
Clarification	Team members need to know what they are trying to build—both what the project includes and what it does not include.
Prioritization	Since there is never enough time to do everything, a vision statement should rank project priorities.
Integration	Your vision statement must complement and support the visions of other company projects. Other projects might serve the same customer markets as yours, and some might have overlapping feature sets. Your vision statement should describe how your project will integrate with other company projects.
Future investment	Not only should your vision statement guide the current project, it should also plan for the future. For example, if developers know that you plan to build a business-to-business site in the next version, they might begin to think about Internet delays and low bandwidth issues as they architect this version. Foresight can save time and money in the future.

When you define the clarification, prioritization, integration, and future investment elements that comprise your vision statement, you should make them S-M-A-R-T:

S = Specific
M = Measurable
A = Achievable
R = Relevant
T = Time-based

Your vision statement should answer the following questions:

- At a high level, what outcome or result do we envision for the project?

- Why are we pursuing this solution?

- Who are our customers?

- What problem does this solution solve for our customers?

- What else is the company doing at the same time?

For example, the following is a hypothetical vision statement for a Web server migration project:

"Our company will replace its current UNIX Apache Web server environment with a Windows 2000 Server and IIS 5.0, a more efficient and flexible solution that will maximize competitiveness in our industry while reducing operational and administrative costs. The company will implement a global Windows 2000 Server domain model and will begin a scheduled deployment program to 20,000 worldwide users at 100 locations by the third quarter of 2001. We will start an enterprise-wide rollout within three months and will be user-complete within 18 months, or the first quarter of 2002.

Implementation will require a conversion and coexistence infrastructure in order to seamlessly move users to the new platform. To accomplish this, we will use Windows 2000 Server integration tools and third-party UNIX conversion tools."

After you draft your vision statement, you should start "selling" the vision and getting the rest of the team involved. Get approval from upper management, incorporate other people's expertise, and get the team excited about realizing the vision. Gather feedback and verify that team members understand the vision and its goals. Then incorporate that feedback into the vision statement, or justify not incorporating it, if necessary.

Scope

To determine the scope of your project, answer the following questions:

- What type of site (for example, business-to-consumer or business-to-business) do we want to build?

- What features can we reasonably implement during the time allotted for this project?

- What features do we want to postpone to a later date?

Project variables, such as resources (people and money), schedule (time), and features (the solution) exist in a triangular relationship, as shown in Figure 4.2.

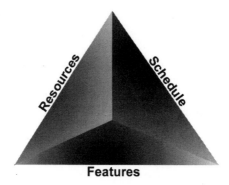

Features

Figure 4.2 Project variables

Setting project scope requires balancing these variables. For example, you might need to eliminate non-critical features in order to complete the project on time or with fewer resources. If eliminating features is not an option, you might need to add resources or extend development time in order to complete the specified features.

Constraints

Identify project constraints by answering the following questions:

- What is the estimated project budget?

- What is the target release date?

- What constrains the project from finishing on time, on budget, or with the functionality we want?

For example, list any time, personnel, budgetary, or other factors that limit project development options in your Project Goals and Requirements document.

Assumptions

List your assumptions so that other team members and management can understand the basis for your design decisions. By making your assumptions known, you also provide the opportunity for others to challenge, correct, and verify your assumptions, if necessary. This feedback can be valuable information for the planning process. For example, you might assume that a Microsoft Windows 2000 Server domain design has been implemented, or that qualified personnel are available, in order to meet the specified schedule. If other team members know that the domain design has not been implemented or that the budget does not provide for more personnel, you need to know that information before you start. These assumptions should be clearly stated in your Project Goals and Requirements document.

Risks

By analyzing risks before you begin a project and implementing methods to mitigate them, you can reduce their impact on your project. The first thing to do when you consider possible project risks is to make a list of the things that can go wrong, then develop strategies for mitigating them. As the project proceeds, your project team can periodically reexamine the risks, review mitigation actions, and decide how well each risk is being managed. The following table lists some examples of high-level project risks and mitigation strategies.

Risk	Mitigation strategy
Site downtime	• Test servers prior to deployment. • Test all applications prior to deployment. • Add server capacity. For more information, see Chapter 6, "Planning for Reliability and High Availability."
Hacker attacks or viruses	Add firewalls to your site architecture. For more information, see the "Security Requirements" section in this chapter.
Power outages, fire, flood, lightning, and so on	Back up your system regularly and store backups in a secure, off-site location. For more information, see Chapter 6, "Planning for Reliability and High Availability."

You should include this type of risk and mitigation assessment in your Project Goals and Requirements document, using risks that are specific to your project. You must determine which risks you are willing accept and which risks you will take specific actions to reduce or eliminate. You can handle risks in a number of different ways, including the following:

- Accept the risk, with no investment of effort or cost. You might want to accept a risk when the cost of mitigating it exceeds your exposure or when your exposure is acceptable.

- Transfer the risk to someone else, or agree to share the risk, if a customer or trading partner is better able to handle it without undue strain.

- Reduce the loss associated with a risk whenever possible. For example, keep a backup local area network (LAN) operational during the deployment of a new network, or provide free training to customers who would otherwise not be trained.

If you encounter significant risks that you cannot mitigate, or risks for which countermeasures are unreliable, you might need to establish and execute contingency plans. When you finish a project, be sure to capture the lessons you learned during the project so that you know what risks to watch for in future projects.

Developing a Conceptual Design

The next step in developing your Project Goals and Requirements document is to analyze and define business processes and data to support your vision statement. You use this information to create a conceptual design that integrates the development of your Commerce Server site with site testing and integration. The following table describes the information that a conceptual design should include.

Section	Describes
Business process diagram(s)	The flow of business processes associated with your proposed site, showing the interrelationship of business processes and functions, including data flows between processes and external sources or destinations
Business data model	Data entities, attributes, relationships, and business rules
Process/location matrix	The physical locations where business processes are performed (if performed at more than one location)
Data flow diagram	The flow of data between processes (if not described in enough detail in the business process diagram)
Physical conceptual design picture	A graphic representation of your applications, interfaces, databases, and hardware platforms

Defining Requirements

It is important to clearly define the following types of requirements in your Project Goals and Requirements document. Your technical team will then use this information to create the functional specification.

Type of requirement	Describes
Business	The business purpose for developing your site
System integration	Requirements for integrating Commerce Server with other software
Security	The type(s) and levels of security you need
Site architecture	Hardware configuration and location, and hardware scalability and availability requirements
Performance and capacity	Requirements for system performance and capacity, the amount of traffic the site must be able to process, and the amount of anticipated growth
System administration	The infrastructure for ongoing management of Commerce Server and other software
International	Requirements to provide for an international audience, if any

Business Requirements

Business requirements describe the business purposes for developing the site, such as the following:

- Sales goals
- Product offerings
- Customers
- Suppliers

Business requirements also describe how you expect the new site to change your current manner of doing business. It is important to understand what you want your site to do and what functions it must perform before you begin development, so that the Development phase can be as efficient, cost-effective, and successful as possible. Your business requirements should include answers to the following questions, among others:

- How do we currently do business?
- What business problem(s) are we trying to solve with this project?
- What are our goals for return on investment with the new site?
- What are our goals for customer relationships?
- What are our goals for supplier relationships?
- What are our goals for each phase (Plan-Develop-Deploy-Manage) of the project?
- Will there be subsequent projects after this particular deployment?
- What technical issues must we address for each phase of the project?
- What new organizational processes do we have to develop if the project is to be successful? What changes do we have to make to current organizational processes? (For example, do we need additional staff to develop or run the system? What training do we need to do when the new system is implemented?)
- What existing processes must be incorporated into the new site?

System Integration Requirements

During the planning process, you need to assess your existing systems and data to determine the most effective methods of integrating them with or converting them to Commerce Server. In addition, you need to plan how to integrate the various subsystems of your e-commerce business. The following table lists some of the questions that you need to answer when you plan for system integration.

Planning question	Recommendation
Should we integrate existing databases and database servers that contain data, such as catalogs and user profiles?	If you plan to maintain separate data sources for your offline and online businesses, establish a system for synchronizing the data. Consider integrating Microsoft Host Integration Server 2000 and Microsoft Application Center 2000 into your system design.
Should we integrate our existing order processing, payment transaction, inventory management, and order fulfillment systems with Commerce Server?	If you plan to integrate these systems, develop Component Object Model (COM) objects to connect them to Commerce Server. Consider incorporating Microsoft BizTalk Server 2000 into your system design.
Do we need to integrate Enterprise Resource Planning (ERP) systems with suppliers and trading partners?	If you plan to integrate ERP systems, you should incorporate BizTalk Server into your system design.
What are our requirements for converting data?	Convert your data from its existing format to a format you can use with Commerce Server. For example, if you have catalog data in a tab-delimited format, you will need to convert it to Extensible Markup Language (XML) or comma-separated value (.csv) file format before importing it into the Product Catalog System.
How much custom development do we have to do?	Although Commerce Server is a full-featured product, it also provides many ways for you to customize those features to suit your business requirements. Examine the features list carefully and read the product documentation before you plan to do custom development.
If we do custom development, should we do it in-house or work with a software development vendor?	Review the information about Microsoft Solution Providers and Partners at http://microsoft.com/commerce.

Security Requirements

Security means managing risks by providing adequate protection for the confidentiality, privacy, integrity, and availability of information, and it is essential to the success of any e-commerce site. Because e-commerce sites handle monetary transactions over the Internet, most sites implement a very high level of security.

To plan security for a Commerce Server site, you must plan how to combat security threats for each feature deployed on your site, selecting the policies and tools to accomplish the level of security you want. You need to configure Secure Sockets Layer (SSL) so that certain pages, such as pages that request credit card information, are served through SSL. To set this up, you need to get a server certificate and configure Microsoft Internet Information Services (IIS) 5.0 to use SSL. For more information about configuring IIS, see http://www.microsoft.com/technet/iis/deploy.asp.

You can also specify a secure host name for each Commerce Server application in the Microsoft Management Console (MMC). The **AuthManager** object uses the secure host name to create links to secure pages. The links can lead to a different Commerce Server application or to a secure section of the same application.

To minimize the probability of a security breach, you must be able to:

- Lock down the site by controlling access to files, pages, and applications with access control lists (ACLs) on files that use the NTFS file system (NTFS).

- Control access to read/run script/write access on various folders defined in your site for IIS security.

- Authenticate site visitors.

When you plan security for your site, you should answer the following questions, among others:

- What are our security risks?

- How severe are those risks?

- How should we structure the site to address security risks?

- What do we want to be secure (user profiles, credit card transactions, Commerce Server Business Desk, catalogs, Active Server Pages (ASP) pages, databases, and so on)?

- Where should we store backups?

- How should we manage security on our site?

- Who should be allowed access to the Web site?

- Who should be allowed access to Business Desk?

- How should we react to a security breach?

- What should we do if our site is forced offline?

You should plan for site security from the beginning and design the site with security in mind. Use the severity levels listed in the following table when you consider the severity of security risks to your site.

Severity of risk	Environment
Low	Stand-alone server in a room with locked doors
Medium	Corporate desktop with intranet connection
High	Anything connected to the Internet
Very high	Monetary transactions conducted on the Internet
Extremely high	Transactions that impact people's lives and privacy (such as medical records and 911 calls) conducted on the Internet

To assess threats to your site, do the following:

1. List the environments (operating systems, networks, and so on) on which each secure item is developed, transmitted, processed, or stored, and describe how they affect your site.

2. List the types of threats to each environment.

3. Measure the risk for each threat, using the following formula:

```
Risk = Damage potential / Probability
```

Damage potential: 1 = little damage potential, 10 = massive damage potential

Probability of threat occurring: 1 = high probability, 10 = low probability

4. Prioritize the threats in order of likelihood and potential damage, and then define mitigating security elements for each threat, balancing the relative costs of implementing additional security versus the business costs of security breaches.

5. Plan how to counter the threats.

A typical e-commerce site architecture can contain multiple security domains, in which you place systems with different security needs. Each domain must be protected by a network filter or firewall. (A firewall is a security checkpoint that separates an intranet from the Internet. Only specific data can pass through a firewall.) The three most common security domains are:

- The Internet.

- A DMZ (derived from the military term *demilitarized zone*) containing the Web servers.

- A secure network on which content is created or staged and secure data is managed and stored. For example, the network on which you develop new ASP pages and then test them before deploying them in your production environment is a secure network.

Consider the following firewall configurations when you plan how to deploy your site:

- Single-firewall solution

- Two-firewall solution

- Three-firewall solution

Single-Firewall Solution

A single-firewall solution can consist of a firewall with three interfaces acting as gateways for three separate networks. In a single-firewall solution, the firewall acts as a host to the DMZ, Internet, and corporate intranet. Figure 4.3 shows an example of a single-firewall solution.

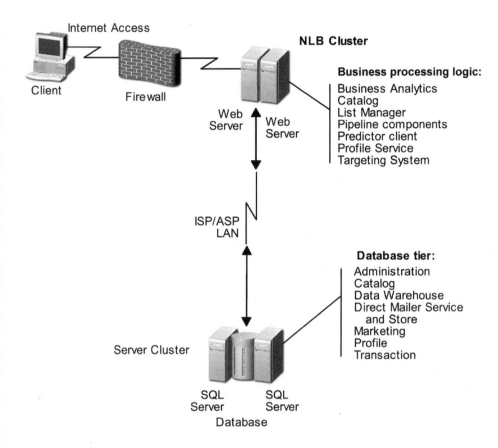

Figure 4.3 Single-firewall solution

Advantages

- The DMZ is separated physically from other networks, thereby stopping any possible intrusions into the DMZ. If someone is able to exploit any publicly accessible server, they still don't have access directly to the intranet.

- There is only one firewall to purchase and manage.

- The intranet isn't dependent on the DMZ to function. If the DMZ has network problems, the intranet doesn't necessarily lose connectivity.

Disadvantages

- SQL Servers are not separated from IIS servers. Hypertext Transfer Protocol (HTTP) and Hypertext Transfer Protocol Secure (HTTPS) are the only protocols allowed from the external network to the DMZ; however, any vulnerability found on the IIS server will jeopardize all of the other servers on the DMZ.

- Communications between SQL Servers and IIS servers still need further security because they are traveling unprotected in the DMZ.

- Some firewall vendors might not support three interfaces.

Two-Firewall Solution

The two-firewall solution is a solution in which a second firewall is placed off of the DMZ network to separate the external DMZ environment and the SQL Servers that it accesses. Creating a staging area also separates your production environment from your development environment. Figure 4.4 shows an example of a two-firewall solution.

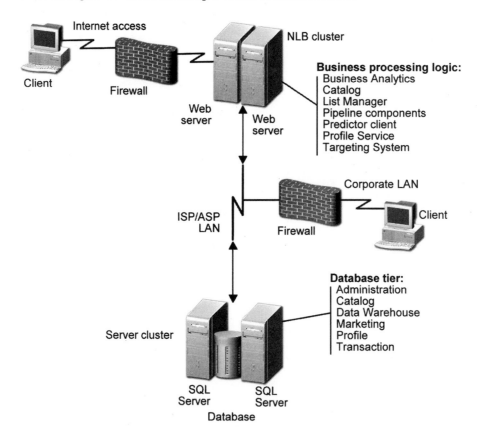

Figure 4.4 Two-firewall solution

Advantages

- You can use a production management network to separate the intranet from the servers and users who run the externally visible DMZ. All of the servers on the DMZ and the SQL Servers are managed by a separate group of users and servers on a different network. This way, the intranet becomes much more difficult for a hacker to access.

- A firewall protects the back-end database servers from vulnerabilities that are not dependent on the relationship between IIS servers and SQL Servers. Such vulnerabilities can result in denial-of-service attacks.

- You minimize the number of computers accessible directly through the Internet by adding two firewalls, thereby making it more difficult to disrupt or abuse the database servers and the Business Desk server.

- Business Desk does not have to run over HTTPS, because the client and server are on the same network.

- Communication between Business Desk and the SQL Servers does not have to be encrypted because the communication never goes over a public wire.

- You can control "spoofing" with the firewalls. (Spoofing is the practice of impersonating another person or computer, usually by providing a false e-mail name, URL, or IP address.) For example, you can tell a server to list only SQL Server requests from one specific Internet Protocol (IP) address. Because both connections are controlled with a firewall, these addresses cannot be spoofed.

- The DMZ is separated physically from other networks, thereby stopping any possible intrusions to the DMZ. If someone is able to exploit any publicly accessible server, they still don't have access directly to the corporate LAN.

- The intranet isn't dependent on the DMZ to function. If the DMZ has network problems, the intranet doesn't necessarily lose connectivity.

Disadvantages

- It is more difficult and costly to maintain two firewalls with different configurations than it is to manage a single firewall.

- Communications between SQL Servers and IIS servers still need further security, because they are traveling unprotected in the DMZ.

- Some firewall vendors might not support three interfaces.

Three-Firewall Solution

The three-firewall solution features two or three firewalls behind one another to create a DMZ that shares bandwidth with the intranet. Figure 4.5 shows an example of a three-firewall solution.

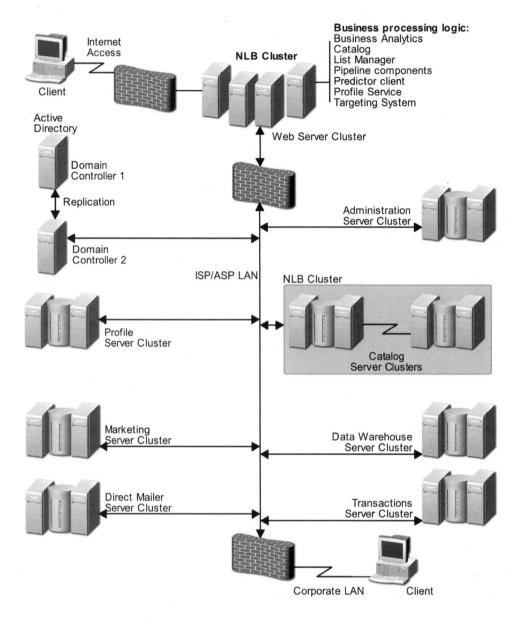

Figure 4.5 Three-firewall solution

Advantages

- The DMZ is separated physically from other networks, thereby stopping any possible intrusions to the DMZ. If someone is able to exploit any publicly accessible server, they still don't have access directly to the intranet.

- You can control spoofing with the firewalls. For example, you can tell a server to list only SQL Server requests from one specific IP address. Because both connections are controlled with a firewall, these addresses cannot be spoofed.

- A layer of protection protects the back-end database servers from vulnerabilities not dependent on the relationship between IIS servers and SQL Servers. Such vulnerabilities can result in denial-of-service attacks.

- You minimize the number of computers accessible directly through the Internet by adding three firewalls, thereby making it more difficult to disrupt or abuse the database servers and the Business Desk server.

Disadvantages

- It is more difficult and costly to configure and maintain three firewalls with different configurations than it is to maintain single- or two-firewall configurations.

- Communications between SQL Servers and IIS servers still need further security, because they are traveling unprotected in the DMZ.

- Connection to the Internet from intranets can be disrupted if certain types of denial-of-service attacks occur in either the DMZ or SQL Server networks.

- Any traffic allowed between the intranet and the Internet is also allowed between the DMZ and the Internet and between the SQL Servers and the Internet. Security ramifications depend on which protocols are allowed by the default security policy of the user.

Be sure to include the following elements in your security planning:

- One firewall between your Data Warehouse, Administration database, and other data stores, and your Business Desk, and another firewall between your Business Desk and Web servers

- Intrusion detection tools

- Ongoing site monitoring

- Strong passwords for site visitors

- Aggressive time-outs

- Method(s) for screening all user input, including parsing for expected user input

- Network architecture to support security requirements, including firewalls, routers, and proxy servers

- Windows 2000 security settings, including authentication methods, disabling of unneeded services, security design of groups and users, NTFS permissions, privileges, and auditing

- IIS security settings, including IP address grant and deny settings, application read, write, and execute permissions, authentication methods, and use of secure communications (such as SSL, HTTPS, and certificates)

- SQL Server security settings to restrict access to Commerce Server databases, especially settings to restrict access to the Administration database, which contains the connection strings and passwords for all Commerce Server databases

- CS Authentication resource properties

- Access control for any data stores that will be shared by intranets and the Internet

- Coding practices for secure sites

- Administrative security policies to protect the e-commerce site, such as password policies, monitoring, and physical control of servers

You should also do the following:

- Protect your domain controllers behind a firewall. Don't put domain controllers on the Internet.

- Create contingency plans, such as setting up redundant hardware, in case the site is forced offline.

For more information about security requirements, see Chapter 6, "Planning for Reliability and High Availability."

Site Architecture Requirements

Your site architecture is the number and configuration of computers that make up your site, including the operating systems and application software installed on each one. You can run a small Commerce Server site (1,000 transactions a day) on one computer with 256 MB of RAM. However, it is better to run Commerce Server on a minimum of three computers: one for your Web server, one for SQL Server, and one for Business Desk site management. Many e-commerce sites start small and grow exponentially with demand, so it is important to plan a solid architecture that meets current and near-term demand, and that will also scale easily.

In addition to the hardware for running your operating environment, you need to plan for hardware to run the environments listed in the following table, as well.

Environment	Function
Development environment	Develop changes to your site.
Test/staging environment	Test all software changes to the site before putting them into production. It is important to maintain a separate site for testing changes to make sure everything works before you install new software in your production environment. The test/staging environment should be an exact duplicate of your production environment.
Redundant operating environment (optional)	Maintain operations in case of malfunctions in your production environment. If it is critical for your site to keep operating at all times, you should consider building a redundant operating environment that can be brought into use immediately when needed. (For information about other options for increasing site availability, see Chapter 6, "Planning for Reliability and High Availability.")

Performance and Capacity Requirements

Performance and capacity requirements are closely linked because performance planning and capacity planning go hand-in-hand. However, each addresses a different perspective. Performance planning addresses the technical aspects of the site, focusing on performance metrics such as ASP page throughput and ASP latency. Capacity planning addresses the business perspective, focusing on maximizing the number of users that a site can handle. For information about maximizing the performance and capacity of an existing site, see Chapter 19, "Maximizing Performance."

Performance

It can be difficult to predict how variables in site design, coding practices, user behavior, and site architecture will combine to affect site performance, so it is important to plan and test the performance and capacity of your site before going into production. If you are upgrading an existing site, you can use site data as a basis for planning the new site. If you are creating a new site, you can use the guidelines provided in this book to set up a test site, on which you can then load, test, and optimize your site before "going live." When defining performance requirements for your site, you need to answer the following questions, among others:

- What are our performance goals for this solution?

- What is the size of the content managed in databases or on Web pages?

- What is the maximum delay (latency) for returning the bulk of the Web pages?

- What are our criteria for measuring the success of our site, in terms of page latency minimums and necessary throughput to survive at peak or stress levels?

- How many servers do we need? How should they be configured?

- How should we balance the load across all of our servers?

Performance plans should include the following:

- A list of items to measure, such as ASP throughput and ASP latency. Select factors that closely match your goals for user experience. For example, if your goal is for users to be able to browse through your catalog quickly, measure the speed at which a catalog browse request is returned.

- Tools and resources for analyzing performance.

One of the most useful tools for analyzing performance on an existing site is transaction cost analysis (TCA), which is a methodology for estimating the cost of each resource as a function of usage profiles, service mixes, or hardware configurations. For more information about TCA, see Chapter 19, "Maximizing Performance."

Capacity

Capacity planning addresses the business perspective of a site, focusing on maximum user capacity. Capacity planning enables you to make sure that your site delivers quality content to users at a rapid speed. If capacity planning is measured incorrectly, users might choose to go elsewhere to find better service, quality, and speed.

When defining capacity requirements, you should answer the following questions, among others:

- What are the typical usage profiles of the users we are targeting with this site?

- How many users do we expect to visit the site each hour and each day? Will those numbers be different on weekends?

- How many users do we expect to visit the site during peak seasons or special promotions?

- How frequently do we expect users to interact with the site? (How many times will they access our home page, and over what span of time, or how many catalog searches do we expect users to make each time they visit our site?)

- How many users need to be supported both near- and long-term?

- At what rate do we expect to grow?

You should review site capacity regularly, to be sure that the infrastructure of your site can maintain and deliver services at acceptable performance levels as you grow and as site content becomes more complex. When you plan site capacity, you need to determine capacity separately for each Commerce Server feature that you plan to use.

Predicting capacity is a little more complex than predicting performance. Before you can predict maximum capacity, you first need to profile expected (or actual) user behavior, and then combine that information with your performance metrics to calculate capacity. User behavior varies from site to site, depending on the richness of the shopping experience (page design, site design, and response time), as well as the types of products being sold and the breadth of the product line. One site might support 1,000 users, while another site with identical hardware might support only 200 users, due to differences in user behavior.

You can project user behavior on your site by providing answers to questions that identify which user operations are to be performed and how often you expect them to be performed over a given period of time. For example, you can design a usage profile to answer the following types of questions:

- What will users do after connecting to the site? Will they view only a few pages or will they browse the site extensively?

- When users browse product offerings, how often will they make a purchase?

Creating a usage profile is the first step in determining site capacity. The key components of a usage profile are:

- The projected length of an average user session.

- The total number of operations performed by the average user during a session.

- A list of commonly used user operations.

- The frequency with which each operation is performed during a session.

In a typical site, for example, the following transactions might account for 10 percent of the types of page requests, but 90 percent of the site traffic:

- Add item and checkout

- Add item and delete

- Browse

- Check zip code

- Default (home page)

- Log in

- Register

- Search (Bad)

- Search (Good)

- View cart

Determine how you expect users to connect to your site and the expected load. Use this usage profile in your testing environment, and then confirm that the profiles are correct when you have collected usage information in the Data Warehouse. For more information about creating usage profiles, see Chapter 19, "Maximizing Performance."

Performance and Capacity Considerations for Site Architecture

You use performance and capacity data to determine the following requirements:

- Number of servers and their roles, including which services, resources, and files each server is to provide; efficient co-location and distribution of services
- Server size (processor, memory, and storage requirements) for each type of server
- Network bandwidth and hardware
- Site architecture, to gain maximum performance from existing servers (For more information about architecting a site to increase its performance, see Chapter 5, "Planning for Scalability.")

The following table describes some diagrams that are helpful for visualizing site architecture.

Diagram	Description
Hardware profile	A description of, and budget for, the hardware needed to implement a site, including diagrams of the expected deployment configuration. This deployment configuration should include the servers on which each software component will reside. Be sure to include network hardware in this description (routers, firewalls, and so on).
Service-to-service architecture	Network diagrams to describe the bandwidth necessary to support the planned throughput, and event-sequence charts (such as the example shown in Figure 4.6) to map the flow of requests through the various systems, so that you can see potential bottlenecks. Generating these diagrams early in the Planning phase can highlight unforeseen problems and bottlenecks.
Server configuration matrix	A network diagram of server roles, data roles, and client roles.

Figure 4.6 shows the type of event-sequence chart you might create to map the flow of requests through your site.

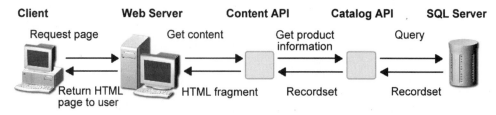

Figure 4.6 Event-sequence chart

Determining User Capacity

You can determine the capacity requirements of your site using the number of expected or actual visitors to your site during a period of time and comparing it with the capacity of the hardware.

For example, if the site receives 500,000 visitors per day at an average session time of 11 minutes, there are an average of 3,800 concurrent users at any given time. The equation is as follows:

```
(500,000 / (24 hours × 60 minutes / 11 minutes per session) = 3,800 users
```

Of course, this does not mean that there will be 3,800 site visitors at any particular time. There might be times when site traffic peaks at a much higher figure. One of the important principles of capacity planning is to use peak activity, rather than average activity, as a baseline. As a rule of thumb, you can account for usage spikes and peaks by multiplying the average number of concurrent users by two (although this multiplier can differ, depending on the nature of your site).

In the previous example, this calculation yields a figure of 7,600 concurrent users at peak periods. If your site experiences peak traffic that is more than twice the average, consider this when you determine where to set your baseline.

If you had already determined the server CPU capacity for your site to be 1,350 users, you would then divide 1,350 into 7,600 to determine how many servers you need to handle peak traffic, as follows:

```
7,600 concurrent users / 1,350 users per server (2 processor) = 6 servers (running
Windows 2000 with 2 x 400-MHz processors)
```

At times of normal use, the load on the six servers would be lower:

```
3,800 concurrent users / 6 servers = 634 users per server
```

This means that your site would be operating at 50 percent of site capacity. Knowing your site capacity is very important, especially for sites that experience usage spikes.

Planning Site Topology

Each site has unique capacity requirements that can be affected by variables such as available hardware and budget, available physical space for servers, and the amount of time your company can afford for the site to be offline. Such requirements directly affect the design and construction of the site's physical infrastructure, the site topology. For examples of site topologies, see figures 4.3, 4.4, and 4.5 in the previous *Security Requirements* section.

The following table lists some of the questions that you need to answer when you plan how to configure site topology.

Planning question	Recommendation
What server operations (like backing up files and content replication) can influence site capacity?	Because TCA measurements don't include operations such as maintenance and system management, you should decide what capacity you need for those activities in addition to the capacity required to handle Web traffic.
How often do we expect usage spikes to occur? How important is it to perform well during such spikes?	The general rule is to plan enough capacity for twice the average number of concurrent users. If you anticipate significant usage spikes that exceed this baseline, plan for surplus CPU, disk, memory, and network capacity. Remember to take future growth into consideration, as well as the possibility of content that is more complex.
How important is it to be operational 100 percent of the time? How often will servers be offline for maintenance?	If 100 percent site availability is critical, plan for system redundancy. Duplicate critical resources and eliminate "single point of failure" areas.
When will we do capacity planning again? What growth do we expect? When should we upgrade the site hardware again? How will content complexity change?	Over time, the average number of concurrent users on a site rises or falls, the content and content complexity changes, and the typical user profile changes. Each of these factors can have a big impact on a site's capacity. Take change and growth into account, and review your capacity plans regularly or whenever these factors change sufficiently enough to impact site capacity.

Scalability

Your initial site design should take future expansion into account. A well-planned site can be cost-effectively expanded, or *scaled*, to accommodate increased site traffic while maintaining performance. The architecture of e-commerce sites is generally divided into two tiers: front-end Web servers, and back-end servers on which database software, data, and operations are located.

You typically scale the front end by scaling horizontally—adding additional, identical Web servers. The Web servers are joined into a farm or cluster, and load balancing is used to distribute user requests evenly across the available servers.

You typically scale the back end first by scaling vertically—upgrading the server and adding mass storage. Then, you can also divide the data by function among two or more servers. For example, the Data Warehouse can be placed on one server and the registered user database on another. With Commerce Server, you can divide functions onto different servers during setup, or do it later using Commerce Server Manager.

Using Commerce Server, you can partition the Commerce Server databases (the databases containing catalogs, campaigns, and so on), and you can add SQL Server databases to the

Data Warehouse. Commerce Server also makes it easy to add Web servers, using Commerce Server Site Packager. You can manage them from one central location.

Issues to consider when planning for scalability include:

- Designing a multi-tier architecture, even if your initial site traffic is low.

- Planning a scaling path for each type of server, each network connection, and each Commerce Server feature, in which you define how you will scale the site when certain thresholds (such as number of concurrent users, memory usage, or disk usage) are reached.

For more information about ways to scale a site's architecture, see Chapter 5, "Planning for Scalability."

Availability

Availability is a measure of fault tolerance for a computer, cluster, or system, and its programs. The measure takes into account both the mean time between failures (MTBF) and the mean time to recovery (MTTR), and includes downtime for both planned and unplanned events. Many e-commerce sites are mission-critical, so they should be designed to be highly available, which means operating at an acceptable service level at least 99.9 percent of the time. Planning for high availability includes defining and testing hardware and software configurations, as well as operational procedures.

Front-end systems are made highly available as well as scalable by using multiple, identical servers, all offering a single address to their clients. Load balancing distributes load across the servers. Building failure detection into the load-balancing system increases service availability. In that way, a server that is no longer offering a service can be removed automatically from the load-balanced set while the remaining servers continue to offer the service.

Back-end systems are more challenging to make highly available, primarily due to the data or state they maintain. They are made highly available by using failover clustering for each partition. Failover clustering assumes that an application can resume on another computer that has been given access to the failed system's disk subsystem. Partition failover occurs when the primary node supporting requests to the partition fails and requests to the partition automatically switch to a secondary node. The secondary node must have access to the same data storage as the failed node. A duplicate e-commerce site can also increase availability by being available at a remote geographic location.

The following table lists some of the questions that you need to answer when you plan a highly available system.

Planning question	Recommendation
What level of availability do we require?	Make this decision by weighing the cost of availability against the business cost of downtime, and determining an appropriate availability level.
How should we monitor availability?	Create a process to determine whether you are meeting your availability goals.
How should we respond to disasters?	Develop a plan for recovering data in the event of a catastrophic failure of all or part of your system. Test your plan by simulating a disaster.

For more information about planning for availability, see Chapter 6, "Planning for Reliability and High Availability."

System Administration Requirements

System administration broadly refers to the infrastructure, tools, and team of site developers and system administrators needed to maintain a Commerce Server site and its services. Many Commerce Server sites are located in hosted environments (co-located with an Internet Service Provider (ISP) or a specialized hosting service), where rich Internet connectivity is available. Consequently, the management and monitoring of the systems must be done remotely. In such a divided architecture, management tasks are split between the ISP and the remote client. The ISP in this case plans the management infrastructure, and the client plans the configuration of Business Desk.

In Commerce Server, *site management* describes what tasks the business manager does using Business Desk. *System administration* describes what tasks the system administrator does using Commerce Server Manager.

When you plan your site management and system administration, you need to answer the following questions, among others:

- Who is going to use Business Desk and for what?

- How is the business manager going to communicate changes to the system administrator (such as requests for customized reports, or a request to run a direct mail job)?

- How are changes to the Web site going to be communicated to the site developer?

Issues to consider when planning a management infrastructure include:

- Placement of Commerce Server, IIS, and SQL Server MMC management computers and a determination of who will use them.

- Placement of cluster management and enterprise management computers, if used, and a determination of who will use them.

- Procedures for routine management tasks, such as content updates, hardware and software upgrades, service packs, and monitoring.

- Tools and utilities needed to manage the site.

- Remote management requirements. The business manager can use Business Desk remotely. Commerce Server Manager can be set up on an administration-only computer (a computer that does not have any other Commerce Server objects installed).

- Security monitoring.

International Requirements

If your site has an international audience, you need to plan how to handle multiple languages and currencies.

When you plan for an international audience, you need to answer the following questions, among others:

- How many currencies do we need to support? What are they?

- How many languages do we need to support? What are they?

- How will local laws affect the way we do business?

- Do we conform to local privacy policies?

- What taxes do we need to collect?

- How should we ship our products internationally?

One of the most important aspects of an international site is planning how to localize the catalog. True internationalization of a site is ideal, but many customers might be happy simply to transact business in a single currency, so long as they can read about what they are buying. There are a number of ways you can accommodate multiple languages, such as using multiple catalogs or even just adding attributes for descriptions in each language.

You need to decide whether to have one Commerce Server store with separate pipelines, catalogs, and so on, for each locale, or to have a separate Commerce Server store for each locale and try to share code between them. Separating the stores would introduce complexity in the back end of the store, with catalogs, prediction, user profiles, data warehousing, and so on.

You should consider the following requirements when you plan an international site:

- Separate content from presentation for easy translation (both for data stores and Web page design)

- Support any SQL Server sort order

- Support high-inflation currencies (where the price of an item or the basket total can become a very large number)

- Take into account variations in credit card validation methods in each country

- Consider classic internationalization/localization issues, such as:

  - Using Unicode to represent text

  - Using the correct date formats, calendars, and currency separators

  - Using appropriate colors, political terms, and so on

For more information about configuring and using the international support of Windows 2000 and the Windows 2000 MultiLanguage Version, see http://www.microsoft.com/globaldev/win2k/setup/default.asp.

Selecting Commerce Server Features

Part of the planning process for your Commerce Server site is to determine which Commerce Server features to use, how to configure those features, and what other Web site functionality you need. Commerce Server is composed of five tightly integrated subsystems, as well as tools you can use to administer and manage your site:

- Administration and Management Tools

- Business Analytics System

- Business Process Pipelines System

- Product Catalog System

- Profiling System

- Targeting System

Administration and Management Tools

Commerce Server provides three tools for managing and administering your installation.

Tool	Description
Commerce Server Business Desk	Hosts business management modules that you use to configure, manage, and analyze your site. For example, you can use Business Desk modules to update pricing information in your catalogs, target new advertisements to specific users, and then run reports to measure how these changes affect site productivity.
Commerce Server Manager	Manages and configures Commerce Server resources, sites, applications, and Web servers. The Microsoft Management Console (MMC), a Windows-based interface that is included in Microsoft Windows 2000, hosts Commerce Server Manager.
Commerce Server Site Packager	Packages a site and its applications and resources into a single file (package), and then moves that file to another environment. Site Packager provides a convenient way for site developers to deliver sites to their customers.

You need to make some decisions about your site to make the best use of these tools. The following table lists some of the questions that you need to answer when you plan how to administer and manage your site.

Planning question	Recommendation
Is our site aimed primarily at customers or at trading partners?	If your site is aimed at trading partners, use the Partner Service, which enables trading partners to manage their accounts.
Do we need to exchange documents with trading partners?	If so, plan to integrate BizTalk Server with your implementation.
What payment options should we support?	Make the necessary arrangements with a banking institution if you plan to support credit card processing.
What currencies do we have to support?	If you plan to localize your site, you need to decide what currencies to support.
How will business managers access Business Desk?	Access to Business Desk should be over a high-speed line.

Business Analytics System

You use the Commerce Server Data Warehouse to collect day-to-day operational data about users who visit your site: user profile data, transaction data, and click-history data. You use Business Desk to analyze the data. For example, you can identify user trends or analyze the effectiveness of a campaign, then update your site to target specific user groups, sell specific products, and so on. The following table lists some of the questions that you need to answer when you plan how to use the Business Analytics System.

Planning question	Recommendation
What data do we need to make key business decisions?	Examine the standard reports available from the Business Analytics System. If you need additional information, you can extend the reporting functionality. There are also a number of third-party software vendors who provide reporting solutions that interact with the Business Analytics System.
Who needs access to the data? How often do they need to see the reports, and how much detail do they require?	You should establish a schedule for running reports. Static reports need to be run regularly so that the data does not become outdated. The schedule for running reports should be coordinated with Data Transformation Services (DTS) tasks.
How often should we process our Web server logs?	This decision depends on the size and nature of the data you store in these logs. The less frequently you process the logs, the larger they will be. Larger log files provide a richer data set, but they also take longer to process. Determine the appropriate processing frequency in your testing environment, and then apply it to your production environment.

Business Process Pipelines System

You use pipelines to define and link together one or more stages of a business process, then run them in sequence to complete a specific task. Each stage of a pipeline contains one or more pipeline COM objects that can be configured to meet your site's requirements.

You can use the pipeline infrastructure to implement several pipeline models: the Order Processing Pipeline (OPP), the Direct Mailer Pipeline, the Content Selection Pipeline, and the Event Processing Pipeline. The following table lists a key question that you need to answer when you plan how to use the business processing pipelines.

Planning question	Recommendation
Do the pipeline components that ship with Commerce Server meet our requirements? If not, should we build our own components or purchase them from a third-party pipeline component developer?	Examine the functionality provided by Commerce Server. If the processing stages do not meet your needs, you can either extend the pipelines yourself or contact a third-party pipeline component developer to purchase pipeline components.

Product Catalog System

You use the Product Catalog System to create catalogs of products and to add and update product data. This system provides both import and export functionality, and enables you to define and modify your catalog schema. The following table lists some of the questions that you need to answer when you plan how to use the Product Catalog System.

Planning question	Recommendation
Do we have an existing product catalog database that can be used directly by our online store? If so, should we continue to maintain the old catalog, or move it over completely to the new Product Catalog System instead?	Synchronizing information in the Product Catalog System with your offline catalog requires development of custom software. Consider integrating your existing catalog system with other features of Commerce Server.
What is the best organizational schema for our catalog?	The Product Catalog System is flexible enough to accommodate a variety of schemas. If you design a new catalog, be sure to provide plenty of opportunities for expanding the schema.
Do we need to provide unique pricing to different groups of customers?	If so, create a custom catalog to which you can apply pricing rules. You should plan custom catalogs in conjunction with planning how to use the Profiling System.
Do we have particularly complex pricing schemes or other requirements beyond the functionality of the Product Catalog System?	Consider using a third-party catalog management solution. A number of catalog solution vendors have integrated their products with Commerce Server to provide additional functionality.
Do we need to exchange catalogs with our trading partners?	If so, include BizTalk Server in your deployment plan, because it provides functionality for exchanging catalogs.
What catalog data should we export to the Data Warehouse?	You should export the information you need to create the reports identified when you planned how to use the Business Analytics System.

Profiling System

In Commerce Server, you use profiles to collect and store information about the users who visit your Web site. The data that forms a profile comes from multiple data sources, such as Web log files and Commerce Server databases. You import the profile data into the Data Warehouse. You can then analyze it and use the results of your analysis to target content to groups of users. The following table lists some of the questions that you need to answer when you plan how to use the Profiling System.

Planning question	Recommendation
Which data store should we use to store profiles, and what data should we store in the profiles?	If you plan to authenticate users with their Windows 2000 security context, you need to store some profile information in Microsoft Active Directory. If you do not plan to do this, use SQL Server to store profile data.
What profile information should we export to the Data Warehouse?	You should export the information you need to create the reports identified when you planned how to use the Business Analytics System. (However, don't export personal information, such as credit card numbers or passwords.)
What information should we collect about users?	You can either collect information from users directly (explicit data) or you can use the Predictor resource to fill in the information you need (implicit data).
Are there existing user accounts that we need to transfer into the Profiling System? If so, do we need to transfer all of the attributes from the current system?	If you are transferring from Site Server 3.0 Membership Directory, use the Directory Migration Toolbox to transfer this information. Don't plan to maintain the Membership Directory after you have migrated to Commerce Server.

You can also use Active Directory as a data source for profile data. Active Directory is the directory service built into Windows 2000. You can use Active Directory to add, modify, delete, and organize your organization's business entities. For example, Windows 2000 user accounts, computer accounts, security and distribution groups, and published resources are all accessible through Active Directory.

The Profiling System can aggregate data from Active Directory and other data sources into a single business entity that you can then use in your Commerce Server implementation. For example, you can store the account number and password of a user in Active Directory and store the rest of the profile information (contact information, credit limit, preferences, and so on) in a SQL Server database. The Profiling System can then assemble data from these two data sources into a single user profile that you can use for targeting and analysis.

Active Directory is a highly robust and scalable technology; however, it is important that you design your site architecture to use it appropriately. The following table lists some questions that you need to answer to determine how you can best use Active Directory in your site design.

Planning question	Recommendation
What data should we store in Active Directory?	Store only non-volatile data in Active Directory.
What volume of data should we store in Active Directory?	You can store up to one million user accounts in a single Active Directory domain. This estimate is based on the following assumptions:
	• One percent (10,000) of the users will be actively using the site at one time.
	• The ratio of the number of items written to Active Directory to the number of items read from Active Directory is no more than 14 percent.
	If you need to accommodate more than one million users in your Active Directory store, you can assemble multiple domains, each containing one million users.
	If you intend to use Active Directory for larger-scale implementations, engage Microsoft Consulting Services (MCS) to assist you with planning how to do this.

Targeting System

You use the Targeting System to deliver content to one or more selected users. The Targeting System includes four distinct subsystems, which you should consider when you plan how to use the Targeting System:

- Content Selection Framework (CSF)
- Direct Mailer
- Expressions (Expression Builder, Expression Evaluator)
- Predictor resource

Content Selection Framework

The Content Selection Framework (CSF) is a framework based on the Commerce Server pipeline architecture. You use the Commerce Server Business Desk Campaigns module to create and schedule marketing campaigns (advertisements, direct mail campaigns, discount campaigns, and other promotions). You can also manage different types of campaigns for multiple customers. CSF can rank, select, and schedule any type of content. The following table lists some of the questions that you need to answer when you plan online campaigns.

Planning question	Recommendation
Do we plan to target campaigns to particular groups of users? If so, what user attributes should we target?	Use the Business Analytics System to determine common buying patterns on your site, and then incorporate this information into the Targeting System. This should be an ongoing process.
What information do we need from the Business Analytics System to make pricing decisions?	Determine your information requirements for the CSF and use this information to evaluate the reports provided by the Business Analytics System.
Should our campaigns use the Predictor resource? If so, what are the key user segments we need to target?	Collect information about usage patterns in the Data Warehouse, use the Predictor resource to identify user segments, and then use this information to update your campaigns.

Direct Mailer

Direct Mailer is a fast, scalable Windows 2000 service that you can use to send personalized e-mail messages from a Web page, or non-personalized mailings from a flat text file, to large groups of recipients. Direct Mailer can be used as a stand-alone process or integrated into the Campaigns modules in Business Desk. Direct Mailer tracks e-mails that have been sent, and clicked, enabling to you to analyze the success of a direct mail campaign. The following table lists some of the questions that you need to answer when you plan your direct mail campaigns.

Planning question	Recommendation
Who should we include in direct mailings? What rules should we use to determine the mailing list?	Use List Manager to create and manage lists of direct mail recipients. Direct Mailer uses mailing lists to create and send pieces of mail to targeted recipients in the list.
How will users tell us they want to be removed from the direct mail list?	Always include an "opt-out" choice in your direct mailings.
How often should we send direct mail?	Establish a schedule and develop a script to automate the process.
Should the direct mail be personalized? If so, what user profile information should we include in the personalization?	Personalized mail is more effective. Design your user profiles to include the attributes you want to use for your direct mail targets.

Expressions

An expression is a condition you can set up to determine, for example, whether or not content should be delivered to a particular set of customers. You use the Expression Builder to create targeting expressions for your marketing campaigns (such as "young adults = ages greater than 16, but less than 25"). You use the Expression Evaluator to create business rules for personalized ad targeting, promotions, direct mail campaigns, and content targeting, based on evaluations of the conditional expressions you created with the Expression Builder. The following table lists a key question that you need to answer when you plan how to use expressions.

Planning question	Recommendation
What experience do we want to create for our users? What business rules should we create to facilitate that experience?	Base your expressions on the personalization requirements developed for the Targeting System. For example, if you have decided to display content based on a referring Uniform Resource Locator (URL), you might create the expression *Referrer equals URL*.

Predictor Resource

You can use the Predictor resource both to recommend products to users online and to fill in missing properties in user profiles. Collect data on at least a few thousand users to get enough data to analyze before you deploy the Predictor resource. The following table lists some of the questions that you need to answer when you plan how to use the Predictor resource.

Planning question	Recommendation
Should we enhance our targeting and provide product recommendations to users?	Implement the Predictor resource by building models of user behavior after you have collected some initial data in your Data Warehouse.
What key user segments should we identify in order to make meaningful recommendations?	Use the Predictor resource to identify meaningful segments, and then view them with the Segment Viewer in Business Desk.
Should we use inference to augment user profile data, or should we make recommendations based only on data explicitly provided by users?	If you plan to infer user properties, use the Segment Viewer in Business Desk in conjunction with the Dependency Network view in Commerce Server Manager to focus on the key user attributes you plan to use to make predictions.

Planning for Migration

You need to plan how to migrate your present operations to the proposed new site, whether you are migrating from existing software or migrating from a completely manual system.

Issues to consider when planning for migration include:

- Migrating authentication methodologies.

- Migrating profiles, such as those for users and products.

- Migrating pipelines and order processing flow.

- Migrating catalogs.

- Migrating the User database or Membership Directory to Microsoft SQL Server or Active Directory.

- Migrating Site Vocabulary to site terms.

- Migrating data center management and site processes.

- Migrating credit card processing.

- Integrating with order processing, inventory, or other existing systems.

Planning for Scalability

This chapter introduces you to concepts for planning how to scale your Microsoft Commerce Server 2000 site. Commerce Server is a highly scalable platform, which makes it easy to add hardware and partition databases or to move processes to enhance performance as your volume of business increases.

A well-designed Web server farm can be expanded (*scaled*) cost-effectively to accommodate sudden increases in site traffic. Web applications must be scalable because you can't predict customer load at any particular time, but you must handle the load as it occurs. With Commerce Server, you can design and build an affordable, highly scalable server farm that will support thousands of concurrent users. When you scale your Commerce Server site, you:

- Increase the number of users each server can handle.

- Increase the number of concurrent users your site can support.

- Provide faster response times.

The following table describes the elements you should consider when planning how to scale your site.

Scaling element	Description
Throughput (per component)	The maximum number of transactions a particular component can handle in a specified length of time. You measure throughput by rate per second (for example, 400 transactions per second).
Load balancing	The distribution of client requests among multiple servers within a server cluster. If a server fails, the load is dynamically redistributed among the remaining servers.
	Of all the scaling elements, load balancing offers some of the most dramatic performance improvements. If you add additional servers and evenly distribute load across them, the throughput of the application can increase in a linear fashion. You can use the Network Load Balancing (NLB) tool, available as part of Windows 2000, to balance the load across all your servers.
Fault tolerance	The ability to deal with failures and faults. The ability to continually handle load is a key component of scalability.
Queuing	The addition of an external component to an application to preserve requests that the application is unable to process immediately. Stored requests are resubmitted when it is possible to process them. If a portion of the application does not need to respond to a request immediately, it is a candidate for a queue.
	Queuing does not improve overall throughput, but it is one method of shifting load. By holding on to excess requests submitted during peak processing times and resubmitting them at a later time, the application can handle more requests than it could handle otherwise.
Throttling	The ability to postpone transactions until a later time. A throttling mechanism is similar to a queue in that it prevents the load from exceeding the maximum throughput rate and enables a component to remain functional during a period of load that would normally be more than it could handle. If an application includes a client that has the ability to retry its request at a later time, it is a candidate for a throttling mechanism.
Locking	The ability to handle contention for shared resources. The techniques you use to deal with locking can affect the amount of load an application can handle.

The following table describes several techniques for scaling your site.

Technique	Description
Scale hardware vertically	Increase capacity by upgrading hardware, while maintaining the same physical footprint and number of servers. Scaling hardware vertically simplifies system administration, but has a higher hardware cost than scaling horizontally or optimizing software architecture. In addition, once you reach maximum capacity on existing hardware, you must begin to scale horizontally.
Scale hardware horizontally	Increase capacity by adding servers. Scaling hardware horizontally enables you to increase hardware capacity at a lower cost. However, once your site becomes too complex to manage, you must begin to scale it vertically.
Optimize site architecture	Improve server efficiency by identifying operations with similar workload factors and dedicating servers to each type of operation. You can significantly improve site capacity by dedicating servers to operations with similar workload factors (rather than to a mixed-operation workload) and optimizing performance. You should plan architectural improvements early in the project life cycle, to enable you to build and operate your site more cost effectively. You can use Microsoft SQL Server 2000 or SQL Server 7.0 to distribute individual Commerce Server components to separate servers.

The result of using these scaling techniques is a highly scalable server farm that you can grow well beyond its original design limitations. The following sections provide you with detailed information about how to scale your Commerce Server site.

Scaling Hardware Vertically

Based on performance and capacity planning benchmarks performed by Microsoft, Commerce Server sites have been found to be characteristically CPU-bound because Commerce Server makes extensive use of data caching to improve site performance. In other words, Active Server Pages (ASP) processing, which is highly CPU intensive, is the primary bottleneck in CPU processing capacity.

Scaling vertically is the process of adding memory, increasing input/output (I/O), and increasing processing capacity, so you can get additional throughput without changing your application architecture. It is common to find Web servers with large amounts of memory that can cache nearly all of the content of an entire Web site. In addition, N-way symmetric multiprocessing (SMP) hardware is readily available in the marketplace. Thus, many methods are available to scale a Commerce Server site vertically.

One method of vertically scaling hardware is to use a higher-class processor to increase processing power so that a single server can accommodate more traffic. Another way you can vertically scale hardware is to run Microsoft Windows 2000 on 8-way SMP servers. The aggregate throughput is higher, but it comes at the cost of diminishing returns on investment. (In other words, per-processor throughput is less on 8-way SMP hardware than on 4-way SMP hardware. You get higher aggregate throughput at a disproportionate increase in cost.)

If you plan to scale your hardware vertically, you should do the following:

Memory

- Add a large amount of memory to decrease disk access and to help improve the I/O throughput of the IIS/ASP server cache content and the NTFS file system disk cache buffers

- Add additional spindles and Redundant Array of Inexpensive Disks (RAID)

I/O

- Scale the hardware with processors up to 4-way SMP hardware, then proceed further with horizontal or architectural scaling techniques

- Add multiple small computer system interface (SCSI) disk controllers to increase disk I/O throughput

- Add multiple 100-megabits-per-second (Mbps) network cards to increase network I/O throughput

- Consider Gigabit Ethernet

Figure 5.1 shows how you might scale from a single Pentium II-CPU server to a dual-CPU server with a Pentium III Xeon-class processor.

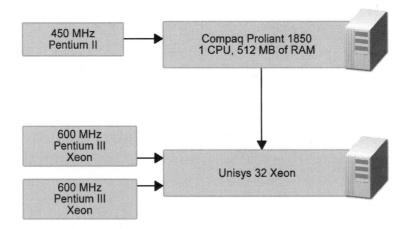

Figure 5.1 Scaling hardware vertically

If you have exhausted vertical scaling techniques, you can try the horizontal scaling techniques described in the following topic.

Scaling Hardware Horizontally

Scaling hardware horizontally increases capacity by adding servers to the server farm. You can then distribute Commerce Server components across multiple servers, thereby increasing capacity.

When you begin scaling horizontally, you add the complexity of having to distribute the load evenly across multiple servers. You must address distribution by using load-balancing tools, such as NLB, Domain Name System (DNS) round robin (network software), and hardware solutions such as Cisco LocalDirector (network/router hardware). The benefits of load balancing include providing redundancy of services and presenting higher aggregated capacity by directing the load to multiple servers.

To effectively scale hardware horizontally, you should not use IIS session variables and you should disable IIS session management, unless you use Cisco LocalDirector. In cases where an application is coded with IIS session management (makes use of session variables), you can use hardware such as Cisco LocalDirector to balance the load because it directs site traffic and sends a client back to the same server each time. For more information about IIS session management, see the "Disabling IIS Session Management and Removing Session Variables" topic.

You can horizontally scale the following components of a Commerce Server server farm:

- **Web servers**. Add more computers to function as Web servers. Externally, you expose the computers by using a common domain name with a single virtual Internet Protocol (IP) address mapped to a load-balancing system. The load-balancing system directs the traffic to multiple servers. Typically, load balancing directs a Transmission Control Protocol (TCP) connection (such as a Hypertext Transfer Protocol (HTTP) request) to a specific server and keeps it directed to the same server until the TCP connection session ends.

- **Active Directory domain controllers**. Add more computers to function as Active Directory domain controllers. Externally, you expose the computers using a common domain name.

Scaling hardware horizontally helps the server farm expand to higher capacity. Further scaling requires architectural improvements. The next section describes how to optimize your site architecture to improve scalability.

Optimizing Site Architecture to Improve Scalability

To improve the architecture of your Commerce Server site, you can:

- Design your site so that static, high-capacity operations (including operations with relatively simple ASP pages) are separated from dynamic operations with heavier load factors but smaller capacity requirements.

- Dedicate servers to each type of operation.

- Optimize the performance of each server.

For example, dedicated servers can process dynamic content, such as ASP and COM+, and run Commerce Server pipeline components, so that the entire bandwidth of the server is used efficiently without interfering with the serving of static Hypertext Markup Language (HTML)/Graphics Interchange Format (GIF) content requests.

Figure 5.2 illustrates a typical site showing how workload might be divided among the available servers.

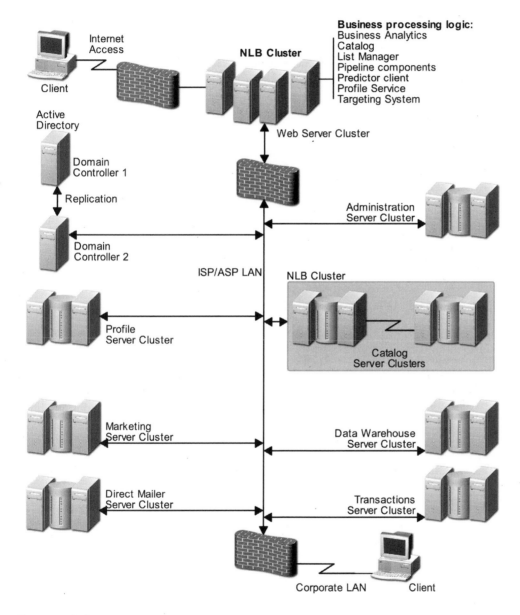

Figure 5.2 Sample site architecture

IIS processes static HTML/GIF content requests many times faster than it processes ASP requests. An IIS server dedicated to processing HTML/GIF content might be able to handle 10,000 concurrent user requests while an IIS server dedicated to processing ASP and

Commerce Server pipeline content might be able to handle only up to 1,000 concurrent user requests.

Another example suggests that most Web-based e-commerce sites process user requests that fall into one of the five categories listed in the following table.

Category	Percentage of customer requests
Browse	80
Search	9
User registration	2
Add item to the shopping basket	5
Check out	4

This example shows that users browse, search, and register nine times more often than they add items to their shopping baskets and check out. Based on this example, in a population of 100,000 users, there should be approximately 10,000 users adding items to their shopping basket or checking out, while 90,000 users are browsing, searching, or registering.

Given the numbers in this example, servers handling static content (browse, user registration, and search operations) can process approximately 90 percent of the traffic, while servers handling dynamic content (add item and check out operations) can process the remaining 10 percent of the traffic. However, because dynamic operations also account for a fewer number of concurrent users, you can decrease the number of these dedicated servers.

There are many situations in which you can use dedicated servers to divide content, such as static content (HTML/GIF), dynamic content (ASP/Commerce Server pipeline), business rules (COM+ components), disk I/O (cache most active files). The following architectural improvements can help you to get even higher performance, with better scalability:

- Disabling IIS session management and removing session variables
- Separating static content from other types of content
- Caching static content
- Caching static look-up data
- Consolidating business rules on dedicated servers
- Using Message Queuing or e-mail to update systems
- Processing requests in batches
- Optimizing SQL Server databases

The following sections provide detailed information about how to implement these architectural improvements.

Disabling IIS Session Management and Removing Session Variables

You must ensure that your application code disables IIS session management and that it does not use IIS session variables, unless you use Cisco LocalDirector. IIS session management consumes a specific amount of memory for each user, consuming more memory as the application stores more values in the session variable (due to an increase in the number of concurrent users). If there are few session variable values, this consumption of memory might not impact performance significantly. On the other hand, if there are a large number of session variable values, such as an object model, memory consumption in IIS session management can impact performance significantly.

For example, if the session variable for each user consumes 1 MB of memory, 1,000 concurrent users consume approximately 1 GB of memory. Based on this example, using session variables severely limits scalability in a case where the computer has 1.5 GB of available memory. Without this memory consumption, it is possible to serve a larger number of concurrent users, up to the limits of the CPU.

Another disadvantage of using session variables is that they reside only on the local server. In other words, the application requires an affinity between the client and the server on which the session variable started, because the session variable resides only on that one server. To maintain the required affinity between the client and server, you must ensure session stickiness (or persistence). This eliminates on-the-fly redundancy (destroying user sessions if a server goes down or needs to be taken offline).

You can configure NLB to enable client-to-server affinity. This sends a client back to the same destination server for each request, providing the load-balancing effect you want. Session variables are local to each server, so the client always sees the correct set of variables and state.

Separating Static Content from Other Types of Content

The following tables compare two server farm methods (non-consolidated and consolidated) of serving 100,000 concurrent users.

Non-Consolidated Server Farm

Operations	Type of content	Percentage of users	Number of Web servers	Number of concurrent users per server	Total number of concurrent users
Browse, search, user registration, add item, checkout	All (static, dynamic, ASP, and so forth)	100	100	1,000	100,000
Totals:	**All**	**100**	**100**	**1,000**	**100,000**

Consolidated Server Farm

Operations	Type of content	Percentage of users	Number of Web servers	Number of concurrent users per server	Total number of concurrent users
Browse, user registration, search	Static	90	9	10,000	90,000
Add item, checkout	Other (dynamic, ASP, and so on)	10	10	1,000	10,000
Totals:	**All**	**100**	**19**	**Not applicable**	**100,000**

Based on the information in the tables, the total number of servers drops from 100 front-end Web servers to 19 front-end Web servers, if you separate the static content from other types of content.

IIS 5.0 processes static HTML/GIF content very efficiently, but processing ASP content requires a significant amount of CPU time, resulting in reduced performance. To most efficiently use the servers, combine operations that have similar load-factor characteristics or capacity requirements and separate those that differ. The numbers in the previous table suggest that you might benefit by using three different servers, one for each of the following categories:

- Browse static HTML/GIF content requests

- Search ASP and user registration requests

- Add item to basket and checkout purchase ASP requests

Caching Static Content

ASP pages render many types of data to HTML that are not highly dynamic, but not truly static, such as product attributes (description, price, and so forth), site announcements, and sale announcements. You can use a process to render these types of information to static HTML pages and serve them up as static HTML/GIF content. This provides for a much higher throughput, and reduces overhead by avoiding ASP processing and SQL Server data retrieval.

If your information is relatively static but some content (such as product price) is driven by a database look-up (such as pricing by zip code) you can use this technique in combination with framing product information in a separate HTML frame from the product price.

Microsoft Scalable Web Cache (SWC) 2.0 provides an excellent caching solution. For more information about SWC, see http://www.microsoft.com/TechNet/iis/swc2.asp. Another solution is to use an Internet Server Application Programming Interface (ISAPI) filter that reads HTML and performs a look-up to an in-memory database, similar to the way early database integration was accomplished using Internet Database Connector (IDC) and HTML extension (HTX) files. This method avoids full ASP processing and retains high-speed serving of HTML pages.

Caching Static Lookup Data

If your data requires dynamic lookups (such as product price based on zip code or user ID) or a database lookup (such as pricing by zip code), you can use an in-memory database to cache the lookup table. This helps reduce overhead associated with retrieving data across a network. You can refresh the in-memory database with a nightly process (or as necessary) to ensure that the dynamic data is up-to-date. This helps reduce overhead associated with retrieving data from the SQL Server database.

On many sites, a page contains an HTML list box/combo box (such as product categories or product compartments) rendered from a lookup table. It is much more efficient to render these records once and cache the HTML fragment globally in the ASP application object than to retrieve them from the lookup table each time they are needed.

When you cache static lookup data, small lookup tables work best. However, you can increase hardware memory capacity to help accommodate larger tables, if you need to do so. You can analyze the IIS and SQL Server logs to determine which lookup tables are accessed most frequently and would benefit most from caching.

Using the Caching Technology Provided by Commerce Server

You can use the Commerce Server **CacheManager** object to set up and use a collection of data caches, in which you can store profile data, catalog data, transaction data, and campaign data for your site.

You can use the **LRUCache** data cache object to create, store, and retrieve name/value pairs (referred to as *elements*) from the cache. When the cache is full, the least recently used (LRU) element is automatically removed from the cache to make room for a new element. Each **LRUCache** object has its own size, which is defined in the Global.asa file. Flushing is performed using an LRU technique, in which each cache is permitted to grow 10 percent larger than its specified size, at which time the cache returns to its specified size by flushing the least recently used items.

You use Commerce Server Business Desk to empty the caches you set up with the **CacheManager** object. After the caches have been refreshed, the next time Commerce Server receives a request for this data, the updated data is loaded into the caches.

For example, you use the Publish Transactions module to update your site with new transaction information, such as new tax rates and shipping methods. The Publish Transactions module refreshes the caches that store transaction information. The next time Commerce Server receives a request for transaction data, the updated data is loaded into the caches.

Consolidating Business Rules on Dedicated Servers

Because an optimized Commerce Server site is CPU-bound, you can improve ASP and Commerce Server pipeline processing performance by reducing CPU utilization. You can reduce CPU utilization by identifying and placing complex, processor-intensive business rules (such as COM+ components) on dedicated servers.

There is a trade-off in performance between in-process execution of components and out-of-process execution of components marshaled by the distributed version of Component Object Model (DCOM). To determine the exact trade-off, you must measure both methods and determine which method works best for your site. If a business rule is processor-intensive and the performance cost is greater than the cost of marshalling by DCOM, you could develop the component as a COM+ component. Dedicating a separate server to COM+ components increases server capacity on the ASP and Commerce Server pipeline components, thereby increasing performance of ASP and Commerce Server pipeline processing.

If a business rule consists of only a few lines of code that is not processor-intensive, it is probably not worth having a dedicated server to run it. In this case, either leave it as an ASP function snippet (saving object activation/invocation costs) or, if the code is complicated ASP code, code it as a COM component using Microsoft Visual C++ and Active Template Library (ATL). Activate the COM component locally by using the "Both" threading model of the ATL wizard.

Using Message Queuing or E-mail to Update Systems

You can use Message Queuing or e-mail to update fulfillment, Data Warehouse, reporting, and other systems, rather than using a database transaction. By using Message Queuing or e-mail, you leverage asynchronous communications to get a high rate of "fire and forget" operations and transactions to avoid latency caused by database operations and transactions such as data retrieval or extended computation.

For example, if a department (or an entirely different company) performs the actual order fulfillment at a different geographical location from the department that receives the order (drop ships), the two locations must frequently communicate new orders and shipping status. Instead of using a database operation or transaction (such as a periodic batch database extract) and sending the results to the remote site, the departments within the company can use Message Queuing services or e-mail to send notifications (such as new orders) to and accept status information from the remote site.

The front-end servers accept the request and quickly hand off the information to Message Queuing or to an e-mail server, which then sends the information to the remote location. This results in a higher rate of processing and faster front-end server response time, updating the remote sites more quickly than by using periodic batch database extracts.

You can also submit Commerce Server orders and receipts to Microsoft BizTalk Server 2000 asynchronously, rather than using an inline database transaction. Doing this enables the ASP page to avoid transaction latency and continue processing. The disadvantage is that the customer does not see an immediate order confirmation number and must wait for a confirmation e-mail or wait until you process and record the orders and receipts in the database. Asynchronously recording Commerce Server orders and receipts works best at sites with periodic load peaks.

Processing Requests in Batches

You can process operations that can be deferred until a later time, such as credit card processing or tax calculations, in batch mode on a dedicated server. For example, most B2C sites can't defer tax calculations because customers need to know the total amount due at the time of checkout, but they can process credit card transactions at a later time. Many B2B sites can defer processing tax calculations until monthly invoices are generated by the accounts receivable system.

Deferring processing enables the front-end servers to process requests at a higher rate of speed and to respond to requests more quickly. You can send failure and exception reports to users through e-mail. In many cases, systems that perform batch processing operations already exist in your business. For more information about interfacing with existing business systems that perform batch processing operations, see Chapter 10, "Integrating Third-Party ERP Systems with Commerce Server Applications."

Planning for Reliability and High Availability

Electronic commerce is a "mission critical" operation, and a significant source of revenue for many companies. When any part of an e-commerce site is unavailable, the company might well be losing money. This chapter describes ways to reduce or eliminate downtime in a Microsoft Commerce Server 2000 environment.

Hardware failure, data corruption, and physical site destruction all pose threats to an e-commerce site that must be available close to 100 percent of the time. You can enhance the availability of your site by identifying services that must be available, then identifying the points at which those services can fail. Increasing availability also means reducing the probability of failure. Decisions about how far to go to prevent failures are based on a combination of your company's tolerance for service outages, the available budget, and the expertise of your staff. System availability is directly dependent on the hardware and software you choose, and the effectiveness of your operating procedures.

This chapter focuses primarily on the hardware and software needed to create a Commerce Server site with no single point of failure. However, operational procedures also can have a significant impact on service availability. To avoid service outages, you must carefully consider service availability for all operating procedures.

Availability is a function of whether a particular service is functioning properly. You can think of availability as a continuum, ranging from 100 percent (a completely fault-tolerant site that never goes offline) to 0 percent (a site that's never available). All sites have some degree of availability. Many of today's companies target "3 9's" availability (99.9 percent) for their Web sites, which means that there can be only approximately 8 hours and 45 minutes of unplanned downtime a year. Telephone companies in the United States typically target "5 9's" or 99.999 percent uptime (5 minutes and 15 seconds of unplanned downtime per year). Although any company might strive for additional uptime for its Web site, significant incremental hardware investment is required to get those extra "9's."

Availability Checklist

You can create an availability checklist to monitor the availability of your site. The availability checklist should contain the items listed in the following table.

Item	Monitors
Bandwidth usage: per day, week, and month	• **Bandwidth**. How bandwidth is being used (peak and idle). • **Usage**. How usage increases (if it increases, when it increases, and how long it increases). You can use this information to project how much bandwidth you'll need in the future. This will enable you to plan for the peak bandwidth you need for a holiday shopping season. You can get bandwidth usage data from managed routers and Internet Information Services (IIS) 5.0 log analysis (using the Commerce Server Data Warehouse).
Network availability	• **Network Internet Control Message Protocol (ICMP) echo pings**. Available from most network monitoring software. Compare your network availability to the level agreed to in your service level agreement (SLA) with your Internet Service Provider (ISP)/data center provider. Request improvement if network availability falls below the level agreed to in the SLA. The formula for measuring network availability is as follows: `(Number of successful ping returns/number of total pings issued) x 100%`
System availability	• **Operating system**. Monitor normal and abnormal shutdowns of the operating system. • **SQL Server**. Monitor normal operation and failover events of Microsoft SQL Server. • **IIS**. Monitor normal and abnormal shutdowns in IIS. The formula for measuring system availability is as follows: `(Period of measurement-downtime)/period of measurement) x 100%`
HTTP availability	• **HTTP requests (internal)**. Monitor Hypertext Transfer Protocol (HTTP) requests issued internally. • **HTTP requests (per ISP)**. Monitor HTTP requests issued from ISP networks (such as AOL, Microsoft MSN, MCI, and Sprint), to track whether or not users of the monitored ISP networks can access your site. • **HTTP requests (per geographic location)**. Monitor HTTP requests issued from different geographic locations (New York, San Francisco, London, Paris, Munich, Tokyo, Singapore, and so on) to track whether or not users from respective areas of the world can access your site. Downtime occurs when the site fails to return a page or returns a page with an incorrect response. The formula for measuring HTTP availability is as follows: `(Number of successful HTTP requests/number of total HTTP requests issued) x 10`

Item	Monitors
Performance metrics (For more detailed information about monitoring performance, see Chapter 19, "Maximizing Performance.")	• **Number of visits (per day/week/month)**. Monitor site traffic information to assess the level of site activity. This data is available from the Data Warehouse. • **Latency of requests for sets of operations and page groups (per day/week/month)**. Compare these metrics to your transaction cost analysis (TCA) test results to see how site performance compares to TCA predictions and to identify system bottlenecks. For more information about TCA testing, see Chapter 19, "Maximizing Performance." • **CPU utilization (per day/week/month)**. Monitor utilization on Microsoft Windows servers, SQL Server servers, IIS/Commerce Server servers, middleware, and so on. Group servers by function to make it easier to track and plan site capacity. • **Disk storage**. Group servers by function and monitor disk capacity (total disk capacity and free space). Review weekly and monthly history, so you can spot trends and plan for expansion. • **Disk I/O**. Group servers by function and monitor disk input/output (I/O) throughput. Compare weekly and monthly history with the disk I/O rating provided by the manufacturer. If the observed I/O nears the disk I/O, consider adding more spindles (adding more drives to the drive stripe set) or redistribute disk I/O to multiple disk controllers. • **Fiber channel controller/switch bandwidth**. Monitor system area network (SAN) fiber channel controller bandwidth. (A SAN is typically used to interconnect nodes within a distributed computer system, such as a cluster. These systems are members of a common administrative domain and are usually in close physical proximity. A SAN is physically secure.) If the observed bandwidth nears the throughput rating provided by the manufacturer, consider adding more controllers and switches to redistribute traffic and get more aggregate bandwidth. • **Memory**. Make sure that the amount of available memory is greater than 4 MB. If the system nears this level during peak usage, add more memory to the server.

Monitoring performance is not strictly part of monitoring availability. However, monitoring performance can sometimes provide advance warning about potential problems that can affect availability if you don't address them.

Designing a Highly Available E-Commerce Site

This section describes how to design a highly available e-commerce site architecture. Today's Internet services require configurations that separate the user interface layer from business processing logic and data, for security reasons. Figure 6.1 shows how many e-commerce sites further isolate business logic from underlying data.

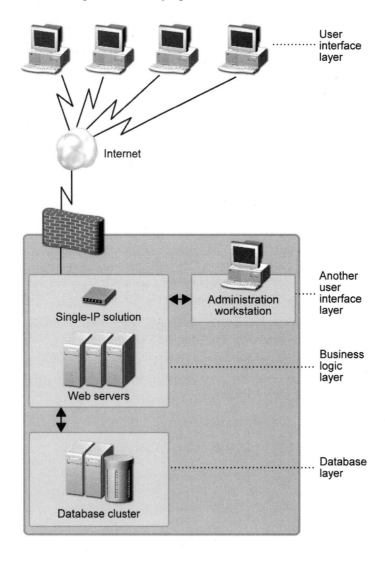

Figure 6.1 Multi-tiered e-commerce site architecture

In a multi-tiered configuration, such as that shown in Figure 6.1, client browsers access Web pages and the Web pages activate associated business logic hosted on a Web server. The persistent data that the business objects require is maintained in a separate database layer (bottom tier).

Data and state information control processing logic and client experience. The following table describes typical strategies you can use at each tier to monitor data and state information.

Tier	Strategy
User interface layer (top tier)	• Low state (doesn't hold much application code state information), unique data stored in cookies or registry. • Wide variety of low-end servers. • Minimize downtime by using additional servers.
Business logic layer (middle tier)	• Web applications, such as the Product Catalog System, Profiling System, and Business Process Pipelines, run on this tier. • Low state, no unique data, inexpensive servers. • Minimize downtime by using software or hardware single-Internet Protocol (IP) load balancing.
Database layer (bottom tier)	• Data that Commerce Server uses is managed and stored in the Data Warehouse on this tier. • System state and data are stored on this tier. • Minimize downtime by using a clustered or replicated configuration.

You design availability into a Web site by identifying services that must be available, determining where those services can fail, and then designing the services so that they continue to be available to customers, even if a failure occurs. There are the following three fundamental strategies you can use to design a highly available site:

• Ensure that operational procedures are well-documented and appropriate for your goals and the capabilities of your staff

• Ensure that your site has enough capacity to handle processing loads

• Reduce the probability of failure

Operational Procedures

One of the most effective means of ensuring site availability can also be inexpensive to implement. Creating well-documented and accurate operational procedures is an effective means of ensuring site availability.

Operational procedures should include the following:

- Change management (For more information, see Chapter 8, "Developing Your Site.")

- Service-level management (For more information, see Chapter 17, "Managing Your Site.")

- Problem management (For more information, see Chapter 18, "Problem Management.")

- Capacity management (For more information, see Chapter 19, "Maximizing Performance.")

- Security management (For more information, see *Designing Secure Web-Based Applications for Microsoft Windows 2000* by Michael Howard, located online at http://mspress.microsoft.com/prod/books/4293.htm.)

- Managing for availability (This chapter discusses availability issues.)

Microsoft has created a knowledge base to describe industry experience and best practices for such procedures called the Enterprise Services Frameworks (Microsoft Readiness Framework, Microsoft Solutions Framework, and Microsoft Operations Framework). You can find more information online at http://www.microsoft.com/technet/ecommerce/ecseries.asp. There is also a wealth of procedural "best practices" available in other locations. For references to additional information, see "Additional Resources" later in this chapter.

When you have a stable set of operational procedures, you can begin to explore ways of improving hardware and software availability. System availability doesn't depend only on how redundant your hardware and software systems are. All of the elements described in the following table determine availability.

Availability element	Consider
Environment	• **Climate control**. Provide adequate climate control and air conditioning. Additional servers, disk storage, and other equipment generate additional heat. If you don't have adequate climate control, you might experience outages due to CPUs overheating. • **Power conditioning (uninterruptible power supply (UPS), surge protection)**. Condition your power and provide surge protection to avoid outages due to power interruptions or brownouts.
Hardware	• **Servers, disks, network interface cards (NICs), and so on**. There are many ways to improve availability by deploying redundant servers, disks, NICs, and so on.
Network	• **Local area network (LAN), wide area network (WAN), routers, firewalls, switches, and so on**. Site availability depends on the availability of network connections to the rest of the world. It is important to deploy a redundant network infrastructure.
Process	• **Change control**. Implement change control by recording change requests, approvals, and implementations. Change control provides historical configuration checkpoints and helps correlate issues with changes in configuration. For more information about processes for managing configuration, see Chapter 8, "Developing Your Site." • **Escalation procedures**. Escalation procedures help reduce confusion about what to do during outages. Maintain a list of contacts for each level of security, so that you can get the necessary help immediately when an outage occurs. • **Service level agreement (SLA)**. It is important to require an SLA from ISPs to guarantee an appropriate level of site monitoring, operations, and availability. • **Staged deployment (move from development to test to staging to production)**. Stage deployments in the appropriate environments to identify failures before they reach the production environment. Set up specific release criteria for each environment, so that you can determine when the application is ready for release to the next environment. For example, the development environment is typically the least restrictive, with a high degree of instability. The test environment should be more stable than the development environment and have better performance. The staging environment should be stable. The production environment should be stable and perform at targeted levels.

Availability element	Consider

Security	• **Physical security (cardkeys, locks, fences, walls).** Depending on the value of the data you are securing, you might want to consider multiple levels of security to protect physical access to your facilities.
	
	• **Software security.** With the increase in hacker activity, it is extremely important to implement software security measures. Consider the following:
	  • Firewalls help restrict network access to servers.
	  • Independent security audits can be helpful for bolstering site security.
	  • Intrusion detection software can alert system administrators to hacks and denial-of-service attacks.
	  • Personnel security can be improved by performing background checks on your personnel, implementing rolling password changes, using biometrics security devices, and so on.
	  • Checking server and client certificates helps ensure the identities of systems with which your site interacts.

Software: application	• **Stable, tested application software that operates correctly, integrates with existing software, and performs at targeted levels.** It is also important to control software versions and manage changes. For more information about managing changes, see Chapter 8, "Developing Your Site."
Software: platform	• **Stable, tested platform software.** In general, you should use only production software. Avoid development or evaluation mode software.

Site Capacity

Site services can become unavailable if site traffic exceeds capacity. Site services can also become less reliable after operating for prolonged periods at peak load. You can scale your server farm to accommodate increased site traffic and to maintain site performance in a cost-effective manner. For detailed information about how to scale a site, see Chapter 5, "Planning for Scalability."

Preventing Failures

To design a highly available site, you must understand potential causes of failure and take steps to eliminate them. The following list contains some of the more common types of failure and the elements that can cause the failure:

- **Application software**. Inferior code quality, vulnerability to service attacks, and platform dependencies that aren't met

- **Climate control**. Air-conditioning units or heating units malfunctioning

- **Data**. Data corruption

- **Electrical power**. Power-conditioning units, UPSs, generator sets malfunctioning

- **Hardware**. Degraded memory chips and CPU, disk hardware, disk controllers, or power supplies malfunctioning

- **Network**. ISPs not complying with SLAs, and routers, firewalls, or network cards malfunctioning

- **Security**. Firewalls, networks, and Web applications not working properly, and attacks from hackers on the Internet

The following table describes failure-reduction techniques for each common type of failure.

Type of failure	Failure-reduction techniques
Application software	• Create a robust architecture based on redundant, load-balanced servers. (Note, however, that load-balanced clusters are different from Windows application clusters. Commerce Server components aren't designed to be application cluster-aware.) • Review code to avoid potential buffer overflows, infinite loops, code crashes, and openings for security attacks.
Climate control	• Maintain the temperature of your hardware within the manufacturer's specifications. Excessive heat can cause CPU meltdown and excessive cold can cause failure of moving parts, such as fans or disk drives. • Maintain humidity control. Excessive humidity can cause electrical short circuits from water condensing on circuit boards. Excessive dryness can cause static electricity discharges that damage components when you handle them.

Type of failure	Failure-reduction techniques
Data	• Conduct regular backups and archive backups offsite. For example, you can archive every fourth regular backup offsite, to save space.

	If your data becomes corrupted, you can restore the data from backups to the last point before the corruption occurred. If you also back up transaction logs, you can then apply the transaction logs to the restored database to bring it up-to-date.
	• Replay transaction logs against a known valid database to maintain data. This technique is also known as "log shipping to a warm backup server." This technique is useful for maintaining a disaster-recovery site (also known as a "hot site").
	• Deploy Windows Clustering. Commerce Server uses data stores such as SQL Server and Microsoft Active Directory. SQL Server provides access to data and services such as catalog search. SQL Server uses Windows Clustering to provide redundancy. Active Directory provides access to profile data and can provide authentication services. Active Directory uses data replication to provide redundancy.
	In general, clustering is more effective for dynamic (read/write) data and data replication is more effective for static (read-only) data.
	• Minimize the probability and impact of a SQL Server failure by clustering SQL Server servers or by replicating data among SQL Server servers.
	If you are using SQL Server 7.0, the full-text search feature is available only in a non-clustered configuration, so you must use a replication strategy for the product catalog. In addition, SQL Server 7.0 is not supported for high availability configurations due to issues with Microsoft Data Access Components (MDAC) 2.6 and Windows Clustering.
	SQL Server 2000 is fully supported for high availability configurations.
	• If you use Active Directory, back up Active Directory stores. (You can do this while Active Directory is online.)
	Use at least two Active Directory domain controllers, with a replication schedule appropriate to your requirements. Restoring a domain controller can be time-consuming and requires that the domain controller be offline. Having peer domain controllers enables you to minimize downtime if you must restore your site from backups.
Electrical power	• Use UPSs. Because UPSs are typically battery-powered, they are useful only for outages that last for short periods of time. Be sure to use a UPS that has the same power rating as your equipment.
	• Use power generators as secondary backups to the UPSs. You can use generators for an indefinite period of time because they are fuel-powered (diesel or gasoline) and you can refuel them if necessary.

Type of failure	Failure-reduction techniques
Network	Implement network redundancy with any combination of the following: • Use multiple NICs, multiple routers, switches, LANs, or firewalls. • Contract with multiple ISPs or set up identical equipment in geographically dispersed locations.
Security	• Contract an independent security audit firm to evaluate your environment. • Deploy intrusion-detection tools. • Deploy multiple firewalls. For the latest strategies and techniques for handling security issues, see http://www.microsoft.com/windows2000/guide/server/features/securitysvcs.asp.
Server	Deploy redundant, load-balanced servers. Single-IP solutions increase site capacity by distributing HTTP requests proportionally, according to each server's capacity for handling the required load. In addition, when you use a single-IP solution, you make sure that users are referred only to operating servers. There are many single-IP solutions available to help you load-balance your servers, such as the following: • Microsoft Windows 2000 Advanced Server and Datacenter Server editions both provide a Network Load Balancing (NLB) service. • Microsoft Application Center 2000 provides Network Load Balancing enhancements (Request Forwarder) to support many users sharing a single-IP address. • Hardware-based load-balancing solutions.
Hardware	Deploy redundant hardware components, such as the following: • Use Redundant Array of Inexpensive Disks (RAID) disk arrays, disk mirroring, and dual disk controllers to minimize disk failures. There are also a number of excellent third-party solutions for reducing downtime related to disk failure. For more information about third-party solutions, see "Additional Resources" later in this chapter. • Use a redundant disk controller. • Use redundant fiber-channel host-bus adapters and switches (for SAN configuration). In the event of an adapter or switch failure, the backup adapter or switch provides an alternate path to the SAN.

The following table lists a number of tools and strategies for reducing downtime due to hardware failures. An "X" in a column means you can use the tool to prevent the indicated type of failure.

Tool or strategy	Application	Data	Network	Server
Clustered configurations	X	X		X
Data backups	X	X		X
Data replication	X	X		X
Dual disk controllers		X		X
Dual power supplies	X	X	X	X
Dual routers			X	
Geographically dispersed data centers	X	X	X	X
Mirrored disks		X		X
Multiple ISPs			X	
Multiple NICs			X	
RAID disk arrays		X		X
UPSs	X	X	X	X

Availability is a continuum that becomes increasingly expensive as you approach 100 percent availability. You must decide what trade-offs and compromises to make to fit your budget. The following table provides a sample framework to help you calculate the benefits of implementing the listed failure prevention strategies. The numbers used in the table are only a guideline. Use your own data and judgment to create a risk-assessment table for your site.

The table lists the types of failures that can occur and the effect of the failure, followed by a calculation of the relative probability number (RPN), using the following formula:

```
RPN = Likelihood of occurrence x Detectability x Severity
```

In which:

Likelihood of occurrence is the number of times an error is expected to occur (from 1 to 10; the higher the number, the more likely the error is to occur). In the following table, this value is represented by the "O" column.

Detectability is the ease with which a failure can be found (from 1 to 10; the higher the number, the harder the failure is to detect). In the following table, this value is represented by the "D" column.

Severity is the degree to which the failure will affect the site (from 1 to 10; the higher the number, the more serious the failure and the more severe the outage). In the following table, this value is represented by the "S" column.

Item	Function	Failure	O	D	S	RPN	Prevention	O	D	S	RPN
CPU (dual)	Application processing	Server might go offline	2	4	7	56	• Monitoring software • Remote-access software • Disable CPU • Reboot	2	2	7	28
CPU (single)	Application processing	Server offline	2	4	10	40	• Monitoring software • Second CPU	2	2	8	32
Drives	Application and data storage	Server offline	5	4	10	200	• RAID 5 controller with hot spare • Monitoring software	2	2	5	20
Firewall	Protection from intrusion and hacking	Information stolen, site altered, or site made inaccessible	4	4	8	128	• Monitoring software • Additional firewall	2	2	4	16
Load balancing	• Balance load on multiple servers • Enable automatic failover if a server goes offline	• All traffic goes to one server • Site inaccessible	4	4	8	128	• Monitoring software • Additional load-balancing	2	2	4	16
Memory	Application processing	Server offline	2	4	7	56	• Monitoring software • Additional server	2	2	7	28
NIC	Network connectivity	Server offline	4	4	8	128	• Dual NIC card • Monitoring software	1	2	4	8
Power supply	Power equipment	Site offline	4	4	10	160	• UPS • Monitoring software	2	2	2	8

Item	Function	Failure	O	D	S	RPN	Prevention	O	D	S	RPN
RAID controller	Data storage	Server offline	2	4	10	80	• Monitoring software • Additional server	2	2	8	32
Router/ Customer Service Unit (CSU)	Connect to partners and customers	• Loss of connections • Inability to process orders or update inventory • Inability to update or manage site	4	4	8	128	• Redundant routers • Monitoring software	2	2	4	16
SQL Server cluster	Data storage	Single-server failure, resulting in slower service	5	4	2	40	• Redundant servers designed into site architecture • Monitoring software	5	2	2	20
Switch	Connect to network	Some or all devices offline	4	4	10	160	• Redundant power supplies • Redundant connection cards • Redundant management card • Monitoring software	1	2	4	8
Web server	Serve Web site application to customers	Site offline	5	4	10	200	• Additional Web servers • Load balancing	2	2	5	20

You can make the business logic layer (middle tier) more resilient by using load-balanced Web clusters to protect servers, services, and the network against failures. Load-balanced clusters enable you to remove an unresponsive server from the cluster so that users won't be directed to a faulty server, and so that the unresponsive server can be repaired. You can combine Round Robin Domain Naming System (RRDNS) with load balancing to produce a scalable and available configuration.

All the nodes in a load-balanced cluster must be on the same LAN subnet and all the nodes should refer to the same IP address. On a site with multiple Web clusters, you must configure multiple load-balanced clusters on different subnets and configure the Domain Name System (DNS) to sequentially distribute requests across multiple load-balanced clusters to increase scalability.

You can make the database layer (bottom tier) more resilient by using a combination of disk redundancy and a sound backup and restoration strategy to protect your data. You can use any of the following methods to make database services more resilient:

- **Clustering**. In Windows Clustering, two servers can share common data and work together as a single system. Windows Datacenter Server supports four servers (nodes) in a cluster. Each node can operate independently of the others.

- **Replication**. You can use SQL Server replication to synchronize your database servers. SQL Server offers replication options such as snapshot replication and transactional replication. Active Directory also uses replication to ensure redundancy.

- **Warm backups**. You can use a single production server to provide read/write access to data, logging all transactions. You then use SQL Server Log Shipping to transfer files to a non-production server that is continuously updated with the transaction log files.

Data must be backed up or replicated to prevent it from being accidentally deleted. The following table describes the two types of data replication.

Type of data replication	Characteristics	Use when
Active	Shares a part of the workload of the primary site and is always online.	Data is extremely critical and the site must always be available.
Passive	Inactive until a disaster takes the primary site out of operation.	Your site can tolerate brief interruptions in data availability while the backup site comes online.

A Highly Available Commerce Server Architecture

Commerce Server uses a full range of options for protecting against network, server, and disk failures. This section describes strategies for constructing small and large highly available Commerce Server sites. You can eliminate any single point of failure by:

- Using multiple instances of servers hosting the business logic layer, fronted by a single-IP solution.

- Clustering SQL Server servers to host data.

- Replicating Active Directory (if used).

Small Commerce Server Configuration

The smallest redundant architecture for Commerce Server separates the business logic layer (middle tier) from the servers in the database layer (bottom tier). A four-server configuration has two identical servers in each tier. You put a single-IP address solution in front of the servers in the business logic layer, to increase availability and to hide site complexities from users. You use SQL Server clustering for the database layer, to increase availability.

All business logic runs on both of the stateless Web servers in the business logic layer in this configuration. An architecture in which all Commerce Server business logic runs on a single server is useful because it maximizes cache usage for a user session. If a customer is directed to a different Web server on the server farm, the new server merely retrieves data and the customer continues shopping. Commerce Server components are persistent for back-end databases, cookies, or Uniform Resource Locator (URL) query strings, so being directed to a different physical server has minimal impact on a customer's shopping experience.

If your site requires a Windows security context for other applications or to protect file system content, you should have at least two domain controllers for each domain on your site. It is important that both domain controllers have consistent data, so the smallest highly available configuration that uses Active Directory for authentication requires two servers at the user interface layer (top tier), two servers for the database layer (bottom tier), and two servers for Active Directory (a total of six servers).

Active Directory uses a replication strategy to ensure consistency among domain controllers in a single domain. The Active Directory processing load is minimal relative to the processing load generated by the authentication filter, so you can also have Active Directory on the same cluster as SQL Server, if necessary. Figure 6.2 shows a small Commerce Server configuration.

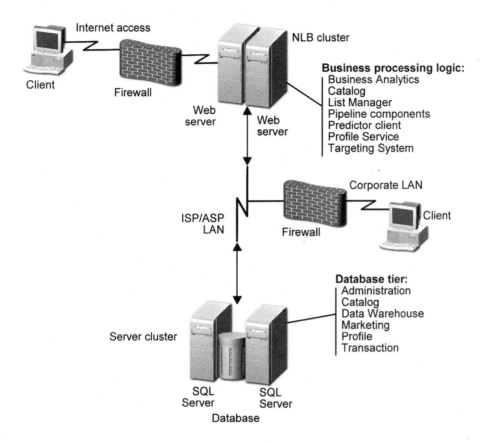

Figure 6.2 Small Commerce Server configuration

Large Commerce Server Configuration

The simplest way for Commerce Server sites to increase capacity is to add Web servers and move component databases onto separate database servers. You then place a single-IP solution in front of the Web services of the business logic layer (middle tier), to increase availability and to hide site complexities from customers. You can use a combination of SQL Server clustering or SQL Server replication to increase the availability of the database layer.

In a large Web farm, all business logic can also run on the stateless Web servers. However, in some environments, you might want to isolate some functions from the site shopping functions.

For example, you might prefer to run pipeline components on a separate Web farm, if the components are particularly CPU-intensive (such as encryption of large files) or if they require access to secure data (such as computing insurance rates while processing social security number, credit history, or medical reports). An example of a CPU-intensive function that you might want to run on a separate server is the generation of analysis models.

You can distribute Commerce Server databases across multiple servers to increase capacity. You should base your availability decisions on the expected usage of each database.

The following table defines typical availability measurements, to help you decide what level of availability you need for your site.

Availability target	Seconds of downtime	Downtime per incident (assuming four incidents per year)
99.9999%	31.536 (approximately ½ minute)	7.5 seconds
99.999%	315.36 (approximately 5 minutes)	1.25 minutes
99.99%	3153.6 (approximately 1 hour)	15 minutes
99.9%	31536 (approximately 9 hours)	2.25 hours

The following table describes the usage profile and impact of failure for each Commerce Server feature. Note that the availability targets shown in the table are typical examples. You might choose different availability targets for your site.

Feature	Usage profile	Failure impacts	Availability target
Catalog	• 100% read-only • Large administrative updates	Shopping not available	99.99%
Content	• 100% read-only • Administrative updates	Degraded browsing experience	99%
Data Warehouse cubes (data structures)	• Fast read/write access required	Reports not available	99.9%
Data Warehouse (import)	• Read/write very large database	Data not current	99%
Directory Service	• 99% read only	Customer authorization not available; shopping by anonymous users only	99.9%
Marketing/Ads/ Discounts	• 100% read-only • Administrative updates	Degraded shopping experience	99%
Transaction	• Read/write • Highest security and availability requirements	Shopping not available	99.999%
User Profile Management	• 97% read • 3% write (modify)	Customer authorization not available; no personalized content; shopping by anonymous users only	99.9%

You can use either SQL Server or Active Directory for authentication on a large site. Either one can support shopping by anonymous users. Figure 6.3 shows an example of a large site configuration.

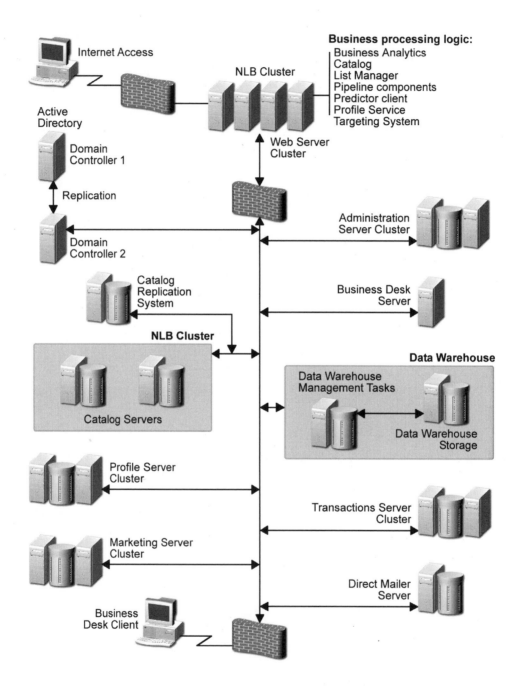

Figure 6.3 Large Commerce Server configuration

Figure 6.3 shows a single Active Directory domain with two domain controllers. The database layer (bottom tier) is shown as being largely run on Windows Clustering. However, this limits you to four nodes in a cluster. If you require more capacity, you should consider the following strategies for the database layer:

- **Catalog**. Add servers to a single-IP solution. Synchronize data using SQL Server replication.

- **Order Form**. Create multiple data partitions and distribute transactions across the partitions. For example, you can implement code to hash a customer's globally unique identifier (GUID) to one of the partitions and then store the customer's order form on that partition.

- **Profiles resource**. Create multiple data partitions and distribute user data across the partitions. Data source partitions use profile properties designated as hashing keys to keep data together. Note that with this architecture, you should create partitions when you set up the site. If you add partitions to a site with existing user profiles, you have to reload user data. Partitioning is useful for both SQL Server and Active Directory profile stores.

Scaling for Active Directory requires multi-forest design with trusts established from the domains in the user forests to the domain in the resource forest. For more information about Active Directory, see http://www.microsoft.com/windows2000/.

Commerce Server Component Design Considerations

The following table contains examples of uptime requirements for Commerce Server functions. Your requirements might be different from those shown in the table; however, you can use the examples as starting points for creating your site architecture.

Commerce Server function	Target uptime	Failure classification
Authentication	99.99%	One retry acceptable
Basket view	99.999%	No acceptable failure rate
Catalog query	99.99%	Two retries acceptable
Personalization	99%	Don't retry
Purchase pipeline	99.999%	No acceptable failure rate
Show advertisement	99%	Don't retry

For examples of business logic that you can use to protect against loss of database connectivity, see "Retry Code Logic" later in this chapter.

Administration Database

You use the Commerce Server Administration database to store configuration information for Commerce Server resources, including global resources shared by all sites, as well as site-specific resources. Connections from objects used to access the database are short-lived and the Global.asa file caches data for later reference. After information is cached, the database connection is no longer needed.

You can make the Administration database redundant with Windows Clustering. You can use either of the following types of configurations to provide redundancy:

- **Active-active configuration**. All nodes are running and hosting a database.

- **Active-passive configuration**. One node is running and hosting a database; all other nodes are idle (in backup mode), ready to run and host the database if the active node fails.

When the IIS application is loaded, the **Application_OnStart** subroutine is called to load the Administration database into the cache. The **Application_OnStart** subroutine loads application variables using the **SiteConfigReadOnly** object, which requires a connection to the Administration database.

If the **Application_OnStart** subroutine fails (for example, if the SQL Server server is failing or simply is not available), you must do one of the following to reload the application variables:

- Run an ASP page that runs all initialization performed by the Global.asa file. This is the least intrusive option. You should use access control lists (ACLs) to protect the ASP page so that only authorized personnel or processes can run it.

- Unload the Commerce Server application from IIS Manager.

- Run the **IISReset** command; this option is intrusive because it resets all ASP applications running on IIS server.

- Reboot the Web server; this is the most intrusive option, because it impacts all applications and services running on the Web server.

You can script all of these options.

Profiling System

You can use the Commerce Server Profiling System to aggregate data from multiple data stores (such as Active Directory (Lightweight Directory Access Protocol (LDAP) version 3.0), SQL Server, or Site Server 3.0 Membership Directory (LDAP version 3.0)). This enables you to store data in the data store that's most appropriate for the usage profile. Directory services are usually optimized for read-only operations, because of inherent security features. SQL Server is optimized equally well for read and write operations, but has fewer inherent security features. You should use Active Directory to store data that is mostly static throughout a user's visit to your site, or data that must be secured with ACLs. Use SQL Server to store data that is volatile throughout a user's visit.

For example, Active Directory is based on a hierarchical LDAP model, which is excellent for fast, single-item retrieval. Attributes stored in Active Directory are easily available to other applications that might be running in the data center. Examples of attributes that might best be stored in Active Directory are *user name*, *address*, and *city*.

In contrast, Commerce Server-specific attributes that are volatile, such as *date of last purchase*, should be stored in a SQL Server database, to take advantage of the capacity of SQL Server to handle high rates of updates. Data availability can vary significantly, depending on what combination of data stores you use to maintain the data.

To generate a large-scale, highly available User Profile Management back end, you should use a hash-based partition cluster of SQL Server servers based on Windows Clustering. Hashing assigns a user to a particular User Profile Management partition. Figure 6.4 shows how you might set up a hash-based partition cluster of SQL Server servers.

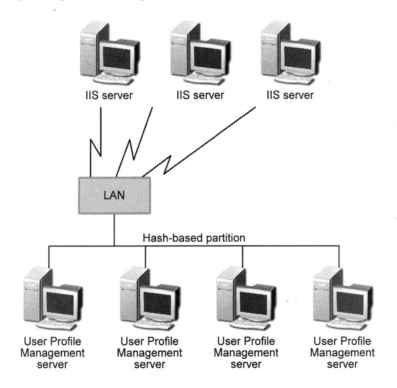

Figure 6.4 Hash-based partition cluster of SQL Server servers

Each User Profile Management server instance shown in Figure 6.4 is actually running Windows Clustering, as shown in Figure 6.5. Figure 6.5 shows Windows Clustering in an active-passive configuration with a shared disk.

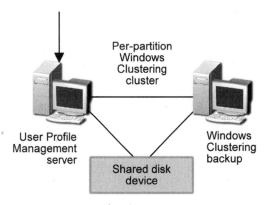

Figure 6.5 Windows Clustering configuration

> **Note** If you use the partitioned architecture described in this section, you should create partitions before you begin. If you add partitions after your site contains user data, you will have to remove and restore user data to be sure that it is stored in the correct partition.

The Profiling System opens a database connection, reads configuration information, and builds a profile configuration cache from that information. Connections to the database are pooled and have built-in retry logic if a connection is lost.

Integrating User Data from Third-Party Data Stores

You can use the Profiling System to integrate data from third-party stores (such as data residing in an Oracle database). Depending on what you want to do, it might be cost effective to set up a highly available configuration for the third-party data store. Be aware, however, that if a read of any of the underlying data sources fails, then the entire operation fails. You can set up redundancy for third-party data stores by creating a virtual server from the multiple data stores. The DSN that the Profiling System uses should then be established with the virtual server.

Aggregating User Data from Multiple Stores

Whenever you must place data into different data stores, there is a risk that one or more of the stores will be unavailable. Figure 6.6 shows an unavailable data store.

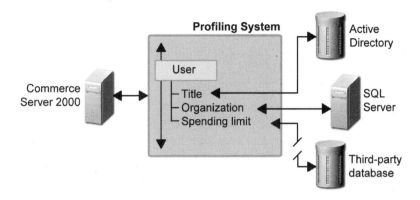

Figure 6.6 Unavailable data store

To protect against this situation, the Profiling System supports the notion of a *loose transaction*. A loose transaction is one in which writes and updates to transacted stores (such as SQL Server and Oracle) aggregated by the Profiling System are committed only if operations to non-transacted stores (Active Directory) succeed.

The following logic example describes how Commerce Server processes loose transactions in a site in which Active Directory, SQL Server, and Oracle stores are all used to store user profile attributes. It is enabled by the *isTransactioned* attribute of the profile definition. The logic example is:

```
Start transaction for SQL Server
Write changes
    Start transaction for Oracle
    Write changes
        Write changes to Active Directory_1
    Commit changes_2
Commit changes_3
```

```
If 1 fails, then 2 & 3 abort.
If 1 succeeds and 2 fails, then Active Directory store is inconsistent.
If 1 & 2 succeed, 3 fails, then SQL Server is inconsistent.
```

The Profiling System does not support two-phase commits.

Product Catalog System

In the Product Catalog System, you can make the Catalogs database redundant by installing it on multiple Web servers fronted by a single-IP solution.

- **Small site**. Use either active-active or active-passive clustering. This configuration will support two nodes running Windows 2000 Server or four nodes running Windows 2000 Datacenter Server.

- **Large site**. Use Network Load Balancing to cluster SQL Server servers and to provide a single, virtual database name for the Catalogs database business logic to access.

  Alternatively, you can use SQL Server replication (either snapshot or transaction, depending on your requirements) to maintain data consistency among SQL Server servers. Figure 6.7 shows how a configuration using Network Load Balancing might look. In practice, Network Load Balancing has been tested with a cluster containing as many as eight SQL Server servers.

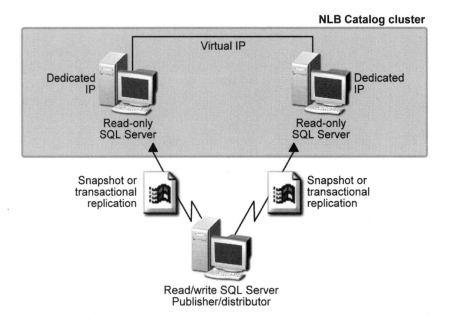

Figure 6.7 Catalogs database cluster using Network Load Balancing

- **Very large sites**. Put a single-IP solution in front of multiple Network Load Balancing clusters. Figure 6.8 shows what this configuration might look like.

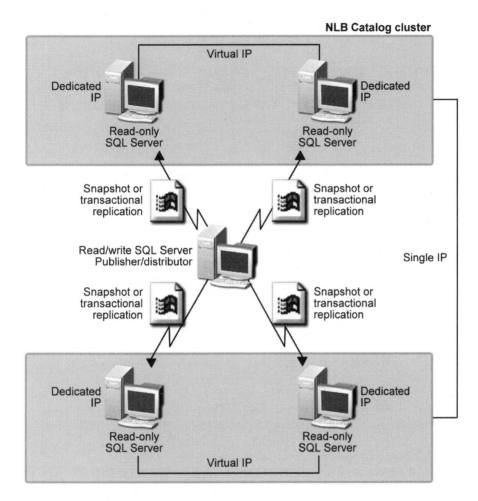

Figure 6.8 Catalogs database for a very large site

The Product Catalog System maintains a continuous connection to database tables. If the connection is lost due to network or database problems, the Product Catalog System will attempt to reestablish the connection.

Targeting System

The Targeting System business logic caches all of its working information, including discounts, advertisements, shipping, and tax information. It caches the Predictor resource Binary Large Object (BLOB). A refresh timer, specified programmatically by the **RefreshInterval** property of the **CacheManager** object, controls the frequency with which the **CacheManager** refreshes a particular cache object. A connection to the database is created each time the cache is refreshed. An existing cache is not discarded until the refresh of the cache has successfully completed. If you absolutely must have an up-to-date cache (or when you start up and there is no cache), you can implement retry logic if a database is unavailable during a refresh operation.

You can install the Targeting System on multiple Web servers and make it highly available using a load-balanced cluster of SQL Server servers. Figure 6.9 shows the smallest database solution that you can use to get the clustering results you want.

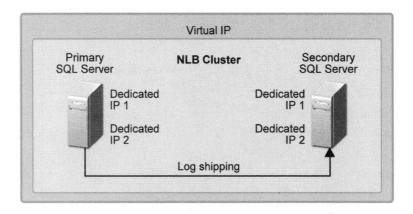

Figure 6.9 Clustering the Targeting System

Direct Mailer

Commerce Server Direct Mailer is a batch process, so it has lower priority than the production components of Commerce Server, such as the Transactions database. Direct Mailer has a higher tolerance for unplanned outages than other Commerce Server features. However, you must manually restart Direct Mailer after a SQL Server server failure to continue from the point at which it was interrupted.

Direct Mailer depends on the SQL Server Agent to run its scheduled jobs, so you must run Direct Mailer on a server that is also running SQL Server. The SQL Server Agent runs a command line that activates a process to create and start a job. That process then runs another service that does the work. If the active Direct Mailer database server fails, the connection will be reestablished with the newly promoted backup SQL Server server when the next SQL Server Agent job starts.

The SQL Server Agent is cluster-aware, so you can install the Direct Mailer database in a Windows Clustering clustered configuration. Because of the architecture of Direct Mailer, you must use an active-passive configuration. Direct Mailer must be installed on the same server as its database, so in a clustered configuration, you must install Direct Mailer twice. Although you can have only one Direct Mailer per site (as specified by the Direct Mailer global resource), you can install Direct Mailer on multiple servers.

You must install the Direct Mailer database on a local instance of SQL Server. You can use SQL Server 2000 local instance setup to do this. After you have installed the Direct Mailer database, you can move it to the virtual cluster SQL Server instance.

Direct Mailer opens a database connection at startup to recover any interrupted jobs. It also opens a database connection for each job. If the database connection is lost, the executing job will fail. Jobs that did not run because Direct Mailer was not working must be manually restarted when the Direct Mailer restarts.

Each job tracks its progress through a mailing list. However, depending on when a failure occurs, the last message sent before the failure can be sent a second time when Direct Mailer restarts. You can configure Direct Mailer to use multiple threads, and it is possible that one duplicate message for each thread will be sent when the Direct Mailer restarts. (The number of duplicate messages is usually equal to as many threads as there are processors.)

Business Process Pipelines

You can install pipeline components on multiple Web servers and make them highly available using a single-IP solution. With Network Load Balancing, you can create a single virtual server from all the servers on which pipeline components are installed. If there is a problem, the server that is not working is automatically removed from the cluster and the load is distributed to the functioning servers in the cluster. Figure 6.10 shows how you might distribute pipeline components.

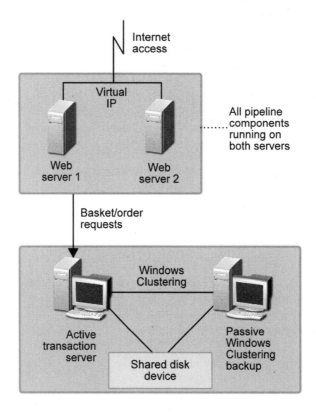

Figure 6.10 Distributed pipeline components

If a pipeline component is CPU-intensive, you can move it to a separate server. There is an expense for sharing data between servers, but that expense might be acceptable if a great deal of processing will be done by the component. For example, a digital media site might encrypt music with a user's public key to prevent piracy. Encryption is CPU-intensive, so it could be worthwhile to move that processing to a separate server. If you did so, you could cluster the servers on which the encryption component is running and activate them by one of the Web servers running other parts of the pipeline. Figure 6.11 shows how you might separate CPU-intensive services from other services.

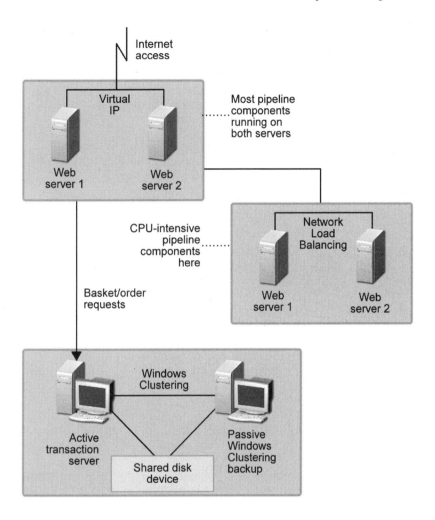

Figure 6.11 Separating CPU-intensive services

You use COM+ pipeline components to access the Order Processing pipeline (OPP). Components are pooled, but there is an initialization, reset, and recycle interface that is called when the **OrderForm** object is recycled into the pool. You can use that interface to release connections, free memory, and so on, when the **OrderForm** object is returned to the pool, and to initialize database connections when components are requested.

The **QueryCatalogInfo** component behaves differently. **QueryCatalogInfo** retrieves product information by invoking a **CatalogManager** object passed as part of the **Context** object. The **CatalogManager** object holds a connection to the database. If the connection is lost, **CatalogManager** will reestablish the connection to the database.

Data Warehouse

The Data Warehouse has two components: offline and online. These two components have very different availability requirements. A very large database that contains imported raw data should be unavailable for querying (offline) while data is being imported. If necessary, it can be clustered. Alternatively, if you don't require a high degree of availability for the database, you can back it up on a regular basis to tape or other permanent media.

Online analytical processing (OLAP) cubes are data structures that the Data Warehouse uses to contain the data you import. (For more information, see Commerce Server 2000 Help or SQL Server Books Online.) Figure 6.12 shows how you can make OLAP highly available, using a clustered configuration. If a node in the cluster fails, the other node will become the primary node.

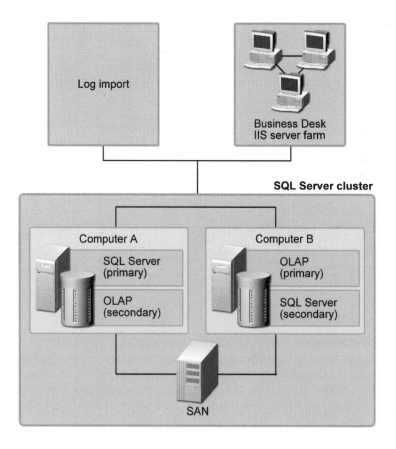

Figure 6.12 Clustering the Data Warehouse

The Data Warehouse opens a database connection for each import and parser Data Transformation Services (DTS) task. The connection is maintained for the duration of the process and then dropped. If the database becomes unavailable during the process, the process will fail, but you can restart it. If a failure occurs during import processing, you must manually delete any data that was only partially imported, and restart all import DTS tasks. If a failure occurs during cube generation, you must manually restart the post-import DTS task.

Operating System Availability

Windows 2000 is designed to be highly available. It contains numerous improvements that provide increased reliability, including Windows file protection, driver certification, application certification, kernel-mode write protection, application dynamic-link library (DLL) protection, a recovery console, and safe boot mode. In addition, key services like IIS and Network Load Balancing have been substantially enhanced to support highly available architectures.

Several types of failures, such as "system hangs", "no-logon," and "network dead" can be attributed to resources running consistently above healthy performance thresholds. "Blue screens" and application failures have also been experienced in certain disk-full conditions. To mitigate these failures on a highly available Windows 2000 platform, you should monitor the system thresholds listed in the following table.

Metric	30-day average	Four-hour average	Peak
CPU utilization	70%	85%	95%
Average available bytes	10 MB	5 MB	5 MB
Disk queue length	1 per non-redundant spindle	2 per non-redundant spindle	3 per non-redundant spindle
Disk used	80%	80%	80%
Network interface using full-duplex Ethernet	60%	70%	70%

Network Load Balancing

Network Load Balancing increases availability by redirecting incoming network traffic to working cluster hosts if a host fails or is offline. As a result, even when existing connections to an offline host are lost, Internet services remain available. In most cases, client software automatically retries the failed connection, and the clients experience only a few seconds' delay in receiving a response. Network Load Balancing is a feature of Microsoft Windows 2000 Advanced Server and Windows 2000 Datacenter Server. For more information about Network Load Balancing, see http://www.microsoft.com/WINDOWS2000/guide/server/overview/internet/adserv.asp.

Application Center provides enhancements to Network Load Balancing, by enabling Network Load Balancing to run on Windows 2000 Server, by providing operations management and monitoring tools, and by providing the Request Forwarder component to facilitate load balancing of customers behind proxy server farms.

When a user accesses a site through a proxy server, the user might appear to Network Load Balancing to have different IP addresses; even when session affinity is enabled, this might cause the user to be directed to different servers. If your site uses session state management at the physical server, this might cause problems. If you use the Request Forwarder in Application Center, the user connection can be forwarded to the server where the user is recognized, regardless of where it is assigned in the server farm.

Web Farm/Active Directory Authentication

When a user accesses a site with multiple Web servers, the request is directed to a particular server, based on load balancing or a round-robin algorithm. When the request arrives at the server, the user is asked to log in.

If you are using Active Directory for authentication, the login is cached by the Internet Server Application Programming Interface (ISAPI) filter and is specific to that server. Commerce Server also places a ticket cookie containing the user ID onto the client server. To enable users to be seamlessly redirected to other Web servers in the farm, you must ensure that sufficient information can be passed to the ISAPI filter on the other servers so that the user can be logged in. You must write custom code to hide this process from the user. To write the custom code, you do the following:

1. Extend the Profiles store to store the password.

2. Capture the password in the Profiles store during login or site registration.

3. Modify the site registration or login page to check for the presence of the ticket cookie.

   If the cookie exists, use the **MSCSAuthManager** object to get the user ID from the cookie and retrieve the username:password from the Profiles store, then pass the username:password back to the ISAPI filter.

To operate a secure data center, you must store the passwords with reversible encryption. Because passwords are captured at the login page and written to the Profiles store, the login page also captures password changes. (However, if Active Directory tools are used to change a password during a browser session, the user will be prompted for login and the new password will be captured.)

   Note You can address the previous authentication issue by deploying Application Center Request Forwarder, which can forward the request prior to authentication being assessed, and can then forward the user to the server that will recognize the user.

Active Directory Availability

Although you need only a single domain controller for each domain, a single domain controller can become a single point of failure. Instead, you can add additional domain controllers to a domain to increase its availability. Active Directory uses a two-way replication strategy to ensure consistency among domain controllers in a single domain. Active Directory domain controllers support multi-master replication, to synchronize data on each domain controller and to ensure consistency of information.

The information stored in Active Directory on every domain controller (whether or not it is a global catalog server) is partitioned into three categories: domain, schema, and configuration data. Each of these categories is in a separate directory partition (also called a *Naming Context*). The directory partitions are the units of replication. The domain data partition contains all of the objects in the directory for the domain. Data in each domain is replicated to every controller in the domain, but not beyond.

If the domain controller is a global catalog server, it also contains a fourth category of information: a partial replica of the domain data directory partition for all domains. This partial replica contains a subset of the properties for all objects in all domains. (A partial replica is read-only; a complete replica is read/write.)

By default, the partial set of attributes stored in the global catalog includes those attributes most frequently used in search operations, because one of the primary functions of the global catalog is to support clients querying the directory. Using global catalogs to perform partial domain replication instead of doing full domain replication reduces WAN traffic.

Figure 6.13 shows replication within a site. Three domain controllers (one of which is a global catalog) replicate schema data and configuration data, as well as all directory objects (with a complete set of each object's attributes).

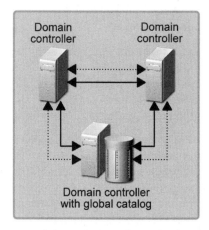

— Schema and configuration data

····· Domain data

Figure 6.13 Replication within site domains

Active Directory attempts to establish a topology that allows at least two connections to every domain controller so that if a domain controller becomes unavailable, directory information can still reach all online domain controllers through the other connection. Active Directory also automatically evaluates and adjusts for changes in the state of the network. For example, when a domain controller is added to a site, the replication topology is adjusted to incorporate the new addition efficiently.

Replication Between Sites

You can also use Active Directory to optimize both server-to-server and client-to-server traffic over WAN links. Having multiple sites can provide redundancy in the event of a geographical disaster. Best practices for setting up multiple sites include the following:

- Set up a site in every geographic area that requires fast access to the latest Active Directory information.

- Place at least one domain controller at every site and make at least one domain controller in each site a global catalog. Sites that do not have their own domain controllers and at least one global catalog are dependent on other sites for directory information and are less efficient.

Disaster Recovery

Every disaster recovery plan must include backup and restoration strategies. When a domain controller fails, either due to environmental hazards or due to equipment malfunction, you should first repair the domain controller itself and then recover the data. Active Directory is able to recover lost data because:

- The database uses log files to recover lost data.

- The directory service uses replication to recover data from other servers in the domain.

There are a variety of tools that you can use to repair the domain controller and recover Active Directory. For more information about Windows 2000 disaster protection, including backups, restores, and repairs, see the *Windows 2000 Server Operations Guide*, which is part of the *Microsoft Window 2000 Server Resource Kit*, available at http://mspress.microsoft.com/books/1394.htm. Also, see Windows 2000 Server Help.

Backup Strategies

You can back up directory data and configuration files to traditional media, such as magnetic tape, or to a separate local or network disk drive. Directories are frequently replicated to provide load balancing, high availability, and localized access in a distributed environment.

It's important to understand the implications of restoring a replica of a directory from tape. Backing up and restoring from tape takes a long time and backed-up data is only current as of the time the backup was created.

In most cases, it is better to rebuild a directory from peer replicas, because the data in the peer replicas is already online and the data is always current.

Restoration strategies

There are two methods of restoring Active Directory:

- **Non-authoritative restore (the default)**. Use when at least one other domain controller in the domain is available and working. After a non-authoritative restore, Active Directory replication automatically begins propagating any changes from other domain controllers that occurred after the time of the backup.

- **Authoritative restore**. Use only when you have accidentally deleted critical data from the local domain controller and the delete has propagated out to other domain controllers.

  Note Do not perform an authoritative restore if the local domain controller is not a working domain controller or if it is the only domain controller in the domain.

Active Directory Monitoring Tools

Active Directory provides the monitoring tools described in the following table.

Active Directory monitoring tool	Use to monitor
Event Log	Information about hardware, software, and system problems. You can use Event Logs to aggregate system uptime by monitoring a combination of system startup, clean shutdown, and "dirty" shutdown events.
Performance Logs and Alerts	Performance counters are contained in categories of objects. You can configure Performance Logs and Alerts to alert you when designated thresholds have been exceeded. You choose the criteria you want reported and the manner in which you want it reported to you.
Replication Monitor	Low-level status and performance of replication between Active Directory domain controllers. Replication Monitor is available in the *Microsoft Windows 2000 Server Resource Kit.*

SQL Server Availability

This section describes three strategies that you can use to create a highly available database layer (bottom tier):

- Clustering
- Replication
- Warm backup

This section also provides examples of retry code logic. For more information about SQL Server availability, see SQL Server Books Online.

Clustering

Two or more SQL Server servers sharing common data form a cluster of servers that can work together as a single server. Each server is called a node and each node can operate independently of the other nodes in the cluster. Each node has its own memory, system disk, operating system, and subset of the cluster's resources. If one node fails, another one takes ownership of the failed node's resources. The cluster service then registers the network address for the resource on the new node so that client traffic is routed to the new server. When the failed server is brought back online, the cluster service can be configured to redistribute resources and client requests.

The following table lists three techniques you can use to make disk data available to more than one server.

Technique	Description
Shared disk	Although no longer requiring expensive cabling and switches, the shared-disk technique, in which multiple servers share the same disk, still requires specially modified applications using software called a Distributed Lock Manager (DLM).
Mirrored disk	More flexible than the shared-disk technique, the mirrored-disk technique is based on each server having its own disks, and using software that "mirrors" every write from one server to a copy of the data on another server. This technique is very useful for keeping data at a disaster-recovery site synchronized with a primary server.
Shared nothing	In a shared-nothing architecture configuration, each server owns its own disk resources. If a server fails, a shared-nothing cluster has software that can transfer ownership of a disk from one server to another. This technique provides the same high level of availability as shared-disk clusters, with potentially higher scalability, because it does not have the inherent bottleneck of a DLM.

SQL Server 2000 provides improved interoperability with Windows Clustering. Prior to SQL Server 2000, SQL Clustering used three rebinding virtual DLLs interjected between every SQL Server or client component and the corresponding kernel DLLs. SQL Server 2000 also contains the following improvements over previous versions:

- Clustering is much easier to manage. It is implemented through the use of SQL Instancing, which removes the need for the virtual mapping layer so that you can directly manage individual components in the cluster environment.

- All SQL Server tools are cluster-aware, which makes the environment significantly more robust. The tools are now integrated, which eliminates the need to coordinate the use of multiple tools. Previously, when you had to use several tools to manage a cluster, any misuse or lack of coordination in using the tools could cause the cluster to fail.

- Clusters can contain up to four nodes (instead of two in previous versions).

- You can now perform rolling upgrades on nodes in a Windows Clustering cluster. Prior to SQL Server 2000, you had to take the entire cluster offline to perform an upgrade. With SQL Server 2000, you can take just one node offline at a time to perform the upgrade, leaving the other nodes online.

- Full-text search is now cluster-aware.

- OLAP can be clustered when you use it with SQL Server 2000. OLAP by itself is not cluster-aware.

Replication

You can use SQL Server replication to synchronize your site's database servers. SQL Server replication options include snapshot replication and transactional replication. You should consider using SQL Server replication to do batch updates if your application logic is aware of the nature of database access.

For example, you can update the Product Catalog System in Commerce Server primarily in batch mode, and have all client access be read-only. Another example is creating and changing the **OrderForm** object a few times from known pipeline components. **OrderForm** objects are frequently read from other pipeline components in the site during check out, for operations like tax and shipping calculations. In both examples, you might consider having a small number of stores updated with reads directed to a bank of read-only servers.

You should also consider using SQL Server replication to keep geographically distributed servers synchronized. Figure 6.14 shows how you might cluster SQL Server servers in the database layer.

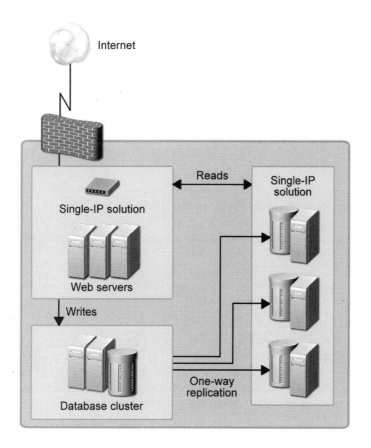

Figure 6.14 Clustering SQL Server servers

If you place Network Load Balancing in front of a group of read-only SQL Server servers, you can use the same server name for the entire cluster. The benefit of doing this is that you can then remove any server in the cluster from service with minimal impact to users. You can also enable replication from the online transaction processing (OLTP) environment to the cluster. Use transactional replication if you require higher transactional consistency to minimize latency between the OLTP server and the load-balanced, read-only servers.

Consider the following for installations of Network Load Balancing query clusters:

- With any installation of Network Load Balancing, there are at least two dedicated IP addresses (one per server) and one virtual IP address. For replication between the OLTP environment and the cluster to work correctly, replication must always be made directly to the dedicated IP addresses (or individual server names) and never be made directly to the virtual IP address or to the cluster name. Because you use Network Load Balancing to balance the load across the cluster, replicating directly to the virtual IP address (or cluster name) would cause transactional inconsistency between servers in the cluster.

- Although you can use either the push or pull metaphor for this configuration, best practice is to push all replication to servers in the cluster. The reason for using the push metaphor is to allow you to manage the distribution jobs centrally and to provide a means of alerting you if one of the servers in the cluster stops responding. (The replication job will fail for the server that stops responding.)

- Because replication is occurring between the OLTP environment and the cluster, you can't set databases on servers in the cluster to read/write. As a result, you must use login permissions to maintain read-only security. All client connections to servers in the cluster must connect through the virtual IP address and have read-only permissions. It is also necessary to ensure that all servers in the read-only cluster include the same subset of logins.

If you want to apply a snapshot to subscribers in the cluster, the best practice is to disconnect servers individually from the cluster, apply the snapshot, and then reconnect each server to the cluster. This produces maximum availability and maintains transactional consistency between servers in the cluster.

Warm Backup

If a single production server provides both read and write access to data, you should log all transactions. You can use SQL Server Log Shipping to transfer files to a non-production server that is continuously updated with the transaction log files. This technique is called *warm backup* because the backup database is always "warmed up" by continuous application of the transaction logs. This option is inexpensive and easy to manage, and provides a strategy for availability in environments where there is some tolerance for downtime.

You can use this method in combination with other strategies described in this section to recover from disaster when availability is particularly critical. You can also use warm backups to keep geographically dispersed data centers reasonably synchronized. In fact, this is an inexpensive way to maintain a synchronized database in a separate data center for site disaster recovery.

Combining Network Load Balancing and SQL Server Log Shipping provides excellent warm failover capability. In this scenario, you can use Network Load Balancing to provide the same IP address to at least two servers. This makes it easier to fail over to the secondary SQL Server server if the primary SQL Server server fails. You direct client applications through the Network Load Balancing cluster to one of the SQL Server servers. If a failure occurs, or when it is time for scheduled downtime, you can use Network Load Balancing to transfer access to another SQL Server server in the cluster. Log Shipping synchronizes the servers, based on the log's shipping frequency.

There are some issues you need to consider when you set up Network Load Balancing and Log Shipping:

- In order to set up Log Shipping within a Network Load Balancing cluster, the SQL Server servers must communicate over a private network that is isolated from the Network Load Balancing network. To create the private network, you must install a secondary NIC into both of the SQL Server servers.

- You must set up Log Shipping with a hard IP address instead of using universal naming convention (UNC) server names, or do one of the following:

  - Create an Lmhosts file to resolve the IP addresses to a UNC server name.

  - Register the IP addresses in Windows Internet Name Service (WINS) to resolve the UNC name, if a WINS server exists on the private network.

- When you set up the SQL Server servers in the Network Load Balancing cluster, the primary SQL Server server is connected to the cluster. You must then disconnect the secondary Log Shipping SQL Server server from the cluster. The servers stay synchronized by having the primary server "log ship" the data to the secondary server.

- If you don't isolate the communications between the SQL Server servers, Network Load Balancing will attempt to communicate directly to the IP address on the second NIC card, causing looped traffic and other problems.

If the primary SQL Server server fails, Network Load Balancing can automatically fail over to a secondary server. Depending on the log shipping frequency, however, best practice is to make the decision to fail over to the secondary server manually. For example, if you have set log shipping to run every five minutes, the secondary server could be as much as five minutes behind (assuming all processes are functioning properly). Failing over the system manually enables you to check to see if the latest transaction log can be applied so that more data can be saved, rather than failing over automatically and perhaps losing up to five minutes' data.

You install stored procedures to facilitate failover when you install SQL Server Log Shipping. For more information about Log Shipping, see SQL Server Books Online.

Retry Code Logic

This section contains examples of retry logic to protect against loss of database connectivity:

- One retry level

```
If (getAuth == error)
    Sleep 1 second
    GetAuth again
Response.write ("Sorry, logins are disabled. Please e-mail questions to mailto:helpdesk.
```

- Two retry levels

```
If (getcatalog == error)
    Sleep 1 second
    Getcatalog again
    If (failed again)
        Response.write ("I'm retrying your query; please wait.")
        Sleep 10
        Getcatalog again
Response.write ("Sorry, our catalog is temporarily unavailable. Please e-mail questions
mailto:helpdesk.")
```

Additional Resources

Information about highly available solutions is available on many third-party Web sites. For more information, you can search for "high availability" on any of the following Web sites:

- http://www.highavailabilitycenter.com/whitepapers.html
- http://www.microsoft.com/enterpriseservices
- http://www.microsoft.com/ISN
- http://www.microsoft.com/apphosting
- http://www.compaq.com
- http://search.dell.com
- http://www.pc.ibm.com/us/netfinity
- http://www.hp.com
- http://www.unisys.com
- http://www.emc.com
- http://www.marathontechnologies.com
- http://www.storagetek.com

Information about fault-tolerant systems is also available on some third-party Web sites. For more information, you can search for "fault tolerant" or "fault-tolerant" on any of the following Web sites:

- http://www.tandem.com
- http://www.sequent.com
- http://www.cisco.com

Also, see the following resources:

- *Microsoft Commerce Server 2000 Installation Guide*
- http://www.microsoft.com/TechNet/maintain/mofovrv.asp
- http://www.microsoft.com/technet/reliable/opmgt.asp
- *Microsoft Windows 2000 Server Resource Kit*

Building the Project Plan

This chapter explains how to create a Project Plan. A Project Plan includes a functional specification; a list of the project team members, including the responsibilities of each person; a project schedule; and a cost estimate. The Project Plan organizes project-planning information, such as tasks, resources, organization, timeframes, and dependencies necessary to complete the project. It contains the information that developers and others who assemble and configure the hardware and develop the site will need.

The Project Plan is refined at the beginning of each phase (Plan, Develop, Deploy, Manage), using Microsoft Project or a similar project-planning tool, to update project information as the project progresses.

To ensure that you have all the essential information you need to build your Project Plan, the following personnel should participate in the planning process:

Personnel	Tasks
Technical	• Create the functional specification
	• Create a project schedule
	• Propose a project budget
	• Propose a list of project team members
Marketing and Sales	• Approve the functional specification
	• Approve the project schedule
Company executives	• Approve the functional specification
	• Approve the project schedule
	• Approve the project budget
	• Allocate resources for development, deployment, and system administration

The following sections provide detailed information about how to build your Project Plan.

Creating a Functional Specification

A functional specification usually contains the following information:

- Summary
- Design goals and justification
- Design
- Compatibility and platform requirements
- Third-party involvement
- Localization
- Deployment and administration
- Issues and risks

The following sections provide guidelines for creating each part of your functional specification.

Summary

- Describe your existing site (if you have one)
- Describe the new site
- Describe your users
- Describe key user scenarios
- Outline navigation through the site

Design Goals and Justification

- Create a list of design goals, including goals for capacity and performance.
- Create a prioritized list of features and functions. Include research, especially market research, to indicate why each feature is necessary.
- List related functionality recommended for future site releases (if any).

The following is a list of questions to consider when you create your feature list:

- Who is the customer for this feature?
- Why would a customer want to use this feature?
- What is the logical flow through the user interface? Is the result what users expect?
- Are there other ways to accomplish the same task or implement the feature? What are they?
- Will the customer have the knowledge necessary to use this feature?

- Is the customer likely to combine the feature with other features or procedures?

- Is the feature or procedure consistent with other features of procedures in the product or in similar products?

- Are any changes needed to make the feature or procedure appropriate to an international market?

- What needs to be changed for different languages?

- Will different versions implement the feature differently in the future?

Design

- Establish coding standards.

- Describe the application architecture (event sequence charts, user authentication, and so on).

- Define your site profile, including the following:

  - Site contents

  - Number of Web pages (dynamic versus static)

- Describe each feature and explain how it will be used. (Cross-reference each feature to your project vision, conceptual design, and requirements, as appropriate.)

- Map each feature to a Commerce Server 2000 function.

- Design the visual interface.

- Determine whether or not settings should be persistent.

Data

- Describe the data architecture (data models, database schemas, and so on).

- Describe how data is to be stored.

- Describe the processes that will be used to transfer, update, and validate data.

- Describe processes for accessing data, and identify who will have access to data and under what circumstances.

Security

- Create a prioritized list of anticipated threats to your system, and then design a mitigation solution for each threat.

- Describe your plan for securing your networks (how users can log on, how resources can be accessed, and who can access them, and so on).

- Describe your plan for application security, including the following:

- Security on software and services

- User authentication and authorization processes

- Membership and other directory schemas

- Describe your plan for securing data, including the following:

  - Database security

  - File/share security

  - Maintaining data integrity

- Describe which Commerce Server, Microsoft Windows 2000, SQL Server, or other product security features you plan to use.

- Describe what measures you plan to use to monitor and authenticate user input.

Compatibility and Platform Requirements

- Specify hardware.

- Describe and diagram the system architecture, including the following:

  - Logical architecture

  - Physical architecture

  - Network architecture

- Identify software and services, and describe why they were chosen.

- List the systems with which the site must interface and describe how you plan to provide connectivity and accessibility to them.

- Describe optimal hardware, software, services, and system settings.

- Determine the boundary conditions with line-of-business systems.

- Confirm disk space requirements.

- Identify incorrect version matches between components.

- Identify shared components, owners, and tracking processes.

- Identify who owns the relationship with component owners.

- Define agreement with component owners.

- Explain how the site will work with various browsers.

Third-Party Involvement

- If you plan to use Microsoft Solution Providers, describe their role and contribution to the solution.

- List all dependencies on third-party components.

Localization

- Identify the parts of the site that require localization (if any). Does the entire site need to be multilingual or only portions of it (such as the catalogs)?

- What languages do you need to support?

- What currencies do you need to support?

Migration

- Describe the migration path from the existing site (if any) to the new site.

Issues and Risks

- What are the project-related issues?

- What are the project-related risks?

Identifying the Project Team

When the functional specification is finished, the technical group must identify the development, deployment, and system administration resources necessary to create and operate the site. Two types of personnel are needed on the project team: those with specific technical skills, and those who can relate the business goals of the company to the implementation of the Web site.

Commerce Server provides a set of features for developing, deploying, and managing Web sites. Each feature area requires specific skills that span three kinds of expertise within an organization.

The following table lists the three distinct roles, provides examples of the tasks that must be performed and the knowledge required for each role, and identifies the Commerce Server tools and user interfaces used by each:

Role	Responsibilities	Required Knowledge	Tools and User Interfaces
Site Developer	• Builds the Web site. • Integrates the Web site with existing line-of-business systems. • Migrates existing e-commerce sites and databases. • Customizes Commerce Server Business Desk. • Adds new modules to Commerce Server Business Desk. • Adds new extension snap-ins to the Microsoft Management Console (MMC). • Creates custom reports. • Extends the Data Warehouse. • Tests and validates site operation in the test environment.	• Dynamic Hypertext Markup Language (DHTML) • Extensible Markup Language (XML) • ActiveX Data Objects (ADO) • HTML Components (HTC) • Active Server Pages (ASP)	• Commerce Server Solution Sites • Commerce Server COM objects • Commerce Server Pipeline Editor • Commerce Server Pipeline Components • Commerce Server Advertisement design-time control (DTC) • Commerce Server Site Packager

Role	Responsibilities	Required Knowledge	Tools and User Interfaces
System Administrator	• Packages and moves sites to the production computer. • Configures and optimizes Commerce Server resources. • Schedules Data Warehouse import tasks. • Schedules Direct Mailer jobs. • Builds new prediction models. • Maintains Commerce Server databases. • Troubleshoots the Web environment.	• Microsoft Windows 2000 • Microsoft SQL Server 2000 or Microsoft SQL Server 7.0 • Internet Information Services (IIS) 5.0 • Commerce Server Setup	• Commerce Server Site Packager • Commerce Server Manager

Role	Responsibilities	Required Knowledge	Tools and User Interfaces
Business Manager	• Creates specifications for developing the Web site. • Determines how the Web site should be updated to meet business goals. • Determines how Commerce Server Business Desk should be customized. • Creates advertising campaigns. • Manages product catalogs. • Analyzes user activity and site effectiveness. • Manages registered users and trading partners. • Creates auctions. • Relates marketing data to the site. • Analyzes site traffic, trends, and so on.	• Business goals, strategies, and processes for creating and running a successful e-commerce Web site.	• Commerce Server Business Desk

Building the Project Schedule

The project schedule clearly identifies how much time and how many resources it will take to develop the site. The schedule should also spell out assumptions, dependencies, and risks. If there is not enough time in the schedule to build the site as designed, it should also specify the trade-offs for altering the design or extending the time necessary to build the site as originally planned.

Part Three: Developing

Microsoft®
Commerce
Server 2000

Developing Your Site

During the Development phase, you design, scope, and develop your site. You also continue to refine the Project Plan and usage, site, and hardware profiles you created during the Planning phase, based on what you learn during the Development phase.

Design and build your site using the Project Goals and Requirements and Project Plan documents that you created during the Planning phase, as shown in Figure 8.1, a high-level view of the development process.

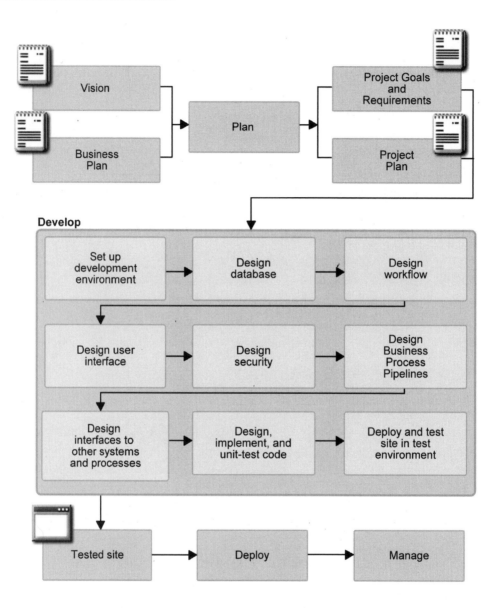

Figure 8.1 Development phase

The results of each task you complete feed back into the previous task. For example, information you discover while designing the workflow and implementing the user interface (UI) is likely to affect your database design.

In the Development phase, you typically set up a development environment in which you develop and unit-test your code. Following successful unit testing, you move your working system or prototype to a staging area for further testing and performance verification. When the site performs acceptably, you are ready to deploy the site into the production environment.

You update your usage profile by becoming more specific about how users will use your site. It is critical to collect data on user visits to your site, such as frequency and duration of visits and usage patterns, if available, to develop a site that meets your business needs.

To update your site profile, you should specify details such as the size of the data to be searched and returned in queries and typical catalog searches. Your site design should specify the size of each Web page and the number of images and links. To account for overhead, you should also determine the security level for each page at this point.

Based on the pages you develop, determine performance targets for each operation. During the Development phase, you must develop a capacity requirement for each operation in terms of transaction rate or operations per second, as well as acceptable user latency. You might want to adjust hardware specifications, based on any new information you discover during the Development phase.

Development Checklist

You should complete the following tasks during the Development phase:

- Decide whether to develop your site "from scratch" (in which case, you'll need a site design) or use your own existing site as a basis. Alternatively, you can use one of the Commerce Server Solution Sites as a basis for development, and then customize your code for that site.

- Establish your configuration management infrastructure. For more information, see the section "Managing Site Configuration" later in this chapter.

- Establish change management processes and infrastructure. For more information, see the section "Managing Change" later in this chapter.

- Analyze data and finalize your database schema using Commerce Server objects and integrating any external databases your site requires.

- Determine the attributes to be stored for each user.

- Design the UI framework.

- Design detailed network architecture.

- Develop operation-specific workflow diagrams and event-sequence charts.

- Design security for each feature.

- Design, implement, and unit-test code, including:
  - Active Server Pages (ASP) code
  - HTML code
  - Custom objects
  - Additional Microsoft Management Console (MMC) snap-ins

- Design business processing pipelines.

- Design interfaces with existing systems and processes (external payment systems, delivery systems, inventory systems, corporate mainframe, and so on).

- Develop test plans. Test your site in a test/staging environment.

- Create load scripts and test scripts, measure the latency for each user operation, then test your site under load and compare response time with performance and availability goals set in the Planning phase.

- Review site readiness. Determining readiness is an exercise in risk management, balancing risks associated with schedule and quality. If you spend too much time correcting all the errors, you risk missing the window of opportunity for the market; if you release the product too soon, you risk losing customers because the quality of your site is too low.

The Development section of this book contains the chapters listed in the following table.

Chapter	Title	Description
9	Developer Notes	- Example describing how to add a feature to one of the Solution Sites - Best practices for using the Profiling System - Conceptual overview of the advertisement scoring system - Description of the Profiles Schema management tools
10	Integrating Third-Party ERP Systems with Commerce Server Applications	Best practices for integrating Commerce Server with existing corporate systems
11	Migrating from Site Server to Commerce Server 2000	Best practices for migrating an existing site built with Site Server to Commerce Server 2000
12	Developing an International Site	Best practices for extending a Commerce Server site for an international audience
13	Integrating Commerce Server with BizTalk Server	How to integrate Commerce Server with Microsoft BizTalk Server 2000

Completing the Development Phase

The following table lists criteria for determining when development is complete and your site is ready for deployment.

Milestone	Action	Timing	Success criteria
Functional test complete	Execute function/feature test cases.	After code freeze.	All tests pass.
Deployment test complete	Install the site in a staging environment, as described in your installation documentation.	After code freeze.	Installation documentation verified.
Manageability test complete	Validate that business managers or site administrators can manage the site, as appropriate.	After code freeze.	All tests pass.
System integration test complete	Validate that the site works in the staging environment with specified software, network, and hardware.	After deployment and functional tests.	All tests pass.
Stress test complete	Validate that the site performs at the specified level of performance when fully loaded (normal load expected), for an extended period of time (usually three to five days).	When system integration tests are successful. Sometimes stress testing is done in conjunction with integration testing, if necessary, to shorten time to market.	System runs at targeted stress level for entire period with no performance degradation or excessive system resource consumption.
Performance test complete	Validate that the site performs well at peak, targeted capacity (peak user and transaction load).	When system integration tests are successful.	System runs at targeted capacity level.
Support process established, staffed, and tested	• Design and implement process for support team to handle expected volume of service calls, including metrics and response time. • Design and deploy support hardware and infrastructure.	Start training before code complete. Support should be in place before any client pilot programs or before you put the site in production.	Customer problems resolved within targeted timeframes.
Escalation process established, staffed, and tested	Design and implement process for support staff to escalate problems to the development team for evaluation and correction, when necessary.	Before any client pilot programs, or before you put the site in production.	Customer problems are solved in a timely manner.
Site approved by program managers, developers, test, and support	Managers and leads of key areas agree that the site meets its design goals and can be supported in a production environment.	Last verification before you deploy the site to production.	Successful deployment of the site.

Selecting a Development Methodology

You can choose any of the following methodologies as the basis for developing your Commerce Server site:

- **Solution Site**. The advantage of using a Solution Site as the basis for your site development effort is that it contains pre-implemented core functionality that has already been tested.

- **SDK sitelet**. The advantage of using an SDK sitelet as the basis for your site development effort is that it is a good starting point for learning how to use each Commerce Server feature, although some features have been omitted, to simplify the code.

- **Microsoft Reference Architecture for Commerce**. The advantage of using Microsoft Reference Architecture for Commerce is that it is similar to a Solution Site, but it is more focused on .NET Enterprise Server integration and is designed to be a reference architecture for .NET Enterprise Servers. For more information about the Microsoft Reference Architecture for Commerce, see http://msdn.microsoft.com/library/techart/ractp.htm.

- **Start from scratch**. Developing your site from scratch might be necessary if your site must be completely customized, and is a valid approach if you have the necessary time and resources. However, this approach is much more time-consuming and means that you must begin at the beginning to test and refine the performance of your new site, instead of implementing proven methods.

Jump-Starting Development with the Solution Sites

If you use a Solution Site as the basis for development, you develop your Commerce Server site in two steps:

- Create a site that interfaces with the Commerce Server application management infrastructure by using Commerce Server Site Packager to unpack one of the Solution Sites.

- Modify the implementation of features in the Solution Site you unpacked and add any new features you identified in the Planning phase.

The choice you need to make before you start development is whether to start with the Blank site or start with one of the scenario-based Solution Sites (Retail or Supplier).

The Blank site is installed in the Commerce Server\Pup Packages folder by Commerce Server 2000 Setup. If you unpack this site with Site Packager, you have a site that is integrated with the Commerce Server application management framework, but does not have any features implemented. The Blank site contains placeholder files that you can use to help you start your development. If you navigate to the Blank site after unpacking, you should see the message, "Hello World, from BlankSite."

The scenario-based Solution Sites, available from http://www.microsoft.com/commerceserver/solutionsites, already have an initial set of features implemented, and you just need to modify those features to meet your specific requirements. The advantage of using a scenario-based Solution Site is that it reduces development time. If there are aspects of the site's design that don't meet your requirements, however, it might be better to start with the Blank site.

The Retail and Supplier Solution Sites provide the most common set of features found in business-to-consumer and business-to-business Internet sites. The two sites employ a common code base and use site configuration information to determine which code path to execute. Site configuration information is retrieved from a data dictionary known as the **Options** dictionary. The **Options** dictionary is a simple name/value pair data structure that contains configuration information retrieved from the Commerce Server 2000 application management infrastructure. The following code snippet shows you how to retrieve the **Options** dictionary:

```
<%
  Dim oOptionsDict, dictConfig
  Set oOptionsDict = Server.CreateObject("Commerce.AppConfig")
  Set dictConfig = oOptionsDict.GetOptionsDictionary("")
%>
```

A complete listing of the items stored in the **Options** dictionary is provided in the reference page for the **AppConfig.GetOptionsDictionary** method in Commerce Server 2000 Help.

The power of a common code base driven by configuration information is that it enables you to prototype your solutions rapidly. For example, by simply changing the *Add items redirect options* value from 0 to 1, you can have your site immediately redirect a customer to the basket page after adding an item to the basket, instead of returning to the page displaying the product. You can set any of the application configuration settings through the App Default Config resource in Commerce Server Manager.

You can change back and forth between the two code paths by making changes with the App Default Config resource. Your development process will be smoother, however, if you start with the Solution Site that most closely matches your site. For more information about setting up the Supplier Solution Site, see Chapter 14, "Deploying Your Site."

Managing Site Configurations

Configuration management is the process of identifying, recording, tracking, and reporting on key system components, called *configuration items* (CIs). You should manage configuration throughout the life of your site. The following table lists the core components of configuration management.

Core component	Description
Configuration item (CI)	Key system component or asset, such as hardware, system software, application software, and documentation. The information you record and track depends on the type of CI, but usually includes the following: • Description • Version • Constituent components • Relationships to other CIs • Location and assignment • Status
Configuration Management database	The single logical data repository for CI information. Whenever possible, this database should be self-maintaining, with automated updates from CIs.

The following table lists the core processes you should use to manage your configuration.

Core process	Activities
Planning	Plan and define the scope, objectives, policies, procedures, and organizational and technical context for managing your configuration.
Identification	Select and identify the structures for all the CIs, including the following: • Owners • Interrelationships • Documentation Assign identifiers to CIs and their versions.
Controlling changes	Accept and track only authorized and identifiable CIs. This process should also ensure that no CI is added, modified, replaced, or removed without an approved change request. For more information about change requests, see the "Managing Change" section.
Status accounting	Report on all current and historical data for each CI throughout its life cycle.
Verification and auditing	Verify the physical existence of CIs to make sure that they are correctly recorded in the configuration management process.

Configuration Items

As you plan development of your site, you should review the CIs that are part of your proposed site. A software component, for example, might either be a stand-alone CI or part of a larger CI. You should answer the following types of questions about each CI:

- Is it practical to manage this component as a CI?

- Is information about the item required by a number of people?

- Will the CI need to be replicated?

- Does this CI depend on others?

- Is this CI likely to change?

- Do we understand how this CI is to be used?

- Are other CIs dependent on the state of this CI?

- Does the CI have adjustable properties?

This section lists some common types of CIs. You might want to track additional CIs associated with your site, as well. You should track any key item associated with the development and management of your site.

Hardware

Track the hardware components that make up the identified CI, such as a server, which might have the following components:

- Server ID
- Date purchased
- Version
- Basic input/output system (BIOS)
- Model
- Firmware
- Serial number

A hard disk drive inside a server would be considered a hardware component CI subordinate to the server hardware CI. The hard disk drive CI might have the following components:

- Hardware component ID
- Primary hardware ID (such as the server)
- Component type
- Date installed
- Version
- Serial number

Software

Track lists of files and versions, build scripts, installation scripts, and settings, such as .ini files, registry settings, or miscellaneous configuration files. For example, a service pack for a software release might include the following components:

- Software CI ID

- Software type

- Application name

- Date installed

- Version

- Service pack

- Hot fix

- Debugging symbols for Windows 2000 and Commerce Server

  You can download Windows 2000 debugging symbols from http://msdn.microsoft.com/downloads/default.asp?URL=/code/sample.asp?url=/MSDN-FILES/027/000/189/MsdnCompositeDoc.xml.

  Commerce Server debugging symbols are located on the Commerce Server 2000 CD in the \bin directory.

Network

You might decide to track anything from a network device, such as a router, to a structured cabling setup. For example, a router CI should include the hardware specifications and inventory of items it contains, such as specific interface cards. It should also include all build and configuration scripts.

User

Track information needed to identify users and their permissions. For example, a CI for a server cluster administrator might include the following:

- User name

- Role

- Contact information

- Backup person when the administrator can't be reached

Configuration Management Database

The Configuration Management database is usually a relational database with associated support tools in which information about the CIs is stored and related. The Configuration Management database should also store information about changes, problems, incidents, and known errors. (For more information about storing incidents in the Configuration Management database, see Chapter 18, "Problem Management.") The Configuration Management database should contain tables such as those described in the following table.

Table	Contains
Line-of–business	The name of the line-of-business (LOB) application described in the Configuration Management database. For example, a Commerce Server Web site is a type of LOB application.
System function	A description of the function performed by each server. For example, one server might be a Web server, one a database server, and so on.
System hardware details	Details of the system hardware.
Physical hardware components	Details of the physical hardware components installed on the server.
Drivers for hardware components	Lists of drivers for each hardware component.
Vendors	Information about each hardware vendor.
System server software	Information about the software installed on the system servers.
Changes	Descriptions of all changes since the functional specification was approved and coding began.
Documents	Information about documents the system administrator needs to manage the application, such as change management documentation, disaster recovery plans, escalation procedures, and so on.
Parameters stored in the registry	Information about parameters stored in the operating system registry for each specific registry key.
Services	Information about services run by the software applications.
Registry entries for the service	Information about registry entries specific to each service identified in the Services table.
Dependent services	Information about services dependent on the primary services. For example, dependent services for the IISADMIN service include the W3SVC, File Transfer Protocol (FTP), and Simple Mail Transfer Protocol (SMTP) services.
Files running the service	Information about .exe, .sys, or .dll files responsible for running the application.
Operational processes	Information about operational processes associated with the application, such as capacity management, configuration management, and change management.
Employees	Information about key personnel responsible for supporting the application.
Roles	Information about each application support role.
Employee details	Contact information for each person listed in the Employee table.

Core Configuration Management Processes

If your configuration management process is an integral part of your development strategy, your processes for managing configurations will be in place before you develop or deploy a new site. Your development team can then use the configuration information as they build the software, to ensure that they have constructed the system correctly. As you move from phase to phase developing your site, you should update your configuration information.

This section describes the following core configuration management processes:

- Identification
- Status accounting
- Verification and auditing

Identification

There are three major tasks in identifying a configuration item:

- Determining CI scope, level, and relationships
- Implementing standard naming conventions
- Recording CI information in the Configuration Management database

The task of identifying CI scope, level, and relationships can vary by environment. The following table describes the three identification factors.

Factor	Description
CI scope	The portion of a site that you intend to manage as a single configuration item. If the scope is too narrow, some parts of the configuration won't be managed properly; if the scope is too broad, the configuration will be too unwieldy to manage. For example, a server might be a configuration item.
CI level	The level of detail you use to describe a CI. If the level of detail is too low, maintenance will be excessive; if the level is too high, the process won't be useful.
	For example, you might optimize the CI level by creating and tracking a build kit for a component rather than tracking each .dll or file separately.
CI relationships	Descriptions of the dependencies between CIs (such as "is connected to", "is a copy of," and "is a part of"). If you identify too few relationships, the Configuration Management database becomes merely an asset database or a list of components; if you identify too many relationships, the database becomes too complex to maintain.

Use standard naming conventions to uniquely identify each CI. For instance, a hardware CI for an e-commerce site that spans multiple data centers could be something like the following:

DDAATTNN, where

DD   = Data center ID
AA   = Application ID
TT   = Server type ID (for example, SQ for SQL Server or WB for Web server)
NN   = Unique identifier (01, 02, and so forth)

You should record CI information in the Configuration Management database. We recommend that you automate this process as much as possible. Microsoft Windows Management Instrumentation (WMI), for example, enables you to identify components within the infrastructure, covering the identification of both infrastructure and software components. For more information about configuration tools, see the "Configuration Management Tools" section later in this chapter.

Status Accounting

It is important to track the status of CIs throughout the time they are in use. The first objective of status accounting is to identify hardware and software and add this information to your site inventory. The best way to do this is to automatically discover the item, identify it, and record it in the site inventory. Automatic procedures for doing this are best, if you have them; however, there might be CIs that you must track manually. The ideal system periodically reruns inventory processes automatically, documenting changes to the configuration as they occur. (For more information about inventory processes, see the "Configuration Management Tools" section in this chapter.) You should, however, check the automated processes on a regular basis. It is a good practice to create a script that periodically extracts the data for you to examine.

Verification and Auditing

The only way to maintain performance standards is to periodically run a comprehensive system audit. You must also verify the physical existence of CIs to make sure that they are recorded correctly. For example, you should audit the builds on all servers at regular intervals, such as once a week, to look for discrepancies. For a description of tools that Microsoft provides to help you manage site configuration, see the section on "Configuration Management Tools" at the end of this chapter.

Managing Change

Managing change is especially important for companies that do business on the Web because of the high rate of change in e-commerce applications and environments. The change management process provides procedures for safeguarding existing services, while safely introducing new services.

Most systems are heavily interrelated, so any changes made in one part of a system can have profound impacts on another. The change management process attempts to identify all systems and processes affected by a change so that everyone affected, such as business managers and system administrators, has an opportunity to mitigate or eliminate adverse effects before the change is put into effect. You should manage changes in all of your environments: production, development, and test/staging.

The categories of assets that you should place under change control include, but are not limited to, hardware, communications equipment and software, system software, applications software, processes, procedures, roles, responsibilities, and documentation relevant to the development, support, and maintenance of systems in the managed environment. In other words, any asset that exists in the environment and is necessary for meeting the service level requirements of the site should be placed under change control.

The following are key components of the change management process:

- Change requests
- Change database
- Change advisory board
- Change process

Change Requests

Change requests are the formal documentation of the change control process, and should include the following elements:

- ID (a unique identifier for the request)
- Configuration item ID(s)
- Reason for change
- Version of components to be changed
- Name, location, and contact information for the person proposing the change
- Date change proposed
- Change priority
- Impact and resource assessment
- Change advisory board recommendations

- Authorization signature, time, and date
- Schedule for implementation
- Details of change builder/implementer
- Implementation time and date
- Review date
- Review results

Change Database

Requests for change are registered and tracked in a central repository, preferably in the Configuration Management database, because the change management and configuration management processes are closely related. If at all possible, you should consider automating the process of adding change requests to the database.

Change Advisory Board

The change advisory board is a cross-functional group that evaluates change requests for business need, priority, cost versus benefit, and potential impacts to other systems or processes. Typically, the change advisory board recommends implementation, further analysis, deferment, or cancellation of the change. The change advisory board should meet regularly — as often as necessary to prevent bottlenecks in implementing changes and decrease the number of urgent changes.

Change Process

You should create a process for making changes, so that all team members for the site understand the escalation path when a change needs to be made. Figure 8.2 shows a sample process for making changes.

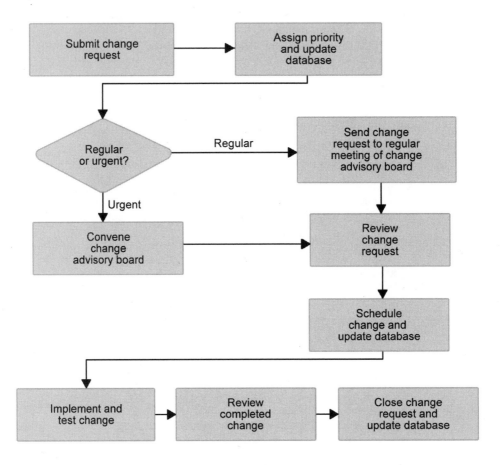

Figure 8.2 Sample change process

The process shown in Figure 8.2 is as follows:

1. The requester submits the change request to the change manager.

2. The change manager reviews the change request, assigns a priority, and enters it in the change database.

   If the change is a regular priority, go to step 4.

   If the change is urgent, go to step 3.

3. The change manager convenes a special meeting of the change advisory board to review the change request. Go to step 5.

4. The change manager sends the change request to the regular meeting of the change advisory board for review.

5. The change advisory board reviews the change request, including the following elements: cost, resources, priority, severity, business commitment, risk, and possibility of recovery.

   If the change is approved, go to step 6.

   If the change is not approved, the process ends.

6. The change manager schedules the change and updates the Change database.

   Scheduling should be done on a single change calendar so that planned changes can be seen in the context of other changes that are being planned or are currently being worked on.

7. The developer implements and tests the change.

8. The change advisory board reviews the completed change.

   If the change is satisfactory, go to step 9.

   If the change is not satisfactory, return to step 7.

9. The change manager closes the change request and updates the Change database.

Development Tools and Resources

The following resources can help you accomplish development tasks:

- Commerce Server 2000 Help
- Commerce Server 2000 Software Development Kit (SDK)
- Commerce Server tools
- Other Microsoft tools
- Configuration management tools
- Other references

Commerce Server 2000 Help

The information listed in the following table is available through Commerce Server 2000 Help.

Section	Explains how to
Setting Up Your Development Workstation	Set up your Commerce Server development environment.
Programming with Commerce Server Objects	Use Commerce Server objects to program your site.
Working with Pipelines	Use Commerce Server pipelines to link one or more components and run them in sequence. Commerce Server provides three pipeline models: the Order Processing pipeline (OPP), the Direct Mailer pipeline, and the Content Selection pipeline (CSP).
Integrating with BizTalk Server	Use BizTalk Server in conjunction with your Commerce Server site.
Customizing Style Sheets	Customize Commerce Server style sheets.
Modifying Your Site for an International Audience	Localize error messages, dates, times, and currencies for an international audience.
Extending Commerce Server	Extend any of the following Commerce Server resources: • MMC extension snap-ins • Commerce Server Business Desk modules • Administrative tools • Pipeline components • Third-party catalogs • Content Selection Framework (CSF) • Custom resources • Custom reports • Commerce Server Data Warehouse logical schema, metadata, or physical data store
Programmer's Reference	Use each Commerce Server object.

Commerce Server SDK

You use the Commerce Server 2000 SDK to develop e-commerce solutions with Commerce Server. The Commerce Server 2000 SDK contains tools, code samples, and documentation that explains how to customize and extend Commerce Server tools.

Before you use the samples and tools in the Commerce Server 2000 SDK, you must download the Microsoft Platform SDK from the following location: http://msdn.microsoft.com/downloads/sdks/platform/platform.asp.

The Commerce Server 2000 SDK is shipped on the Commerce Server 2000 CD. You can access it from the Start Menu at Start/Program Files/Microsoft Commerce Server/Software Development Kit if you use the Complete installation option.

The SDK contains the samples listed in the following table.

Folder	Sample	Demonstrates how to
Business Analytics	Create SchemaObject.vbs	Use the OLE DB Provider for Commerce Server to modify the Business Analytics System logical schema.
	• Analysis – New dynamic OLAP report script.sql • Analysis – New dynamic SQL report script.sql • Analysis – New static OLAP report script.sql • Analysis – New static SQL report script.sql	Create new reports of various types in the Business Analytics System.
	Schema Tool	Use the OLE DB Provider for Commerce Server to access the logical schema of the Data Warehouse.
Management	BizDesk	Use XML data islands, including Business Desk HTML Components (HTCs) for site administration.
	BizDesk Installer	Automate the process of adding configuration information for a new module to an existing Business Desk installation.
	PuP Resource	Package a specified set of tables from a single SQL Server database.
	ResourceConfig	Add the configuration information for a custom resource to the Administration database.
	Site Status	Extend the Commerce Server Manager interface and open or close the Commerce Server installations into which this MMC extension snap-in is installed.
	Widgets	Construct pages for the various HTCs provided with the Business Desk Framework.

Folder	Sample	Demonstrates how to
Marketing	Dbscripts	Remove the following tables and related objects from a SQL Server database: • Campaigns-drop.sql • Expression-store-drop.sql • Listmanager-drop.sql
	Debug	Dump the contents of a CSF cache and trace the scoring logic applied to a content request.
	Headlines	Extend the Targeting System using custom CSF cache loading and scoring components.
Order Processing	MinMaxShip	Add a new pipeline component to the OPP.
Privacy	DeleteDetailedData.vbs	Use the OLE DB Provider for Commerce Server to delete detailed data about a particular user from the Data Warehouse.
	Disconnect Detailed Data.vbs	Use the OLE DB Provider for Commerce Server to disassociate detailed data about a particular user without deleting the data itself.
Sitelets	Ad	Use the Profiling System in combination with the Targeting System to display targeted advertisements.
	Auction	Use the **Auction** object to implement Winning Bid auctions.
	Catalog	Use the Product Catalog System to offer catalog browse and search functionality.
	Discount	Offer targeted discounts during order processing.
	Order	Implement an order capture process.
	Passport	Integrate Passport Single Sign-In (SSI) capability with the Profiling System.
	Profile	Use the Profiling System to register and authenticate users.

In addition to the samples, the AppConsts.idl file in the SolutionSites folder provides constants used by the Solution Sites.

The SDK also contains the tools listed in the following table.

Tool	Use to
ATL Pipe Wizard	Install a new wizard in your Microsoft Visual C++ 6.0 installation to automate the creation of Commerce Server pipeline components.
Membership Migration	Migrate user profiles from a Site Server Membership Directory into a Commerce Server 2000 user profile store.
Migration: Ad Server	Migrate campaigns from Site Server Ad Server to the Commerce Server 2000 CSF.
Registration	Register pipeline components for stage affinity.
VB Pipe Wizard	Install a new wizard in your Microsoft Visual Basic 6.0 installation to automate the creation of Commerce Server pipeline components.

Commerce Server Management Tools

You can use the Commerce Server tools described in the following table to develop your site.

Commerce Server tool	Use to
Commerce Server Business Desk	Host business management modules for managing and analyzing your site. For example, you can update pricing information in your catalog, target new ads to specific users, and then run reports to measure how these changes affect site productivity with Business Desk.
Commerce Server Manager	Manage and configure Commerce Server resources, sites, applications, and Web servers. The MMC hosts Commerce Server Manager.
Commerce Server Site Packager	Package a site, including applications and resources, into a single file (package) so you can move the site to another environment. Site Packager provides a convenient way for site developers to move sites to staging and production environments or to deliver sites to customers.
Pipeline Component Wizard	Automate the creation of Commerce Server pipeline components. The Pipeline Component Wizard consists of a group of files that you add to a Visual C++ installation to create object definition and implementation files. These files contain the function prototypes for all of the interfaces you need to create a fully functional pipeline component. In addition, the Pipeline Component Wizard creates a property page for your project, to which you add the controls through which users set component properties.
Solution Sites	Build a site. After you install Commerce Server, you can unpack one of the Solution Sites, and then use it as a foundation for building your own site.
	When you purchase Commerce Server, you receive the Blank site to help you build your own custom site. Also, the following Solution Sites are also available for download from http://www.microsoft.com/commerceserver/solutionsites:
	• **Retail Solution Site**. Commerce Server resource for building a retail site.
	• **Supplier Solution Site**. Commerce Server resource for building a Microsoft Active Directory-enabled supplier site.

Other Microsoft Tools

The Microsoft tools listed in the following table can also be helpful for developing your site.

Microsoft tool	Use to
Microsoft Management Console (MMC) snap-in for Microsoft Windows 2000	Determine the status of a server or workstation. For more information, see http://www.microsoft.com/WINDOWS2000/library/howitworks/management/mmcover.asp.
Microsoft Visual InterDev	Develop Web sites. For more information, see http://msdn.microsoft.com/vinterdev/.
Microsoft Web Application Stress (WAS) tool	Simulate Web stress for sites under load. For more information, see http://webtool.rte.microsoft.com/.
Microsoft Windows 2000 Server Resource Kit support tools	Isolate, diagnose, and in some cases repair problems. For more information, see http://www.microsoft.com/windows2000/library/resources/reskit/default.asp.
Network Monitor	Detect and troubleshoot problems, and analyze data on LANs and WANs. Network Monitor is a component of Microsoft Systems Management Server (SMS). For more information, see http://msdn.microsoft.com/library/psdk/netmon/portalnm_6ilu.htm.
SQL Profiler	Capture SQL Server events from a server and save them in a trace file for analysis and problem diagnosis. For more information, see http://www.microsoft.com/SQL/productinfo/bizopsoverview.htm.
System Monitor	Collect and view data about hardware and system service usage. For more information, see http://msdn.microsoft.com/library/default.asp?URL=/library/psdk/winbase/sysmonauto_3jqd.htm.
Visual Studio Analyzer	Analyze performance, isolate faults, and analyze the structure of distributed applications. Visual Studio Analyzer is one tool in the Microsoft Visual Studio 6.0 suite of tools. For more information, see http://msdn.microsoft.com/library/periodic/period99/analyzer.htm.

Configuration Management Tools

The following table describes the configuration management tools that Microsoft provides.

Tool	Description
Windows Management Instrumentation (WMI)	Part of the Windows 2000 platform, WMI helps you manage your enterprise systems, applications, and networks. For more information, see http://www.microsoft.com/TechNet/Win2000/mngwmi.asp.
Microsoft Visio 2000 Enterprise Edition	Helps you monitor your network, manage network user accounts, and get a hierarchical view of your directory structure. For more information, see http://www.Microsoft.com/catalog/.
Metabase Editor (MetaEdit)	Helps you edit Internet Information Services (IIS) 5.0 configuration files. For more information, see http://msdn.Microsoft.com/library/winresource/ssreskit/.

Other Resources

The following table lists other resources you might find useful for developing your site.

Resource	Provides
Third-party software	The latest information about software developed especially to work with Commerce Server 2000. For more information, see http://www.microsoft.com/commerceserver.
Sysinternals	Advanced utilities, technical information, and source code related to Windows 2000 internals. For more information, see http://www.sysinternals.com.

Related Web Sites

The following table lists related Web sites that contain design tips and code samples, tools that you can download, and sample sites.

Site	Provides
http://www.microsoft.com/frontpage/default2.htm	Information about installing and maintaining Microsoft FrontPage Server extensions on multiple platforms.
http://support.microsoft.com/support/search/c.asp?spr=	The latest articles about FrontPage Server extensions and using FrontPage in conjunction with IIS.
http://www.asptoday.com	Free daily articles on writing ASP code.
http://www.microsoft.com/sql/bizsol/commerce.htm	Materials to help you deploy and maintain a reliable, high volume e-commerce site.
http://www.microsoft.com/globaldev/default.asp	Suggestions and tips for adapting software for an international audience.
http://msdn.microsoft.com/workshop/server/nextgen/nextgen.asp	Tips for constructing your Web site to reach beyond the English-speaking community.
http://www.microsoft.com/technet	Updates and information for the system administrator.
http://www.rainbow.com/isg/products/cs_1.html	Information about Rainbow Technologies' CryptoSwift, a tool for improving secure Web server response time.
http://msdn.microsoft.com/xml/general/xmltools.asp	A list of tool vendors that offer generalized XML support.
http://www.microsoft.com/mind/1198/ado/ado.htm	Tips and sample code for accessing SQL Server through ADO and ASP, in the article, "Top Ten Tips: Accessing SQL Through ADO and ASP," by J.D. Meier.
http://homer.rte.microsoft.com	Information about WAS, a Web stress tool that realistically simulates multiple browsers requesting pages from a Web application.
http://www.microsoft.com/BackStage/whitepaper.htm	Information about optimizing Web server performance.
http://vcmproapp02.compaq.com/ActiveAnswers/global/en/home	A dynamic set of tools, e-services, and information to help you plan, deploy, and operate business solutions.
http://msdn.microsoft.com/vstudio/centers/interop	A number of resources, learning tools, and a complete end-to-end sample application for developers who want to learn how to integrate Windows-based applications with other platforms, including IBM mainframe, AS/400, Unix, structured and unstructured data sources, and Enterprise Resource Planning (ERP) systems.

Developer Notes

The features that you can implement with the Microsoft Commerce Server 2000 software are limited only by your imagination. Many procedures for developing an e-commerce site using Commerce Server are described in Commerce Server 2000 Help, the Commerce Server 2000 Software Development Kit (SDK), and other chapters in this book. This chapter supplements that information with the four sections described in the following table.

Section	Describes
Gift Certificate Feature	How to add a Gift Certificate feature to the Retail Solution Site
Profiling System Utilities	Functionality and operation of two tools you can use to develop profiles: • Profiles Schema Mover • Site Terms Viewer
Profiling System: Operational Considerations	Guidelines for using the Profiling System
Advertising Scoring and Selection	How the advertising engine leverages the Content Selection Framework (CSF) to determine which advertisements to display on a Web site

Gift Certificate Feature

This section describes how the Contoso, Ltd. company described in Chapter 2 ("A Retail Scenario") added a Gift Certificate feature to its site. (Before reading this chapter you should be familiar with the basic features and implementation details of the Retail Solution Site described in documentation available at http://www.microsoft.com/commerceserver/solutionsites. You should also read Chapter 2, to see how Contoso decided to implement its site.)

Contoso identified the data requirements listed in the following table for its gift certificates.

Data requirement	Value and type
Certificate identification	Eight-digit alphanumeric code (primary key) (**string**)
Purchaser information	Name and contact information (**string**)
Value of certificate	Currency value (**currency**)
Recipient	Name and contact information (**string**)
Current balance	Currency value (**currency**)
Date of purchase	Date (**date**)

Contoso's gift certificates can be used only for online shopping. The gift certificates issued by the online store can't be used to make purchases from their mail order catalog. The Contoso team did recognize, however, that when they issued an online gift certificate, they also had to adjust the revenue and liability accounts of their accounting system accordingly.

Contoso decided to add the new gift certificates feature to its online catalog. They set the minimum value for a gift certificate at $20, with value increments of $5 up to a maximum of $300. Each gift certificate contains a unique redemption code that customers use to make purchases. Contoso will mail (or e-mail if the purchaser provides an e-mail address for the recipient) the gift certificate, including the redemption code and instructions for using it to make a purchase, to the recipient.

When recipients log in to use their gift certificates, they can either register or shop as guests. To make purchases with their gift certificates, they simply select the Gift Certificate option on the Order Summary page. When they select this option, they are redirected to the Gift Certificate Redemption page and asked to enter the certificate redemption code. Customers can't use only part of a gift certificate's amount to make a purchase; they must use the full amount on their purchases.

The Contoso team made the implementation decisions listed in the following table for their gift certificate feature.

Requirement	Implementation decision
Site management	Add Commerce Server Business Desk modules to the Orders category.
Site administration	Create a new site resource to set the connection string for the gift certificates data source.
Profile information	Store contact information and account balance data in Microsoft SQL Server 2000 in a table added to the Contoso_Commerce database.
Site implementation	Add two new pages: • **A page for buying a gift certificate**. Similar to Contoso's shipping address form, but with additional boxes for the e-mail address and for entering a message to include with the gift certificate. • **A page for purchasing merchandise with a gift certificate**. Enables customers to enter their gift certificate redemption codes.
Order processing	Add a new pipeline component to the Checkout pipeline.
Accounting updates	Create a Component Object Model (COM) object that communicates asynchronously with the accounting system, using Microsoft Host Integration Server 2000.
Management reports	Create the following dynamic and static reports: • Gift Certificate Sales Report • Gift Certificate Percentage Report (percentage of total online sales) • Number of Gift Certificate Purchases (added to the Order Events report) • Gift Certificate Buyers (static)
Targeting requirements	Display a gift certificate advertisement to previous gift certificate buyers. This is a house ad.

The modifications Contoso made to implement gift certificates on its site are described in the following sections.

Business Desk Modifications

The development team decided to add three Business Desk modules to manage gift certificate sales. They placed these modules in the Orders category in the Business Desk navigation pane, and provided the features listed in the following table.

Feature	Implementation
List and delete current gift certificates	**List sheet**
Create and edit gift certificates	**Edit sheet**
Update gift certificate caches	**Refresh**

To implement the necessary changes in their Business Desk, the development team followed the steps outlined in the "Building Business Desk Modules" section of Commerce Server 2000 Help. The following steps summarize what the development team did:

Note These steps are also summarized in the Instructions.txt file, located in the path *<installation location>*\SDK\Samples\Management\BizDesk\Instructions.txt.

1. Add a new configuration file.

   The team first added a new configuration file, named GiftCerts.xml, to the ContosoBD\config directory. The following excerpt from the file shows the action "View Certificates" and the ASP files associated with this new module:

   ```
   <config xmlns="x-schema:bdmodule-schema.xml">
     <actions>
   <action id='orders/cert_list.asp''helptopic=''cs_ft_certs_EXTN.htm''>
   <name>Certificate List</name>
   <tooltip>View Certificates</tooltip>
     <tasks>
       <task icon=''taskopen.gif'' id=''open''>
         <postto action=''orders/certstatus_view.asp''
                         formname=''selectform'' />
   <name>&lt;U&gt;O&lt;/U&gt;pen</name>
   <key>o</key>
   <tooltip>Open Certificate</tooltip>
   </task>
   </tasks>
   </action>
   ```

2. Add a module entry to the master configuration file.

   Because the Contoso team decided to add the new modules to the Orders category, they had to add the following module entry to the moduleconfigs section of the master configuration file, Bizdesk.xml:

   ```
   <moduleconfig id="GiftCerts.xml" category="orders" />
   ```

3. Implement **list sheet, edit sheet**, and **refresh** functions.

   The team implemented the three functions in the following Active Server Pages (ASP) files:

   - **Cert_list.asp**. This file implements a list sheet and is based on the Orderstatus_view.asp file included with Commerce Server.

- **Cert_edit.asp**. This file implements an edit sheet and is based on the Orderstatus_list.asp file included with Commerce Server.

- **Refresh.asp**. This file refreshes the cache provided by the Retail Solution Site and is included with Commerce Server.

4. Extend Business Desk Help.

The team created four new Help files to extend the Business Desk Help system delivered by Commerce Server. They also extended the index and table of contents of the Business Desk Help system to make it easier for business managers to find the new Help topics. They made the following additions to the Bizdesk.hhc and Bizdesk.hhk files, which are installed in the Business Desk\docs folder (for example, Retailbizdesk\docs):

- Added content to Business Desk Help.

  The development team decided that the Help topics should appear in the "Orders" section of the Business Desk Help system, so they added their entries after the Object entry for the Orders topics. They also decided to follow the same organizational scheme employed in the Help system, so that their topic structure would appear consistent with the Help topics delivered by Commerce Server.

  The following entries are a sub-set of the values they added to the Bizdesk.hhc file:

```
<LI>
<OBJECT type="text/sitemap">
<param name="Name" value="Workflow for Gift Certificate
        Management">
<param name="Local" value="htm/cs_bd_orders_xygh.htm">
</OBJECT>
<LI>
<OBJECT type="text/sitemap">
<param name="Name" value="About Certificates">
<param name="Local" value="htm/cs_bd_orders_iaaz.htm">
</OBJECT>
....
```

- Added index entries for new Help topics.

  To make sure that new topics are referenced in the Business Desk Help index, they added the following entries to the Bizdesk.hhk file:

```
<LI> <OBJECT type="text/sitemap">
        <param name="Name" value="gift certificates">
        <param name="Name" value="Certificate Workflow">
        <param name="Local" value="htm/cs_bd_orders_xygh.htm">
        </OBJECT>
<OBJECT type="text/sitemap">
        <param name="Name" value="gift certificates">
        <param name="Name" value="About">
        <param name="Local" value="htm/cs_bd_orders_iaaz.htm">
        </OBJECT>
```

Site Resource Modifications

The development team decided to add a new resource for system administrators to use to manage the databases in which gift certificate information is stored. They named this resource *Certificates*. The Certificates resource uses the Generic Properties dialog box as described in "Levels of Integration" in Commerce Server 2000 Help.

The only configuration information required for the Certificates resource is the connection string for the Certificates database. To add this resource, the development team created the SQL script CertificatesInit.sql, which they based on the SiteStatusInit.sql file included with the Commerce Server 2000 SDK. This SQL script makes the changes needed to include the Certificates resource in the Commerce Server Site Packager file (with a .pup extension) that the team used to move the finished site from the development environment to the test and production environments.

The following excerpt is from the CertificatesInit.sql script:

```
IF NOT EXISTS(SELECT s_ClassName FROM SystemProps WHERE s_ClassName = ''Certificates''
insert into SystemProps (s_Name, s_ClassName, s_ResourceType, f_ResourceFlags, f_PupFlag
s_ProgIDSnapin) VALUES
('''',''Certificates'',''Certficates'',6,0,''Shoesnet.CertResource'')

IF NOT EXISTS(SELECT s_PropertyName FROM ExtendedProps WHERE s_PropertyName =
''s_AppName'' )
insert into ExtendedProps VALUES
(''Certificates'',''s_AppName'',0,1,0,''Contoso'',8200,'''',''s_AppName'')
```

Site Page Modifications

The development team consulted the marketing team to decide on the best way to position the new gift certificate feature. They consulted the site designers to see how to best present it. This consultation concluded with the following decisions:

- The team added a Gift Certificate page on which customers can purchase new gift certificates.

- The marketing team created an advertisement for gift certificates to display to registered users who had previously purchased gift certificates. This advertisement was displayed on the home page.

- The link to the new Gift Certificate page appeared on the menu that is displayed on all pages, and the advertising banner included a click-through link to the Gift Certificate page.

- The team integrated purchases made with a gift certificate into the checkout process by including an option button on the Summary page.

- Gift certificates were added to the Contoso online catalog. These items included a **not-taxable** property that the tax component checked to calculate the tax for orders that include gift certificates.

Checkout Pipeline Modifications

The development team decided to create a new pipeline component, called **GiftCert**, to reduce the billing amount on the order form when a purchase is made with a gift certificate. They added this new pipeline component to the Payment stage of the Checkout pipeline. The following table summarizes the values read and values written by the **GiftCert** component (three values read and one value written).

Values read	Values written
certificate_code	Billing_amount
redemption_amount	
billing_amount	

COM Object Development

The development team identified the following requirements for a new COM object they created:

- Create a unique identifier for each new online certificate.

- Update the online and back-end databases with new balance information when a gift certificate is created or used to make a purchase.

The development team implemented the new COM object with the following attributes:

- It creates the unique identifier by first generating a globally unique identifier (GUID) and using a hashing algorithm to develop a four-digit alphanumeric code to append to the first four characters of the recipient's last name.

- It updates the back-end system asynchronously by calling a Host Integration Server connector object and passing in the sales and gift certificate information.

- It uses COM+ queuing.

- It implements the "Both" threading model and aggregates the **Free Threaded Marshaller** object.

Profile Modifications

The Contoso development team decided to create a new profile for the gift certificates. The gift certificate profile stores recipient identification, including the recipient's address. The profile is stored in Contoso's SQL Server database.

Report Modifications

The development team based the new dynamic reports on a SQL Server Analysis cube. The static report, Gift Certificate Buyers, is based on a SQL query. They also created a new cube named *Certificates*. The development team then created the Extensible Markup Language (XML) framework for the new dynamic reports, in the manner described in "Creating Dynamic Reports Using Cubes" in Commerce Server 2000 Help.

After adding the new Analysis cube and XML framework, the development team used the Analysis – New Dynamic OLAP Report.sql script provided in the SDK\Samples\Business Analytics\Scripts directory to add the report definition to their Commerce Server Data Warehouse.

The team also created the SQL script for generating the static reports, based on the example in "Creating Custom Reports" in Commerce Server 2000 Help.

Site Term Modifications

To display the Certificates advertisement to customers who previously purchased gift certificates, the development team added a new site term, called *Certificate Buyer*. They used the Site Terms Editor module in Business Desk to do this. The new site term has the properties listed in the following table.

Property	Values
Name	Certificate_Buyer
Display Name	Certificate Buyer
Term Names	No, Yes
Term Display Name	No, Yes

The development team mapped the new Certificate Buyer site term to one of the custom properties of the **User** object.

Campaign Modifications

The development team used the Campaigns modules in Business Desk to create a new advertising campaign for the gift certificates. The campaign contained a single house ad targeted to customers for whom the expression Certificate_Buyer = Yes evaluates to True. They added registered users to the Certificate_Buyer group by exporting the Gift Certificate Buyers static report to the List Manager module, and then targeting the certificates ad to this group. The click Uniform Resource Locator (URL) for this new advertisement is the Certificates page.

Deployment Summary

The Contoso development team used the tools listed in the following table to deploy and replicate the new gift certificate feature.

Feature elements	Deployment tool	Replication tool
New site pages	Site Packager	Microsoft Application Center 2000
New Business Desk modules	Site Packager	Application Center
New pipeline component	Setup program	Setup program
New database	Site Packager	SQL Server replication
New COM component	COM+ application	Application Center

After the team finished testing the new gift certificate feature, they deployed the changes in their production environment by packaging the new version of the site using Site Packager. This new package included the site pages, Business Desk modules, and site data. They created a Microsoft Windows Installer file to set up the new **GiftCert** pipeline component on the servers in their Web farm. Because the COM+ object is implemented as a COM+ Queued Component, they added the object to a COM+ application. This made it possible to use the Application Center Deployment Wizard to deploy the object to all of the servers in the Web farm. (For more information about using the Application Center Deployment Wizard, see Chapter 15, "Deploying Content.")

Profiling System Utilities

The profile schema for a Commerce Server site is stored and maintained in the Profiles database. By default, this database is named *<SiteName>*_COMMERCE when you unpack a site. A profile schema is a hierarchy made up of the following nodes:

```
Catalog
Business Object Profile
    Business Object Profile Attribute (to store Data Warehouse class name)
    Group
    Property
    Property Attribute
    Data Ref (to store linked Data Member name)
    Data Source
        Source Info (to store Data Source Partition settings such as default partition flag and
    connection string)
            Source Info Attribute
                Data Object
                Data Member
```

The root node is named Catalog, and you must have a minimum of two catalogs for the Profiling System in any Commerce Server site:

- Profile Definitions catalog

- Site Terms catalog

The nodes are provided by default in the Site Packager file for the Blank Solution Site. The Profile Definitions catalog stores the business object profile schemas, such as User Object, Address, and Organization, as well as the data source settings. The Site Terms catalog stores the site term definitions.

The Commerce Server 2000 Resource Kit CD contains the tools listed in the following table to help you develop profiles.

Tool	Description
Profiles Schema Mover	A compiled Microsoft Visual Basic application that enables you to define and configure the profile schema in one Commerce Server environment (such as your development environment), then migrate it to another (such as your test or production environment). You can also use this tool to change the data source connection strings for the target environment when you migrate the schema.
Site Terms Viewer	The Site Terms Viewer is a Visual Basic script that shows how to access site terms programmatically.

This section describes the architecture of these two tools and describes how to use the Profiles Schema Mover to import and export a profile schema.

Note The term *profile schema* represents the entire set of schemas for a site's Profiling System and does not denote the schema for an individual profile, such as user object, address, and organization, which represent the business entities of the site. Schemas for individual business entities are always called *business object profile schemas*.

Profiles Schema Mover

You use the Profiles Schema Mover tool to migrate the profile schema you configured in one Commerce Server site environment to another Commerce Server site environment.

Note The Profiles Schema Mover tool does not migrate the business object profile data or the physical database tables and Lightweight Directory Access Protocol (LDAP) classes used to store the business object profile data. It simply automates the process of manually creating the profile schema (profile definitions, data sources, and data members) using Commerce Server Manager.

If you create a data object or a data member through Commerce Server Manager, the specific database table/column or LDAP class/attribute is visible only to the Profiling System. You must create the necessary database tables or LDAP classes to expose them before you migrate the data objects and members.

Installation

The Profiles Schema Mover tool is a stand-alone application (.exe file), and there are no additional resource files or dynamic-link libraries (DLLs) that you need to install. To use it, copy the executable file to the server on which Commerce Server is installed.

The Profiles Schema Mover tool is written in Visual Basic and references the following type libraries:

- Microsoft Commerce 2000 Configuration Type Library

- Microsoft Commerce 2000 BizData Admin Type Library

- Microsoft XML, version 2.0

- Microsoft ActiveX Data Objects 2.5 Type Library

- Microsoft OLE DB Service Component 1.0 Type Library

- Active DS Type Library

    Note The type libraries provided by Commerce Server are automatically installed and registered on the server where Commerce Server is installed.

Operation

You run the Profiles Schema Mover tool on the server on which Commerce Server is installed because it must interact directly with the run-time services and components that Commerce Server provides. You must run the Profiles Schema Mover tool in the environment in which the profile schema is located. If you want to copy the profile schema from one environment to another, you must first run the Profiles Schema Mover tool in the source environment to export the schema, and then run the tool in the destination environment to perform the import.

Figure 9.1 shows the user interface (UI) for the Profiles Schema Mover tool.

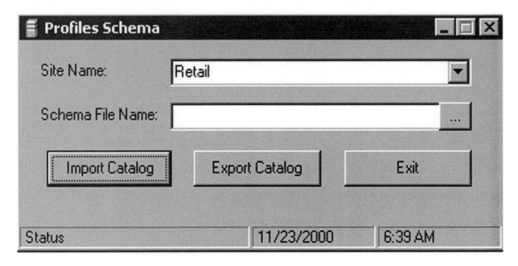

Figure 9.1 Profiles Schema dialog box

The following sections provide a detailed description of how to export and then import catalogs.

Exporting a Catalog

Clicking the Export Catalog button in the Profiles Schema dialog box shown in Figure 9.1 generates a single XML file describing the profile schema settings for the Commerce Server site selected in the Site Name box. The XML file generated follows the Commerce Server profiles XML schema format. To export a catalog, the tool does the following:

1. Obtains a list of sites.

2. Connects to the data store.

3. Obtains profile and data source names.

4. Obtains profile definitions.

5. Obtains the Site Terms catalog.

6. Saves the profile schema XML document.

Obtaining a List of Sites

The Site Name box in the Profiles Schema dialog box contains the names of sites found in the Administration database for the Commerce Server environment in which the Profiles Schema Mover tool is running. The tool obtains a list of sites by using the **Commerce.GlobalConfig** object to retrieve global configuration settings stored in the Administration database. The following code demonstrates how to retrieve the settings:

```
Dim oGlblCfg As New GlobalConfig
    Dim rsSites As New Recordset

    oGlblCfg.Initialize
    Set rsSites = oGlblCfg.Sites
    For Each Site In rsSites.Fields
        SitesList.AddItem Site.Name
    Next
```

The tool uses the **Commerce.SiteConfigReadOnly** object to access the site configuration
settings for the selected site. It calls the **Initialize** method of the
Commerce.SiteConfigReadOnly object to load the configuration settings for the site and site
resources from the Administration database and return them in the **Fields** property of the
SiteConfigReadOnly object instance.

The tool then reads this property and retrieves the connection string from the Profiles data
store (defined in the **_BizDataStoreConnectionString** property of the Profiles global
resource in Commerce Server Manager).

> **Important** The Profiles Schema Mover tool manipulates the site schema
> programmatically by using the **Commerce.BusinessDataAdmin** object (BDAO). The
> **Commerce.BusinessDataAdmin** object is provided in the Microsoft Commerce 2000
> BizData Admin Type Library (BizDataManager.dll), but is currently not documented.
>
> Using the **Commerce.BusinessDataAdmin** object to modify the profile schema is not
> supported; at this time the only supported approach for modifying the profile schema is to
> use the Profile Designer UI in either Commerce Server Manager or in Business Desk. The
> UI enforces the appropriate validation rules during the creation and modification of a
> profile schema. If you bypass these validation rules by using the
> **Commerce.BusinessDataAdmin** object, your profile schema may be corrupted,
> preventing your site's Profiling System from working properly.

Connecting to the Data Store

After the Profiles Schema Mover has obtained a connection string to the Profiles data store, it
calls the **Connect** method for the **Commerce.BusinessDataAdmin** object, passing in the
connection string to establish a connection to the data store. The following code demonstrates
how to connect to the data store:

```
Public Function LoadBDAO(sSiteName As String) As BusinessDataAdmin
  Dim objSiteCFG As New SiteConfigReadOnly
  Dim objBDAO As New BusinessDataAdmin
  Dim sDSN As String
  objSiteCFG.Initialize gSiteName
  sDSN = objSiteCFG.Fields("Biz Data_
                    Service").Value.Fields_
                    ("s_BizDataStoreConnectionString").Value_
                       objBDAO.Connect sDSN
  Set LoadBDAO = objBDAO
End Function
```

The **Commerce.BusinessDataAdmin** object interface exposes and describes the internal structure of the profile schema in XML format. The Microsoft Extensible Markup Language (MSXML) version 2.0 parser handles the XML Document Object Model (DOM) manipulation, though this can be changed to use the later version of the MSXML parser.

Obtaining Profile and Data Source Names

To export a profile schema from its data source, the Profiles Schema Mover tool first calls the **GetCatalog** method for the **Commerce.BusinessDataAdmin** object. This method returns an XML DOM object that contains a list of catalogs, as well as a list of business object profiles and data sources belonging to each of the catalogs, as defined in the following profile schema for the site:

```
Set objBDAO = LoadBDAO(gSiteName)
Set CatalogsDoc = objBDAO.GetCatalogs
```

For example, if you use the Profile Schema Mover tool to export a schema for the Retail Solution Site, the following XML would be returned:

```
<Document xmlns="urn:schemas-microsoft-com:bizdata-profile-schema">
    <Catalog name="Profile Definitions" displayName="Profile Catalog"
     description="Profile Definitions">
        <Profile name="Address" displayName="Address"
         description="Addresses"/>
        <Profile name="BlanketPOs" displayName="BlanketPOs"
         description="Blanket Purchase Orders"/>
        <Profile name="Organization" displayName="Organization"
         description="Organization Object"/>
        <Profile name="UserObject" displayName="User Object"
         description="User Object"/>
        <Profile name="TargetingContext" displayName="Targeting Context"
         description="CSF Targeting Context"/>
        <DataSource name="UPM_SQLSource"
         displayName="ProfileService_SQLSource" description="Source"
         sourceType="OLEDB-ANSI"/>
    </Catalog>
    <Catalog name="Site Terms" displayName="Site Terms">
        <Profile name="MSCommerce" displayName="Site Terms"
         description="Site Terms for Microsoft Commerce Server"
         isProfile="0"/>
    </Catalog>
</Document>
```

Obtaining Profile Definitions

The **GetCatalog** method returns only the Catalog node and its immediate child nodes, Profile and DataSource. To generate an XML document representing the entire definition of the profile schema, the tools adds the remaining child nodes (such as Group, Property, Attribute, Data Object, and Data Member) to the XML document. To do this, the Profiles Schema Mover tool iterates through each Profile node and retrieves all of its child nodes as well as the elements beneath the child nodes.

The tool obtains an XML DOM object representing each individual Profile node and its child nodes by calling the **GetProfile** method for the **Commerce.BusinessDataAdmin** object, passing in the Profile name. The profile is passed in the *<Catalog Name>*.*<Profile Name>* format (for example, Profile Definitions.Address). After a complete structure is obtained, the tool replaces each Profile node represented as `<Profile … />` in the XML DOM document obtained by the **BDAO.GetCatalog** method, as follows:

```
<Profile …>
    <Attribute …/>
    <Group …>
        <Property …>
            <DataRef …/>
            …
            <Attribute …/>
<Attribute …/>
            …
        </Property>
        <Property …>
            …
        </Property>
    </Group>
    <Group …>
        …
    </Group>
</Profile>
```

The Profiles Schema Mover tool performs the same operation on each DataSource node in the Profile Definitions catalog.

Obtaining the Site Terms Catalog

After the Profiles Schema Mover tool has obtained the catalog for each data source, it must process the Site Terms catalog to carry out the same operation on its Profile nodes. It uses the following code to do this:

```
' Process each catalog
Set Catalogs = CatalogsDoc.selectNodes("//Catalog")
  For Each Catalog In Catalogs
  ' Get the catalog name
    CatalogName = Catalog.getAttribute("name")

  ' Get each profile and add it to the XML document
    sProfileXSL = "//Catalog[@name='" & CatalogName & "']/Profile"
    Set Profiles = CatalogsDoc.selectNodes(sProfileXSL)
      For Each Profile In Profiles
          ProfileName = CatalogName & "." & Profile.getAttribute("name")
            Set ProfileDoc = objBDAO.GetProfile(CStr(ProfileName))
            Set ProfileNode = ProfileDoc.selectSingleNode("//Profile")
            Set NewChild = Catalog.replaceChild(ProfileNode, Profile)
      Next

  ' Get each data source and add it to the XML document
    sDataSourceXSL = "//Catalog[@name='" & CatalogName & "']/DataSource"
    Set Datasources = CatalogsDoc.selectNodes(sDataSourceXSL)
      For Each DataSource In Datasources
        DataSourceName = CatalogName & "." _
        & DataSource.getAttribute("name")
        Set DataSourceDoc = objBDAO.GetDataSource(CStr(DataSourceName))
        Set DataSourceNode =
          DataSourceDoc.selectSingleNode("//DataSource")
        Set NewChild = Catalog.replaceChild(DataSourceNode, DataSource)
      Next
  Next
```

Saving the Profile Schema XML Document

Finally, the Profiles Schema Mover tool calls the **CatalogsDoc.Save** method to save the profile schema XML document.

> **Note** The **Commerce.BusinessDataAdmin** object also exposes the method **ExportCatalog** to export the profile schema in XML format. This method works specifically with Site Packager to generate and package the profiles XML schema in a Site Packager file.
>
> For this reason, the **ExportCatalog** method includes the primary partition setting for the site data source, but leaves out the settings for any other partitions from the profiles XML schema it generates. The Profiles Schema Mover tool implements its own logic (described in the previous "Obtaining the Site Terms Catalog" topic) to include the settings for all

data source partitions and to export the complete "picture" of the site profile catalog in the generated profiles XML schema.

Importing a Catalog

When you click the Import Catalog button in the Profiles Schema dialog box shown previously in Figure 9.1, the selected profile schema settings for the Commerce Server site selected in the Site Name box are loaded. To import catalog code, the Profiles Schema Mover tool:

1. Loads and validates the XML document.

2. Selects a data source for the import.

Loading and Validating the XML Document

The Profiles Schema Mover tool parses the content of the selected file and loads it into the XML DOM object for processing. If the file loads properly, the tool next verifies that the loaded XML document is correctly formatted, by ensuring that the namespace Uniform Resource Identifier (URI) element of the loaded XML document is set to the following address: urn:scheams-microsoft-com:bizdata-profile-schema.

Before initiating the import process, you can use the Profiles Schema Mover tool to change the data source connection strings specified in the import profiles XML schema to match the configuration settings used in the target site environment. A data source connection string is specified in the *connStr* attribute of the **SourceInfo** element in the import profiles XML schema. In the partitioned data source environment, the **SourceInfo** element is created for each partition. The connection string attribute is also specified for each partition.

For example, you could represent the import profiles XML schema for a site with two SQL data sources and two partitions created on the first SQL data source, as follows:

```
<DataSource name="UPM_SQLSource" displayName="ProfileService_SQLSource" description="Source"
sourceType="OLEDB-ANSI">
<SourceInfo name="SQLSource_Partition1" isDefault="1" connStr="Provider=SQLOLEDB; Data
Source=CSITS;Initial Catalog=RETAIL_COMMERCE;User ID=SA;Password=;Extended
Properties=;Network Library=DBMSSOCN" />
<SourceInfo name="UPM_SQLSource_Partition2"
  connStr="Provider=SQLOLEDB.1;Password="";Persist Security Info=True;User
  ID=SA;Initial Catalog=RETAIL_COMMERCE2;Data Source=CSITS">
  <Attribute name="Username" displayName="" />
      <Attribute name="Password" displayName="" />
</SourceInfo>
...
</DataSource>
  <DataSource name="UPM_SQLSource2"
    displayName="ProfileService_SQLSource2" sourceType="OLEDB-ANSI">
...
</DataSource>
```

Selecting a Data Source for the Import

The Profiles Schema Mover tool iterates through each DataSource node in the import profiles XML schema, reads the connection string attribute (*connStr*) of each partition element under the DataSource node (**SourceInfo**), and then displays the results. Figure 9.2 shows how the Profiles Schema Mover tool displays the data sources.

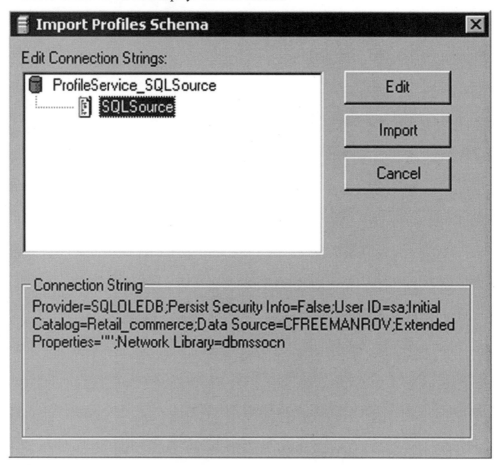

Figure 9.2 Import Profiles Schema dialog box

You can select a specific data source partition in the tree view control to display the connection string currently specified in the import profiles XML schema. Click the Edit button to open a dialog box in which you can edit the connection string for the selected data source partition.

The Profiles Schema Mover tool determines the appropriate dialog box to display, based on the type of data source (OLEDB-ANSI SQL source or LDAP directory) you select. The following code sample illustrates how the tool determines which dialog box to display:

```
Dim oDataLinks As DataLinks, oConn As ADODB.Connection
Dim SourceInfo As IXMLDOMElement, Source As IXMLDOMElement
...
Set SourceInfo = gXMLDoc.selectSingleNode("//DataSource[@name='" &
    sSourceName & "']/SourceInfo[@name='" & sSourceInfoName & "']")
  If Not SourceInfo Is Nothing Then
    sConnStr = SourceInfo.getAttribute("connStr")
    Set Source = SourceInfo.parentNode
    sSourceType = Source.getAttribute("sourceType")
      If StrComp("OLEDB-ANSI", sSourceType, vbTextCompare) = 0 Then
        Set oDataLinks = New DataLinks
        Set oConn = New ADODB.Connection
        oConn.ConnectionString = sConnStr
        oConn.Properties.Item("Persist Security Info").Value = True
        oDataLinks.hWnd = Me.hWnd
        'PROMPTAGAIN:
        If oDataLinks.PromptEdit(oConn) Then
          oConn.Properties.Item("Persist Security Info").Value = True
          sConnStr = oConn.ConnectionString

            If InStr(1,sConnStr,"Integrated Security", vbTextCompare) > 0 _        Then
               MsgBox "Windows NT Integrated security is not supported._
                 You_must use SQL Server authentication.  Use a specific_
                 user name and password.", vbCritical, "Profile schema"
                 'GoTo PROMPTAGAIN:
             End If
          SourceInfo.setAttribute "connStr", sConnStr
         End If
       ElseIf StrComp("LDAPv3", sSourceType, vbTextCompare) = 0 Then
         Set gXMLNode = SourceInfo DlgLDAP.Show 1, Me
       End If
     End If
 End If
```

After you have adjusted the data source connection strings in the import profiles XML schema to match the target Commerce Server site environment, you click the Import button in the Import Profiles Schema dialog box (Figure 9.2) to begin the import.

Once again, a programmatic manipulation of the site profile schema is done using the **Commerce.BusinessDataAdmin** object, and its **ImportCatalog** method is made available to update the profile schema by importing the XML document, as shown in the following code:

```
Dim objBDAO As New BusinessDataAdmin
...
Set objBDAO = LoadBDAO(gSiteName)
objBDAO.ImportCatalog gXMLFileName
```

Deployment Scenarios

The scenarios in this section describe how to migrate a profile schema from one site to another. Note that the term *Commerce Server environment* denotes one instance of Microsoft Windows 2000 Server on which Commerce Server is installed.

Migration Across Multiple Commerce Server Environments

In this scenario, two Commerce Server sites (Site A and Site B) are installed in two different Commerce Server environments. The Profiles Schema Mover tool is used to migrate the profile schema from Site A into the Profiles data source of Site B. The tool is installed in both Commerce Server environments. The installation in the environment of Site A is used to generate the profile XML schema file, and the installation in the environment of Site B is used to import the XML file into the Profiles data store of Site B. Figure 9.3 shows an example of migration across multiple Commerce Server environments.

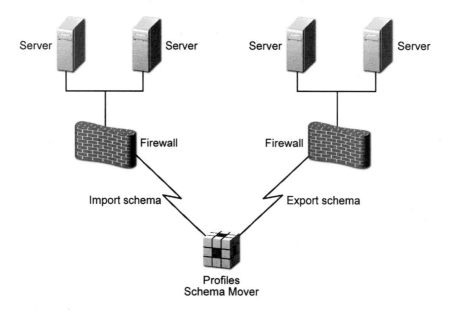

Figure 9.3 Migration across multiple Commerce Server environments

This scenario represents a project environment in which a site's profile schema is maintained in the development environment and any schema changes made in the development environment are then migrated to the other environments, such as the test environment, staging environment, and production environment.

The Profiles Schema Mover tool is especially useful if you make a large number of changes to the profile schema, because it eliminates the time you would otherwise have to spend applying the same changes manually in the different environments, using Commerce Server

Manager or Business Desk. The Profiles Schema Mover tool enables you to generate a single XML file that represents the entire profiles schema of the site, and then migrate the changes to multiple environments, without errors, by simply importing a XML file.

Migration Within a Single Commerce Server Environment

In this scenario, both Site A and Site B are installed in a single Commerce Server environment, thus sharing the same Administration database. This scenario is possible because each individual site in the Commerce Server environment has its own Profiles data store. Changing the profile schema for Site A does not impact the profile schema for Site B. In the Administration database, the global configuration data is maintained once and shared by both sites, but site configuration data, such as the connection string for the Profiles data store, is maintained separately for each site. Figure 9.4 shows migration within a single Commerce Server environment.

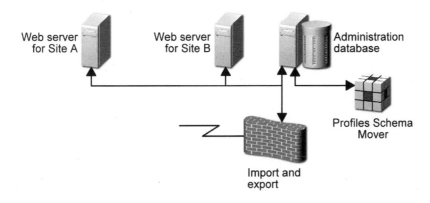

Figure 9.4 Migration within a single Commerce Server environment

Site Terms Viewer

The second tool provided in the Profiles Schema Manager directory of the Commerce Server 2000 Resource Kit CD is the Site Terms Viewer script. This script illustrates how you can programmatically access a site's profile schema and display a list of all site terms and their values at the command line.

The implementation of this script is relatively simple. The script reads a site name as an argument from the command line prompt. It then uses the **SiteConfigReadOnly** object to retrieve the connection string for the site's Profiles data source from the Administration database, and establishes a connection through the **Commerce.BusinessDataAdmin** object, as follows:

```
' Get the BDAO connection string
Set SiteCFG = CreateObject("Commerce.SiteConfigReadOnly")
SiteCFG.Initialize SiteName
ConnStr = SiteCFG.Fields("Biz Data _
Service").Value.Fields("s_BizDataStoreConnectionString").Value
' Create Biz Data Admin Object
Set BDAO = CreateObject("Commerce.BusinessDataAdmin")
BDAO.Connect ConnStr
```

The site terms settings are all stored in the Site Terms catalog node within the profile schema, and the **Commerce.BusinessDataAdmin** object accesses these settings using XML. By default, the Site Terms catalog contains one Profile node named *MSCommerce*, and each individual site term is defined as a single Property node under this Profile node. The values for each site term are then defined as attributes belonging to the corresponding Property node. Using the Retail Solution Site as an example, the Site Terms schema is represented as the following XML:

```
<Catalog name="Site Terms" displayName="Site Terms">
  <Profile name="MSCommerce" displayName="Site Terms" description="Site_
  Terms for Microsoft Commerce Server" isProfile="0">
    <Group name="UserSiteTerms" displayName="User Site Terms">
    <Property name="AccountStatus" displayName="Account Status"_
    description="Account Class" propType="STRING" isDefaultNull="0"_
    isExported="1" isRequired="1" isSearchable="1">
     <Attribute name="1" displayName="Active Account"_
       description="Active"_/>
     <Attribute name="0" displayName="Inactive Account"_
       description="Inactive" />
    </Property>
    <Property name="UserRole" displayName="User Role" description="User_
    Role" propType="STRING" isDefaultNull="0" isExported="1"_
    isRequired="1" isSearchable="1">
 ...

    </Property>
 ...

    </Group>
    <Group name="CalendarSiteTerms" displayName="Calendar Site Terms">
      ...
      </Group>
  </Profile>
</Catalog>
```

Using the **Commerce.BusinessDataAdmin** object, the Site Terms Viewer script retrieves the MSCommerce profile XML schema from the Site Terms catalog. Then the script iterates through each site term defined in the Property node of this profile, and displays each site term value defined in the Attribute node of each property, as shown in the following code:

```
' Get the Site Terms Catalog
Set SiteTermsXML = BDAO.GetProfile("Site Terms.MSCommerce")

' Get a list of the site terms and display them
Set Terms = SiteTermsXML.SelectNodes("//Property")
For Each Term in Terms
      wscript.echo Term.GetAttribute("displayName")
      Set Values = Term.SelectNodes("Attribute")
      For Each Value in Values
          wscript.echo "    " & Value.GetAttribute("displayName")
      Next
Next
```

To run the Site Terms Viewer script, use the **Cscript** command from the command line. The syntax for running the script is as follows:

```
cscript "<directory path>\SiteTerms.vbs" "<Site Name>"
```

For example, you might type the following command: `cscript "C:\SiteTerms.vbs" "Retail"`

Profiling System: Operational Considerations

This section describes the choices and caveats developers need to consider before they design and effectively use the Commerce Server Profiling System. It describes the following:

- Profile definition keys
- Design considerations
- Run-time considerations
- Ways to manage pre-existing accounts in Microsoft Active Directory stores
- User profile import Data Transformation Services (DTS) tasks

Profile Definition Keys

You must define one or more keys for every valid profile definition. You can identify unique, primary, join, and hashing keys by examining the **Key** type property in the Advanced Attributes section in the Profile Designer module of Business Desk or in the profile definition of the Profiles resource in Commerce Server Manager. This section describes how to define the following keys:

- Unique key
- Primary key
- Join key
- Hashing key

Unique Key

Every profile definition property marked as a key has the *Unique Key* attribute turned on. Only properties of **string** or **numeric** data types can be marked as keys. A profile definition can have any number of keys, although from a performance and memory perspective, it is better to have as few keys as possible.

All core profile object management operations in the Profiling System (**CreateProfile**, **GetProfile**, **GetProfileByKey**, **DeleteProfile**, **DeleteProfileByKey**) work with key members only. The Profiling System does not guarantee the uniqueness of properties that are marked as unique keys. Instead, it relies on constraints on objects in the underlying data stores (tables for relational databases or classes for directory stores) to implicitly enforce uniqueness.

Primary Key

Every profile definition must have exactly one unique key property marked as a primary key. You should mark the profile property most commonly used to operate on profile object instances as the primary key.

A primary key is identified by a red "P" or a green "D" (for a dual primary and join key) that precedes the property in the Profile Designer module of Business Desk or in the profile definition of the Profiles resource in Commerce Server Manager.

Join Key

Every profile definition must have exactly one unique key property marked as a join key. For optimal performance, you should also mark the primary key on the profile definition as the join key. If you don't provide a value for the join key property when you create the profile object, then the Profiling System automatically generates a value for this member.

A join key is identified by either a blue "J" or a green "D" (for a dual primary and join key) that precedes the property in the Profile Designer module of Business Desk or in the profile definition of the Profiles resource in Commerce Server Manager. The Profiling System uses the join key property to assemble profile object fragments stored in multiple data stores. Join key property values are replicated across all data stores.

Note After the join key property has been committed to the underlying stores, it can't be updated.

Hashing Key

Every profile definition can have one unique key property marked as the hashing key. The profile aggregation layer uses the hashing key property to hash a profile object to a unique partition within a data source. The presence of a hashing key property is the only way to indicate that instances of a profile definition will be stored across multiple partitions of a data source. The absence of this property results in all profile instances being stored in the default partition.

You should mark the join key on the profile definition as the hashing key. For optimal performance, you should mark the same property as the primary key, the join key, and the hashing key.

You can identify a hashing key by examining the Advanced Attributes/Hashing key in the Profile Designer module of Business Desk or in the profile definition of the Profiles resource in Commerce Server Manager.

Note After the profile object has been committed to the underlying stores, the hashing key property value can't be updated.

Important For partitioned ANSI SQL stores only, profile object retrieval operations based on a non-hashing key and the **GetInfo** method of the **ProfileObject** object could fail. However, this is not true for LDAP version 3-compliant stores.

Figure 9.5 displays the Key type drop-down box and the Hashing key check box.

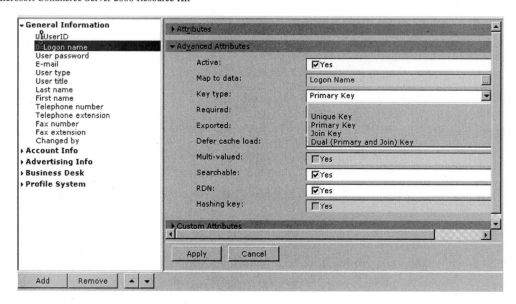

Figure 9.5 Profile definition keys

Profiling System Design Considerations

This section describes the following considerations for designing effective profile definitions:

- Keys
- Recommended data type mappings
- Other considerations

Keys

Choosing the appropriate key members can help you maximize the performance of the Profiling System. To effectively define keys in the profile definition, answer the following questions, and then use the table to find the corresponding guideline.

- **Question 1**. Should the primary key property be updateable after the object has been committed to the underlying stores?

- **Question 2**. Should the data be partitioned within a data source?

Guideline	Question 1	Question 2
Use the same property as the primary key and the join key.	No	No
Use the same property as the primary key, the join key, and the hashing key. This configuration maximizes the performance of Profiling System operations in partitioned scenarios.	No	Yes
Do not use the same property as the primary key and the join key.	Yes	No
Do not use the same property as the primary key and the join key. However, use the same property as the join key and the hashing key. This configuration provides sub-optimal performance for profile object operations based on a non-hashing (or non-join) key property.	Yes	Yes

Recommended Data Type Mappings

The following tables list the recommended mappings between Profiling System data types and the data types supported by SQL Server, Oracle, Active Directory, and Membership Directory.

ANSI SQL Stores

Profiling System data type	SQL Server data type	Oracle data type
BOOL	smallint	number
NUMBER	int	number
FLOAT	float	number
STRING/PROFILE/PASSWORD/ SITETERM	nvarchar	nvarchar2
CURRENCY	money	number
DATETIME/DATE/TIME	datetime	date
BINARY	varbinary	raw
LONGTEXT	ntext	nclob
IMAGE	image	blob

LDAP-v3 Stores

Profiling System data type	Active Directory data type	Membership Directory data type
BOOL	boolean	integer
NUMBER	integer	integer
STRING/PROFILE/ PASSWORD/SITETERM	string (Unicode)	UnicodeString
CURRENCY	LargeInteger	integer
DATETIME	string (GeneralizedTime)	generalizedTime
BINARY	string (Octet)	binary
LONGTEXT	string (Unicode)	UnicodeString
IMAGE	string (Octet)	binary

Note For ANSI SQL stores, the Profiling System supports multi-values only for the **string** data type. For LDAP-v3 stores, the Profiling System supports multi-values for all data types, except **longtext** and **image** data types.

Other Considerations

The following table describes other items you should consider to define effective profile definitions.

Design consideration	Description
Restrictions on **WHERE** clauses	OLE DB Provider for Commerce Server requires that all properties in the **WHERE** clauses of queries passed to it map to the same underlying store. This restriction becomes important when you design profile definitions that aggregate data across multiple data objects.
Non-encrypted storage	The Profiling System does not store any properties in encrypted format in the underlying data stores. If you want to restrict access to data, you must consider storing sensitive data in secure data stores such as Active Directory.
Data size limitations	For a detailed description of each of the data types exposed by the Profiling System, see "Profile Definition Components," located in the following path "Administering Commerce Server/Running the Profiles Resource/About the Profiles Resource/Profile Definitions/" in Commerce Server 2000 Help.
Valid characters in object names	Profile definition object names such as **ProfileDefinitionName**, **ProfilePropertyName**, and so on, can contain only alphanumeric characters and the underscore (_) character.

Profiling System Run-Time Considerations

This section describes the following Profiling System run-time considerations:

- CSOLEDB handles
- Accessing properties
- Transaction support
- Data size validation

CSOLEDB Handles

You must always store handles to the Profiling System and OLE DB Provider for Commerce Server at application scope. You should do this because the CSOLEDB handles were designed so that they create an object once in the Global.asa file, store the object at application scope, and then use the object on every ASP page. The CSOLEDB handles coordinate the concurrency issues that arise from processing multiple queries simultaneously. They also manage the fault-tolerance of connections to underlying stores for reliable query processing.

Accessing Properties

The Profiling System provides a number of mechanisms to access profile object properties. For example, the following are different ways of accessing the **GeneralInfo.user_id** property of a **ProfileObject** object named **oUser**:

- Access using standard Microsoft ActiveX Data Objects (ADO) notation:

```
oUser.Fields.Item("GeneralInfo").Value.Item("user_id").Value
oUser.Fields("GeneralInfo").Value("user_id").Value
```

- Access using extended dot notation:

```
oUser.Fields("GeneralInfo.user_id"
```

- Access using smart dispatch notation:

```
oUser.GeneralInfo.user_id
```

The performance difference between these options is insignificant.

Transaction Support

The Profiling System, by default, does not transact write operations across multiple data stores. More specifically, it does not support executing a two-phase commit protocol across transactional data stores.

The Profiling System provides loose support for transactions. The data aggregation layer brackets INSERT, UPDATE and DELETE data store operations that aggregate across multiple stores in a transaction, and commits them only after all data store operations have succeeded against non-transactional data stores (such as directory stores).

You can enable loose support by creating a custom attribute named *IsTransactioned* in the profile definition and setting it to "True." If this attribute is absent or you set it to "False," this feature is disabled.

Figure 9.6 shows the *IsTransactioned* custom attribute being added to the UserObject profile in the profile definition of the Profiles resource in Commerce Server Manager.

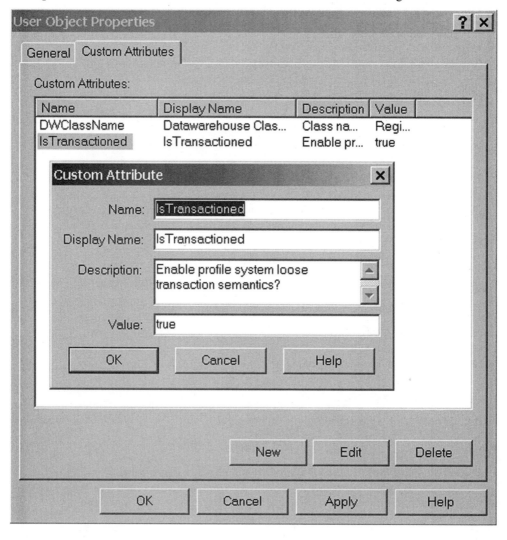

Figure 9.6 IsTransacted custom attribute

Data Size Validation

The Profiling System does not perform any data size validations, and depends on the underlying data stores to perform the validation.

Managing Pre-Existing Accounts in Active Directory Stores

To leverage pre-existing accounts in Active Directory, you must configure the search container and search scope of Active Directory data sources appropriately. Configuring the search container and search scope correctly enables the Profiling System to find the pre-existing accounts for directory operations such as object creation and object retrieval. At the beginning of every search operation, the Profiling System determines the starting container for the search operation and whether it should perform a one-level search or a sub-tree search.

This section describes the following:

- Starting container for directory operations

- Search scope

Starting Container for Directory Operations

The Profiling System provides three levels of support for defining the starting search container:

- **ParentDN**

- *DefaultParentURL*

- *Parent URL*

These levels are arranged in a hierarchy that determines the precedence for searching. The following three topics are arranged according to this hierarchy.

ParentDN

The **ParentDN** property is optionally added to the profile definition to specify the distinguished name (DN) of the starting search container. If used, this property allows the container to be specified for an individual profile and overrides the settings for the *DefaultParentURL* and *Parent URL* attributes. Specifying this property provides the most granular level of control.

DefaultParentURL

The *DefaultParentURL* attribute is added as a custom attribute to the profile definition, as shown in the following figure. The value of this attribute is relative to the *defaultNamingContext* custom attribute specified for the data source. This value is used as the starting search container for all profiles (of this definition type) that do not have a different value specified in a **ParentDN** property. This attribute overrides the *Parent URL* attribute. Figure 9.7 shows the *DefaultParentURL* attribute being added to the UserObject profile.

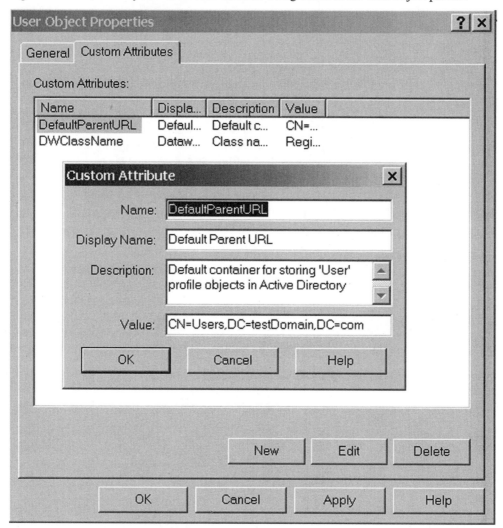

Figure 9.7 DefaultURL custom attribute

Parent URL

You can configure the *Parent URL* attribute through the System Attributes tab in the Properties dialog box for the LDAP data source that is using the Profiles resource of Commerce Server Manager. The value of this attribute is the DN of the starting search container. Figure 9.8 shows the *Parent URL* attribute being added.

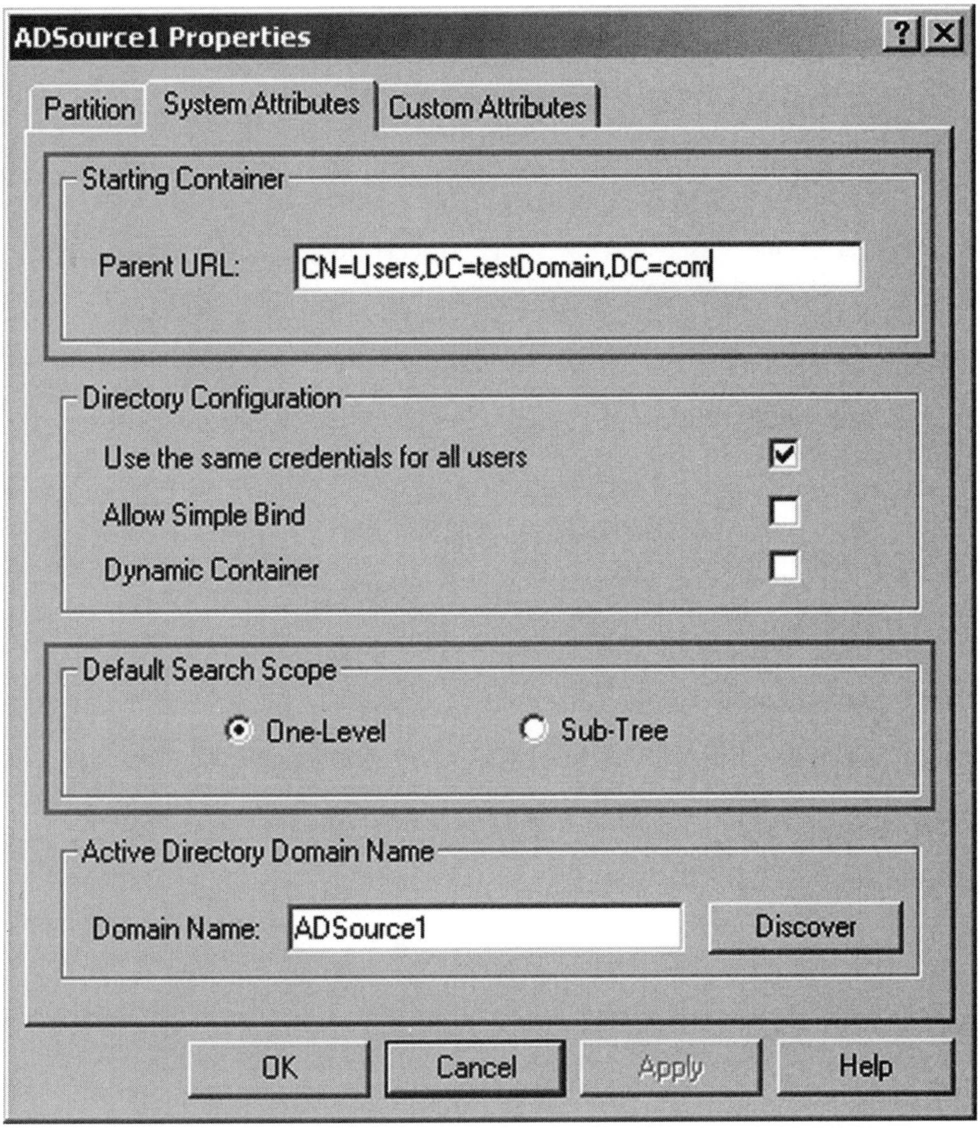

Figure 9.8 Parent URL and default search scope

As an example, assume that existing accounts are stored in the CN=Users,DC=testDomain,DC=com directory path. One way to direct the Profiling System to read accounts from this container is to set the *Parent URL* attribute of the Active Directory data source to CN=Users,DC=testDomain,DC=com. The Profiling System will perform all subsequent directory operations against this container unless overridden by the *DefaultParentURL* attribute or the **ParentDN** property.

Search Scope

The search scope depends on whether the client operation is a bulk operation (invoking a SELECT query against an OLE DB Provider) or a single-instance operation (invoking the **GetProfile** method of the **ProfileService** object). Bulk operations always set the search scope to sub-tree (sub-directories of the specified *Parent URL* attribute are also searched). Single instance operations default to one-level search scope (sub-directories are not searched). You can configure the client operation as sub-tree search scope using the Profiles resource of Commerce Server Manager, as shown in the preceding figure.

User Profile Import DTS Task

The User profile data import DTS task imports profile data into the Data Warehouse. By default, this DTS task imports only the Address and UserObject profiles.

Importing New Profile Types

To import other profiles supplied by Commerce Server, or new custom profiles, use the Profiles resource in Commerce Server Manager to add the custom attribute, *DWClassName*, to the profile definition. The value of the *DWClassName* attribute is the name of the class in the Data Warehouse where the profile data will be imported. A property named **date_last_changed** must also be defined for the profile if it will be imported.

To specify the data members of a profile to be imported, use the Profile Designer module in Business Desk to select the Exported check box in the Advanced Attributes section for each property to be imported. By default, the property is imported into a data member of the same name. To specify a different data member in the Data Warehouse class, add the attribute, *DWMemberName*, to the property in the Custom Attributes section of the Profile Designer module.

When you create a new profile type, you must also create a source table with matching properties, in addition to specifying the profile data source and the profile definition. You do not have to explicitly create the destination class and data members in the Data Warehouse. When the User profile data import DTS task is run, it automatically creates these, if they do not already exist, based on the two custom attributes specified earlier.

Profile Mappings

The following tables list the source to destination mappings for the Address and UserObject profiles.

Address Profile

Address profiles are stored in the Addresses table in the Commerce Server database. By default, the Addresses table (source) is mapped to the **Address** class (destination) in the Data Warehouse.

Source column	Source data type	Destination column	Destination data type
g_address_id	nvarchar (510)	Id	uniqueidentifier (16)
i_address_type	int (4)	AddressType	int (4)
u_address_name	nvarchar (510)	AddressName	varchar (255)
u_city	nvarchar (510)	City	varchar (255)
u_country_code	nvarchar (510)	CountryCode	varchar (255)
u_country_name	nvarchar (510)	CountryName	varchar (255)
u_first_name	nvarchar (510)	FirstName	varchar (255)
u_last_name	nvarchar (510)	LastName	varchar (255)
u_postal_code	nvarchar (510)	PostalCode	varchar (255)
u_region_code	nvarchar (510)	RegionCode	varchar (255)
u_region_name	nvarchar (510)	RegionName	varchar (255)
u_tel_extension	nvarchar (510)	TelephoneExtension	varchar (255)
u_tel_number	nvarchar (510)	TelephoneNumber	varchar (255)
d_date_created	datetime (8)	DateCreated	datetime (8)
d_date_last_changed	datetime (8)	DateLastChanged	datetime (8)

UserObject Profile

UserObject profiles are stored in the UserObject table in the Commerce Server database. By default, the UserObject table (source) is mapped to the **RegisteredUser** class (destination) in the Data Warehouse.

Source column	Source data type	Destination column	Destination data type
g_user_id	nvarchar (510)	UserId	varchar (255)
i_user_type	int (4)	UserType	int (4)
u_first_name	nvarchar (510)	FirstName	varchar (255)
u_last_name	nvarchar (510)	LastName	varchar (255)
u_email_address	nvarchar (510)	Email	varchar (255)
u_tel_number	nvarchar (510)	TelephoneNumber	varchar (255)
d_date_registered	datetime (8)	DateRegistered	datetime (8)
i_account_status	int (4)	AccountStatus	int (4)
d_date_created	datetime (8)	DateCreated	datetime (8)
d_date_last_changed	datetime (8)	DateLastChanged	datetime (8)

Advertising Scoring and Selection

The advertising selection engine in Commerce Server uses the Content Selection Framework (CSF). At the center of the framework are pipeline objects that describe a linear ordering of stages and components used in content selection: loading, filtering, initial scoring, scoring, selecting, recording, and formatting. This section focuses on the scoring and selection stages of the Advertising pipeline, which is included with the Commerce Server Solution Sites.

> **Note** The information in this section applies to the default Advertising pipeline configuration and might not be applicable if you have reconfigured or replaced the standard components in the pipeline.

Commerce Server supports the delivery of two main types of advertisements: house ads and paid ads. The key difference between these ads is that paid ads are *goaled*—that is, a certain number of impressions, clicks, or other events must be served within a given time period. A house ad, on the other hand, is assigned a *weight* that controls how frequently it should be delivered relative to all other house ads active in the system. Paid ads take priority and are served until they begin to run ahead of their goals, at which time house ads are also served. You can determine how paid ads are selected by adjusting their goals, while house ads are selected based on the probabilities and random number generation that determine their weight. You target both paid ads and house ads to site users in the same ways.

Campaign Goals and Item Goals

When you create an advertising campaign in Business Desk, you must specify whether the advertisements should be goaled at the advertisement item level or at the campaign level (campaign-goaled is the default). With campaign goaling, you must specify the total number of events (impressions, clicks, or other events, such as downloads) to serve across all advertising items in the campaign. Then for each advertising item, you specify a weight. The weight is considered relative to the weights of all other advertising items in the campaign. The total number of events scheduled for the campaign is distributed to the advertising campaign items in the campaign based on their weights, and each item then runs using those goals. In contrast, for item-goaled campaigns, you specify the number of events scheduled for each ad item in the campaign independently.

For example, if Contoso, Ltd. created a campaign to show advertisements for a brand of shoes, this campaign might have a goal of displaying 1,000 advertisements over a two-week period. If the campaign were made up of 10 different advertisements, all 10 advertisements would be displayed 100 times each during the two weeks. Contoso could also set a goal for each advertisement to be displayed 100 times during the two-week period. The first example is campaign-goaled, while the second is item-goaled.

You can change the way a campaign is goaled at any time. If you turn an item-goaled campaign into a campaign-goaled campaign, the number of events scheduled for each ad is used to derive the item weights and vice-versa.

Initial Scoring

Advertisements that have passed through the filter stage of the Advertising pipeline require scores to be assigned. Scoring is actually split into two pipeline stages, one to assign the initial score to each advertisement, and one to augment those scores by applying multipliers (targeting).

For house ads, the initial score for each ad is simply the assigned weight for the house ad. The weight for each ad is relative to the weights of all the other house ads. For example, if there are three house ads in the system, two with a weight of 1 and one with a weight of 2, then all else being equal, the first two ads will have a 25 percent chance of being served and the second ad will have a 50 percent chance of being served. Of course, targeting may change the scores before the selection stage is reached, thus altering the probabilities.

Paid ads are assigned an initial score based on how the ad is performing against its goals. The goal is the number of events (impressions, clicks, sold events, or others) that should be served in a given amount of time. This calculation is referred to as Need of Delivery (NOD). The basic formula for this calculation is:

```
Need of Delivery =    (Events Scheduled / Time Periods Total)/
                      (Events Served / Time Periods Elapsed)
```

Need of Delivery represents the ratio of the scheduled delivery rate (average events / sec over the entire run) compared to the actual delivery rate observed so far. A Need of Delivery score greater than 1.0 means the ad is running behind schedule, while a score less than 1.0 means the ad is ahead of schedule. Because all ads are scored using this same formula, the result is a fair distribution in the overall delivery of paid ads. If the ad inventory is oversold (that is, more events are scheduled during a given period than can actually be delivered), then all the ads should under-deliver on their goals proportionally.

Notice that this formula is undefined when no time periods have yet elapsed or when no events have yet been served. You can avoid the first situation by assuming one time period has already elapsed even though it hasn't, as the **CSFNeedOfDelivery** component uses seconds as the time period. To avoid the second situation, when no events have yet been served, you should set the Need of Delivery to a very large number (such as one million) to force an initial delivery event. After that first event has been served, the ad will subsequently be scored using the formula.

The **NeedOfDelivery** component is also responsible for ensuring that the ad is currently active. That is, if the ad has time of day or day of week schedule restrictions, then it is scored to zero if it is currently outside of those times.

If a Content Selection pipeline does not have any component in the initial scoring stage, then each advertisement is assigned an initial score of 1.0.

Scoring (Targeting)

Scoring in a Content Selection pipeline means applying multipliers to the ad item scores. A multiplier greater than 1.0 will increase the likelihood of the ad being selected, while a multiplier less than 1.0 will decrease it. You can disqualify an advertisement entirely by applying a multiplier of zero. The scoring components in a standard Advertising pipeline are the **CSFEValTargetGroups** and **CSFHistoryPenalty** components.

A *target group* is a collection of expression-action pairs. With the exception of the *Sponsor* action, each action corresponds to a pair of multipliers. One multiplier is applied if the expression evaluates to True, and the other is applied if the expression evaluates to False. The default multipliers are listed in the following table.

Action	Multiplier
Target	True 1.2
	False 1.0
Require	True 1.0
	False 0.0
Exclude	True 0.0
	False 1.0
Sponsor	True 1.0 (exclusive)
	False 0.0 (not configurable)

The *Require* and *Exclude* actions are filters that disqualify an ad if the filter isn't met. The *Target* action, on the other hand, is fuzzier. It will increase the advertisement's score if the expression evaluates to True, but will not affect the score if it evaluates to False. You can change any of these multipliers (with the exception of the *Sponsor* action) in the Pipeline Editor module using the property page of the **EvalTargetGroups** component. For example, you might want to change the *Target* action so that it decreases the score of advertisements for which a targeted expression result is False by using a multiplier such as 0.85.

The *Sponsor* action is a little different. Sponsorships are used to give an ad or set of ads exclusive access to the target. If for any given ad request one or more ads have a sponsorship expression that evaluates to True, then only those ads that have a sponsorship expression that evaluates to True will be eligible for selection on that request. Sponsorships are common in the advertising industry. An advertiser may pay a premium to sponsor your site's home page, for example, and the ads for that advertiser should be the only ones eligible for selection on that page.

If more than one target group is associated with an advertisement, then the target group that evaluates to the largest multiplier is the one that is actually applied. You can think of this as a logical "Or" operation on the target groups (target group one .OR. target group two .OR. target group three, and so on). An important consideration to keep in mind is that *Require* and *Exclude* actions apply only to the target group(s) they appear in and will not prevent the ad from being displayed if the ad is also targeted using other target groups that evaluate to a non-zero multiplier. However, when any sponsorship expression result is True, then all ads and target groups without a sponsorship expression are automatically scored to zero.

The **CSFHistoryPenalty** component assigns a penalty to ads that have recently been selected for the current user in order to avoid "banner-burnout." The more recently an advertisement has been selected, the greater the penalty. You can specify the number of recent ads to be penalized and the range of penalties to apply using the property page of the **CSFHistoryPenalty** component.

The **CSFHistoryPenalty** component also enforces exposure limits. An exposure limit is the maximum number of times an advertisement can be shown to a given user. Whether this is a session limit or a persistent user limit depends on how you store the history string.

To use the **CSFHistoryPenalty** component, you must ensure that the **CSFLoadHistory**, **CSFRecordHistory**, and **CSFSaveHistory** components are also in the pipeline and configured appropriately. **CSFLoadHistory** and **CSFSaveHistory** allow you to select a means of storing the user history. This history is stored in a string that contains a comma-delimited list of the advertisement IDs of ads already displayed to the user (oldest first). The maximum length of the history string (in ad IDs) can be specified on the property page of the **CSFRecordHistory** component. If you want this history string to be persisted across user sessions, you should configure **CSFLoadHistory** and **CSFSaveHistory** to use the UserProfile option. If session history strings meet your requirements, you can use either the HTTP Cookie or ASP Session options, as appropriate. A final option is to create a custom implementation of persisting the history strings and to remove the **CSFLoadHistory** and **CSFSaveHistory** components from the pipeline.

Selection

After the initial scoring and targeting is complete, the selection stage of the Advertising pipeline is reached and the **CSFSelectWinners** component is run to pick the winning ad or ads. The **CSFSelectWinners** component determines whether to serve a paid ad or a house ad based on the maximum Need of Delivery for all paid ads not disqualified for a request. If the maximum Need of Delivery is greater than the threshold value, then the component serves a paid ad; otherwise it serves a house ad.

The threshold value is 0.95 by default and corresponds to all advertisements being at least 5 percent ahead of their goals before a house ad is served. You can configure this threshold using the property page of the **CSFSelectWinners** component. If you find, for example, that your ad campaigns are falling short of their goals but house ads are being mixed in during the ad runs, then you might want to lower the threshold score so that ads must be farther ahead of their goals before any house ads are mixed in.

After the **CSFSelectWinners** component determines a paid ad should be served, it selects the ad with the highest score. However, if a house is to be served, then the scores of all house ads are taken to be relative probabilities and the winner is selected randomly based on those probabilities. For example, if a house ad is to be served and there are three house ads with scores of 1.0, 2.0, and 3.0, then the ads will have selection probabilities of 17 percent (1/6), 33 percent (2/6), and 50 percent (3/6) respectively.

Note that if there are no eligible house ads and no eligible paid ads with a Need of Delivery above the specified threshold, then paid ads with Needs of Delivery less than the threshold will be eligible for selection.

Ad selection also takes into account a **PageHistory** string. The **PageHistory** string is a comma-delimited list of the ad IDs of those ads that were already selected on the page. This string is used to prevent the same ad from being selected multiple times on the same page when more than one call to the **GetContent** method is made on that page. The **PageHistory** string is also used to avert industry collision, which is defined as ads from different advertisers who are in the same industry appearing on the same page. (To prevent this, you specify a tag describing an ad's industry at the time you create the ad.)

Troubleshooting Ad Scoring and Selection

The file TraceScores.asp in the path SDK\Samples\Marketing\Debug in the Commerce Server 2000 SDK, contains a routine that, when used together with trace mode enabled (CSO.Trace = True), produces trace information showing the final score for each ad along with all of the score modifications made to each ad. This information, together with an understanding of how the **SelectWinners** component chooses ads to serve, is useful in troubleshooting and debugging ad selection problems on your site.

For more information about the TraceScoresasp file, see "Ads or discounts do not appear on the Web site" in the "Troubleshooting Commerce Server" section of Commerce Server 2000 Help.

Integrating Third-Party ERP Systems with Commerce Server Applications

Integrating Microsoft Commerce Server 2000 with existing Enterprise Resource Planning (ERP) systems, such as SAP, J.D. Edwards OneWorld®, PeopleSoft, and other corporate systems, is often critical to successfully implementing a Commerce Server application. E-Commerce data and business rules often exist on the ERP system. For accuracy and consistency, data and business rules residing on the ERP system need to be accessible from the Commerce Server application or copied (mirrored) to the Commerce Server application.

This chapter describes several techniques for making ERP data available to Commerce Server applications, including batch downloads, real-time connectors, queued connectors, and mirrored updates. The technique you choose depends on the requirements of your site, the availability and performance of your ERP system, and the availability of the different types of integration connectors available to your ERP system.

Figure 10.1 shows a common high-level architecture for integrating an ERP system with a Commerce Server application.

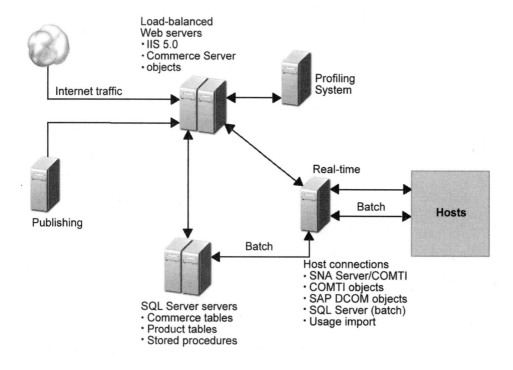

Figure 10.1 Sample physical architecture for integrating an ERP system with a Commerce Server application

E-commerce data, such as the following, often exists on the ERP system and must be made accessible to the Commerce Server application:

- Customer data

- Product catalog date (including SKU numbers, vendor information, and availability)

- Product inventory levels

- Pricing data

- Order status and history

Additionally, algorithms and business rules, such as the following, usually exist on the ERP system and must also be made accessible to the Commerce Server application:

- Taxation rules
- Credit card processing policies
- Product authorization rules
- Pricing algorithms
- Shipping algorithms

Finally, data from the Commerce Server application, such as the following, must be sent back to the ERP System:

- Customer orders

- Web customer profiles and customer updates

It is important to decide which system should own the data; in most cases, it will probably be the ERP system.

Integration Techniques

There are four common techniques for integrating data on ERP and Commerce Server applications:

- Batch downloads

- Real-time connectors

- Queued connectors

- Mirrored updates

Batch Downloads

Using a batch download is a common technique for copying ERP-managed data from an ERP system to a Commerce Server application. Batch downloads often work well for the product catalog, customer data, and pricing data, and can also work well for inventory and order-status data. Fundamental to this technique is the idea that the ERP system owns the data.

On a regular (usually nightly) basis, the subset of data needed by the Commerce Server application is deleted from the Commerce Server application and refreshed with data from the ERP system. To accomplish this, you must extract the required data from a specific ERP system and copy it to the Commerce Server application. If you are using the Commerce Server Product Catalog System, you will probably use the Product Catalog objects and other objects to do this. If you aren't using the Product Catalog System, you can import data directly into Microsoft SQL Server tables using the Bulk Copy Program (BCP) or Data Transformation Services (DTS).

Figure 10.2 shows how data is extracted from an ERP system and copied to high-end SQL Server servers used by the Commerce Server application.

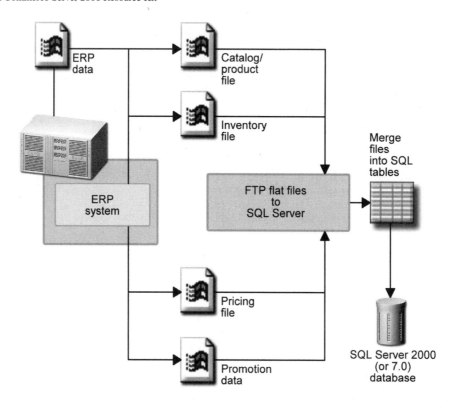

Figure 10.2 Transferring data from an ERP system to a SQL Server database

Depending on the volume of data and the hardware you use to perform batch downloads, the transfer process can take from a few minutes to several hours. To keep the Commerce Server application available while the download is in progress, you should deploy two versions of the Commerce Server application database: the *online* version and the *offline* version.

If you do this, the Commerce Server application can direct all processing to the online database while the batch download is taking place. When the scheduled extract of ERP data is finished, you can begin the Commerce Server data import process and direct it to the offline database. When the update is complete, you update a global variable in the Commerce Server application to direct all processing to the offline database. The offline (updated) database then becomes the new online database and the target of Commerce Server application requests. The former online database becomes the new offline database, which is the target of the next download. Thus, by alternating between the two databases, you can ensure that your application is available even when the nightly batch downloads are in progress.

Figure 10.3 shows how you can increase system availability during a batch download by using two copies of the database, designating one as "online" for processing requests and the other as "offline" for batch updates. When the update is complete, you use a global variable to switch the two databases.

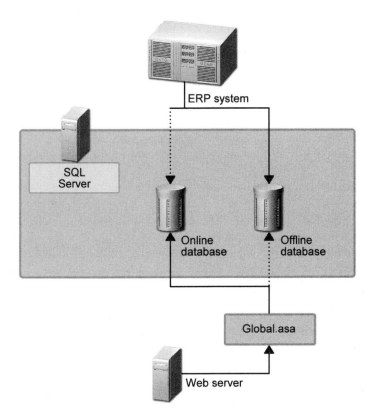

Figure 10.3 Using two copies of the database to ensure system availability

The batch download is one of the most popular techniques for synchronizing data between an ERP system and a Commerce Server application. Consider the following points if you decide to use the batch download technique:

- You usually have to write custom scripts to export the subset of data needed by the Commerce Server application from the ERP system and import it into the Commerce Server application.

- The batch download technique is relatively straightforward and, if you incorporate the online/offline database strategy, you can update at any time, while still keeping the Commerce Server application available at all times.

- The batch load technique minimizes the performance burden on the ERP system. Because the data extract causes a measurable increase in processing on the ERP system, you can minimize its impact by scheduling the data extract during a time of low activity.

- Using the batch load technique separates the Commerce Server application from the performance or maintenance schedule of the ERP system and separates the ERP system from the processing requests of the Commerce Server application.

- The batch load technique works well for data that becomes stale slowly, or at least remains valid for the period between data refreshes.

  Product and pricing data usually must be updated only once in a 24-hour period.

  Product inventory data might need to be updated more often. For example, a customer who is ordering a software package is reassured by seeing an inventory level of 231 copies available as of 4 A.M. that morning and completes the order. But, if only 7 copies were available at 4 A.M., the same customer, believing that the software is likely to be sold out, might decide to check availability on another site. Items that have been restocked since the last update would still appear at their low, pre-restock levels until the next nightly batch download.

- If you have data that becomes stale quickly, you can conduct full data downloads nightly and conduct incremental downloads more frequently.

  For example, you can download the entire product catalog, pricing, and inventory data nightly, but update inventory data every hour. Although some data still might become stale between downloads, discrepancies will be much smaller using this technique.

- You can combine ERP data with data from other external sources before downloading it to the Commerce Server application in one batch.

  For example, you might want to combine ERP catalog data with product images, technical specifications, customer testimonials, or cross-sell data.

- You can simplify the batch download and achieve greater scalability if you put the data to be downloaded into a separate database, to be treated as read-only by the Commerce Server application. Doing this enables the batch load scripts to send all database tables to the offline database without doing any other data transfers.

Of all the techniques described in this chapter, the batch download technique is probably the fastest and easiest way to begin integrating your systems. The batch download technique also enables you to better control system security by limiting access between the DMZ connected to the firewall and the corporate network to the single ERP integration server, rather than opening access to all of the production servers. You should use a separate server to drive the process, rather than adding batch processing to the load on the production servers.

You can write an application in Microsoft Visual Basic that you schedule to run through the SQL Executive on the server you use to manage the data transfer process (the "ERP integration server"). This application should do the following:

- Move required data from the ERP system to the Commerce Server application. This includes:

  - Transferring data files from the hosts and Microsoft Windows 2000-based servers using the File Transfer Protocol (FTP). You can use the Internet Transfer Control to do this.

  - Using BCP functions (taken from the DB-Library for Visual Basic) to transfer data from text files into SQL Server. You can also use the DTS included in SQL Server 7.0 or SQL Server 2000 to do this. For more information about DTS, see http://microsoft.com/sql.

  - Starting SQL Server stored procedures for data processing.

  - Changing ASP global application variables or the Global.asa file after you have moved new product data into production. This tells the application that the download is complete; the online database then becomes the offline database, and vice versa.

- Move required data from the Commerce Server application to the ERP system. This includes:

  - Transferring order records (and other data, as appropriate) that are new since the previous batch download from SQL Server to text files.

  - Transferring the order text files to the ERP system, using FTP. You can use the Internet Transfer Control to do this.

  - Marking order records as *uploaded* when you have received verification that the transfer is complete.

A data transfer application must perform thorough error checking and data validation to ensure data integrity. The Internet Transfer Control included in Visual Basic 6.0 provides FTP transfer functionality. You can use DB-Library for Visual Basic to access BCP and SQL Server functions. Visual Basic also provides error handling, error checking, and transaction integrity to the application.

Real-Time Connectors

Another effective technique for integrating ERP systems with Commerce Server applications is to use a real-time connector. To use a real-time connector, however, the ERP vendor or a third-party vendor must provide the connector software. If you are integrating with SAP, you can get the SAP DCOM connector from http://www.sap.com. For access to an IBM CICS host-based system, you can use Microsoft Host Integration Server 2000. Support for real-time connectors from other ERP vendors varies; check the Web site of your ERP vendor or check with a technical representative for more information about the real-time connectors that they provide.

In general, real-time connectors wrap the programming interfaces on the ERP system with a COM+ component executed in real time. The COM+ component is essentially a proxy object that can then be instantiated and called from any ASP page in the Commerce Server application by the **Server.CreateObject()** method.

Figure 10.4 shows the architecture of a Commerce Server application using the SAP DCOM connector to make real-time calls to SAP.

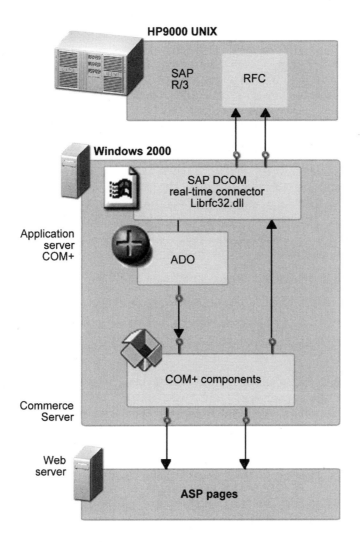

Figure 10.4 A Commerce Server application using the SAP DCOM connector to make real-time contact with an ERP SAP system

Using a real-time connector, any application programming interface (API) functionality in the ERP system becomes available to the Commerce Server application synchronously and in real time. Even if an API for a specific function is not available, ERP systems can provide hooks for writing custom API functions, which can then be wrapped by a COM+ proxy object and made available to the Commerce Server application.

If the connector software is available, using real-time connectors can be a powerful and useful method; however, you should consider the following points before using this technique:

- Processing requests from the Commerce Server application can impact performance of the ERP system. It is very important that you analyze performance before you begin integrating the two systems. ERP systems are usually tuned to serve only tens to hundreds of users, but a Commerce Server application can expose the ERP system to thousands of additional users. You must prepare for that additional load on your ERP system before you integrate the two systems.

- You must test and monitor the performance of real-time calls. Monitor both Web servers and application servers for performance during stress testing.

- You should test performance beyond expected traffic levels to the point where system performance begins to erode significantly. The symptoms of a breakdown will then be much easier to recognize, should it occur in a production environment. The Microsoft Web Application Stress (WAS) tool, available at http://webtool.rte.microsoft.com, is an excellent tool for testing performance.

- Real-time connector software must be available for the targeted ERP system.

- You usually incur additional software and licensing fees when you use real-time connectors.

- If you decide to use real-time connectors, you should start implementing them very early in the development cycle.

  In a medium-to-large organization, different groups usually own the ERP system and the Commerce Server application. Additionally, ERP developers often know little about Commerce Server applications, and Web developers often know little about the APIs in ERP systems, so the integration effort has to be a joint project. Agreeing on priorities, coordinating development and test schedules, and coordinating software installations and server reboots can require additional time.

- You must have a high-speed network link between the Commerce Server application and the ERP system. If your Commerce Server application must be highly available, the high-speed network link must also be redundant.

- The performance of the ERP system can impact the Commerce Server application.

  If the ERP system doesn't respond to processing requests, the Internet Information Services (IIS) 5.0 worker thread making the call will be blocked. Because a COM+ object controls the ERP API call, the IIS ASP timeout setting won't take effect and the thread will be left waiting until the call completes. Tens or hundreds of nearly simultaneous requests to slow-running proxy objects could overload a Web site until all available worker threads are waiting and the ASP request queues are full. For this reason, a high-performing ERP system is essential to make synchronous calls successful.

- The maintenance schedule of the ERP system can affect the performance and functionality of the Commerce Server application. To avoid hanging IIS worker threads while connection attempts time out, you should use a global application variable to control access attempts to real-time calls.

- Remember that the hardware and software powering ERP systems is usually several times more expensive per processing cycle than that powering a Commerce Server application. Consequently, there is usually greater resistance to adding hardware to the ERP system to enable greater Web functionality.

- In general, it is difficult to guarantee the performance of API calls to the ERP system at any time from a Commerce Server application.

  For this reason, the batch download technique is often combined with the real-time connector technique to provide a hybrid solution. You can load product catalog, pricing, order, and inventory data nightly, update it hourly, and make it available to all customers, while offering real-time access to data such as order status and inventory only to your more privileged customers.

Figure 10.5 shows how a Commerce Server application might be integrated with a real-time connector to a host-based CICS system, combined with nightly batch downloads.

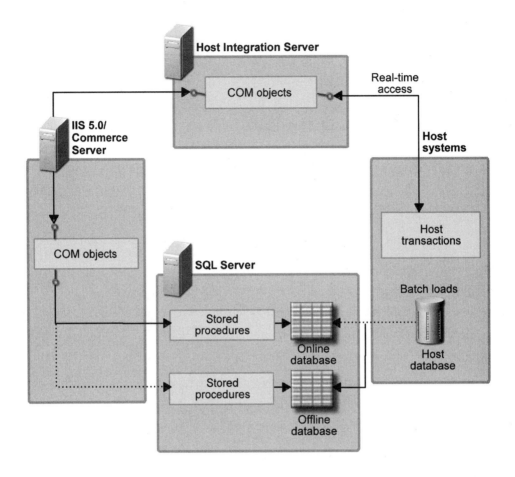

Figure 10.5 Combined real-time and batch integration between a Commerce Server application and a host-based CICS system

Queued Connectors

The queued-connector technique for integrating a Commerce Server application with an ERP system is similar to the real-time connector technique. The key difference is that the queued-connector technique adds a queuing technology to make the calls asynchronous. The queued-connector technique, like the real-time connector technique, employs a proxy object to access the ERP API. However, instead of having the ASP page call the proxy object directly, the ASP page calls an object or function that places a request for the proxy object on Message Queuing. The Message Queuing message is sent to a listening server application that then invokes the proxy object to perform the requested function.

Figure 10.6 shows an ASP page calling a COM+ component that places an ERP request into a Message Queuing message, thus allowing the ASP page to complete quickly. The Message Queuing message gets delivered to the target server, where a Listener service picks up the message and executes the request.

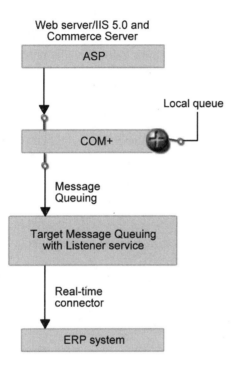

Figure 10.6 Using a queued-connector

The queued-connector technique works well for tasks like submitting orders to an ERP system or requesting order status from an ERP system. It also resolves some of the most important issues associated with making synchronous calls directly to an ERP system, such as the following:

- The performance and maintenance schedule of the ERP system has much less impact on the performance of the Commerce Server application than it does with the real-time connector technique. The IIS worker thread no longer calls directly into the ERP system, but simply makes a call to place a message on Message Queuing. This call executes quickly and doesn't block the IIS worker thread.

- If the ERP system is high performing and responsive, the request is delivered to the Listener service and executed at a speed that makes it appear to be executing in real time.

- If the ERP system is performing slowly, requests are placed in a queue and then executed. As long as the average speed at which the ERP system can process requests is faster than the average speed of incoming requests, performance should be acceptable. The net result is that spikes in the numbers of requests are flattened without over-burdening either the Commerce Server application or the ERP system.

- If the ERP system is taken offline for maintenance, requests can still be made and placed in the queue. The Commerce Server application can continue to function, even though the ERP system is offline.

- A custom Listener service can be built to limit the number of concurrent requests made to the ERP system, schedule the times at which calls to the ERP system are made, or prioritize the calls to the ERP system by type of request or by customer privileges.

The primary limitation of the queued-connector technique is that the calls are asynchronous. ASP requests to the ERP system always get queued; these requests can be executed almost immediately or not until much later.

The architectural challenge in implementing this technique is that the asynchronous model only lends itself to the techniques and functions associated with input parameters. Return parameters, such as error codes, only indicate whether the request was successfully queued, not whether the request was successfully executed. To provide results to the original caller, you must use an out-of-bounds mechanism, such as that outlined in the following steps:

1. An ASP page calls an **OrderSubmit** object to submit an order.

2. The **OrderSubmit** object allocates a unique request ID and places the request into a message queue. It also writes a record to a local SQL Orders table, recording the order and setting the status to Pending.

3. The ASP page dynamically displays the request ID to the customer and informs the customer that the order has been accepted.

4. At some later time, the Message Queuing service delivers the message to the target server.

5. A Listener service picks up the message with the request ID and invokes a proxy object to submit the order to the ERP system in real time.

   If an error occurs, the listener can retry, put the message back into the queue, or write an error to a log file.

6. The proxy object calls the ERP system and submits the order. It then updates the status in the local SQL Orders table to Accepted.

7. At any time, the customer can invoke an ASP page to query order status. The ASP page then checks the local SQL Orders table and returns the contents of the order, along with the status (Pending or Accepted).

Although the queued-connector technique can be implemented with any queuing technique, it works best with Message Queuing. In addition, you can facilitate development with COM+ by leveraging queued components in the implementation.

Mirrored Updates

The mirrored updates technique is another method for integrating ERP systems with Commerce Server applications, but it requires software event support on the ERP system. As events occur on the ERP system (inventory is updated, customers are added, product pricing is changed), they can be trapped and transmitted over a real-time connector to the Commerce Server application.

You can mirror updates from the ERP system constantly throughout the day to the back-end databases of the Commerce Server application. All processing requests related to Commerce Server application traffic are directed to SQL Server database servers, so there is no longer any reason to call directly into the ERP system.

When you use the mirrored updates technique, ERP system performance and maintenance schedules have only minimal effects on the Commerce Server application, and vice versa. The routines mirroring the events between the two systems are the only performance inhibitors. You can also add a queuing mechanism to the mirroring routines to limit the impact of ERP system updates on the Commerce Server application. A queuing mechanism also guarantees that all updates reach the Commerce Server application, whether or not the network link between the systems is available or the Commerce Server application has been taken offline for maintenance.

You should consider the following points before using the mirrored updates technique:

- You must have ERP real-time connector and event support.

- This technique works best if you add queuing to the implementation to prioritize the updates, limit the number of concurrent updates, and make sure all updates are completed, regardless of network availability.

- This technique minimizes, but doesn't eliminate performance risks. When you implement this solution, you should still monitor performance on both the ERP system and the Commerce Server application. Any performance impact will probably affect the Commerce Server application data servers, due to additional row updates.

- You can combine this technique with the batch download technique. If you do, batch downloads can be done nightly, thereby guaranteeing that data is always synchronized. Mirrored updates can then occur throughout the day, keeping the data synchronized until the next batch download occurs.

Figure 10.7 shows mirrored updates occurring between the ERP system and a Commerce Server application.

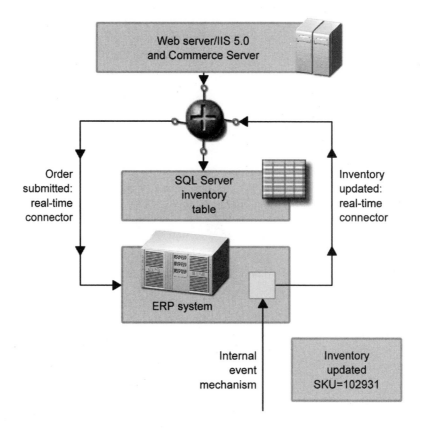

Figure 10.7 Mirrored updates

Figure 10.7 shows an *inventory-updated* event occurring in the ERP system. It triggers a call across a real-time connector to an inventory COM+ object of the Commerce Server application. The inventory COM+ object then mirrors the update in the local SQL Server database. In the Commerce Server application, an *order-submitted* event triggers a call across a real-time connector to place the order in the ERP system.

You can extend the mirrored updates model on the Commerce Server application by leveraging COM+ events to start multiple autonomous COM+ components. These components perform multiple Commerce Server-related tasks in response to an ERP event.

General Considerations and Best Practices

This section describes general considerations and best practices for using integration techniques in the following areas:

- ERP systems and Commerce Server business rules

- Pricing and promotions

- Shipping, taxation, and credit card authorization

- Product catalog

- Replication

- Physical architecture (highly scalable)

ERP Systems and Commerce Server Business Rules

The ERP system normally contains business rules for such key commerce functionality as pricing and promotions, taxation, shipping, inventory management, and credit card authorization. You must identify each of the business rules and decide whether to mirror each one in the Commerce Server application or provide a real-time call for it to the ERP system. Consider the following as you make your decision:

- The type of business rule

- The frequency with which the business rule must be invoked

- The costs and risks associated with invoking the business rule directly, in real time

- The cost to mirror the business rule

This decision also depends on your organizational priorities.

In general, however, it is better to mirror frequently used business rules in the Commerce Server application. For example, pricing algorithms based on customer history are often table-driven and computationally expensive because they must be recalculated frequently. The best way to handle pricing algorithms is by moving the pricing data to the Commerce Server application using the batch download technique. You then create a COM+ component and/or stored procedure within the Commerce Server application to mirror the ERP business rule.

Credit card processing, on the other hand, occurs much less frequently, so you can either call this functionality in real time from the Commerce Server application or leave it for the ERP system to process after the order has been uploaded. If you leave it for processing by the ERP system, you can use a standard Commerce Server component to verify the card number.

Pricing and Promotions

The ERP system often contains a complex set of pricing business rules based on each of a company's customers. When you use this functionality, you might need to address the following variables:

- Quantity

- Customer and customer volume history

- Current availability

- Product market status (discontinued, recalled, and so on)

- Sales goals

- Advertisements and promotions

All of these items can influence pricing business logic. In some industries, pricing is also controlled by regulatory agencies. Consider the following suggestions when you deal with pricing issues:

- Use the pricing models and templates from the ERP system and mirror changes to the Commerce Server application.

- Establish a real-time connection to the ERP system only if any combination of customer, quantity, and SKU in the Commerce Server application falls outside the templates mirrored from the ERP system.

- Make sure you understand custom pricing. Apply the 80/20 percentage rule whenever possible. In other words, if you can accommodate most of your customers (80 percent or more) with a defined pricing logic, focus your development on that work.

- If you provide the capability for long-lived shopping carts (shopping carts that a customer can save and return to at a later date), pricing on products can change between the time the SKU was added to the cart and the time the purchase takes place. You can avoid problems if you include the pricing algorithm in the Order Processing pipeline (OPP) and invoke it just prior to check out.

Shipping, Taxation, and Credit Card Authorization

Shipping, taxation, and credit card authorization functions are each important to a Commerce Server application, but are also often provided by the ERP system. Because these functions occur only once per order, and near the end of a transaction, they make good candidates for real-time connections.

However, if you must provide these functions from the Commerce Server application, several third-party software developers provide components that you can use for this purpose. For a list of products, see http://www.microsoft.com/commerce.

Product Catalog

The Commerce Server Product Catalog System is a key part of the Commerce Server product. Its terms, attributes, category definitions, associations, and hierarchies provide powerful searching capabilities not found on ERP systems. You should perform early evaluation and prototyping using the Commerce Server product catalog during batch imports.

If you have to use another technique for building your catalog, then you should design the product database to match the structure of the corresponding ERP system as closely as possible. Doing so will simplify data transfer between platforms and make it easier to mirror the business logic in the ERP system. You should also consider the following points:

- You must develop a process to add content and add data to the product catalog as it is being built from the ERP system. The ERP system contains product SKUs, prices, and basic product details. However, to sell products on the Web, you must provide more detailed data, including images, multimedia, and so on. As the catalog is copied from the ERP system, add content to the data before serving it on the Web.

- The cleanest way to deliver the product catalog is to have a read-only copy of the catalog on the Web. This provides performance gains, because the Catalogs database can then be optimized for Web delivery.

- Design a scheduled update process. In some cases, the product catalog must be updated nightly, but there are two ways to handle updates: rebuild the entire catalog nightly or just apply the daily changes to the database.

Replication

Although it is possible to use replication as an ERP integration technique (writing custom applications to bypass the ERP vendor's recommended API or setting up replication between the ERP system's database and the Commerce Server Application database), it is definitely not recommended. You should not try to directly access database tables on the ERP system.

Many ERP systems support API access only to managed data and specifically don't permit direct access to the underlying tables. In addition, many ERP vendors specifically warn against replication because they might need to change the underlying table structures in future releases.

Physical Architecture

The Microsoft .NET architecture supports many different physical configurations that also support a highly scalable Commerce Server application with ERP integration. Figure 10.8 shows the logical architecture of a three-tier Commerce Server application with ERP integration. The ERP integration shown in Figure 10.8 includes batch downloads and a real-time connector.

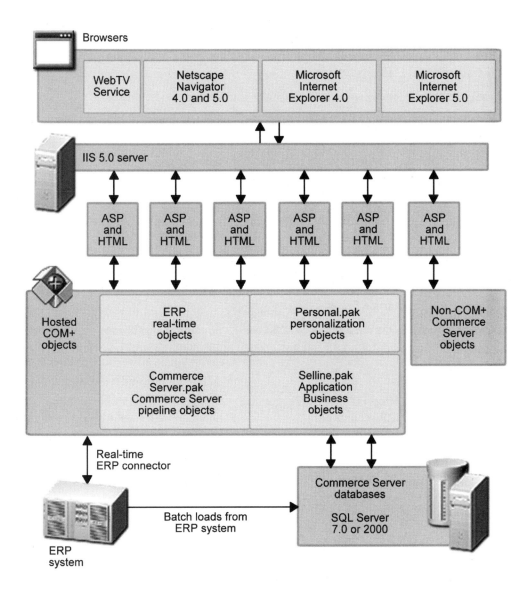

Figure 10.8 Highly scalable Commerce Server application integrated with an ERP system

Figure 10.8 shows the Web portion of a Commerce Server application. In this example, there are multiple Web servers, a set of clustered SQL Server servers, and an ERP system (the host) on the back end. The Web servers:

- Host the user interface (HTML and ASP pages).

- Host lightweight COM+ components called by the ASP pages.

- Provide the logic that requests data from the SQL Server servers, which provide the tables needed to build a shopping basket.

There is a membership environment that controls authentication, user accounts, and user profiling. The following table describes each component of the system shown in Figure 10.8.

System component	Services	Description
Web servers	IIS 5.0 COM+ Commerce Server Pipeline objects Commerce Server	Contain the ASP files of the site.
SQL Server servers	SQL Server 2000 (or SQL Server 7.0)	Provide all database services for the site, including customer, product, and pricing information, as well as the tables for shopping baskets and receipts.
ERP Commerce objects	ERP integration software provided by ERP vendors Custom-built integration objects	Provide Internet order processing and integration. This may be a combination of vendor-supplied objects and custom objects.
ERP system		Provides business management.

Integrating with SAP

Figure 10.9 shows a network diagram of an SAP system application with an integrated Commerce Server application.

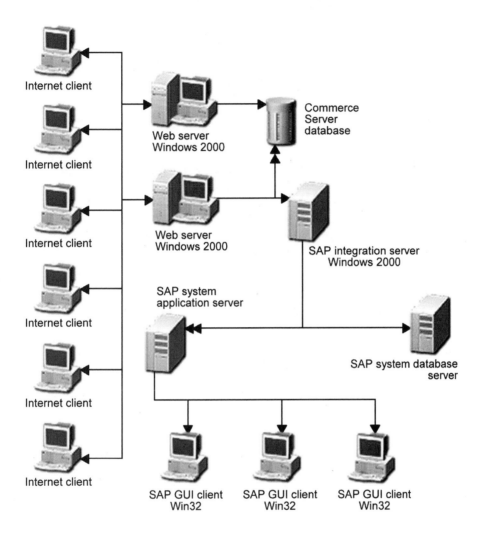

Figure 10.9 SAP system with integrated Commerce Server application

This section explains the following points to consider when you integrate a Commerce Server application with an SAP R/3 system:

- Using the SAP DCOM connector
- Integrating a product catalog
- Integrating item pricing
- Integrating inventory data
- Integrating orders

SAP DCOM Connector

The bridge between the Windows 2000 platform and the SAP business object framework is the SAP DCOM connector. You can download the DCOM connector from the SAP Web site: http://www.sap.com/solutions/technology/bapis/resource/software/dcom/rfcsdk.exe. For detailed installation instructions and programming procedures and considerations, see the article "SAP DCOM Connector: Expanding SAP Business Processes," by Homann, Rogers, and Russo, in *SAP Technical Journal*, Vol. 1, No. 2. You can also find the article online at http://www.mysap.com/solutions/technology/bapis/com/dcom_mag/dcom_mag.htm.

You use the DCOM connector to write a COM component to access existing Business APIs (BAPIs) or custom-developed remote function calls (RFCs) in SAP R/3 on any SAP-supported platform. The COM component with which you access SAP resides on the SAP integration server (see Figure 10.9). The SAP DCOM connector package contains an Object Builder Wizard, which eliminates the need to write large amounts of C++ code using native SAP RFCs. The components you create with the wizard are COM+ components that are reusable by other applications.

The DCOM connector process is as follows:

1. An ASP page calls the generated DCOM connector object directly, or calls a custom business object that wraps the DCOM connector object so that it can provide custom functionality.

2. If the ASP page did not call the DCOM object directly, the DCOM connector call is automatically sent by COM+ to the SAP integration server.

3. The DCOM connector object on the SAP integration server calls a BAPI object or custom-written RFC.

4. The BAPI gets the results from the SAP environment and returns them to the calling object or ASP page.

5. The results are returned to the Visual Basic business object.

6. The results are returned to the ASP page.

Figure 10.10 shows an example of this process.

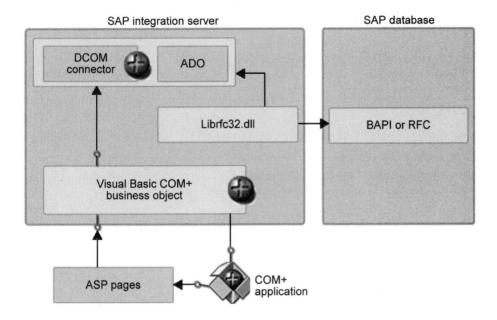

Figure 10.10 Using the DCOM connector

The example in Figure 10.10 shows an availability query being made to SAP for a particular product, using the following process:

1. The ASP page calls the Visual Basic business object, which in this case wraps the DCOM connector object that resides in a COM+ package on the SAP integration server.

2. The DCOM connector object uses the SAP interface DLL (Librfc32.dll), which you can use to interface with any SAP system, regardless of the host platform.

3. The BAPI checks the tables and assembles an internal table of product availability for a selected warehouse, which is sent back to the DCOM connector object.

4. The product availability data is wrapped into a Microsoft ActiveX Data Objects (ADO) recordset, and is then passed back through the COM+ package.

The approach in this example works well as long as the ERP system is able to process all of the incoming requests. However, because Web traffic can surge unpredictably, this might not always be the case. In such instances, it is better to use a Commerce Server database synchronized in real time with the SAP application server instead of using the DCOM connector.

Product Catalog

You can use the following techniques to integrate a product catalog between Commerce Server and SAP:

- Batch download product catalog data

- Batch download incremental catalog changes

- Mirrored updates

- Real-time connections

In each of these techniques, the product catalog data obtained from SAP can be enriched with other site data, such as the path to an image for the product SKU, other technical data not residing on the SAP system, additional descriptions of the product, or cross- or up-sell product numbers.

Batch Download Product Catalog Data

You can export product catalog data from SAP by scheduling a custom extract program on the SAP R/3 system to extract relevant product data from the SAP tables into a comma-separated value (CSV) file, XML file, or flat file. You can then import that file into the Commerce Server product catalog. Figure 10.11 shows how you can use a batch download to transfer catalog data from SAP to Commerce Server.

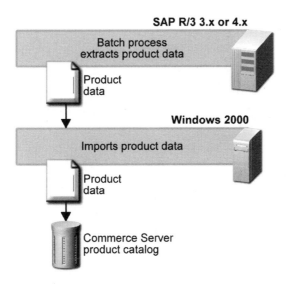

Figure 10.11 Using a batch download to transfer product catalog data from SAP to Commerce Server

Figure 10.12 shows a second way of doing this, which can only be used with version 3.x or 4.x of SAP R/3. In this scenario, you run a Windows 2000 scheduled process that uses the provided BAPI to extract product catalog data from SAP. You can then place the extracted product catalog data directly into a Commerce Server product catalog.

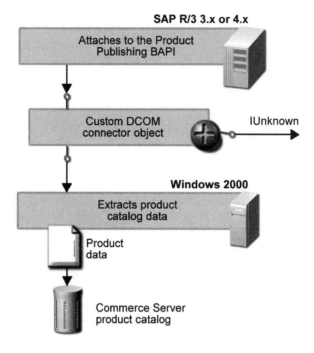

Figure 10.12 Placing extracted catalog data directly into the product catalog

Batch Download Incremental Catalog Changes

Incremental changes to product catalog data on an SAP system can be reflected using a batch method, which can reflect changes almost in real time. The process looks exactly the same as that shown in Figure 10.11, except that the SAP batch process extracts only changed product data to send to Commerce Server instead of sending all product data.

Mirrored Updates

You can use either of the two mirrored update techniques shown in Figure 10.13 to send more immediate notification of changes to the product catalog. Both techniques for synchronizing data use SAP Application Link Enable (ALE) to notify the Commerce Server application of product changes by means of the IDOC message *MATMAS02 IDOC*.

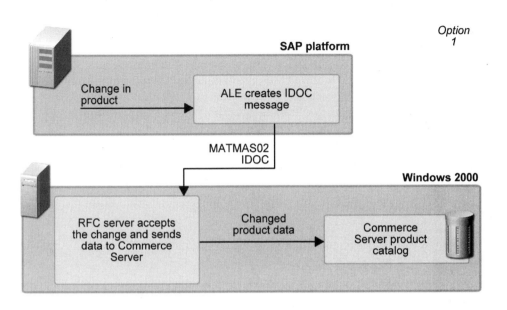

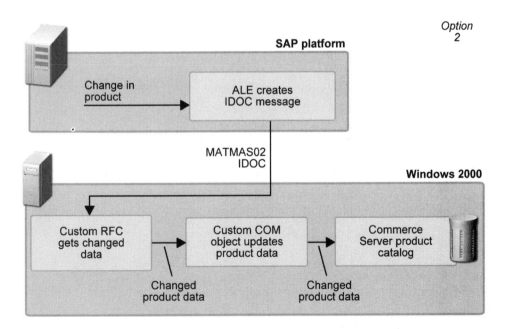

Figure 10.13 Updating the product catalog using mirrored updates

You can combine the mirrored-update technique with the batch-update technique, or you can use it by itself.

Item Pricing

Integrating item pricing can be a greater challenge than integrating catalog data, depending on how the pricing scheme is configured in SAP and at what point in the order process you decide to apply the pricing calculations. In some business-to-business (B2B) scenarios, you must deal with complex pricing formulas, such as contract pricing by customer, quantity discounts, and discounts on items ordered in relation to other items on the order. Some of these complex pricing formulas can be difficult to replicate in the Commerce Server application. This section describes the following ways to integrate pricing information for items:

- Batch download item prices
- ALE-triggered price change download
- Real-time pricing integration

Batch Download Item Prices

You can batch download item prices by customer, item, and quantity. To do this, you must first build pricing logic into the Commerce Server application to calculate the prices. Figure 10.14 shows the process for batch downloading item prices.

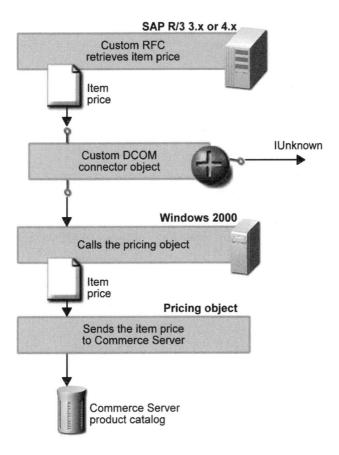

Figure 10.14 Batch downloading item prices

In this scenario, a scheduled Windows 2000 process retrieves pricing data from SAP by means of a DCOM connector object that wraps a custom RFC to retrieve the data. When the data has been retrieved, a custom-built object is invoked to place the pricing data into the Commerce Server database.

ALE-Triggered Price Change Download

You can attach an Application Link Enable (ALE)-triggered price change download to a user exit when customer/item combination-specific prices change. This scenario requires that you build pricing logic into the Commerce Server application to calculate the pricing. Figure 10.15 shows how this technique works.

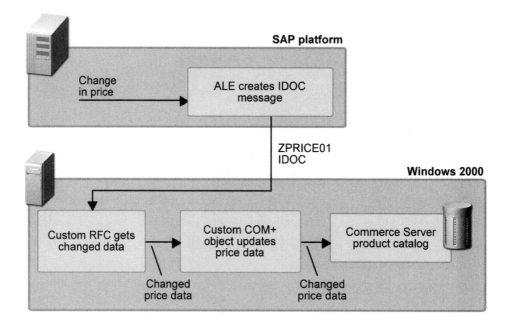

Figure 10.15 ALE-triggered price change download

In this scenario:

1. A price change for a customer/item combination is detected when a user exits.

2. A custom IDOC message (in this example, *zprice01*) is created and passed to the ALE subsystem.

3. ALE invokes a custom RFC to pass the custom IDOC data to the SAP COM object for an ABAP-generic RFC server.

4. The custom RFC calls a custom COM object to place the data into the Commerce Server item pricing tables.

Real-Time Pricing Integration

You can access pricing for an order in real time by invoking a pipeline component calling the SAP SalesOrder_Simulate BAPI. Figure 10.16 shows how you would do this.

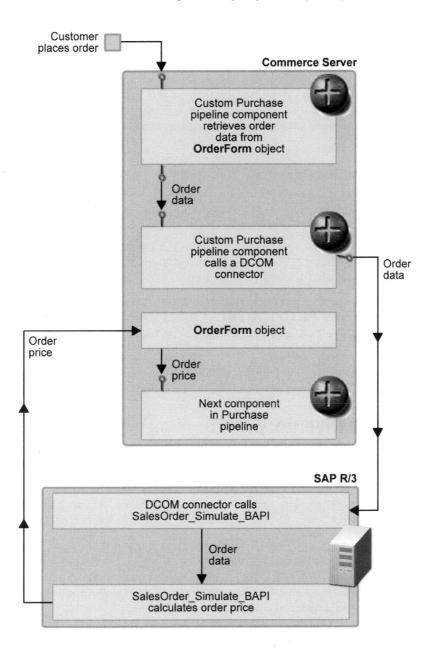

Figure 10.16 Real-time pricing integration

In this scenario, you update pricing for items in the order at the time the customer confirms the purchase. This technique uses SAP for all pricing calculations. To use real-time pricing integration, you must create a custom pipeline component to call a previously created SAP

DCOM component to invoke the SalesOrder_Simulate BAPI. When all of the item pricing and order costs have been retrieved from SAP, the Commerce Server **OrderForm** object is updated with the new data.

Inventory Data

This section describes the following methods of integrating inventory data:

- Batch download inventory data

- Batch download inventory changes

- Mirrored updates using ALE

- Real-time connections

These techniques are similar to those described for integrating the product catalog, except that inventory data is generally much more volatile than product catalog data. For this reason, you must carefully plan how to integrate this data.

If you expect a low volume of traffic, you can use the real-time connection, in which the DCOM connector transmits order data to the Product Availability BAPI. The Commerce Server application can then use the same inventory data used by SAP.

If you expect medium-to-high traffic volumes, integration becomes significantly more complex. In a high-volume situation, you probably should use a combination of the batch, batch plus changes, and ALE integration techniques described in this section.

Batch Download Inventory Data

In the batch download scenario, you extract SAP inventory data using a custom Advanced Business Application Programming (ABAP) report program to place the data into an XML file, a flat file, or a CSV file on the target system. A Windows 2000 service or scheduled program then either reads the extracted data and places it directly into the Commerce Server database, or uses the Commerce Server Catalog objects to place it in the Commerce Server database.

The batch download is generally run once a day and is particularly useful if you can allocate a certain percentage of inventory exclusively to the Commerce Server application. A disadvantage of this technique is that inventory data can be out-of-date by the time the next cycle runs. Figure 10.17 shows the batch download scenario.

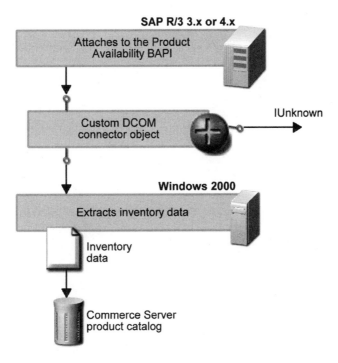

Figure 10.17 Batch download scenario

You can initiate another version of the batch download with a Windows 2000 scheduled process, as shown in Figure 10.18.

This scenario differs from the SAP-initiated batch scenario in that the batch download process is controlled from the Windows 2000 server instead of being scheduled from SAP. This gives the Commerce Server system administrator greater control over the timing of the batch update. However, this type of process must be coordinated with the SAP Basis administrators so that conflicts in the extraction process don't adversely affect the main SAP batch system processing.

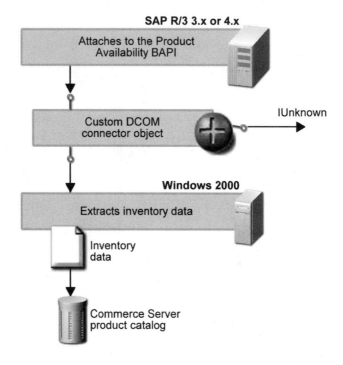

Figure 10.18 Batch download using a Windows 2000 scheduled process

Batch Download Incremental Inventory Changes

In addition to the nightly batch download, you can develop an inventory update process to download inventory changes to the Commerce Server application more often. The process looks exactly the same as the regular change process shown in Figures 10.17 and 10.18, except that the SAP batch process is configured to extract only changed inventory data to send to Commerce Server, instead of sending all inventory data.

Mirrored Updates Using ALE

You can also download inventory data on a real-time basis to the Commerce Server Application database. You can use this technique by itself as the primary technique for replicating inventory, or in conjunction with a batch download technique. Figure 10.19 shows the mirrored update technique using ALE.

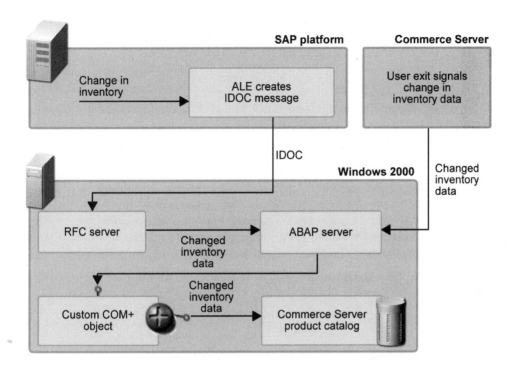

Figure 10.19 Mirrored updates using ALE

Real-Time Connections

A real-time connection scenario uses the DCOM object in a Commerce pipeline object to return the current inventory value in SAP in a real-time fashion. However, this method should be used with caution, because it can adversely affect performance on the SAP application servers.

Orders

There are several batch, synchronous (real-time), or asynchronous (queued) techniques that you can use to integrate orders from a Commerce Server application into SAP.

If you use a batch technique to send orders to SAP, you first must convert Commerce Server order data to an IDOC format, which you can then send to SAP by means of the IDOC interface. This technique requires little or no customization of SAP programs and can be administered easily by SAP system administrators.

To use a real-time order interface technique, you must create a SAP DCOM connector object to communicate with the SalesOrder_CreateFromDat1 BAPI.

If you expect relatively low order volumes, you can create a custom pipeline component to get the order data from the Commerce Server **OrderForm** object, map the data to the ADO recordsets required by the DCOM connector object, and then call the DCOM connector object to pass the data to SAP in real time. When you use this technique, you can generate an e-mail message, fax, or phone call to notify the customer if the order fails in SAP.

If you expect medium-to-high volumes of orders, you can pass the order number to a COM+ queued component, then return control to the pipeline to get faster execution. However, if you do this and the order fails in SAP, you can't notify the customer in real time.

If you expect very high volumes of orders, you should use a more controlled asynchronous method to update SAP. You can pass the order number through Message Queuing to a waiting service optimized for ERP order integration. The service can then update SAP with the order data. Again, a disadvantage to this approach is that you can't notify customers of order failures in real time.

As an alternative to using an asynchronous ERP integration service, you can use Microsoft BizTalk Server 2000 to pass the message to the appropriate Application Integration Component (AIC). The AIC can then map the passed XML document to the parameters necessary for the BAPI call in SAP.

Because SAP error information won't be sent to the customer in real time if you use one of the asynchronous techniques, you must design an asynchronous technique to notify customers if a SAP error occurs. One suggestion is to contact customers by e-mail with instructions to call a customer service representative or check the order status online.

This section describes the following techniques for integrating Commerce Server orders with SAP:

- Batch integration using IDOC

- Real-time integration using the DCOM connector

- Integration using queued connectors

- Mirrored updates using Message Queuing

- Mirrored updates using BizTalk Server

- Real-time integration using custom COM objects and DCOM connector objects

Batch Integration Using IDOC

When you use IDOC to batch upload Commerce Server order data to SAP, you extract order data and convert it to an IDOC format, then send it to the SAP IDOC processor. You generally use this technique with applications that do not require real-time order processing by the SAP system. Figure 10.20 shows the batch integration process using IDOC.

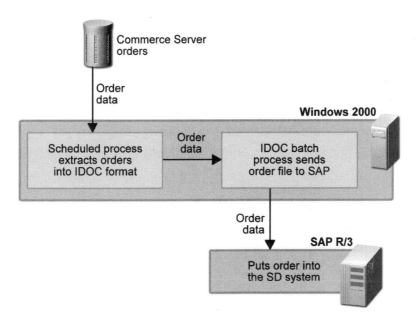

Figure 10.20 Batch integration process using IDOC

Real-Time Integration Using the DCOM Connector

To send Commerce Server order data to SAP in real time, you can use the process shown in Figure 10.21.

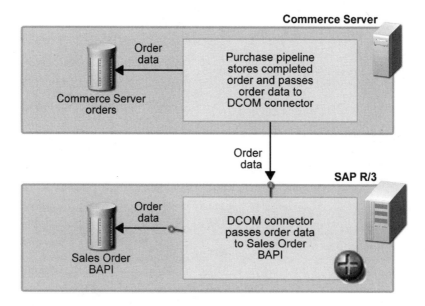

Figure 10.21 Real-time integration process using the DCOM connector

When the Purchase pipeline accepts an order, a custom pipeline component maps the order form data to the parameters required by the SAP DCOM connector object for the Sales Order BAPI. When the mapping is finished, you invoke the DCOM connector technique to create the order in SAP.

If the order is rejected, the pipeline component then fails the entire transaction and notifies the customer that an error has occurred. You should use this technique only if you expect low order volumes.

An example of code for a Visual Basic pipeline component object that can create an order in SAP is located on the Commerce Server 2000 Resource Kit CD in the file SAP_sales_order.txt. The code in the example is the minimum that you would need to write to implement this process; the code you need to successfully implement the BAPI call at your site might be different, depending on how your SAP system is configured. Because you can use the DCOM Connector Wizard to create the DCOM connector, the example doesn't show the original C++ code used to create the object. .

Integration Using Queued Components

When you use the queued component technique to send order data from Commerce Server to SAP, you pass the order number to a COM+ queued component from a custom pipeline component in the Purchase pipeline. When you use this technique, Commerce Server doesn't have to wait until SAP processes the order before returning control to the customer.

COM+ invokes the queued component with the order number as the passed parameter. The queued component then uses Commerce Server objects to read the saved order and move the order data to the parameters required by the SAP DCOM connector object. Finally, you invoke the **OrderCreate** method and the order is created in the SAP system.

If an error occurs in the SAP update process, you must use an out-of-bounds mechanism to inform the customer of the error, so that the customer can initiate a correction.

Figure 10.22 shows the integration process using queued components.

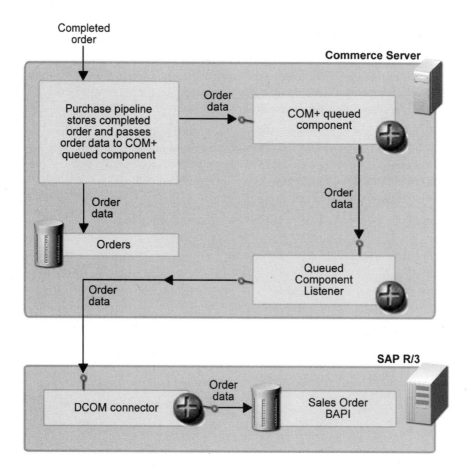

Figure 10.22 Integration using queued components

You can find an example of code that creates a Visual Basic COM+ object to create an order in SAP on the Commerce Server 2000 Resource Kit CD, in the file SAP_create_order.txt. In this code example, the SAP order is created from the **OrderForm** object retrieved from the Commerce Server order tables.

Mirrored Updates Using Message Queuing

If you decide to use the mirrored updates technique with Message Queuing to download orders from Commerce Server to SAP, you use a custom pipeline component to place the order number in the message queue. The order is stored in the Commerce Server database and the customer is notified.

An asynchronous SAP updating service containing application server throttling reads the message queue and finds a new order number to process. The service then instantiates a custom Visual Basic object that uses Commerce Server objects to read the saved order and copies the order data to the parameters required by the SAP DCOM connector object.

After the parameters have been properly set up, the service invokes the **OrderCreate** method to create the order in the SAP system. If an error occurs in the SAP update process, an out-of-bounds mechanism is used to notify the customer.

Figure 10.23 shows the mirrored update technique using Message Queuing.

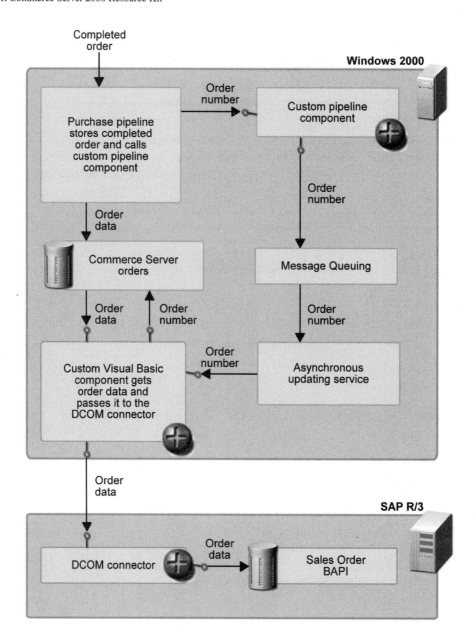

Figure 10.23 Mirrored update using Message Queuing

Mirrored Updates Using BizTalk Server

Another technique is to download orders from Commerce Server to SAP using mirrored updates with BizTalk Server. To do this, you can create a custom pipeline component in the Purchase pipeline to create an XML document from the **OrderForm** object data and submit the document to BizTalk Server. BizTalk Server then instantiates the specified channel to pass the XML order document to the AIC that is responsible for updating SAP with the new order data.

This logic follows many of the same principles used by the batch download technique. In fact, you can use this technique in conjunction with the batch download technique to provide greater control of the download to SAP.

Figure 10.24 shows the mirrored update technique using BizTalk Server.

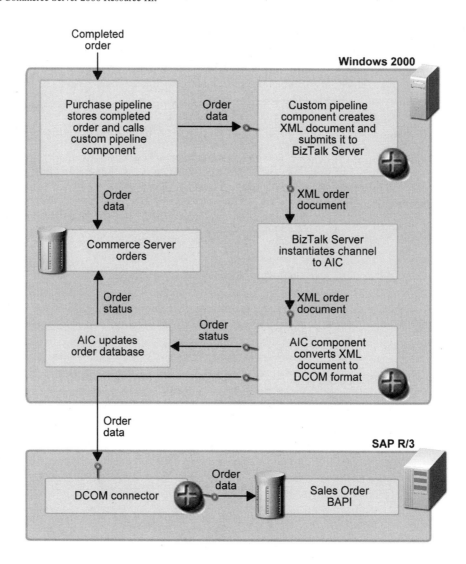

Figure 10.24 Mirrored update using BizTalk Server

You can find an example of Visual Basic COM+ code that creates pipeline component pseudocode to create the XML document from the **OrderForm** object on the Commerce Server 2000 Resource Kit CD in the file SAP_mirrored_update.txt.

Real-Time Integration Using Custom COM Objects and DCOM Connector Objects

If you decide to download orders in real time using custom COM objects and DCOM connector objects, use Commerce Server ASP pages to request and display real-time order status for order header and detail records. You use custom Visual Basic COM objects to wrap the call to the generated DCOM connector object that calls the Sales Order BAPI methods.

Because real-time queries are generally less CPU- and database-intensive, a site with low-to-medium order volume can make real-time inquiry calls to the SAP application server with little performance degradation. However, it is sometimes easier to wrap complex calls in a COM object.

Figure 10.25 shows the process of real-time integration using custom COM objects and DCOM connector objects.

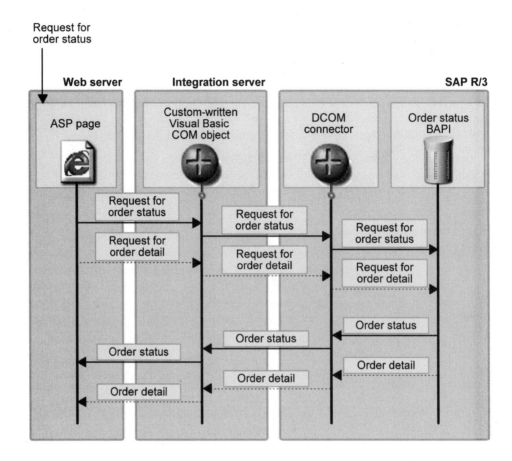

Figure 10.25 Real-time integration using custom COM objects and DCOM connector objects

You can find a code example containing Visual Basic COM+ code snippets on the Commerce Server 2000 Resource Kit CD, in the file SAP_realtime_integration.txt. The example contains functions that return order header records in summary form and return order detail records, and a function that creates a disconnected recordset to contain the summary order header records.

Integrating with J.D. Edwards OneWorld

This section describes the following techniques used to integrate Commerce Server with J.D. Edwards OneWorld:

- OneWorld **COM** wrapper objects

- Product catalog and pricing

- Orders

OneWorld also supports other integrations, such as the Microsoft Integration Solution. The Microsoft Integration Solution uses the following technologies for integrating with software such as Commerce Server:

- **OneWorld Message Queuing Adapter**. An asynchronous integration using Message Queuing and XML-based documents.

- **OneWorld Orchestration Adapter for BizTalk Server 2000**. An Application Integration Component (AIC) written with COM that exposes predefined transactions into OneWorld using OneWorld COM wrapper objects.

OneWorld also supports XML through the following APIs:

- **XML CallObject**. An API used for synchronous requests to OneWorld.

- **XML Transactions**. An API used for asynchronous requests to OneWorld.

- **XML Z-Table Inquire**. An API that uses an Index passed in an XML document to retrieve records from a Z-Table and returns the result in an XML string.

The OneWorld XML APIs support well-formed XML documents. OneWorld also supports UTF-8 and UTF-16 Unicode standards for inbound and outbound information. J.D. Edwards provides XML schemas for each type of XML document API. OneWorld can also return an XML CallObject Template for a specific business function. This template contains an XML document with required elements for calling the requested business function. No data or environment information is returned.

Before you attempt to integrate sales orders, a product catalog, pricing, or other function, it is important to understand how OneWorld performs these functions.

OneWorld processes are based on Master Business Functions (MBFs). OneWorld Master Business Functions can be accessed from a Windows 2000 platform through several different configurations. OneWorld can process XML documents, and can be called directly with COM through the OneWorld COM server. In most cases, you can leverage existing MBF, but OneWorld also provides development tools to create new, custom business functions depending on your business requirements.

When you have decided which integration solution to use (batch download, real-time connectors, and so on), you must then decide which business functions to implement for the functionality you want to integrate. You use the OneWorld GenCom client tool to create the OneWorld COM wrapper objects used by the OneWorld COM Server to access the business functions within OneWorld.

Figure 10.26 shows a network diagram consisting of a OneWorld system application with a Commerce Server application integrated into the entire system.

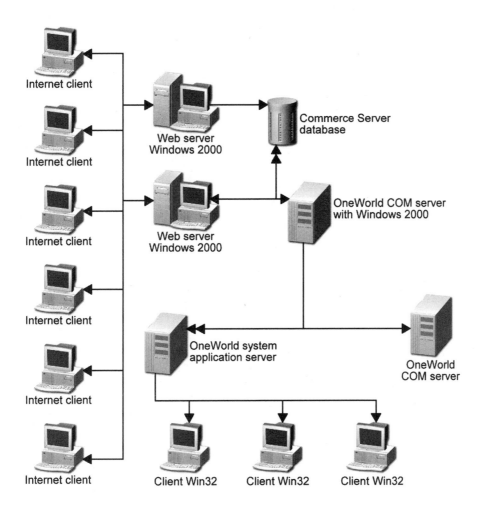

Figure 10.26 Network diagram showing how Commerce Server integrates with OneWorld

OneWorld GenCom Component Wrapper

The bridge between the Windows 2000 platform and the OneWorld MBFs is the OneWorld COM server. The OneWorld GenCom client tool and server components are shipped with OneWorld software. Detailed documentation describing how to use the OneWorld GenCom client tool to create OneWorld COM wrapper objects to OneWorld business functions is contained in the *Interoperability Manual* that comes with OneWorld. You can also use outbound Z-Table processing or the Universal Batch Engine (UBE) to provide batch interface capabilities with OneWorld.

The process for using a generated OneWorld COM object is as follows:

1. An ASP page calls the generated OneWorld COM object directly, or calls a custom business object that wraps the OneWorld COM object.

2. The OneWorld COM object call is automatically sent by COM+ to the OneWorld COM server.

3. The OneWorld COM object on the OneWorld COM server calls a particular OneWorld MBF or custom-written business function.

4. The business function gets the results from the OneWorld environment and returns them to the calling object or ASP page.

Figure 10.27 shows the process for using the OneWorld COM object.

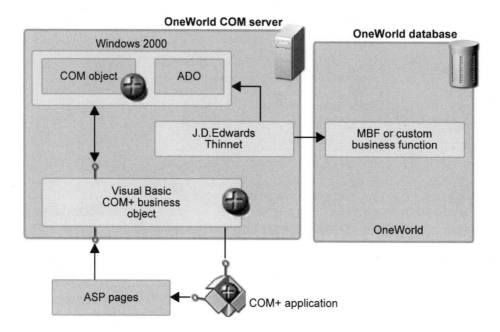

Figure 10.27 Using the OneWorld COM object

Figure 10.27 also shows an inventory query being made to OneWorld, as follows:

1. An ASP page calls a Visual Basic business object, which in this case wraps the OneWorld COM object that resides in a COM+ application on the OneWorld COM server.

2. The OneWorld COM object runs through the low-level J. D. Edwards thinnet interface protocol, which interfaces with any OneWorld system regardless of the host platform.

3. The business function checks the availability of the requested item and returns the results to the OneWorld COM object.

4. The results are wrapped in an ADO recordset by the COM+ wrapper object and passed back through the COM+ package.

Product Catalog and Pricing

You can use the following techniques to integrate a product catalog or pricing data between Commerce Server and OneWorld:

- Batch download data from OneWorld

- Mirrored updates

- Real-time integration

Using any of these techniques, product catalog data retrieved from OneWorld can be enriched with other data, such as images, additional product descriptions, or other technical data that doesn't reside on the OneWorld system, before it is presented to customers.

Batch Download Data from OneWorld

To download product catalog data from OneWorld using the batch download technique, you have to schedule a custom UBE extraction program to pull the relevant product data from OneWorld tables into a Z-Table (a temporary interface table for imports and exports) that can be imported into the Commerce Server product catalog. Unless the pricing scheme is extremely complicated, pricing data can also be placed into the UBE program. Figure 10.28 shows the process of downloading product catalog data using the batch download technique.

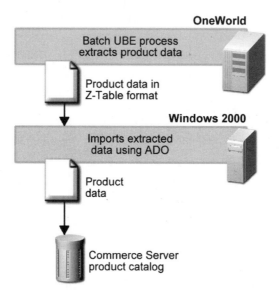

Figure 10.28 Downloading product catalog data using the batch download technique

Another way to download product catalog data using the batch download technique is by means of a Windows 2000 scheduled process that calls a wrapped custom business function of the OneWorld COM object to extract product catalog data directly from OneWorld tables. Extracted data can then be placed directly into a Commerce Server product catalog. Figure 10.29 shows the process for this batch download technique.

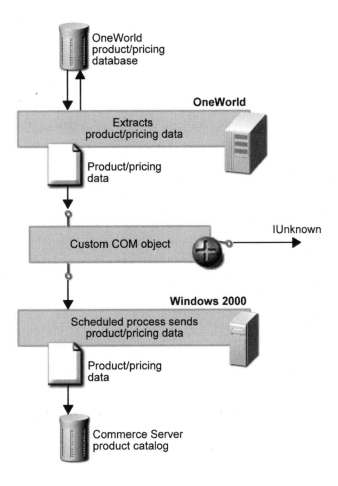

Figure 10.29 Downloading product catalog data using the OneWorld COM object

The process for downloading incremental changes to the product catalog is similar to that shown in Figures 10.28 and 10.29.

Mirrored Updates

If you need more immediate notification of changes to the product catalog than you can get from a batch technique, you can use the mirrored update technique to integrate product data. This technique leverages the outbound processing technology in OneWorld to notify Commerce Server about product changes. You can handle mirrored updates for inventory, pricing, order status, and other data in a similar manner. Figure 10.30 shows the process for mirrored updates.

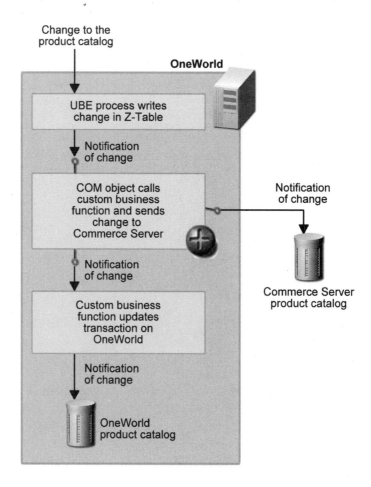

Figure 10.30 Mirrored updates

You can use the mirrored update technique by itself or you can combine it with the batch download technique.

The outbound trigger mechanism in OneWorld is single-threaded and can be a performance bottleneck. To optimize performance, you can assemble all of the parameters received from the OneWorld trigger to the outbound DLL and place the message into a message queue. A code example showing how to do this is located on the Commerce Server Resource Kit CD in the file JDE_mirrored_update.txt.

Real-Time Integration

You can use the real-time technique to immediately download a product price from OneWorld to Commerce Server. Figure 10.31 shows the process for this real-time technique.

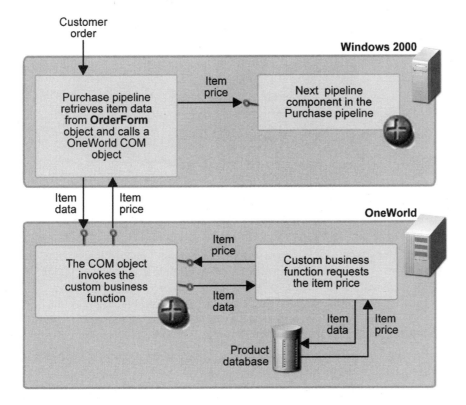

Figure 10.31 Real-time downloads

Using real-time downloads, prices for the items in an order are calculated only when the order is ready for purchase. Prices are configured in OneWorld, not in the Commerce Server Product Catalog System. This technique also relies on a custom pipeline component that calls a previously created OneWorld COM object created with the GenCom client tool. The OneWorld COM wrapper object then invokes the OneWorld custom business function to obtain pricing information. After the item prices and order costs are retrieved from OneWorld, the Commerce Server **OrderForm** object is updated with the new data.

Orders

You can use any one of the following techniques to upload Commerce Server orders to OneWorld:

- Batch download using the Z-Table

- Real-time integration using the OneWorld COM object in the Purchase pipeline

- Integration using queued connectors

- Mirrored updates using Message Queuing

- Mirrored updates using BizTalk Server

You can design batch techniques for sending Commerce Server orders to OneWorld by exporting Commerce Server order data to a Z-Table format. The Z-Table can then be processed by a custom UBE, which places orders into OneWorld by means of the batch interface in Batch mode. This technique requires little customization of OneWorld programs.

If you use a real-time (synchronous) technique to download order data from Commerce Server to OneWorld, you must use the GenCom client tool to create a OneWorld COM object to communicate with the master business functions (MBFs) required for sales order entry.

If you expect only low order volumes, you can create a custom pipeline component to get the order data from the Commerce Server **OrderForm** object, map the data to an ADO recordset, and invoke the COM object generated by the GenCom tool for sales order entry. The OneWorld COM object can then download the order into OneWorld synchronously. When you use this technique, you can easily alert customers if an order fails during processing by OneWorld.

If you expect medium order volumes and want to ensure faster execution, you can pass the order number to a COM+ queued component, then return control to the pipeline. However, if you use this queued technique, you can't notify a customer in real time if the order fails in OneWorld; you have to notify the customer by a generated e-mail message, fax, or phone call.

If you expect high order volumes and want to update OneWorld in a more controlled, asynchronous manner, you can pass the order number through Message Queuing to a Listener service optimized for ERP order integration. The service then picks up the message and calls the OneWorld COM object to update OneWorld with the order data.

As an alternative to using an asynchronous ERP integration service, you can use BizTalk Server to pass the message to the appropriate AIC. The AIC can then map the passed XML document to parameters necessary for the OneWorld COM wrapper object call into OneWorld. Alternatively, it can transform and pass a OneWorld-specific XML document directly into OneWorld using Message Queuing or the XML CallObject API.

If you use any of the asynchronous techniques, including the batch download Z-Table technique, you can't send OneWorld error information to customers in real time. You have to devise an asynchronous technique to notify customers if you use any of these techniques.

Batch Download Using the Z-Table

If you place extracted Commerce Server order data into the appropriate Z-Table, you must then run a UBE to import Z-Table data into OneWorld by means of the business functions used to create sales orders. You usually use this technique with applications that do not require real-time order processing by the OneWorld system.

Figure 10.32 shows how you would use a Z-Table for the batch download technique.

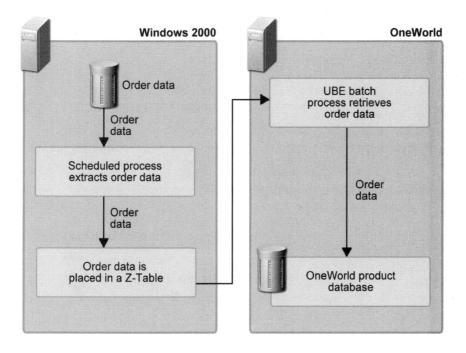

Figure 10.32 Batch download technique using a Z-Table

Real-Time Integration Using OneWorld COM Objects in the Purchase Pipeline

Using the real-time integration technique, as soon as the Purchase pipeline accepts an order, a custom pipeline component maps **OrderForm** object data to the parameters required by the OneWorld COM wrapper object for the Sales Order MBFs. After the data is mapped, the OneWorld COM object is invoked to create the order in OneWorld. If the order is rejected for any reason, the pipeline component fails the entire transaction and notifies the customer that an error has occurred.

You can use this technique in a low-volume site, because the volume of traffic does not adversely affect application server performance. Figure 10.33 shows real-time integration using the OneWorld COM wrapper object.

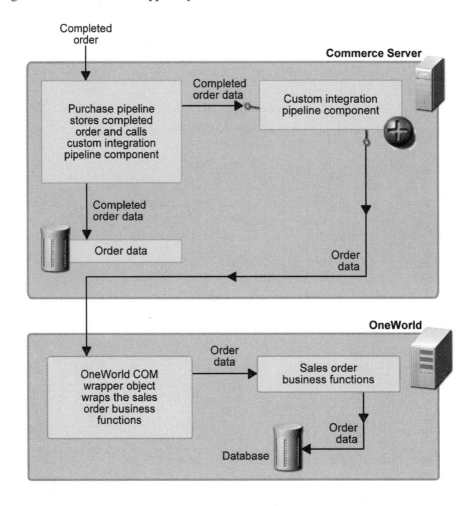

Figure 10.33 Real-time integration using the OneWorld COM object

The file JDE_sales_order.txt, located on the Commerce Server 2000 Resource Kit CD, contains a script and batch file that shows how to create a OneWorld **COM** wrapper object to wrap the business function and data structures used to retrieve updated catalog data. The file JDE_sales_order.txt also contains an example of Visual Basic COM+ code illustrating a Commerce Server Purchase pipeline function that calls a generated OneWorld **COM** object to wrap the sales order business function.

Integration Using Queued Connectors

When you use queued connectors to download order information from Commerce Server to OneWorld, the Commerce Server application does not have to wait until OneWorld processes the order before returning control to the customer. Using this technique, you pass the order number to a COM+ queued connector from a custom pipeline component in the Purchase pipeline. The queued connector then uses Commerce Server objects to read the saved order and map the order data to the parameters required by the OneWorld **COM** object. The **OrderCreate** method creates the order in the OneWorld system. If an error occurs in the OneWorld update process, you have to use an out-of-bounds mechanism to inform the customer that an error has occurred.

Figure 10.34 shows the process of using queued connectors to download order information from Commerce Server to OneWorld.

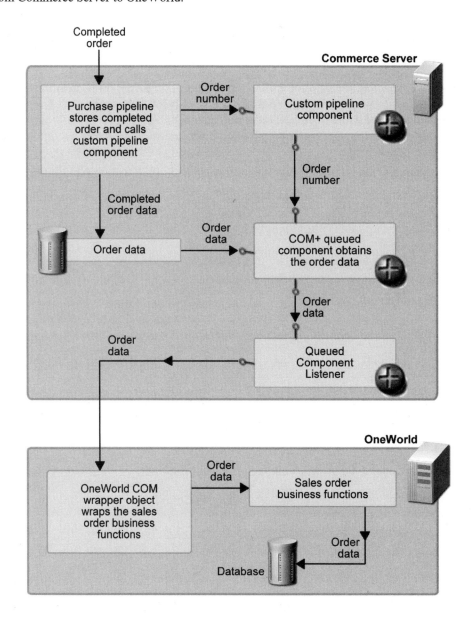

Figure 10.34 Using queued connectors to download order information

The file JDE_create_order.txt, located on the Commerce Server 2000 Resource Kit CD, contains an example of code for a Visual Basic COM+ object that creates an order in OneWorld from a Commerce Server **OrderForm** object. The only items passed to the function are the order number and the ADO connection string to the Commerce Server database. This object could be placed in a COM+ application marked as *Queued*. Most of the code is similar to that found in the JDE_sales_order.txt file.

Mirrored Updates Using Message Queuing

When you use Message Queuing with the mirrored updates technique, you use a custom pipeline component to place the order number in the message queue. The order is also stored in the Commerce Server database and a confirmation is displayed to the customer. An asynchronous OneWorld updating service with application server throttling reads the message queue and picks up the order message. The updating service then instantiates a custom Visual Basic object that uses Commerce Server objects to read the order data and map it to parameters required by the OneWorld **COM** object. The OneWorld **COM** wrapper object then invokes the **OrderCreate** method to submit the order to OneWorld. If an error occurs during order submission, you must use an out-of-bounds process to notify the customer.

Figure 10.35 shows the process for using mirrored updates with Message Queuing.

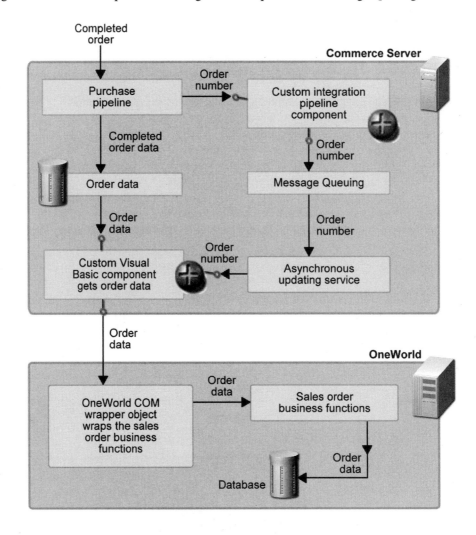

Figure 10.35 Using mirrored updates with Message Queuing

Mirrored Updates Using BizTalk Server

When you use the mirrored updates technique with BizTalk Server, a custom pipeline component in the Purchase pipeline creates an XML document from **OrderForm** object data and submits the document to BizTalk Server. BizTalk Server then instantiates the specified channel, which passes the XML order document to the AIC responsible for updating OneWorld.

This technique is similar to the asynchronous service technique. In fact, you can use this technique with the asynchronous updating service to get better control of the data being downloaded to OneWorld.

The file JDE_orderform.txt, located on the Commerce Server 2000 Resource Kit CD, contains pipeline component pseudocode that creates the XML document from the **OrderForm** object. It also contains application integration component pseudocode that creates the OneWorld order from the XML document.

Figure 10.36 shows the mirrored updates process using BizTalk Server.

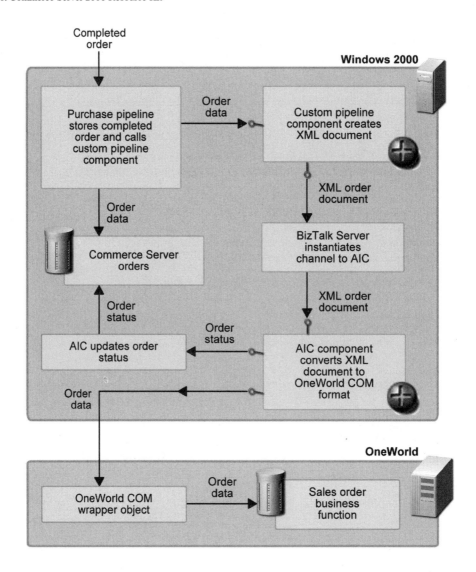

Figure 10.36 Mirrored updates using BizTalk Server

Migrating from Site Server to Commerce Server 2000

Migrating an e-commerce site developed with Microsoft Site Server 3.0 or Site Server 3.0 Commerce Edition (SSCE) to a site based on Microsoft Commerce Server 2000 requires careful planning. You must first analyze how your site uses each Site Server feature before you can determine its migration path. Most SSCE features have corresponding features in Commerce Server, but some Site Server 3.0 features do not.

Although Site Server 3.0 and SSCE provide excellent deployment platforms, neither can take advantage of Microsoft Windows 2000 technology, which includes advances in directory services, clustering, and administration. By using Commerce Server, you can leverage the advantages of Windows 2000 Server, including its comprehensive set of Web and Internet services that are compatible with the latest Web technologies, from simple site hosting to advanced Web applications and streaming media services.

Commerce Server also works with Internet Information Services (IIS) 5.0 to provide robust and powerful e-commerce services. IIS 5.0 provides your Web site with an interface for interacting with the authentication engine of Windows 2000. IIS also provides an interface to the networking protocol layer and the front end for servicing client requests. This seamless interface allows IIS services to interact with Commerce Server as a collection of ASPs, HTML, dynamic HTML, and other objects.

Active Directory

Instead of maintaining a separate membership directory, as you did with your Site Server 3.0 or SSCE site, Commerce Server uses the Windows 2000 Active Directory service to provide membership services. Active Directory provides a hierarchical view, increased extensibility and scalability, and distributed security that large organizations require. When you use Active Directory, you don't have to implement and manage additional directory services, so you can save on administrative and hardware costs. Active Directory integration provides single sign-in per-user authentication instead of tying security to a certain incoming IP address and requiring users to log on again to provide their names.

You can scale Active Directory from a small installation with a few hundred objects to a very large installation with millions of objects. Active Directory also provides an extensible schema, which contains a definition for every object that can exist in a directory service.

Commerce Server Site Packager

Commerce Server includes a new deployment tool called the Commerce Server Site Packager, which you use to package all of the contents of a Commerce Server site, and install the same site on another Web server. Site Packager packages all the content, scripts, configuration information, and all other relevant data about a site into a binary file, which can then be transported to other servers for unpacking. This facilitates the installation of your site across an entire server farm. Site Packager can be run from a command-line interface so you can easily incorporate it into scripts for building new servers.

Commerce Server Business Desk

Commerce Server Business Desk is a Web-based site management tool that hosts business management modules. You can use these modules to perform tasks, such as the following:

- Make changes to a site, such as changing content, updating a catalog, or targeting new ads to users

- Run reports to measure site productivity

Profiling System

SSCE used various types of records to store user attributes. Commerce Server provides a Profiling System that stores user attributes. You can use Active Directory and the Profiling System to create a virtual map of all attributes, thus making it appear to applications as though all user information is located in one physical database. Applications no longer have to ensure that a particular type of user data is sent to the correct database.

For example, an application requesting all user information receives user name, password, address, telephone number, e-mail address, and all other available data. In addition, the Profiling System can access the personalization store to retrieve a specific user's favorite color, stock symbols, or similar preferences.

It is important to note that the Profiling System does not create a new database. It manages the location of data stored in existing databases, and provides an interface to the data for applications. The Profiling System also caches recently or frequently used records.

With Commerce Server, you can store user attributes using either Active Directory or a Microsoft SQL Server database. If your site requires authorization and a security context for each user, then security attributes should be stored in Active Directory. If your site tracks personalization information for a user, that information can be stored in a SQL Server database. Commerce Server can locate and provide requested user data from either location.

If you require both authentication and personalization, the Commerce Server Profiling System can aggregate data between Active Directory and the SQL Server database. User authentication information, such as user name and password, can be stored in Active Directory, while the personalization attributes, such as favorite color and last time visited, are stored in a SQL Server database.

Before You Migrate

To migrate from Site Server to Commerce Server, you use the same methodology that you use to develop a new site:

- Plan

- Develop

- Deploy

While you plan for migration, it is also a good time to plan a full upgrade of your site. During the Planning phase, you should review requests for enhancements and analyze existing Web log data to determine what your customers need. Refer to the Commerce Server *Getting Started Guide* to plan site features that take advantage of the Commerce Server Profiling System, Product Catalog System, Targeting System, Business Analytics System, Business Process Pipelines, and the Commerce Server Data Warehouse.

When migrating your site from Site Server to Commerce Server, you can perform many activities in parallel, as shown in Figure 11.1.

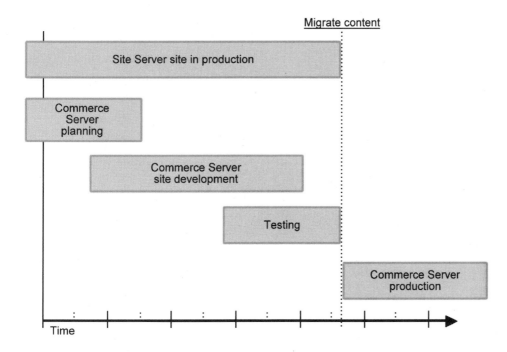

Figure 11.1 Migration timeline

Planning the Migration

As you plan how to migrate your site from one application to another, be sure to read this chapter thoroughly. The following table contains a list of questions you must answer as you plan your migration strategy.

Subject	Question
Features	• What features of Site Server or SSCE do you use?
Risk management	• What risks are involved in upgrading your site to Commerce Server?
	• Do you expect to have periods of downtime? If not, what steps are you going to take to guarantee that your site continues to function?
	• What is your fallback plan?
Site upgrade	• Are you planning to take this opportunity to upgrade your site in other ways? For example, is it time to upgrade your servers to take advantage of the newest technologies?
	• Are you going to add hardware or reconfigure networks?
Timing	• What is your window of opportunity? How long will it take to migrate to Commerce Server?
Resources	• How much effort will it take to perform the migration?
	• How many people do you need to do the work?
	• Who are the people?
Knowledge transfer	• Who knows the most about your current site?
	• Are there additional people who need to have this information? If so, how are you going to transfer and preserve that knowledge?
Deployment	• How do you plan to deploy your new site?
	• Have you provided for each of the necessary environments (development, test, staging, and production)?
	• Have you planned how to implement operational procedures you need for the new site?
Testing	• Who will test the functionality and behavior of the site in the development and test environments?

The following table lists the types of items you must consider when planning your migration.

Item	Consider
Data	User profiles, receipts, orders, shopper records, product catalog, and so on
Static site content	HTML, GIFs, and so on
Application logic	ASP pages, pipeline/Microsoft Transaction Server (MTS)/middleware components
Content deployment	Using Microsoft Application Center 2000 for content replication
Content search	Commerce Server provides product catalog searching capabilities, but not content searching; Windows 2000 Index Server provides intranet searching
Platform software	Commerce Server requires Windows 2000 Server and SQL Server 7.0 or SQL Server 2000
Integration with existing third-party software	Software for processing credit cards and orders, calculating taxes, and managing inventory, shipping, fulfillment, and other information that flows between your site and existing systems

Your migration plan should contain at least the following elements:

- Site architecture diagrams

- Feature analysis

- Supporting software

- A plan for moving existing software and features forward

- Acceptance tests for the migrated site

- Operational plan for managing and operating the new site once it's in production

Before beginning your migration, see http://www.microsoft.com/siteserver for the latest system upgrades and installation instructions. Currently, you must do the following:

- Upgrade your existing Site Server 3.0 or SSCE site to use Site Server Service Pack 4 (SP4)

- Upgrade your SQL Server installation to the latest version compatible with Commerce Server (SQL Server 7.0 or SQL Server 2000)

- Save your Web site usage logs in World Wide Web Consortium (W3C) format and archive them for import to the Commerce Server Business Analytics System

Feature Analysis

As you begin to conduct a feature (or *gap*) analysis of your current site, with migration to the Commerce Server platform in mind, you should ask the following questions:

- What is our current functionality?

- What features of SSCE are we using?

- Which features does Commerce Server offer?

- Which features does Commerce Server not offer?

- What new features of Commerce Server should we use?

The following table shows how Site Server and SSCE features map to Commerce Server features.

Site Server/SSCE features	Commerce Server 2000 features or related resources
Active Channel Multicaster/Active Channel Server (ACM/ACS)	No equivalent functionality.
Ad Server	Campaigns modules, which include added functionality. You can use the Ad Server Migration tool located in the Commerce Server 2000 SDK to migrate Ad Server from Site Server to Commerce Server. For more information, read about the Directory Migration Toolbox in "Developing Your Site" and "Migrating the Membership Directory" in Commerce Server 2000 Help.
Analysis – import	Data Warehouse.
Analysis Report Writer	Business Analytics System. Microsoft Office Web tools are used by Business Desk to display reports. For details about how to create custom reports for existing data in the Data Warehouse, see Commerce Server 2000 Help.
Catalog	Product Catalog System.
Commerce Interchange Pipeline (CIP)	Microsoft BizTalk Server 2000.
Content Analyzer	No equivalent functionality.
Content Replication (deployment)	Available from Application Center and from third parties. You can find the latest information about content replication software developed especially to work with Commerce Server at http://www.microsoft.com/commerceserver.
Cross-sell functionality	The Product Catalog System and Campaigns modules contain cross sell functionality. However, there is no direct migration path.
Direct Mail	Commerce Server Direct Mailer.
Dynamic Directory	Windows 2000 Server Internet Locator Service (ILS) (though it doesn't support dynamic replication).

Site Server/SSCE features	Commerce Server 2000 features or related resources
Knowledge Manager	Future release of Microsoft technology.
Personalization & Membership	Profiling System. Use the Membership Migration tool in the tools section of the Commerce Server 2000 SDK for this migration.
Order Processing Pipeline (OPP)	Business Process Pipelines (pipeline components and Pipeline Editor).
Posting Acceptor	Windows 2000 Web Distributed Authoring and Versioning (WebDAV).
Predictor	Predictor resource, which includes added functionality.
Promotions	Promotions and campaigns.
Publishing Wizard	No equivalent functionality.
Rules	Expressions and ASP code.
Search	Commerce Server provides search capabilities on product catalog information. Windows 2000 Index Server provides search capabilities for intranet search. For more information about companies who provide capabilities for Internet browsing, see http://www.microsoft.com/commerceserver/.
Site Vocabulary	Site terms (flat structure).
Tag Tool	No equivalent functionality.
Transactions	Use the Transaction Migration tool found on the Commerce Server 2000 Resource Kit CD to migrate from Site Server to Commerce Server.

When you have finished your feature analysis, chosen which Commerce Server features to use, and decided which data items to migrate, you should answer the following questions:

- What tools do we need to perform the migration?

- What tools are available?

- What modifications do we need to make to the code?

- What testing do we have to do?

Migration Strategies and Scenarios

This section describes how to perform your migration in five phases. Before you begin, however, you should keep the following migration strategies in mind:

- Start with the Blank Solution Site provided by Commerce Server if you are migrating from SSCE to Commerce Server.

- Design your catalog schema early in the development process.

- Identify the trade-offs between using Windows 2000 Active Directory and SQL Server for your site. Based on performance and scale projections, begin building your profile storage system.

- Focus on migrating to equivalent site functionality instead of trying to incorporate every new Commerce Server feature at the beginning. Later, you can add other Commerce Server features.

- Upgrade SSCE to a Windows 2000 Server platform using Site Server 3.0 Commerce Edition, Service Pack 4 (SP4). This will make your migration easier because Commerce Server requires Windows 2000 Server. Windows 2000 provides a 30 percent to 100 percent performance improvement for SSCE sites, as well.

- Migrate your SQL Server 6.5 or SQL Server 7.0 database to SQL Server 2000 to get clustered, full-text-search database support. The Commerce Server Product Catalog System uses the full-text-search capability built into SQL Server 2000. Although you can use SQL Server 7.0, the best practice is to use SQL Server 2000 because it fully supports clustering of the free-text indexes.

Plan to do your migration in the five phases described in this section.

Phase 1: Set Up Commerce Server in Your Test Environment

Your goals for a successful migration should include the following:

- Minimal customer disruption

- A fully tested destination platform with all functionality validated at production-level stress loads before going into production

- Sustained viability of the existing test platform used for pre-production testing and staging throughout the migration process

The migration technique described in this section accomplishes these goals. This technique assumes the following:

- The existing SSCE site is in production close to 100 percent of the time.

- You currently have a test/staging environment that can handle your current production load as a failover system, if necessary.

- You have access to additional hardware, network, and physical infrastructure on a short-term basis to use during the migration. If you don't have access to the necessary additional hardware, you can substitute your test platform for the additional hardware.

   Note   Before you begin Phase 1, back up your entire system and thoroughly test your backup restoration procedure.

In Phase 1, you set up a new test/staging platform to continue supporting the existing SSCE-based production site. You then rebuild the old test platform using Commerce Server to act as your pre-production environment. Figure 11.2 shows the state of the network during Phase 1.

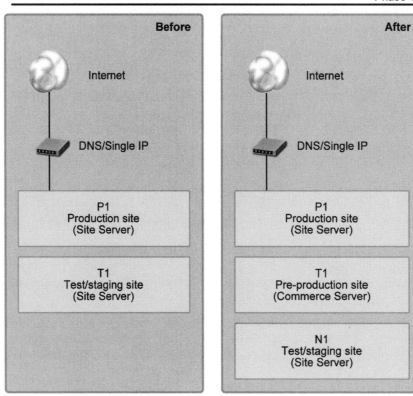

Figure 11.2 State of network during Phase 1

In Phase 1, you do the following:

1. Build out your new production environment (N1) as a clone of your existing test environment (T1) and install SSCE. Your N1 environment will be made up of additional hardware that is not already in use in one of the existing site environments (development, test/staging, or production). Those environments should remain intact during this process.

    The Domain Name System (DNS) should continue to point at your existing production environment (P1), with no changes yet. The following work items are typical of the work that you need to do in this step (though this list might not include everything you need to do):

    *   Build the hardware and network

    *   Install Microsoft Windows NT 4.0 Server

    *   Install SSCE

- Install Windows NT service packs

- Install SSCE service packs

- Using build-out scripts, add extended attributes to the Membership Directory

- Configure the Ad server

- Configure the Personalization & Membership feature

- Configure the Web server(s)

- Install site files

- Install extensions to the site database

- Configure the marketing system

- Configure the analysis engine

- Configure reports

- Configure the transaction system

- Verify that the site is fully functional in all respects

2. Test and confirm that N1 is also an exact copy of your test environment (T1).

- Confirm that all pages work as expected, including ads, promotions, cross sell, personalization, transactions, logging, and data storage

3. Make N1 your SSCE test site.

- Update Content Replication System (CRS) jobs to post new code to the new test platform

- Notify your production staff of the change in test platforms

4. Rebuild the T1 environment as a Commerce Server site (Windows 2000, SQL Server 2000, Commerce Server, and so on). For instructions about how to do this, see the Commerce Server installation instructions located at http://support.microsoft.com/support/commerceserver/2000/install/default.asp.

- Format the hardware disk drives

- Follow product instructions for installing Windows 2000 Server on each server

- Configure the appropriate servers for Windows 2000 Active Directory

- Follow instructions for installing SQL Server 2000 on the appropriate servers

- Follow instructions for installing Commerce Server on the appropriate servers

- Configure the appropriate servers for Windows 2000 ILS for caching support

5. Test Commerce Server in your T1 environment by testing it with the Blank site after you have unpacked it in Site Packager.

Phase 2: Migrate Site Code and Content

In Phase 2, you deploy the migrated SSCE-based site to Commerce Server on the T1 environment. Figure 11.3 shows the state of the network during Phase 2.

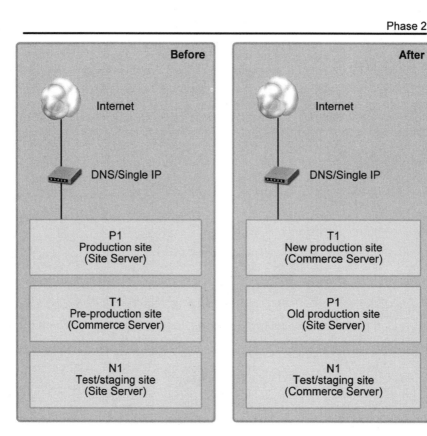

Figure 11.3 State of network during Phase 2

In Phase 2, you do the following:

1. If you currently use personalization, you must migrate user data into a store that the Commerce Server Profiling System can use (SQL Server or Active Directory). You can use the Membership Migration tool (Directory Migration Toolbox) located in the Commerce Server 2000 SDK to help you do this migration.

   - If you use a Windows NT 4.0 domain for authentication, see the document *Upgrading a Windows NT Domain* in Windows 2000 Server Help for instructions about upgrading the Windows NT 4.0 domain to Active Directory.

- If your site contains personalization data not contained in the Windows NT 4.0 SAM or in the Membership Directory, you must move the data to another store. See Commerce Server 2000 Help for information about suitable stores and how to do this.

- If you currently use an LDAP store that supports LDAP 3.0, the Commerce Server Profiling System can treat the existing store as a source for user information, but Commerce Server won't be able to authenticate users against the store. To authenticate users, you have to supplement this store with another store (SQL Server or Active Directory) that Commerce Server can use for authentication. When you build a Commerce Server user profile, you must define a common join key that the **ProfileService** object can use to pull the appropriate attributes for a specified user from multiple stores.

- If you currently use a SQL Server database to store personalization and authentication data, you might be able to use the existing store for the **ProfileService** object. For additional information about how to use an existing SQL Server-based user attribute store with Commerce Server, see "Adding a New Data Source" in Commerce Server 2000 Help.

2. Migrate Ad Server system data, schedule, and tags. See the description of the Ad Server Migration tool later in this chapter for more information about how to do this.

3. Convert content tags to Commerce Server expressions.

4. Import historical logs into the Data Warehouse for use by the Analysis modules and Predictor resource. For instructions about how to do this, see "Importing Data into the Data Warehouse" in the "Running the Data Warehouse" section in Commerce Server 2000 Help.

5. Migrate user transactions from the receipts table using the Transaction Migration tool found on the Commerce Server 2000 Resource Kit CD. If your site contains a significant number of receipts, you can modify the Transaction Migration tool to import only the last "n" number of transactions or transactions that occurred after a specified date.

6. Migrate distribution lists using the StaticExport.vbs script found on the Commerce Server 2000 Resource Kit CD.

7. Re-create usage analysis reports to be used by the Data Warehouse and the Business Analytics System. For instructions about how to do this, see "Creating Custom Reports" in Commerce Server 2000 Help.

   Refer to the VCTurbo_CS2K folder on the Commerce Server 2000 Resource Kit CD for details about how to migrate existing SSCE code to run on Commerce Server 2000.

8. Convert rule-builder logic into scripts that use expressions.

9. Convert all scripts using the catalog system to use a Commerce Server catalog object.

10. Implement the Discount pipeline, as appropriate. For more information, see "About Content Selection Pipelines" in Commerce Server 2000 Help.

11. Implement the Advertising pipeline, as appropriate. For more information, see "About Content Selection Pipelines" in Commerce Server 2000 Help.

12. Configure your system-monitoring tool to check for the new event and performance monitor values generated by Commerce Server, as appropriate.

13. Create a backup package of your site.

14. If you used Secure Sockets Layer (SSL) certificates, make sure that they are enabled on the new Commerce Server servers.

15. Deploy and test any required third-party or custom components.

Phase 3: Move Your New Commerce Server 2000 Site into Production

When you have a fully functional pre-production environment up and running, the next step is to move the Commerce Server site into production. Figure 11.4 shows the state of the network during Phase 3.

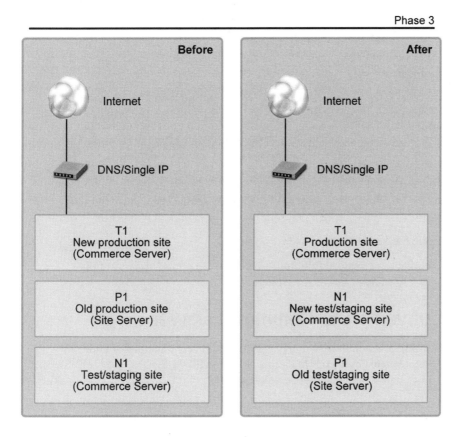

Figure 11.4 State of network during Phase 3

In Phase 3, you do the following:

1. Thoroughly test all site functionality in your pre-production (T1) environment.

   You can use the Web Application Stress (WAS) tool (located at http://homer.rte.microsoft.com) to test load against the new production site. Best practice is to perform a full transaction cost analysis (TCA) on the new site to verify that it will successfully support your current and projected loads. For more information about TCA, see Chapter 19, "Maximizing Performance."

2. Rebuild your production test/staging (N1) environment as a Commerce Server test/staging site. (This becomes the temporary test facility for your Commerce Server site.)

3. Unpack your new Commerce Server site in your new test/staging site (N1) environment.

4. Confirm that directory migration components are in place and ready to begin migrating users when the new Commerce Server site goes live.

5. Import any additional production log files generated since Phase 2.

6. Confirm that the content deployment technologies you have implemented are fully functional.

7. Test all functionality on both Commerce Server sites (the production environment (T1) and the test environment (N1)).

8. During a period of minimal usage, change the DNS and/or Single Internet Provider (IP) solution entry points to your new production (T1) Commerce Server environment.

9. Enable directory migration components to support real-time and batch migration of users from the old Membership Directory (if appropriate).

10. Test all functionality of your site from an external client to confirm full functionality.

    If the site fails, roll DNS/single IP back to your SSCE P1 environment and determine what went wrong.

    When the problem has been identified and resolved, repeat Step 7 in this phase.

After 24 hours, if the site has remained fully functional, you can consider the site fully operational on the new Commerce Server-based platform.

Phase 4: Convert P1 to Commerce Server

Converting your existing production environment (P1) to Commerce Server is a relatively simple procedure, but it is most important to do this cleanly, with the least impact to site users.

There is a brief period during which you can move back to your Site Server site should a failure occur. The exact duration of this period depends greatly on your site's transaction volume. As a general rule, you should be able to go back to your Site Server site within 24 hours, if the Commerce Server site is failing for any reason.

> **Caution** If you revert to Site Server, there is no way to transfer the transactions performed on the Commerce Server site back into Site Server. The migration tools can't do bi-directional synchronization. This means that transactions recorded on the new Commerce Server site will be lost if you have to move back to your Site Server site.
>
> In addition, user information changed during the time the Commerce Server site was in production will not be reflected back to the old SSCE-based site.

If you used the Membership Directory in conjunction with your old SSCE-based site, you should maintain at least a read-only instance of the Membership Directory that is capable of supporting the ongoing migration of users to the stores used by the Commerce Server site until user migration is complete.

Figure 11.5 shows the state of the network during Phase 4.

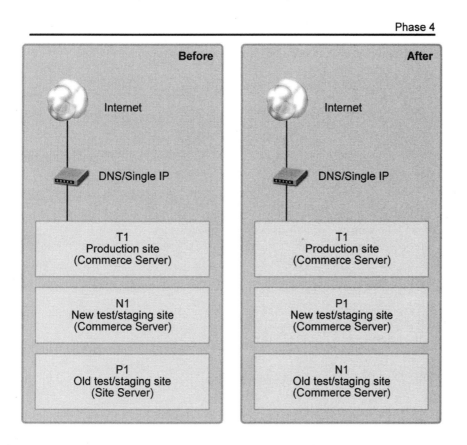

Figure 11.5 State of network during Phase 4

Convert your old production environment (P1) to Commerce Server by doing the following:

1. Rebuild the old production (P1) environment as a Commerce Server test/staging site. (This will then become your new test environment.)

2. Unpack the latest copy of your site to the new test/staging environment (P1).

3. Test all functionality of P1 to be sure it successfully functions as the test environment.

Phase 5: Decommission the N1 Environment

When you have a fully functional Commerce Server production (T1) and test environment (P1), you can decommission the old test/staging site (N1), dismantle the hardware, and return it to its previous use.

Fallback Plan

One important aspect of managing the risks of downtime or data loss to your site during migration is to prepare a fallback plan. A fallback plan should describe the potential problems that might arise during the migration process, such as the following:

- Hardware problems, including hardware configuration
- Software problems, including platform software configuration
- Performance
- Interfaces with your existing corporate systems
- Third-party software issues (for example, pipeline components that do not work)

You should back up the following data during and after the migration:

- Product catalog
- New accounts
- Edited accounts
- Transactions
- Order history
- Inventory information
- Any site-specific, custom data

The following table describes mitigation strategies for a number of failure scenarios.

Failure	Mitigation strategy
Errors or failure while setting up the new production site	Perform thorough testing before moving the new software into production, including stress and load testing. Consider "soft" testing or beta-testing your site by pre-deploying it from the test environment to allow a limited number of users time to encounter any bugs before moving your new site into production.
Failure while moving your site from the test environment into the production environment	Create a plan for immediately reverting back to the old site. Test this scenario, if possible, by taking your production site offline, then bringing it back online. You can use your disaster recovery plan for this effort.
Failure of the new site in production	Consider logging transactions of critical data items, such as orders and user profiles, in a format that can be readily re-imported by the old site. This might require tool development and should be considered when estimating the development effort.

Developing

This section provides general development-related information and describes development best practices for migrating an SSCE site to Commerce Server. Be sure to see Commerce Server 2000 Help, the Commerce Server 2000 SDK, and the other development chapters in this book for suggestions and best practices for developing ASP pages and other site components.

Consider using the Blank Solution Site shipped with Commerce Server to prototype your new site. Two additional Solution Sites (Retail and Supplier) are available for download from http://www.microsoft.com/commerceserver/solutionsites. All three Solution Sites provide examples of best practices for coding sites with Commerce Server. Consider using a Solution Site as the basis for coding your site if your site is sufficiently like one of them, rather than migrating code and components from your existing site.

> **Note**   Even if you use a Solution Site as the basis for developing your site, you will still have to migrate user and product catalog data.

The site development process consists of the following steps:

1. Port Web pages from Site Server to Commerce Server.

2. Develop new components or pages.

3. Configure migration tools.

4. Modify sample code for tools.

5. Run migration tools.

6. Unit test all new code.

7. Perform integration testing.

8. Perform acceptance testing at full scale and load in staging area.

The tools in the following table can assist you with migration.

Use this tool	To
SQL Server DTS	Process data before writing custom components. For more information about the SQL Server DTS tool, see SQL Server Books Online.
Membership Migration tool	Migrate user data from the Membership Directory to stores used by the Commerce Server Profiling System. This tool is available in the Commerce Server 2000 SDK. For more information about this tool, see "Personalization & Membership" later in this chapter.
Ad Server Migration tool	Migrate data and schedules. This tool is available in the Commerce Server 2000 SDK.
Transaction Migration tool	Migrate transaction data. This tool is available on the Commerce Server 2000 Resource Kit CD.
Catalog Migration tool	Import a catalog from either an Extensible Markup Language (XML) file or a comma-separated value (CSV) file. You must first write code to export your SSCE custom catalog into one of these formats. The script MigrateCatalog.vbs, which is located on the Commerce Server 2000 Resource Kit CD, is an example of a catalog import script for importing the Volcano Coffee catalog. It provides a migration path from a SSCE online store to a Commerce Server catalog. Also, for more information about migrating a catalog, see the VCTurbo_CS2K folder on the Commerce Server 2000 Resource Kit CD.

Migrating Site Server 3.0 Features

Most Site Server 3.0 features have corresponding features in Commerce Server and the Microsoft .NET Enterprise Servers environment. However, some features, including Active Channel Multicaster (ACM), Tag Tool, and Content Analyzer, do not.

This section provides tips for migrating the following Site Server 3.0 feature areas to Commerce Server:

- Analysis
- Content management
- Knowledge management
- Personalization & Membership

Analysis

Commerce Server contains the following components for performing business analysis:

- Data Warehouse

- Business Analytics System

The Commerce Server Business Analytics System and Data Warehouse features are not compatible with the Analysis package found in Site Server 3.0. Commerce Server has many standard reports that might meet your reporting requirements. If you need custom reporting capabilities, you can write your own (for examples, see "Creating Custom Reports" in the "Extending Commerce Server" section in Commerce Server 2000 Help). There are also a number of vendors who provide comprehensive reporting products that work well with Commerce Server. For information about these vendors and their products, see http://www.microsoft.com/commerce server/.

You can also create new reports using information in your log files. For more information, see Commerce Server 2000 Help. If you need to import custom data into the Data Warehouse and report on it, you must create a custom Data Transformation Services (DTS) task to import the data before you create a custom report to report on the data.

To maintain continuity, you must import existing logs into the Data Warehouse. You need to import only enough data to satisfy your existing trending periods. For example, if you usually track performance for 90 days, you need to import 90 days' worth of historical data into the Data Warehouse.

The following table describes the migration path for Site Server analysis features.

Feature	Migration path
Analysis – Import	Data Warehouse. To migrate, you:
	• Save log files.
	• Import log files (for last "n" days).
	• Create custom-import DTS scripts, if necessary.
Report Writer	Business Analytics System. The Commerce Server 2000 SDK provides examples of several types of custom reports.
Content Analyzer	No equivalent functionality.

Figure 11.6 shows a timeline for migrating the Analysis functions from Site Server 3.0 to Commerce Server 2000.

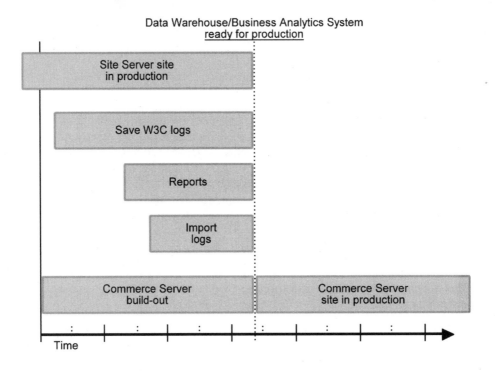

Figure 11.6 Timeline for migrating Analysis functions

Content Management

You can use the Commerce Server Site Packager and Application Center to deploy content. The following table describes the migration path for Site Server content management features.

Feature	Migration path
Content Replication (deployment)	• Use Site Packager to deploy simple site installations. • Use Application Center to replicate content over a local area network (LAN). • Use the Content Replication System (CRS), which is shipped with Application Center, to deploy on a wide area network (WAN).
Posting Acceptor	WebDAV.
Publishing Wizard	No equivalent functionality.
Tag Tool	No equivalent functionality.

For information about how to deploy content using the Commerce Server platform, see Chapter 15, "Deploying Content."

Knowledge Management

Commerce Server contains the following knowledge management components:

- Commerce Server Direct Mailer

- Catalog search

- Site terms

This section describes how to migrate the following Site Server knowledge management components to Commerce Server:

- Direct Mail

- Search

- Site Vocabulary

Commerce Server contains no equivalent functionality for the following Site Server knowledge management components:

- ACM/ACS

- Knowledge Manager

Direct Mail

Commerce Server Direct Mailer is faster and more scalable than the Site Server 3.0 Direct Mail function. In addition, it is easier to integrate and manage, and you can personalize it. The following table describes the migration path for Site Server Direct Mail features.

Feature	Migration path
Dynamic distribution lists	Migrate users, then create a dynamic report of the users using the Commerce Server Business Desk Reports module. Import the list of users into the List Manager module from the Reports module.
Static distribution lists	Export static distribution lists from the SSCE Membership Directory to a CSV file for import by the List Manager module, in the following format:

```
Mailto, [GUID], [message format], [language], [URL]
```

Use the StaticExport.vbs script on the Commerce Server 2000 Resource Kit CD as a prototype for creating CSV files for import into the Direct Mailer database.

Figure 11.7 shows the Direct Mail conversion process.

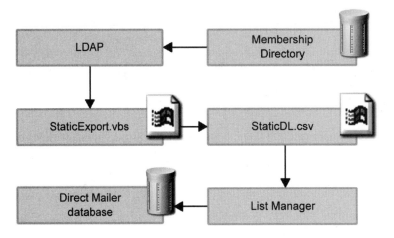

Figure 11.7 Direct Mail conversion process

Search

Site Server provided the following three types of searches:

- **Catalog searches**. The Commerce Server Product Catalog System provides search capabilities on product catalog information. In addition to improved scalability and performance, it also supports probabilistic ranking, "find similar," and natural-language queries. If you use SQL Server 2000 with Commerce Server, you also receive free-text search capabilities without adding an external search engine.

- **Intranet searches**. Windows 2000 Index Server provides search capabilities for intranet search. The Commerce Server Business Desk Help Search feature uses the Index Server. For more information about Index Server, see http://www.microsoft.com/ntserver/web/techdetails/overview/IndxServ.asp.

- **Internet searches**. Neither Commerce Server nor Windows 2000 Index Server provide Internet search capabilities. For information about companies who provide capabilities for Internet searching and indexing for use with Commerce Server sites, see http://www.microsoft.com/commerceserver/.

Site Vocabulary

Commerce Server provides a site terms feature, which you use to create a list of specific values pertinent to your site. You then assign each value to a profile property as the property type. For example, you can create a site term named *City*, then display possible locations in a drop-down list from which customers make a selection. The site terms feature is a flat structure. To migrate from Site Server 3.0 Site Vocabulary (which is a hierarchical structure) to Commerce Server site terms, consider the following options:

- Flatten the hierarchy of your Site Vocabulary structure
- Recreate Site Vocabulary entries as site terms
- Use SQL Server for large Site Vocabulary trees

Personalization & Membership

Commerce Server contains the following components that map to certain SSCE Personalization & Membership features:

- Profiling System
- Expressions

This section describes how to migrate the following Site Server Personalization & Membership features to Commerce Server 2000:

- Authentication
- Dynamic Directory
- Lightweight Directory Access Protocol (LDAP)
- Membership
- Personalization
- Rules

Authentication

Commerce Server supports the following authentication modes:

- **Windows Authentication**. AuthFilter controls site access through access control lists (ACLs).
- **Custom Authentication**. Using AuthFilter basic services, you create a custom authentication process to control site access.
- **Autocookie**. Anonymous users can access the site. AuthFilter generates a persistent cookie (MSCS Profile ticket) to track an anonymous user.

For more information about AuthFilter, see Commerce Server 2000 Help. For more information about authentication, see Chapter 14, "Deploying Your Site."

If you store user IDs and credentials in Active Directory, you can use any form of authentication supported by Windows 2000 and Internet Information Services (IIS) 5.0, including the following:

- NTLM

- Kerberos

- Digital certificates

- Basic HTTP authentication

- HTTP forms authentication

- Cookie authentication

- FormsAuth

If you want to use data in the Membership Directory for authentication, you must migrate it to Commerce Server.

Note Distributed Password Authentication (DPA) is not supported; however, Commerce Server works with Passport. For more information about Commerce Server/Passport interoperability, see "Integrating with Passport" in the "Extending Commerce Server" section in Commerce Server 2000 Help.

Dynamic Directory

Site Server ILS Services are now available in Windows 2000 Server. It replaces the Site Server ILS Services/Dynamic Directory. Note that the current version shipped in Windows 2000 Server does not support replication between service instances, so it is not a true fault-tolerant system. If you used the Site Server ILS as a store for session state information, and your Commerce Server site requires the same functionality, store your data in a SQL Server 2000 database to maintain high availability. If you choose to use the Windows 2000 Server ILS, you must recreate your ILS/Dynamic Directory schema when you migrate from Site Server to Commerce Server. For more information about using Windows to migrate Site Server ILS Services/Dynamic Directory to Commerce Server, see the *Windows 2000 Resource Kit*.

LDAP

If your site has an application that requires LDAP, it can continue to use the LDAP interface to Active Directory, as long as the attributes the application needs are located in Active Directory.

Membership

The following table lists options for migrating your Membership Directory from Site Server to Commerce Server.

Migration option	Description
Windows 2000 Server Active Directory	• Active Directory is required for access control list (ACL)/ access control entry (ACE)-based access control to static content through group permissions.
	• Active Directory is the best option for storing attributes that don't change often (such as names).
	• Active Directory is necessary to support deployments requiring access control of files that map to groups of users.
	• Performance is better when you have large volumes of read activity, with minimal write activity.
	• Active Directory provides better security than SQL Server. Commerce Server leverages Windows 2000 security if you use Active Directory.
SQL Server	• SQL Server relies on the application to control content.
	• Support for groups is limited to approximately 200 members, due to the way group information is stored.
	• Tune SQL Server for equal read and write performance.
	• SQL Server is supported for authentication.
	• SQL Server is the best option for managing data that changes frequently (last visit, favorites, and so on).
Combined Active Directory and SQL Server	• The combination of Active Directory and SQL Server 2000 provides both access control (Active Directory) and enhanced performance for data that changes often (SQL Server).
	In this scenario, you would store data associated with user credentials and other stable data in an Active Directory store. You would store the remaining attributes in a SQL Server database.
LDAP	• The Commerce Server Profiling System only supports using LDAP stores as a property store.
	• CS Authentication doesn't work with LDAP providers.

The following steps outline the process for migrating your Site Server Membership Directory to Commerce Server. For more detailed information about migrating your Membership Directory, see the description of the Membership Migration tool in the Commerce Server 2000 SDK.

1. Determine whether you need on-demand user migration (in which you migrate users on a real-time basis, as they log in to your site) or batch user migration (in which you migrate the entire user database, using a batch method to download the data).

   If you need on-demand migration, you can install the migration objects on the Web servers and use the sample Login.asp as an example of how to trigger a migration on demand.

   If you need batch migration, you can install the migration objects on a stand-alone server, then start the sample client to move users across.

2. Decide which members and which attributes to migrate. This is an excellent opportunity to review and revise your membership structures, if necessary.

3. Determine which Membership Directory attributes are used for all current users.

4. Create Commerce Server user profile equivalents for the Membership Directory user attributes you want to migrate.

5. Modify the Membership Migration tool, if necessary.

6. If necessary, migrate groups using the Membership Migration tool.

7. Create a migration configuration XML file using the Migration ProfileBuilder helper function of the Membership Migration tool.

8. Design tests and test a small population of users.

9. Reapply ACLs on Commerce Server files and directories, as appropriate, after groups are migrated.

The following table shows which property stores provide features comparable to those found in the Membership Directory.

Option	Active Directory	SQL Server	LDAP
User properties	Yes	Yes	Yes
Authentication supported	Yes	Yes	No
Groups	Yes	Yes	No
File access control	Yes	No	No

Figure 11.8 shows the timeline for migrating the Membership Directory.

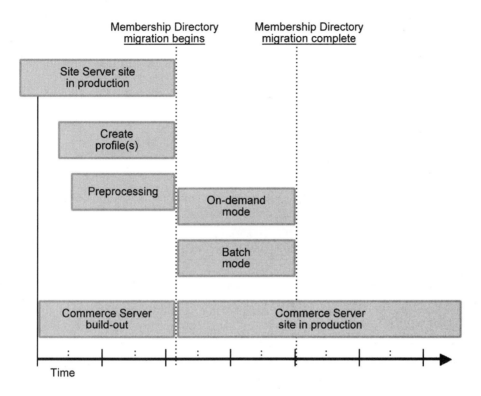

Figure 11.8 Membership Directory migration timeline

The timeline in Figure 11.8 shows that preparatory work is completed prior to migration. Migration occurs after the Commerce Server site goes live.

Membership Migration Tool (Directory Migration Toolbox)

You use the Membership Migration tool (Directory Migration Toolbox) to migrate membership data from Site Server to Commerce Server. You can use it for incremental migration of user profiles (on demand, as users log in), as well as batch migration. This means that users can log in and be migrated in real time even when batch migration mode is running in the background. This removes the need to take your site offline to migrate the Membership Directory.

Figure 11.9 shows the architecture of the Membership Migration tool.

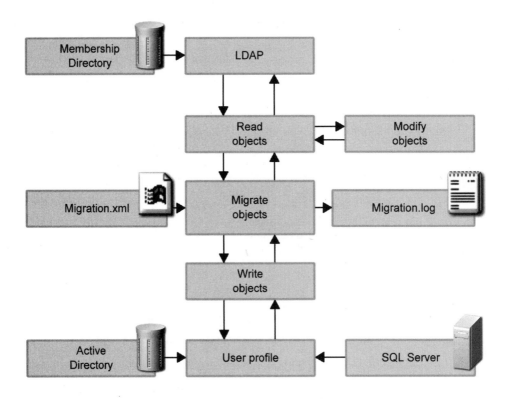

Figure 11.9 Membership Migration tool architecture

The Membership Migration tool is structured as a set of COM objects and configured by means of an XML migration profile. In addition, the Membership Migration tool includes the source code for all of the components so you can modify them to meet your needs. The source code for these components is located at Microsoft Commerce Server\SDK\Tools\Membership Migration after you install Commerce Server using the **Complete** option or **Custom** option with **SDK** selected.

Although the Commerce Server Profiling System supports groups, the implementation depends on the capability of the Profiles data store. You must use the Active Directory to implement groups the same way they were implemented in your Site Server Membership Directory.

You can use Active Directory to create groups and assign ACLs and ACEs to files and directories. However, the implementation is not completely the same. Active Directory limits a group to 5,000 objects. This limit is necessary because of the manner in which the contents of the group are replicated between instances of the domain controllers. Although this limitation will be addressed in future versions of Active Directory, you might have to perform a work-around to migrate your Membership Directory in the meantime.

You can use the Membership Migration tool to create subgroups, and then add user profiles to the subgroups. To preserve space for additional growth and subgroups, the tools fill 4,500 user profiles per subgroup.

Important   You must set up Active Directory in native mode. Do not set up Active Directory in mixed mode; if you do, Active Directory will not create the required groups hierarchy.

Personalization

The Commerce Server **UserProfile** object replaces the Site Server Active User Object (AUO). The **UserProfile** object is compatible with the **IADs** ADSI interface, and should be instantiated in the Global.asa file. For more information about the **UserProfile** object, see Commerce Server 2000 Help. For more information about ADSI, see http://www.microsoft.com/windows2000/library/howitworks/activedirectory/adsilinks.asp.

The Commerce Server Profiling System provides the following functionality:

- Abstracts data location

- Integrates with the Targeting System and the Business Analytics System

- Evaluates expressions in run time

You perform the following steps to migrate from Site Server to Commerce Server:

1. Migrate all code that uses the AUO to use the **UserProfile** object for each ASP.

2. Instantiate the **UserProfile** object in the Global.asa file.

Rules

Commerce Server expressions are named conditionals that evaluate to **True** or **False**. Commerce Server expressions combined with ASP pages are equivalent to Site Server rules. Expressions provide better reuse than rules.

Business Desk contains the Expression Builder, which is fully integrated with the Targeting System and the Content Selection Framework (CSF). To migrate from rules to expressions, you must re-create rules logic as expressions and wrap the expressions in ASP code. For more information about creating expressions, see Commerce Server 2000 Help.

Migrating SSCE Features

You can migrate most SSCE features directly to Commerce Server 2000. SSCE functionality is a superset of the Site Server functionality described in the previous section. This section provides tips for migrating the following SSCE feature areas to Commerce Server:

- Ad Server
- Online store
- Pipelines
- Predictor
- Promotions
- Transaction data

Ad Server

In Commerce Server, functionality corresponding to SSCE Ad Server has been moved to the Targeting System and is accessed from within Business Desk instead of running as a stand-alone management interface, as it did in SSCE. The Ad Server system has been extensively revised.

To migrate Ad server functionality from SSCE to Commerce Server, do the following:

- Migrate ad data
- Migrate ad schedules
- Change ad tags to expressions

Use the Ad Server Migration tool, AdServerMigration.exe, to perform your migration and recode Site Server rules as Commerce Server expressions. The Ad Server Migration tool is available in the Commerce Server 2000 SDK in the SDK\Tools\Migration\Ad Server path in the Commerce Server installation folder.

Online Store

The Commerce Server Product Catalog System is very flexible. It can support imports by means of XML files, CSV files, or Catalog application programming interfaces (APIs). To migrate your SSCE online store to a Commerce Server product catalog, do the following:

1. Create a new catalog in the Product Catalog System.

2. Map your online store structure to your catalog structure. The VCTurbo_CS2K folder, located on the Commerce Server 2000 Resource Kit CD, provides an example of how to do this mapping. The VCTurbo site is a sample site created to demonstrate a performance enhancement to the Volcano Coffee site originally included with SSCE. The script MigrateCatalog.vbs, which is available on the Commerce Server 2000 Resource Kit CD,

migrates the Volcano Coffee Turbo (VCTurbo) catalog from an SSCE online store to a Commerce Server 2000 catalog. The script migrates the catalog by directly calling the catalog APIs.

3. Export your SSCE online store to an XML file, including the following:

   - Products to the Commerce Server catalog

   - Product attributes

   - Product families to Commerce Server product definitions

   - Departments to Commerce Server categories

4. Import the XML file into the Product Catalog System.

To migrate the VC Turbo catalog, do the following:

1. Create definitions.

2. Associate product ID.

3. Create variant values.

4. Create new catalog.

5. Create a department.

6. Migrate product information.

Now, you can use Business Desk to manage your newly migrated catalog.

VC Turbo does not use Personalization & Membership; it uses shopper tables. Therefore, this migration example does not migrate your users. You can migrate users with the Membership Migration tool.

Pipelines

You use pipelines to serialize actions that result in a completed order. For a detailed description of all the pipelines that Commerce Server offers, see Commerce Server 2000 Help and the Order Processing sitelet in the Commerce Server 2000 SDK. There are also several sitelets in the SDK that might be helpful to you as you plan your migration.

The following Site Server pipelines have changed in Commerce Server:

- **Order Processing Pipeline (OPP)**: The Commerce Server OPP API is the same as it was in SSCE. However, most of the underlying pipeline data structures have changed. There is a backward-compatible mode available so that existing pipeline components can be used in the Commerce Server site. However, when you run in compatibility mode, you have to run the entire pipeline in compatibility mode. You can't select compatibility mode at the stage level.

  If the existing pipeline component uses data in the dictionary, it will function as expected. The only data types and formats that have changed are addresses and currency. If the old pipeline component looks for data in a specific location or database table, however, you must rewrite it to use the new data storage locations used in Commerce Server. If possible, use pipelines in native mode to take advantage of the new features of COM+, such as object pooling.

- **Commerce Interchange Pipeline (CIP)**: BizTalk Server has replaced the SSCE CIP pipeline. For information about BizTalk Server, see http://www.microsoft.com/biztalkserver.

Predictor

The Commerce Server Predictor resource provides intelligent and automatic selection of cross-promotional items by correlating the items that a customer has ordered with a database of items that similar customers have ordered previously. The Predictor resource examines the database to find orders that are similar to the current customer's order, and generates a list of recommended products, ensuring that none of the products are already in the current customer's order.

In SSCE, the predictor engine was usually used in conjunction with the intelligent cross-sell function. In Commerce Server, the role of the Predictor resource has been greatly expanded to support the following application scenarios:

- Product area recommendations

- User cluster visualization

- User attribute prediction

Wait to create Prediction models until your new Commerce Server site has been in production for several weeks, because the Predictor resource requires data from the Data Warehouse that was not tracked in the Site Server analysis engine.

Promotions

Commerce Server supports the types of promotions listed in the following table.

Promotion type	Description
Cross sell	A type of promotion in which customers are presented with a list of products related to products they have already purchased. This feature is part of the Product Catalog System.
Intelligent cross sell	A type of promotion in which customers are presented with a list of products based on past purchase behavior and the products they are currently viewing or have added to their baskets. You use the Predictor resource to implement intelligent cross-sell promotions.
Discount	A type of promotion in which shoppers are invited to save money on products or product groups if they meet certain conditions (such as two items for the price of one or discounts for members of a purchasing group). In Commerce Server, discounts have a targeting component and a display component. The Commerce Server 2000 SDK contains a sitelet demonstrating how to implement various discounts.
Up sell	A type of promotion in which shoppers who have purchased one type of item are urged to upgrade to a better version. For example, a shopper who has purchased silver jewelry is shown the same item in gold.

Transaction Data

It is technically possible to migrate SSCE transaction data to Commerce Server 2000. The Commerce Server 2000 Resource Kit CD contains a Transaction Migration tool to help you migrate your transaction data from SSCE to Commerce Server.

The primary reason for converting transaction data is so that you can use a single console (Business Desk) to handle customer support issues. You can also have historical information available for generating reports. If you don't need this data, or if you can obtain it through an existing application, it's probably not worth the effort to move the old data across.

If you decide to migrate SSCE transactions to Commerce Server, use the Transaction Migration tool. The Transaction Migration tool migrates only transaction data (orders and receipts). Transaction data depends on customer and product data, so you must migrate all customer and product data before you use the Transaction Migration tool to migrate transaction data.

Figure 11.10 shows how you might migrate transaction receipts, using the Transaction Migration tool.

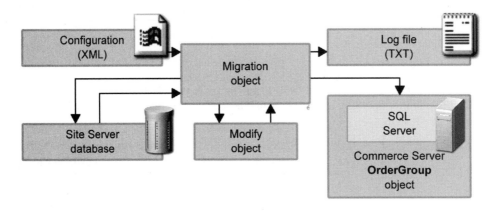

Figure 11.10 Migrating transaction receipts with the Transaction Migration tool

Deploying

The "Migration Strategies and Scenarios" section earlier in this chapter contains a step-by-step scenario for migrating to Commerce Server from a Site Server platform. In addition to that section, review the sources for deployment information listed in the following table.

Source	Contains
Commerce Server 2000 Help	Suggestions for configuring hardware as well as information about how to use Business Desk, Commerce Server Manager, and other key Commerce Server components.
Deployment section of this Resource Kit	Best practices for deploying a Commerce Server site.
http://www.microsoft.com/commerceserver	Latest updates on migration issues and information about third-party vendors.
http://www.microsoft.com/technet	Information about Windows 2000, SQL Server 2000, Commerce Server, and best practices. Select the product you want from the Navigate by Product drop-down list on the left side of the screen.
http://www.microsoft.com	Downloads of tools.
Commerce Server 2000 Resource Kit CD	Downloads of tools and code examples.
Commerce Server 2000 SDK	Code samples, sitelets, and other deployment assistance.

Developing an International Site

This chapter describes best practices for offering multiple languages and currencies when you develop a site for an international audience. Your goal should be to make it easy for your customers to change language or currency at any time without losing context (that is, without being redirected to another page that contains different content). There are several ways to implement multiple languages and currencies. Which one you choose depends on your preferences and on project constraints.

The Microsoft Commerce Server 2000 sample site, a chocolate shop named *Sweet Forgiveness*, located on the Commerce Server 2000 Resource Kit CD. The Sweet Forgiveness site is multilingual and supports multiple currencies. It incorporates several of the methods described in this chapter.

Using Multiple Languages

Most companies would benefit from the ability to offer customers a choice of languages in which to interact with their site. However, many companies either ignore the issue or address it by deploying several versions of their site. For example, Amazon.com provides several versions of its site (Amazon.de and Amazon.nl).

If all versions of a site could be updated simultaneously, having multiple versions would not be a problem. However, in most cases, each version must be updated separately, which can cause the versions to differ significantly. For example, the English version of Amazon.com is much richer in functionality than the German and Dutch versions. Such significant differences can cause confusion for the project team and make the site difficult to manage. This section discusses ways to create a single, multilingual site.

Language-Dependent Strings

There are two types of language-dependent strings used in e-commerce sites:

- Product information

- Site information (including HTML content in advertisements and discount descriptions)

Product Information

Product information strings are the collection of language-dependent properties pertaining to products, such as name and description. Product information should be stored in the product catalog and should be available in all the languages your site supports because a multilingual product catalog is much easier to manage than separate catalogs for each language.

To manage language-dependent properties, simply adjust your code for each property to identify the language in which it is to be displayed. For example, your product might contain a property called **short_description**, which you want to display in English, French, and Dutch. To do this, you can rename **short_description** to **short_description_en** for the English version, **short_description_fr** for the French version, and **short_description_nl** for the Dutch version. When you display the product description, you can then adapt your code to select property **short_description** plus the language code (en for English, fr for French, or nl for Dutch). The language code can be a parameter entered by the user or a property of the user profile.

Site Information

Site information is the collection of strings that the site must display, such as "Product of the Week," "Search," and "OK." You can store the whole set of displayable strings in different languages in a database or in an Extensible Markup Language (XML) file. XML is the better choice because it's more portable. For example, you can send an XML file to a translator by e-mail, if necessary. For an example of how to use an XML file to store displayable strings in different languages, see the Rc.xml file in the Sweet Forgiveness site, which contains all its site information in strings.

The Global.asa file reads the XML file when the application starts. The strings are stored in the Commerce Server **MessageManager** object, which has application scope, thus ensuring that every server in your Web farm has its own copy of the string set for every language.

When a string must be displayed on the site, you can retrieve it from the **MessageManager** object with the following method call:

```
mscsMessageManager.GetMessage(sStringName, sLanguage)
```

To speed up page execution, you can store strings that are displayed often, like menu bars (which are really concatenations of individual strings), in the **CacheManager** object for later retrieval. When you do this, the **MessageManager** object has to look them up only once.

You can use the same technique for other displayable strings, such as descriptions of discounts that you can't change in Commerce Server Business Desk.

Caching

The Commerce Server Solution Sites use the **CacheManager** object extensively. Essentially, the **CacheManager** object is an extended **Dictionary** object, which stores strings in name/value pairs.

If you examine the Solution Site code, you'll see that the name part of a name/value pair is called a *cache key*. If you decide to implement multilingual pages, you need to make cache key generation language-specific. You can do this with the following code:

```
sCacheKey = sCatalogName & sCategoryName & CStr(iPageNumber) & sLanguageCode
```

Using language-specific cache key generation makes the language code part of the cache key, so that the **CacheManager** object can detect which language to display.

Choosing the Language

A basic site scenario, often used in Europe, is to offer users a choice of language on the first visit. A user must click a link or a button to produce the site in the chosen language. The choice is then stored either as a property in the user profile or stored in a cookie on the user's computer so that the appropriate language appears immediately whenever the user revisits the site.

In another scenario, some sites try to guess a user's language preference by looking up the country extension from the IP address. For example, if the user is surfing from proxy.myprovider.co.uk (a U.K.-based provider), they assume that the user speaks English. This is often a convenient strategy, but it is not necessarily the most accurate. For example, many tourists browse the Web from cybercafés when they visit other countries. Other users browse from a .com, .net, or similar address, that doesn't have any obvious relationship to a particular language.

In a third scenario, your site can check the default language setting for users who use Microsoft Internet Explorer. The drawback to this scenario is that many users install the English version of Internet Explorer and then don't change the language settings, even though English might not be their native language. The issue of cybercafés arises in this scenario, too. If a cybercafé using Internet Explorer sets local language parameters, your site will assume that travelers logging in from that location want to view your pages in that language, rather than their own.

The best solution for most sites is probably to use the first scenario: to let the user choose a language, which is then saved in the user's profile. The next time the user logs in from any location, the site will automatically switch to the user's preferred language.

Changing Languages

Multilingual sites should enable the user to change from one language to another on every page. The Sweet Forgiveness sample site does this with a drop-down list from which users can select a new language on any page on the site. Some sites display images of national flags that users can click to select the corresponding language.

Some multilingual sites allow changes in language only on the site home page, which means that users must return to the home page from other locations in the site to select a new language. This method is easy to implement, but less user-friendly than letting users change languages on any page to retain the context of the operation being performed.

There are four ways to encode language context:

- Use a client-side cookie to store the active language code

- Encode the language code in the URL

- Store the language preference in the user profile

- Use pre-generated pages

The method you use depends on project constraints and developer preferences.

Using a Client-Side Cookie with Language Codes

Using a client-side cookie is the easiest way to encode a language context, where permissible. To do this, you simply store a language code (en, fr, nl, and so on) in the cookie and read the cookie on every page that displays language-dependent strings. You can even make the cookie persistent by having it expire on some date far in the future, such as January 1, 2100, so that the site is always aware of a user's language (assuming that the user agrees to make the cookie persistent, of course).

It is best to use this technique only in situations where you can control cookie acceptance, such as proof-of-concept or company-internal projects. If there is a single user whose browser doesn't support cookies, such as a microbrowser in a cell phone, this technique will fail.

Encoding the Language Code in the URL

You can embed the language code in the URL, similar to the way in which the Solution Sites generate the session ID ticket. This means adapting the **GenerateURL** function to add the language code to every link you create, so that the site displays the correct language. For example, you have to call **GenerateURL** for every link so that:

```
http://commercesitename.tld/mypage.asp
```

becomes

```
http://commercesitename.tld/mypage.asp?lang=nl
```

Every page can then simply read the *lang* parameter.

Note   You can't encode the language code with static HTML pages, because HTML pages can't pass any input parameters to other pages.

Storing the Language Preference in the User Profile

Another option for encoding language preferences is to keep a user's language in the user profile. Doing this requires that you add a **language** property to the user profile, which you must then update if a user changes languages. This is a cost-effective method of storing language preferences, because the only performance cost involved is retrieving and updating the profile.

Using Pre-Generated Pages

If your site contains mostly static HTML pages, then using pre-generated pages is another option for encoding language on your site. Pre-generated pages don't have to pass language identification to other pages, because the context of the pages (the directory that the pages are in) provides that capability. Pre-generated pages can link to other pages without providing language information. In addition, pre-generated pages don't have to read cookies, URL parameters, or user profiles to determine which language to display. You can even render pre-generated pages in static HTML.

To pre-generate your pages in all the languages you support, you can put all your pages in a /source directory and mark all strings that can be pre-generated with delimiters in your ASP code. For example, you might specify the Search button as:

```
<INPUT TYPE=SUBMIT VALUE="[[=Search]]">
```

In this fragment, [[=Search]] is a mnemonic for a word that will be translated. You must write a page generator that reads all the pages in the /source directory, looks up the delimited mnemonics using the **MessageManager** object, translates them, and saves the translated pages in a language-specific directory. Using our example of a site supporting English, French, and Dutch, you would read pages from /source and generate pages in the /en, /fr and /nl directories. This process can be automated to run once or twice a day, or whenever you update your site.

The page pre-generation approach saves time at run time and does not rely on the **CacheManager** object. In addition, it can significantly boost performance if your site has many static pages (pages that perform no logic other than to call the **MessageManager** object to look up strings) because now those pages can become truly static HTML pages rather than ASP pages. Putting those static pages on dedicated servers that serve only static content can enhance performance even further.

Using Multiple Currencies

The issues related to supporting multiple currencies are similar to, but simpler to solve than, the multilingual issues. You can support many currencies and let users switch back and forth between them, or you can display prices in all currencies at the same time. For some e-commerce sites, displaying prices in multiple currencies at the same time might be useful, but for the majority of sites, especially business-to-consumer (B2C) sites, the first method is easier.

Product Pricing

You should store product pricing information in only one currency (the *reference* currency), if possible. For example, you can store your prices in U.S. dollars or European euros, and then recalculate prices in other currencies in real time, as needed. In order to recalculate prices based on the reference currency, you need an exchange rate table that specifies the rates for other currencies in comparison to the reference currency. The exchange rate table should contain the following fields:

- Currency symbol
- International Standards Organization (ISO) currency code
- Exchange rate
- Display format

The following example shows what an exchange rate table might look like.

Currency symbol	ISO currency code	Exchange rate	Display format
$	USD (U.S. dollar)	1.0	####.##
£	UKP (U.K. pound sterling)	1.2	####.##
F	BEF (Belgian franc)	0.023	######,00
€	EUR (European euro)	0.9	####.##

When your site displays a price, it recalculates the price based on the exchange rate and displays it with the associated currency symbol and display format.

Important If you store search results and product detail pages with the **CacheManager** object, you must make the currency part of the cache key or you will retrieve the wrong results when you try to display pricing in a different currency.

Different Prices for Different Locales

Some projects require different pricing for different locales. For example, a specific car might cost DM 100,000 in Germany, but only $40,000 in the U.S. However, that is locale-specific pricing, not currency-specific pricing. A German customer living in the U.S. should be charged the same price for the car, whether it is viewed in Deutsche Marks or U.S. dollars.

Different prices for different locales will, in most cases, require explicit pricing in the product properties, requiring you to keep several prices in your catalogs. You can do this by creating custom catalogs with the Catalog Editor module in Business Desk, or you can add locale-specific pricing properties to your catalog schema. The goal is to create inviting, market-oriented pricing that customers find appealing. For example, instead of simply multiplying a U.S. item price of $9.95 by a conversion factor, which can produce an odd price in Belgian francs (such as 457 francs), it is better to create a custom catalog for Belgium that contains a price tailored to the Belgian market (such as 450 francs).

Different Discounts for Different Locales

The notion of providing different discounts for different locales is similar to maintaining different pricing for different locales. However, locale-specific discounting does not require custom catalogs or multiple price properties. Instead, you can set up the Commerce Server Purchase pipeline and Content Selection pipeline to perform different discounts based on locale. This is not a currency-related issue, although at first glance it might look like one. For more information about Commerce Server pipelines, see Commerce Server 2000 Help.

Changing Currency

The issues associated with changing currency are similar to the issues associated with changing language. The Sweet Forgiveness sample site contains a drop-down list from which users can choose currency in the same manner that they choose language. For the purposes of demonstration, the currency is always passed through the URL, as is the language.

You can provide an active currency in any of the following ways:

- **Use a client-side cookie to store the active currency code**. As with changing languages, using a client-side cookie is the easiest way to encode a currency context. The only downside to this approach is the aversion some users have to the use of cookies. Also, roaming users will have to reenter their data.

- **Encode the currency code in the URL**. Use the same **GenerateURL** function that you use to change languages to include the active currency.

- **Store the currency code in the user profile**. Storing the appropriate currency code in the user profile is an option, but every page that displays currency information then needs to invoke the user profile. If a user's profile data is already cached, this is a reliable and speedy method. The user's settings are then available from any location.

Configuring International Locale Settings

You can set up a site to use a different language from your development language. For example, you might develop your site in English, but want to use a copy of your English site to set up a French site. To set up a site using a different language:

- Set the Windows 2000 system locale. In the **Control Panel**, set the options in **Regional Options** for the new locale. You must set locale separately for each computer and enable display and input of text in a given code page, as well as define default settings specific to the locale, such as currency, numeric format, and date and time formats.

- Set up SQL Server collation settings. SQL Server collation settings are set when you set up SQL Server and you can't reconfigure them after installation. The collation settings determine which code page and sort orders will be accepted by the database for non-Unicode data. (The database schema determines whether or not the data is Unicode.)

- Change the following Commerce Server site properties in Commerce Server Manager, using the App Default Config resource:

  - **Site default locale**

  - **Page encoding charset**

  - **Unit of Measure for Weight**

  - **Currency: Base currency locale**

  - **Currency: Base currency code**

  - **Currency: Base currency symbol**

  If you plan to display more than one currency, you also need to configure the following properties for each additional currency:

  - **Currency: Alternate currency options**

  - **Currency: Alternate currency conversion rate**

  - **Currency: Alternate currency locale**

  - **Currency: Alternate currency code**

  - **Currency: Alternate currency symbol**

  - **Currency: Currency display order options**

For more information about configuring the App Default Config resource, see the "Configuring App Default Config Resource Properties" topic in Commerce Server 2000 Help.

After the Windows system locale is set up, SQL Server will default to the corresponding collation when you set it up. (Code page and sort orders match the locale.) When you set up

Commerce Server, the Commerce Server databases support the code page you have configured. You can change any of the settings in the App Default Config resource in Commerce Server Manager.

After you unpack Business Desk or use one of the Solution Sites, the following site configuration properties are based on the system locale and should not need to be changed:

- **Site default locale** (formats for numbers and dates).

- **Base currency locale**.

  Note   The **Base currency symbol** and **Base currency code** properties are not set the same way.

- **Page encoding charset** (set to the default charset that supports the language associated with the system locale). The encoding charset is used in Business Desk header files to set the charset for each page.

If you unpack a localized site with Commerce Server Site Packager on a system configured for the same locale, you shouldn't have to change any settings, unless you are displaying multiple currencies. All other settings are included in the Site Packager package. Be sure to review all settings before publishing your site.

For example, if you install an English site on a Korean system, you can enter Korean language characters into Business Desk without making any other changes.

If, however, you want to run a site in a different language on a system configured for your development language, such as a French site on an English system, you need to reconfigure the following settings:

- Set **Default site locale**, **Base currency locale**, and **Page encoding charset** properties to **French**

- In the BDHeader.asp and BDXMLHeader.asp files:

  - Remove "<%@ LANGUAGE=VBSCRIPT%>"

  - Uncomment "<%'@ LANGUAGE=VBSCRIPT CODEPAGE=1252 %>" and set the code page to the correct value for French

  Note   The Catalogs modules use the **Base currency symbol** and **Base currency code** properties when creating currency properties.

Integrating Commerce Server with BizTalk Server

With the arrival of the Internet, the pattern of electronic commerce has dramatically changed. In particular, the Internet has introduced many new ways of trading, enabling interaction between groups that previously could not economically afford to trade with one another. The exchange of information takes the form of fulfilling requests for items such as quotes, bids, catalogs, purchase orders, order confirmations, shipping documents, invoices, and payment information.

Building business-to-business (B2B) e-commerce systems presents many challenges. Typically, each company stores its data and documents in formats that can be different from the formats that other participating companies use. Companies need a way to connect internal line-of-business applications and vendors with systems that improve customer service and reduce operating costs. By automating and integrating business and data-exchange processes between buyers and sellers, companies can increase efficiency, reduce errors, and lower costs.

You can integrate Microsoft BizTalk Server 2000 with Microsoft Commerce Server 2000 to build B2B e-commerce networks with your vendors. Your vendors can then send you catalogs of their products and fill orders for products that you are selling on your site.

BizTalk Server Overview

BizTalk Server provides a standard gateway for sending and receiving documents across the Internet, as well as a range of services that ensure data integrity, delivery, security, and support for the BizTalk Framework and other key document formats. BizTalk Server features include the ability to design and use XLANG schedules (executable business-process files), integrate existing applications, define document specifications and specification transformations, and monitor and log run-time activity. BizTalk Server provides these features in two main subsystems:

- BizTalk Messaging Services
- BizTalk Orchestration Services

BizTalk Messaging Services

BizTalk Messaging Services enable you to do the following:

- Receive incoming documents

- Parse the documents to determine their format

- Extract key identifiers and identify document-specific processing rules

- Deliver documents to their destinations

- Track documents

- Map data

- Generate and correlate receipts

- Ensure data integrity and security

This section describes the following BizTalk Messaging Services:

- Receive functions

- Transport services

- Data parsers

- Data validation services

- Document delivery services

- Security

Receive Functions

The Receive functions provided in BizTalk Server enable a server to poll for business documents that are posted at specified locations. The following table shows the Receive functions supported by BizTalk Server and where they are configured.

Receive function	Configure using
File	BizTalk Server Administration
Hypertext Transfer Protocol (HTTP)	ASP page
Hypertext Transfer Protocol Secure (HTTPS)	ASP page
Message Queuing	BizTalk Server Administration
Simple Mail Transfer Protocol (SMTP)	Microsoft Exchange script

Transport Services

BizTalk Server supports a core set of transport services that enable a server to send documents to organizations or applications. Documents can be sent whether or not the recipients are capable of communicating directly with the server by means of a Component Object Model (COM) interface. BizTalk Server supports the following transport services:

- Application integration components (AIC)
- File
- HTTP
- HTTPS
- Message queuing
- SMTP

Data Parsers

BizTalk Server supports data parsers for a variety of document standards, such as ANSI X12, UN/EDIFACT, and valid, well-formed Extensible Markup Language (XML). BizTalk Server also supports BizTalk Framework 2.0. For more information about BizTalk Framework 2.0, see the Microsoft BizTalk Server Web site at http://www.microsoft.com/biztalk/. BizTalk Server also provides parsers for flat files; you can register and use your own custom parser components.

Data Validation Services

BizTalk Server validates data by verifying each instance of a document against a specification. You create specifications in BizTalk Editor; specifications can be based on industry standards (such as EDIFACT, X12, and XML) or on flat files (delimited, positional, or delimited and positional). If a document does not match the specification, it is placed into a suspended queue for further analysis.

Document Delivery Services

BizTalk Server uses configurable BizTalk Messaging Services properties to provide reliable document delivery. You can configure these properties to do the following:

- Set service windows for sending documents
- Send or receive receipts
- Set the number of send retries
- Set the time between retry attempts

BizTalk Server supports the use of BizTalk Framework-compliant envelopes to provide reliable messaging features. For more information about BizTalk Framework 2.0, see the Microsoft BizTalk Server Web site at http://www.microsoft.com/biztalk/.

BizTalk Server queues documents to a central location. If a server fails, rollover mechanisms enable a new server to take control of the documents and process them.

Security

BizTalk Server supports encryption and digital signatures. Public-key encryption technology is supported for all documents that you transmit using BizTalk Server Transport Services. BizTalk Server also supports decryption and signature verification for the documents that it receives.

BizTalk Orchestration Services

BizTalk Orchestration Services integrate long-running business processes with the applications that run the business processes. BizTalk Orchestration Services can handle complex transactions that require weeks or months to complete, not just minutes or hours.

Integration is handled by an executable business-process file called an *XLANG schedule*. Additional services run XLANG schedule instances. You can also implement concurrent actions within a single XLANG schedule.

BizTalk Orchestration Services support the following implementation technologies:

- BizTalk Messaging Services
- COM components
- Message Queuing Services
- Windows Script components

XLANG Language

XLANG is a language that describes the logical sequence of a business process, as well as the implementation of the business process using various technology components or services. The XLANG language is expressed in Extensible Markup Language (XML).

XLANG Schedules

An XLANG schedule is a business process that you implement by connecting each step in the process to a technology such as a Component Object Model (COM) or Windows Scripting Component, or to another service that can execute the step.

A service called the XLANG Scheduler Engine then runs the XLANG schedule. The engine controls the instantiation, execution, dehydration, and rehydration of an XLANG schedule, or multiple instances of one or more schedules.

Dehydrating schedules reduces the load on the computer that is hosting the schedule. When a schedule is *dehydrated*, all state information in the Microsoft SQL Server database is stored while the XLANG Scheduler Engine waits to receive a message before it executes the next action in the business process.

When the XLANG Scheduler Engine receives the message, it rehydrates the schedule by retrieving all state information for the XLANG schedule instance from SQL Server.

Common Business-to-Business Requirements

Although each business-to-business (B2B) site is different, many requirements are common to all sites. These requirements include the following:

- Catalog exchange and management

- Order management and order workflow

- Secure exchange of business documents

- Integration of existing business applications

- Advanced product pricing and product configuration

BizTalk Server and Commerce Server offer a number of core features that can help companies satisfy these requirements in a timely, cost-effective manner. This section describes how to exchange and manage catalogs and orders.

Catalog Exchange and Management

The catalog stores the products and services that a company procures through a B2B application. A catalog must be accurate, current, complete, extensible, and flexible. In many scenarios, the catalog also has to support multiple vendors.

Commerce Server and BizTalk Server offer a number of features that can help you manage your catalog. Figure 13.1 shows how you can use products from multiple vendors in a catalog management scenario.

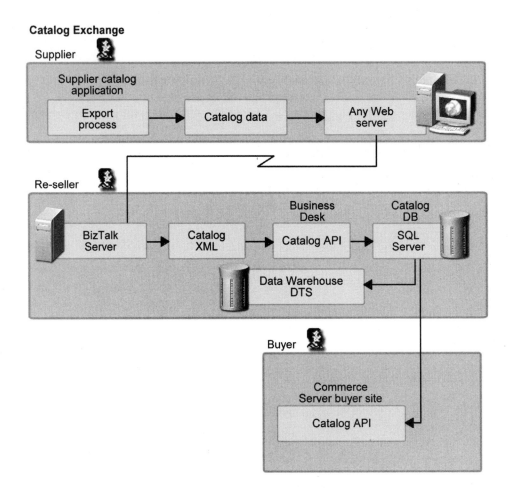

Figure 13.1 Catalog management scenario

In this scenario, the B2B site hosts catalogs from a number of suppliers. Buyers can purchase products and services from the supplier catalogs through the B2B site. Catalog exchange and management are major issues in this situation. For example, the B2B application might host catalogs for hundreds of suppliers. It is likely that each supplier will send catalog data to the B2B application in a different file format. This poses a significant challenge to the system administrator of the B2B site, who must convert the various formats into a single one that can be used on the B2B site.

BizTalk Server and Commerce Server can facilitate catalog management. Both products include features that specifically address common B2B catalog management challenges, such as the following:

- Catalog mapping tools

- Commerce Server XML format for catalogs

- Catalog import, export, and exchange tools

- Application Integration Components (AIC)

You can use these tools to streamline the process of aggregating catalog data in various formats into a single, consistent format, thereby eliminating the need to write costly mapping scripts for each supplier that hosts a catalog on your B2B site. In addition to lowering catalog management costs, these tools can also significantly reduce the time it takes to bring a new supplier online.

Catalog Mapping Tools

The BizTalk Editor and Mapper tools provide easy-to-use, drag-and-drop interfaces that you can use to define and map catalog formats. These tools can greatly reduce the time it takes to define the structure of various supplier catalogs, and also to graphically define maps between different catalog schemas.

BizTalk Editor

You can use BizTalk Editor to create, edit, and manage specifications using XML. You can base these specifications on industry standards (such as EDIFACT, X12, and XML) or on flat files (delimited, positional, or delimited and positional).

Using BizTalk Editor, you can graphically create catalog schema definitions for each supplier, thereby reducing the time it takes to define the structure of various supplier catalogs. BizTalk Editor supports a number of file formats that can describe most catalog formats.

BizTalk Editor creates specifications by interpreting the properties of records and fields contained in a file. Specifications represent the structured data as XML, regardless of the original format. In addition, specifications that you create or modify with BizTalk Editor provide common data descriptions that BizTalk Mapper can use to transform data across dissimilar formats. The specifications provide data portability across business processes.

BizTalk Mapper

BizTalk Mapper is a transformation design tool that enables you to create a correspondence between the records and fields in two different specification formats. BizTalk Mapper supports complex structural transformations from records and fields in a source specification tree to records and fields in a destination specification tree.

The cross-reference and data-manipulation functionality creates a map that provides a set of instructions that define the relationship between the two different specification formats. (You use BizTalk Editor to define the specification formats.)

BizTalk Messaging Service uses a map within a channel to specify how data existing in a document in a given format is transformed into data in a document conforming to a different format. *Channels*, which are named sets of properties, identify the document source and define the processing steps performed by BizTalk Server to deliver the document to the destination designated by the messaging port with which the channel is associated.

BizTalk Mapper uses links and functoids that enable complex structural manipulation between source data elements and destination data elements to accomplish this translation.

Functoids are similar to Microsoft Visual Basic controls that can be dragged onto the map itself. You use BizTalk Mapper to graphically represent the structural transformation relationship between the source data elements and destination data elements.

Functoids use predefined formulas and specific values, called *arguments*, to perform calculations. BizTalk Mapper runs these calculations based on the designated order of the records and fields. By selecting a functoid from the Functoid Palette, dragging it to the mapping grid, and linking it to elements in the source specification and destination specification trees, you can combine data, modify dates or times, concatenate data, or perform other operations. Figure 13.2 shows the Functoid Palette in BizTalk Mapper.

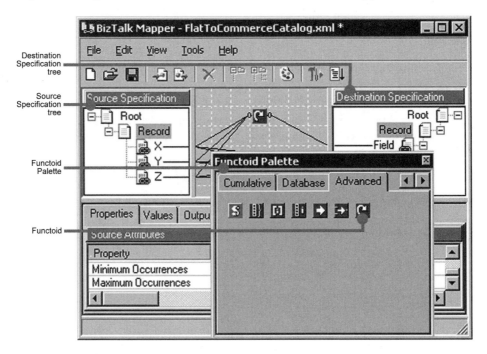

Figure 13.2 Functoid Palette in BizTalk Mapper

You can use the Value Mapping functoid in two different types of mapping scenarios:

- Mapping from a Commerce Server catalog specification to a flat schema

- Mapping from a flat schema to a Commerce Server catalog

Mapping from a Commerce Server Catalog to a Flat Schema

Commerce Server site managers need the ability to map data from a Commerce Server catalog to a flat schema. You use the Value Mapping (Flattening) functoid to do this. The following code is an example of three records in a Commerce Server catalog:

```
<Root>
  <Record>
    <Field Name="X" Value="1"/>
    <Field Name="Y" Value="2"/>
    <Field Name="Z" Value="3"/>
  </Record>
  <Record>
    <Field Name="X" Value="4"/>
    <Field Name="Y" Value="5"/>
    <Field Name="Z" Value="6"/>
  </Record>
  <Record>
    <Field Name="X" Value="7"/>
    <Field Name="Y" Value="8"/>
    <Field Name="Z" Value="9"/>
  </Record>
</Root>
```

The following code is an example of a flat schema:

```
<Root>
  <Record X="1" Y="2" Z="3"/>
  <Record X="4" Y="5" Z="6"/>
  <Record X="7" Y="8" Z="9"/>
</Root>
```

In this mapping scenario, it is important to maintain the one-to-one correspondence between the three records in the catalog and the three records in the flat schema. Figure 13.3 shows a map that maintains this correspondence.

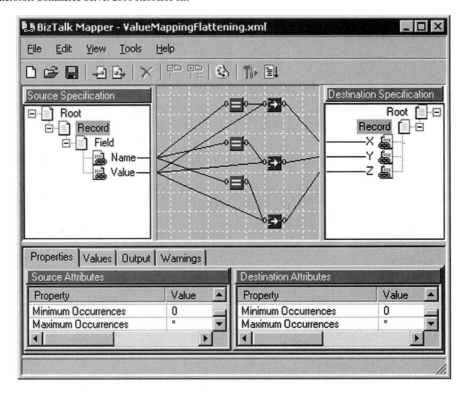

Figure 13.3 Mapping from a Commerce Server catalog to a flat schema

Mapping from a Flat Schema to a Commerce Server Catalog

You can use the Looping functoid to map a flat schema to a Commerce Server catalog. For more information about flat schemas and Commerce Server catalogs, see "Using the Value Mapping (Flattening) Functoid" in BizTalk Server 2000 Help.

Figure 13.4 shows a flat schema mapped to a Commerce Server catalog.

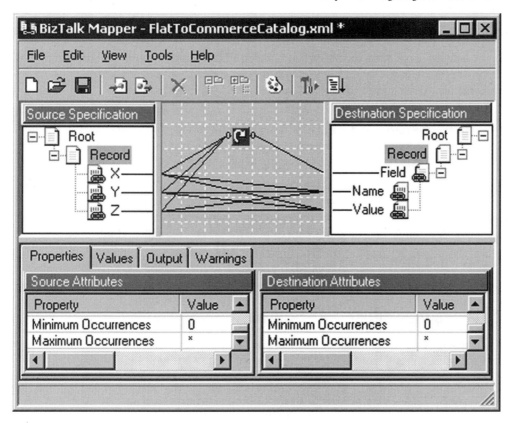

Figure 13.4 Mapping from a flat schema to a Commerce Server catalog

Generating Catalogs in the Commerce Server XML Format

A product catalog must exist in the XML or CSV format required by Commerce Server before Commerce Server can import it successfully. If the vendor supplying the catalog is using Commerce Server to produce the catalog and BizTalk Server to deliver the catalog, the process is quite simple. A business manager can select a catalog and send it to a vendor.

However, if the vendor doesn't use Commerce Server to produce the catalog, you can still use BizTalk Server to import the catalog to your Commerce Server application. You can take advantage of the Mapper tool in BizTalk Server, using the Looping functoid, to convert the product catalog from its native format to the XML format required by Commerce Server.

If vendors don't use BizTalk Server, they must devise a proprietary solution to convert their catalog format to the XML format required by Commerce Server. For more information about the XML format required by Commerce Server, see "Catalog XML Structures" in Commerce Server 2000 Help.

Catalog Import, Export, and Exchange Tools

You can import catalogs into Commerce Server databases in XML or comma-separated value (CSV) file format from external sources. For example, if you have catalogs in other databases, you can import them into a Commerce Server database, and then use Business Desk to manage them.

You might want to export a catalog if, for example, you are selling products wholesale, and you want to make your catalog available to retailers. Or you might want to export a catalog to another application, such as an inventory system or a pricing system. You can export your catalogs in XML format.

You can use BizTalk Server to exchange catalogs with your vendors. After you convert a catalog to an XML document, BizTalk Server processes it to save the XML catalog file in a shared folder on the destination computer on which Commerce Server is installed. If the destination computer is on a local area network (LAN), then BizTalk Server does not need to be installed on the destination computer. However, if you use HTTP to send the catalog, then BizTalk Server must be installed on the destination computer.

Import Catalogs from Other Data Sources

To convert a catalog to XML or CSV format, you can use your existing database management system to save the catalog in XML or CSV format, or you can write a Visual Basic script to convert the catalog for you.

You normally use the Catalog Editor module of Business Desk to import a catalog. However, you can also use the **ImportXML** method of the **CatalogManager** object to programmatically import a catalog that is already in XML format into the Commerce Server Catalogs database. For more information about this method, see "CatalogManager.ImportXML" in Commerce Server 2000 Help.

To verify that your catalog XML file conforms to the proper schema, do the following:

1. Edit the root element in your catalog XML file so that it references the catalog XML-Data Reduced (XDR) file provided in the Commerce Server root installation folder. For example:

   ```
   <MSCommerceCatalogCollection xmlns="x-schema:C:\Program Files\Microsoft Commerce
   Server\CatalogXMLSchema.xml">
   ```

2. Open your catalog XML file in Internet Explorer. Internet Explorer verifies that the XML file conforms to the specified schema and provides diagnostic errors if it does not conform.

If you have BizTalk Server installed on the same computer as Commerce Server, you can use an AIC to automate the process of importing XML catalogs into Commerce Server as they arrive from vendors using BizTalk Server.

Export Catalogs

You can export a catalog to a known path or a shared folder called CommerceCatalogs on the computer on which Commerce Server is installed. Exporting a catalog can enable you to share your catalog with a business partner, or outsource the development and maintenance of your catalogs.

Before you can export a catalog, you must create a shared folder on Commerce Server, or you must know the name of a directory on the server that you can access. You can then use Business Desk to export the catalog to the shared folder or the directory.

Exchange Catalogs

After you save an XML catalog file on the destination computer, you use Business Desk to import the catalog from the shared folder on the destination computer. You can then publish the catalog on your Web site. You can also use the Catalog Editor module in Business Desk to edit the newly imported catalog, if necessary. For information about importing a catalog using Business Desk, see "Importing a Catalog" in Commerce Server 2000 Help.

You can set up BizTalk Server to automatically transform an incoming catalog to Commerce Server. Figure 13.5 shows how BizTalk Server processes an XML catalog file.

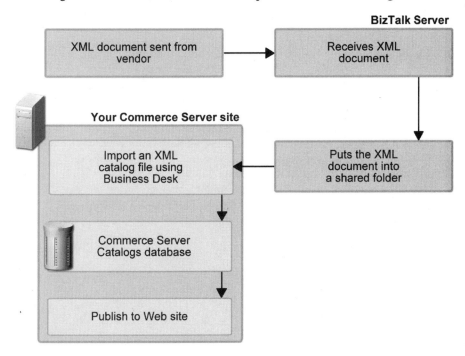

Figure 13.5 Processed XML catalog file

Application Integration Components

Application integration components (AIC) are COM objects that the BizTalk Server state engine calls to deliver data to an application. If you configure a messaging port in BizTalk Server to include the use of an AIC for application integration, this component is automatically instantiated and passed the requisite data. The component then determines how to communicate this data back to the application. You can use private API calls, invoke other COM objects, use database writes, or other methods to do this.

An AIC typically serves as an integration point between BizTalk Server and a back-end application that cannot be accessed directly from BizTalk Server. The AIC functions both as the integration point and as a simulated back-end application. The messaging port passes a purchase order, which is received from the buyer system, to the AIC. The AIC transforms the purchase order message into an invoice message and submits it to a channel in BizTalk Messaging Services on the seller system.

If you have BizTalk Server installed on the same computer as Commerce Server, you can use an AIC defined by BizTalk Server to automate the process of importing XML catalogs into Commerce Server through BizTalk Server. For information about creating an AIC, see "Creating the Application Integration Component (AIC)" in BizTalk Server 2000 Help.

Order Management

Your order fulfillment process might be managed by an internal order management system within your private network, a remote distribution and fulfillment center, or a vendor that provides an outsourced fulfillment service. Companies that run successful e-commerce sites quickly realize the need to integrate their Web order-capture process with their order fulfillment process.

You can submit orders to BizTalk Server in several different ways, depending on your needs. You can use mapping to submit orders, you can use a variety of protocols to submit orders, or your trading partner can create a Commerce Server site or a non-Commerce Server site to receive the submitted orders. For additional methods of integrating Commerce Server order processing with your existing systems, see Chapter 10, "Integrating Third-Party ERP Systems with Commerce Server Applications."

Order Routing Manager

Commerce Server supports both internal routing and routing through BizTalk Server. The Order Routing Manager is a design-time component that you can use to define, configure, and maintain a RoutingConfig table. You can use the RoutingConfig table to route the following methods:

- **INT** (internal)
- **BTS** (BizTalk Server)

You use the **INT** and **BTS** methods with the components required for routing.

Splitter Pipeline Component

The **Splitter** is a pipeline component that creates a collection of Shipment dictionaries (each pointing to a collection of references to line items). You can configure the **Splitter** to create the required data structures by taking the Shipping method and Vendor ID properties as input. The required data or input distinguishers (for example, `shipping_method_id and shipping_address_id`) are the keys in the required data structure or dictionary.

You can use the **Splitter** to specify the input distinguishers and then use the associated dictionary item as the input. By specifying the input distinguishers, you add a column to the product catalog indicating the source of the product. At this point, you need to use the associated dictionary item as the input distinguisher that you configure on the **Splitter** component. The **Splitter** creates multiple dictionaries (one for each source of the product).

You can implement the **Splitter** using the catalog vendor ID feature based on the product type. If you do this, you must create a separate catalog for each source and then assign each catalog a vendor ID to specify the source for the catalog products. Commerce Server then automatically places the items into separate order forms when a customer adds them to the shopping cart (order group). This splits the order into groups of items, which you can then send to different back-end systems.

ShippingMethodRouter Component

The **ShippingMethodRouter** is a run-time component that iterates through the Order Routing dictionaries to invoke the components specified by the **ShippingMethodManager** object. The router components are the following:

- **CommerceRouter**. Wraps the **OrderGroup.SaveAsOrder** method.

- **BTSRouter**. Wraps the **GenerateXMLForDictionaryUsingSchema** method.

The router components are followed by a submit call to BizTalk Server. Figure 13.6 shows how the **Splitter** and the **ShippingMethodRouter** component work with other objects to process shipments.

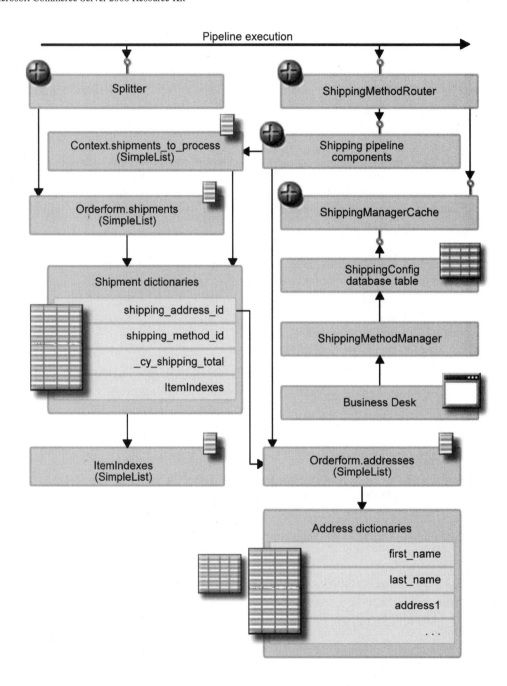

Figure 13.6 Processing shipments with the Splitter and ShippingMethodRouter

Order Form Integration

Order form integration is the process of splitting an order form into multiple purchase orders, then using BizTalk Server to send them to the appropriate vendors. The Commerce Server Solution Sites include conditional code for submitting per-vendor purchase orders to BizTalk Server, thus enabling the purchase orders to be sent to the appropriate vendors. This functionality is built into the Solution Sites, and is configured using Commerce Server Manager.

Associating a Vendor with Each Catalog

When you set up an agreement with a vendor, the vendor ID is automatically made available to Commerce Server. The vendor ID is the organization name that you specify for the vendor when you create a destination organization for the source server. For more information, see "Creating Source and Destination Organizations on the Source Server" in Commerce Server 2000 Help.

Commerce Server uses the vendor ID associated with a product catalog to identify the vendor for each product in an order. It does this by identifying the product catalog associated with the product, and then identifying the vendor associated with that catalog. Commerce Server can then construct purchase orders on a vendor-by-vendor basis, and use BizTalk Server to deliver those purchase orders to the corresponding vendors.

You usually use Business Desk to manually associate vendors with catalogs. Commerce Server displays the vendor ID in Business Desk. It also displays those vendors that support the same document type as your organization supports, and thus have compatible document routing. You can then use Business Desk to associate the vendor ID with the catalog.

You can associate more than one catalog with a vendor. You can also specify a vendor at the product level; however, if you do this you must also customize the _Additem.asp page (if you are developing with the Retail Solution Site). For instructions for adding the vendor ID to a catalog, see "Setting Up Your Catalogs for BizTalk Server" in Commerce Server 2000 Help.

Commerce Server also provides a COM object designed to assign vendors to catalogs programmatically. This object, called the **CatalogToVendorAssociation** object, also provides methods to, for example, retrieve a list of available vendors, and to return vendor information for a particular catalog. For more information about this object, see "CatalogToVendorAssociation Object" in Commerce Server 2000 Help.

Sending Orders to BizTalk Server

A common e-commerce scenario is to collect a group of catalogs from various drop-ship vendors and present them to users as one catalog. When users place orders on your site, the **Splitter** component separates the line items in any given order (basket) into logical groups so that each line item can be routed to the appropriate vendor for fulfillment. This logical separation of an order should be completely transparent to the users.

The **Splitter** identifies the fulfillment vendor for each line item in an order, and then groups vendors with the appropriate **OrderForm** objects. As the existing pipelines (Plan, Product, Purchase, and so forth) are operating against the **OrderForm** object, the order processing happens on a subset of the **OrderGroup** object (based on how the order will be routed internally). When a customer adds an item to a basket, it must be added to the default **OrderForm** object to ensure that there is only one **OrderForm** object within each **OrderGroup** object.

Figure 13.7 shows how Commerce Server processes an order and then sends it to BizTalk Server.

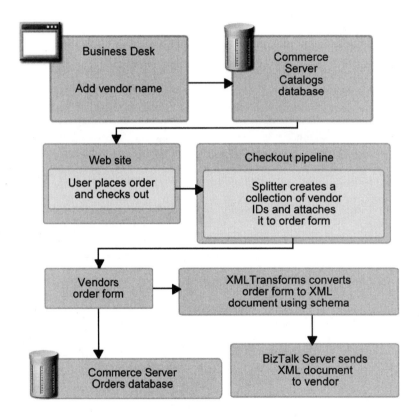

Figure 13.7 Commerce Server processes an order and sends it to BizTalk Server

To create an order for processing by Commerce Server, a customer does the following:

1. Adds items to the basket.

   Commerce Server reads the Commerce Server database and retrieves vendor names for the items.

2. Proceeds to check out.

To process the order, Commerce Server does the following:

1. The Commerce Server Checkout pipeline processes the order. For each line item (product) in the order, the Splitter component determines whether your company supplies the product or whether a vendor with whom you have a trading agreement supplies it. The Splitter component creates a list of vendors and attaches it to the order form.

2. Commerce Server determines whether the BizTalk Options property (in the App Default Config resource) is set to "1."

   If the BizTalk Options property is set to "1," Commerce Server reads the list of vendors and bundles the line items for each vendor.

3. Commerce Server converts the order form into one or more XML documents to be sent to BizTalk Server.

   When Commerce Server converts the order form (using the XMLTransforms process), it creates one XML document for each vendor. To convert the order, Commerce Server uses the schema named POSchema.xml, which is associated with the site.

   If you add one or more fields to the order form, by default Commerce Server does not include the new fields in the XML document that it sends to BizTalk Server. To add the new fields on the order form, you must edit POSchema.xml, an XDR (XML-Data Reduced) format file, and re-associate the XML file with the document in BizTalk Server. You must also transfer the XML file to BizTalk Server and re-associate it. You use BizTalk Editor to edit POSchema.xml.

4. Commerce Server sends the XML documents to BizTalk Server.

Processing Received Orders

You can submit orders to BizTalk Server in several different ways. You can use mapping to submit orders, you can use a variety of protocols to submit orders, or your vendor can create a Commerce Server site or a non-Commerce Server site to receive the submitted orders.

If you choose to have your vendor set up a Commerce Server site to receive orders, you can set up the site using the _Recvpo.asp page that receives XML documents from BizTalk Server. When _Recvpo.asp receives an XML document, it starts the XMLTransforms process and converts the XML document back to an order form. Commerce Server then runs a pipeline on the order form. After the pipeline processes the order form, the order is saved to the Commerce Server database. By using _Recvpo.asp, you can use Commerce Server objects to redirect the XML to your order management system. For information about the components in _Recvpo.asp, see the "Pipeline Component Reference" section of Commerce Server 2000 Help. For information about _Recvpo.asp, see the Commerce Server Solution Sites Help.

Figure 13.8 shows how an XML document is sent from your BizTalk Server and processed by the vendor's Commerce Server site.

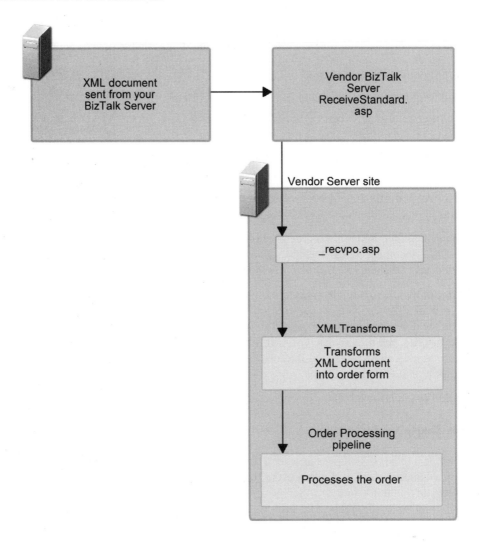

Figure 13.8 XML document processed by vendor's Commerce Server site

You can also set up Commerce Server to process and send order forms to a queue. You then set up your BizTalk Server (or the BizTalk Server at the vendor installation) to poll the queue. If you use this configuration, you can install BizTalk Server and Commerce Server on separate servers. Figure 13.9 shows a configuration with Commerce Server and BizTalk Server installed on separate servers.

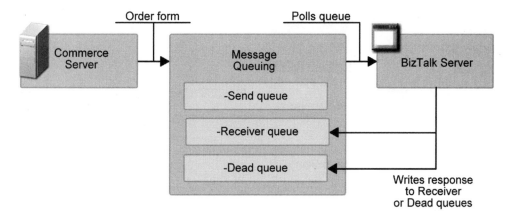

Figure 13.9 Order forms processed in a queue between Commerce Server and BizTalk Server

Integrating Commerce Server and BizTalk Server

By integrating BizTalk Server with your Commerce Server installation, you can contract with vendors to receive catalogs of their products, and then fill orders for their products that you sell on your site. Although it is not required that both you and your vendors install BizTalk Server, the following business scenario explains how to set up BizTalk Server systems for both you and your vendors.

This business scenario describes how a wholesaler manually sends a Commerce Server catalog to a retailer using the Catalog Editor module in Business Desk. Business Desk then accepts the order from a consumer or business buyer using the Retail Solution Site and passes the order to BizTalk Server.

A custom AIC is used to import the catalog on the retailer's server. After the wholesaler makes changes to its catalog, the catalog is submitted to BizTalk Server over HTTP. The retailer automatically receives the catalog and deploys it onto the production site.

When a customer makes a purchase at the retailer's site, the purchase is automatically sent to the wholesaler for fulfillment. BizTalk Server converts the XML-based order into an EDI representation of a purchase order (for example, an EDI X12 850). The result is written to a file location for tracking purposes. A BizTalk Server file receive function monitors this file location, and then converts the file into a Purchase Order Acknowledgment (for example, an EDI X12 855). The status is extracted and posted to the Commerce Server Orders database by an AIC. The customer can check the Web site to determine whether the order has been shipped. Figure 13.10 shows the workflow for a purchase order exchange.

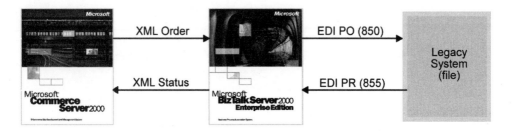

Figure 13.10 Workflow for a purchase order exchange

The following sections describe the implementation steps required to achieve Commerce Server and BizTalk Server catalog exchange and purchase order integration.

Configuring Commerce Server and BizTalk Server to Send and Receive a Catalog

In the following configuration, for simplification purposes, two sites are unpacked on a single computer. One site is named *Wholesaler* and represents the wholesaler who has generated a catalog that needs to be sent. The wholesaler sends the catalog through BizTalk Server to a retail site. The retail site, named *Retailer*, represents the retailer who is receiving the catalog.

In a production implementation, you probably would implement Commerce Server and BizTalk Server on separate systems for scaled-out scenarios. Your Commerce Server system will most probably be more active than your BizTalk Server system because many shopping page hits result in only a single or limited number of purchase orders. Several purchase orders, however, would be generated if a shopper picked products from different vendors. The Commerce Server and BizTalk Server combination is designed to split up these orders and process the order transformation and delivery individually for each vendor.

To configure Commerce Server and BizTalk Server, you do the following:

1. Set up the environment.

2. Configure the site options on the wholesaler site.

3. Copy CatalogXmlSchema.xml to the BizTalkServerRepository.

4. Create the catalog document definition.

5. Configure Receivestandard.asp to receive the catalog.

6. Modify the home organization.

7. Create the retailer organization.

8. Create the catalog application for the wholesaler organization.

9. Create the wholesaler messaging port to the retailer organization.

10. Create the CatalogImportChannel and retailer receive port.

11. Test your configuration.

These steps are described in the following sections. For detailed information about these configuration steps, see "Using BizTalk Server and Commerce Server" in Commerce Server 2000 Help.

Setting Up the Environment

To set up the environment, you do the following:

1. Follow the BizTalk Server installation instructions to install BizTalk Server.

2. Follow the Commerce Server installation instructions to install Commerce Server.

3. Unpack the Retail Solution Site and name it *Retailer*.

4. Unpack the Supplier Solution Site and name it *Wholesaler*.

5. Import a catalog to the Wholesaler site.

Configuring the Site Options on the Wholesaler Site

You use the App Default Config resource to set properties that enable Commerce Server and BizTalk Server to work together.

To enable Commerce Server to exchange catalogs through BizTalk Server, you must specify the properties listed in the following table in Commerce Server Manager.

Property	Value
BizTalk Catalog Doc Type	Catalog
BizTalk Options	1
BizTalk Source Org Qualifier	Catalog
BizTalk Source Org Qualifier Value	Wholesaler
BizTalk Submit Type	1

After you modify the BizTalk Server properties in the previous table, unload the application from memory.

Copying CatalogXmlSchema.xml to the BizTalkServerRepository

The schema of the XML document you are transferring must be available through Windows Web Distributed Authoring and Versioning (WebDAV) to BizTalk Server through the repository. To make the XML document schema available to BizTalk Server, do the following:

1. In **BizTalk Editor**, import the **XDR Schema** file. Specify the path to the **catalogxmlschema.xml** file in *<drive>*:**\Program Files\Microsoft Commerce Server**.

2. Store the file to **WebDAV**, and then save the file in the **Microsoft** folder.

Creating the Catalog Document Definition

In this step, you create a document definition representing a catalog in a messaging port. A document definition provides a pointer to a specification that defines the catalog.

In BizTalk Messaging Manager, in Document definitions, you should modify the boxes in the following table to integrate Commerce Server with BizTalk Server.

Box	Value
Document definition name	Catalog
Document specification	Select this check box, and then browse to the **Catalogxmlschema.xml** file on the **WebDAV** repository.

Configuring Receivestandard.asp to Receive the Catalog

On the Retailer site, the file Receivestandard.asp receives XML documents and calls an interchange submit. You must modify this file (on the Retail site, because it receives the catalog) to call a specific channel. The name of the channel called by Receivestandard.asp must match the name of an existing channel. To ensure that the name matches, you must change the following code.

Modify line 89 of Receivestandard.asp, from:

```
SubmissionHandle = interchange.submit(1, PostedDocument)
```

To:

```
SubmissionHandle = interchange.submit(1,PostedDocument,,,,,"catalogimportchannel")
```

This takes the **PostedDocument** object, which is the exported catalog, and submits it to the **catalogimportchannel** object.

Modifying the Home Organization

The organizations that you create using BizTalk Messaging Manager represent the vendors with whom you exchange documents. A special organization type, called the *home organization*, represents your company.

BizTalk Messaging Manager creates the home organization for you automatically. When you configure the home organization, you can rename it to make it easier to identify as your company.

In BizTalk Messaging Manager, in Organizations, you should modify the boxes in the following table.

Box	Value
Home Organization	Wholesaler
Custom identifier	Catalog
Qualifier	Catalog

Creating the Retailer Organization

Organizations other than the home organization represent an external vendor or a business unit of a vendor. You can create any number of organizations. You can designate a vendor organization either as a source organization in a channel or as a destination organization in a messaging port.

In BizTalk Messaging Manager, in Organizations, you should modify the boxes in the following table.

Box	Value
Organization	Retailer
Custom identifier	Catalog
Qualifier	Catalog
Value	Retailer

Creating the Catalog Application for the Wholesaler Organization

The applications that you create for your home organization enable you to identify and track the flow of documents between BizTalk Server and actual internal applications within your company. You can designate only applications of the home organization as the source or destination for documents within your company.

For example, you might create a messaging port that designates a vendor organization as the destination for documents that your company sends. Then, when you create a channel for that port, rather than designating your home organization as the source, you designate a specific internal application within your company where the documents originate.

To complete the integration between Commerce Server and BizTalk Server, in BizTalk Messaging Manager, you would add an application to the Wholesaler organization named *CatalogApplication*.

Creating the Wholesaler Messaging Port to the Retailer Organization

A *messaging port* is a set of properties that you use to configure BizTalk Server so that it transports documents to a specified destination, using a specified transport service. You use the New Messaging Port Wizard to create a new port for sending a catalog from the Wholesaler to the Retailer.

In BizTalk Messaging Manager, in Messaging ports, modify the boxes in the following table.

Box	Value
Messaging Port name	CatalogPort
Destination Organization	Retailer
Primary transport	http://<*computer name*>/retailer/receivestandard.asp
Envelope information	None
Security information	None
New Channel name	CatalogApplication
Organization Identifier	Catalog/Wholesaler
Inbound document definition name	Catalog
Log inbound document	In native format

In BizTalk Messaging Manager, in Advanced Configuration, modify the boxes in the following table.

Box	Value
URL	http://<*computer name*>/retailer/receivestandard.asp
User name	<*domain*>\<*username*>
Password	<*user password*>

Creating the CatalogImportChannel and Retailer Receive Port

You configure the retailer receive port to use an AIC/scriptor.

In BizTalk Messaging Manager, in Messaging ports, modify the boxes in the following table.

Box	Value
Destination Organization	Retailer
Primary Transport	Application Integration Component
Component name	BizTalk Scriptor
Organization Identifier	Catalog/Retailer

After you modify the boxes, you create the channel that uses the retailer receive port.

A *channel* is a set of properties that you use to configure BizTalk Server to process a document that it receives. After a channel has processed a document, it is passed to its associated messaging port or distribution list to be transported to the specified destination. You can create one or more channels for a port or distribution list.

In BizTalk Messaging Manager, in Channels, modify the boxes in the following table.

Box	Value
Channel name	CatalogImportChannel
Organization	Retailer
Organization Identifier	Catalog/Retailer
InboundDocumentDefName	Catalog
OutboundDocumentDefName	Catalog
Log Inbound Document	In native format

In a BizTalk Scriptor, the **OrderForm** object is used to pass in the contents of the XML document. Use the **scripting.filesystemobject** object to write out the XML document to a file. To modify the scriptor, use the following code:

```
function MSCSExecute(config, orderform, context, flags)
sOutput = orderform.Value("working_data")

Dim fso, MyFile
Set fso = CreateObject("Scripting.FileSystemObject")
Mydrive = "c:\commercecatalogs\"
MyDate = cstr(Date)
MyTime = cstr(Time)
Filename = MyDate & MyTime & ".xml"
FileName = Replace(FileName, "/", "")
FileName = Replace(FileName, ":", "")
Filename = Mydrive & FileName
Filename = Replace(Filename, " ", "")
Set MyFile = fso.CreateTextFile(Filename, True)
MyFile.WriteLine(soutput)
MyFile.Close
set appcfg = createobject("commerce.appconfig")
set catalogmanager = createobject("commerce.catalogmanager")
appcfg.initialize("retailer")
set optdict = appcfg.getoptionsdictionary("")
connstr = optdict.s_CatalogConnectionString
catalogmanager.initialize connstr, true
catalogmanager.importxml Filename, TRUE, FALSE

    MSCSExecute = 1    'set function return value to 1
end function

sub MSCSOpen(config)
    'optional open routine
end sub

sub MSCSClose()
    'optional close routine
end sub
```

Testing Your Configuration

You use the Catalog Editor module in Business Desk to send a catalog from the Wholesaler site. BizTalk Server then automatically imports the catalog into the Retailer site. To send a catalog to the Retailer site, do the following:

1. In Commerce Server Business Desk, in Catalogs, in the Catalog Editor module, select a catalog that you have imported.

2. Send the Catalog to the Retailer vendor that you created using the BizTalk Messaging Manager.

Processing a Commerce Server Purchase Order Through BizTalk Server

A Commerce Server application accepts an order from a consumer or business buyer. The order is then passed to BizTalk Server. The configuration steps in the "Configuring Commerce Server and BizTalk Server for Sending and Receiving a Catalog" section earlier in this chapter must be complete before you do the tasks described in this section.

To process a Commerce Server purchase order through BizTalk Server, you do the following:

1. Configure the site options for the Retailer site.

2. Copy POSchema.xml to the WebDAV repository.

3. Configure the PurchaseOrder document definition.

4. Add the identifier to the retailer organization.

5. Configure a vendor for the imported catalog.

6. Create a WholesalerPO application for the wholesaler organization.

7. Create a new messaging port to an application.

8. Create a new channel that uses the WholesalerPO as the messaging port.

9. Test your configuration.

Configuring the Site Options for the Retailer Site

You use the App Default Config resource to set properties that enable Commerce Server and BizTalk Server to work together.

To enable Commerce Server to exchange purchase orders through BizTalk Server, you must specify the properties in the following table.

Property	Value
BizTalk PO Doc Type	PurchaseOrder
BizTalk Options	1
BizTalk Source Org Qualifier	MyCompany
BizTalk Source Org Qualifier Value	Retailer
BizTalk Submit Type	1

After you modify the properties in the previous table, unload the application from memory.

Copying POSchema.xml to the WebDAV Repository

The schema of the XML document you are transferring must be available through WebDAV to BizTalk Server through the repository. To copy the XML document to the WebDAV repository, do the following:

1. In BizTalk Editor, open the *<drive>*:\inetpub\wwwroot\wholesaler\poschema.xml file.

2. Store the file to WebDAV, and then save the file in the Microsoft folder.

Configuring the PurchaseOrder Document Definition

A document definition represents a business document in a messaging port, channel, or distribution list. In this scenario, the document definition represents a purchase order. This document definition provides a pointer to a specification that defines the purchase order.

In BizTalk Messaging Manager, in Document definitions, modify the boxes in the following table.

Box	Value
Document Definition name	PurchaseOrder
Document specification	Select this check box, and then browse to the POSchema.xml file on the WebDAV repository that you imported in Step 2.
WebDAV Repository reference	http://*<computer name>*/BizTalkServerRepository/DocSpecs/Microsoft/poschema.xml

Adding the Identifier to the Retailer Organization

Organizations other than your home organization represent an external vendor or a business unit of a vendor. In BizTalk Messaging Manager, in Retailer Organization, modify the boxes in the following table.

Box	Value
Custom Identifier name	PurchaseOrder
Qualifier	MyCompany
Value	Retailer

Configuring a Vendor for the Imported Catalog

After you have added the identifier to the Retailer organization, you are ready to configure a vendor for the imported catalog. To configure the vendor, do the following:

- In Business Desk for the Retailer site, in Catalogs, in the Catalog Editor module, open the imported catalog, and change the vendor ID of the catalog to Wholesaler.

    Notes   If the Wholesaler organization doesn't appear, there is a mismatch between what you have entered on the site options, and the identifier that you have configured for the organization.

    The function **sVendorsAsOptions** () in the Dlg_vendorpicker.asp file is used to retrieve a list of vendors for this operation, and also for a catalog send operation.

Creating a WholesalerPO Application for the Wholesaler Organization

The Application tab is available only on the Wholesaler organization. Normally you wouldn't attempt to send something to your home organization from your own BizTalk Server computer, and therefore wouldn't perform this step. However, in this single server scenario, you need to create a port to an application so that you can send this purchase order to your home organization.

To create a WholesalerPO application for the Wholesaler organization, do the following:

- In BizTalk Messaging Manager, edit the Wholesaler Application, and add an application named *WholesalerPO*.

Creating a New Messaging Port to an Application

You need to create a messaging port that you can use to configure BizTalk Server to transport a purchase order that is submitted through BizTalk Server over HTTP.

In BizTalk Messaging Manager, in Messaging ports, modify the boxes in the following table.

Box	Value
Messaging Port name	WholesalerPO
Application	WholesalerPO
Transport type	HTTP
Address	http://<computer name>/wholesaler/_recvpo.asp
	The transport type specifies the transport service that BizTalk Server uses to convey documents to the destination designated in the messaging port. Transport properties can also include a specific address to which the data is sent. The address properties vary depending on the transport type selected.

Creating a New Channel that Uses the WholesalerPO as the Messaging Port

A channel is a set of properties that you can use to configure BizTalk Server to process a document. After a channel has processed a document, it is passed to its associated messaging port or distribution list to be transported to the specified destination. You can create one or more channels for a port or distribution list.

In BizTalk Messaging Manager, in Channels, modify the boxes in the following table.

Box	Value
Channel name	RetailPO
Organization identifier	PurchaseOrder/Retail
InboundDocumentDefName	PurchaseOrder
OutboundDocumentDefName	PurchaseOrder

In BizTalk Messaging Manager, in Advanced Configuration, modify the boxes in the following table.

Box	Value
URL	http://*<computer name>*/wholesaler/_recvpo.asp
Username	*<domain>\<username>*
Password	*<user password>*
Use HTTP proxy	Leave this check box cleared.

Testing Your Configuration

You can test your configuration by logging onto your Retail site and making a purchase. After you have made a purchase, you can use the Orders modules in Business Desk to view your order status information. You use order status codes to track the location of an order in the order process and to determine where an order might be blocked or have unresolved problems.

An order status code identifies a name with a code for a specific area of the order process. For example, if a customer ordered two CDs and two t-shirts 8 weeks ago, you can view order status codes and track the order's location in the ordering process. There are three default order status codes:

- 4 (New Order)
- 2 (Saved Order)
- 1 (Basket)

To test your configuration, do the following:

1. Log on to the http://*<computer name>*/retailer site.

2. Add items to your basket, and then make a purchase.

3. In Business Desk, in Orders, in the Orders Status module, search for all orders you made on the Retailer site.

If your Commerce Server and BizTalk Server applications are integrated correctly, there should be a purchase order in the Wholesaler site for the purchase that you just made on the Retailer site.

Part Four: Deploying

Microsoft
**Commerce
Server** 2000

Deploying Your Site

During the Deployment phase, you install hardware and software and then test performance against the criteria set in the Planning and Development phases. The following personnel should be involved in the deployment phase:

- Site developers
- Testers
- System administrators

You deploy your site using the Project Goals and Requirements and Project Plan documents that you created during the Planning phase. Figure 14.1 shows a high-level view of the deployment process.

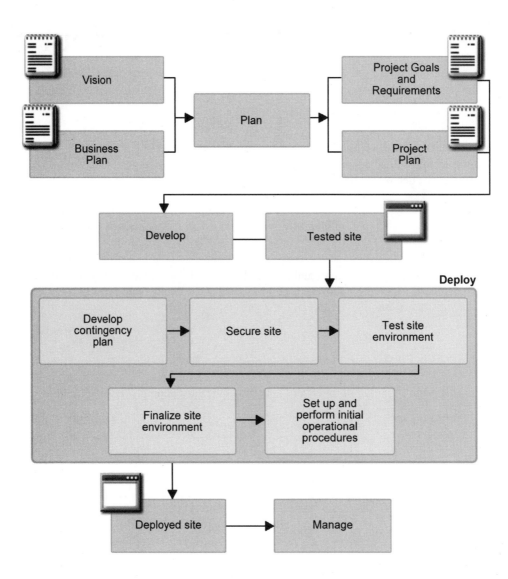

Figure 14.1 Deployment phase

During the Deployment phase, you perform the tasks listed in the following table.

Task	Consists of
Implement your contingency plan	Implementing the initial phases of your contingency (or risk management) plan. For example, you identify the data that you need to back up for a full recovery.
Deploy your site	Installing the hardware and software required to run the Web site, deploying your platform software, installing Microsoft Commerce Server 2000, deploying Commerce Server features, and unpacking your application.
Secure your site	Securing your Commerce Server files, Commerce Server Business Desk, and databases and implementing the Commerce Server authentication method for your site.
Test your site environment	Testing the recovery time of your hardware, verifying your backup services are running, and testing that the failover configuration works.
Finalize your site environment before production	Removing extra logging that you used for debugging purposes, performing a final audit of the hardware and software, verifying that the current configuration is documented, and determining the process the deployment team will use to resolve problems when the site goes live.
Set up and perform initial operational procedures	Holding daily meetings with the development, test, and deployment teams to make sure the site is behaving as expected, revisiting the usage profile to determine how users are actually using your site, and performing initial backup and recovery testing of the production site.

The Deployment section of this book contains the chapters listed in the following table.

Chapter	Title	Description
14	Deploying Your Site	• Deployment checklists
		• How to implement your risk management plan
		• How to deploy your site, including its architecture, hardware, and software
		• How to secure your Commerce Server site, including how to implement Commerce Server authentication
		• How to finalize your site environment before production
		• How to perform initial operational procedures
15	Deploying Content	• Deployment tools
		• How to deploy content using Microsoft Application Center 2000
		• Examples illustrating how to use deployment tools in three different sites: small-to-medium, medium-to-large, and global
		• Examples illustrating how to deploy the following types of content: campaigns, campaign items, expressions, COM+ applications, and databases
16	Testing Your Site	• A general methodology for testing software
		• Specific information about testing your Commerce Server site

Deployment Checklists

Before you deploy your site, review the following checklists to ensure that your planning is complete:

- Site architecture checklist
- Availability checklist
- Site development and testing checklist
- Business process checklist
- Platform security checklist
- Commerce Server security checklist

Each checklist is described in the following topics.

Site Architecture Checklist

Before you deploy your site, make sure you have planned and implemented your site architecture. Check for the following:

- A Microsoft Windows 2000 Server network is in place, containing at a minimum one Microsoft Active Directory domain controller. Windows 2000 Advanced Server is recommended if you are using Network Load Balancing or creating server clusters, both of which increase the availability of your site.

  Ideally, you need two computers to handle Active Directory efficiently. They would serve as replicated domain controllers. Your other computers would then join the domain.

- The Windows 2000 domain architecture for the Commerce Server servers has been determined and is documented.

- Server names, roles, ports, and required services are identified and documented.

  If possible, do not change the names of your servers.

- The necessary Internet domain names and Internet Protocol (IP) addresses have been obtained.

- Windows 2000, Internet Information Services (IIS) 5.0, and Microsoft SQL Server security models have been determined.

- Internet Explorer version 5.0 or later is installed. Business Desk client computers require Internet Explorer 5.5.

- Firewalls and proxy servers are in place.

- Initial users, groups, permissions, and policies are set up.

- Server hardware is installed at the site.

- Client hardware for Business Desk client computers is installed at the site.

- Network hardware and connections are in place and connectivity to the Internet has been established.

- Replacement hardware is available at the site.

- Windows 2000 Terminal Services has been set up, if you plan to use remote computers for Business Desk sessions.

Availability Checklist

Before you deploy your site, make sure you have planned for protecting against server failure using a combination of the following methods:

- Geographically dispersed data centers.

- Dual uninterruptible power supplies (UPSs).

- Data backups.
- Clustered database servers. In Windows Clustering, two servers sharing common data form a cluster that works as a single system.
- Data replication. Microsoft SQL Server replication is used to ensure synchronization among the database servers for a site. SQL Server offers replication options that include snapshot replication and transactional replication.
- Network load-balanced clusters for Web servers. Network Load Balancing provides availability and load balancing for Web (IIS/ASP-based) applications.

For additional information about high availability, see Chapter 6, "Planning for Reliability and High Availability."

Site Development and Testing Checklist

Before you deploy your site, make sure you have completed your site development and testing. Check for the following:

- Site development is complete.
- The site is packaged.
- A list of site resources has been documented.
- Names have been determined for site servers.
- Database names, user names, and passwords have been determined.
- Testing is complete. You have tested for the following items: .
  - Browser compatibility
  - Content
  - Databases
  - Data validity and integrity
  - Links
  - Performance
  - Query response time
  - Routers
  - Search options
  - Server load
  - System recovery
  - Visual consistency

  You have tested the performance of your site using the Microsoft Web Application Stress (WAS) tool.

- An independent, outside company has completed a security audit of your site. Such a review is an effective means for discovering security risks.

For more information about testing your site, see Chapter 16, "Testing Your Site."

Business Process Checklist

Before you deploy your site, make sure you have planned and implemented your business processes. Check for the following:

- Workflows have been determined and tested.

- System administrators have received initial training and business managers, the primary users of Business Desk, have completed the Business Desk tutorial or have received other training that covers the specific tasks they are to perform using Business Desk.

- The server environment team has been identified and operational procedures have been determined (for example, change request, change control log, server update, maintenance schedules, and problem escalation procedures).

Platform Security Checklist

The platform security checklist addresses the following topics:

- Windows security

- IIS security

- Physical security

- Personnel security

Windows Security

The security features in Commerce Server are built upon security features in Windows 2000. For more information about Windows 2000 security, see Microsoft's security Web site, located at http://www.microsoft.com/technet/security/tools.asp.

The following tables contain information about the tasks you should perform to configure security settings in Windows to help make your Web site more secure.

File System

You can use the tasks listed in the following table to make your file system more secure.

Task	Reason
Use NTFS	The NTFS file system (NTFS) is more secure than the file allocation table (FAT) system. For information about converting your computer's hard disk from FAT to NTFS, see Windows 2000 Server Help.
Review directory permissions	By default, Windows creates new folders and assigns Full Control permissions to the Everyone group.
Set access control for the IUSR_<*computer name*> account	Setting access control for this account will help limit the access anonymous users have to your computer.
Store executable files in a separate directory	Storing executables in a separate directory makes it easier to assign access permissions and auditing.
Check NTFS permissions on network drives	By default, Windows creates new shared resources and assigns Full Control permissions to the Everyone group.

User Accounts

You can use the tasks listed in the following table to make your user accounts more secure.

Task	Reason
Review user accounts often	Check for new accounts that were not created by a valid administrator. Review the rights given to the IUSR_<*computer name*> account. All users gaining anonymous access to your site have their rights assigned to this account. You can also use auditing to monitor when and who changes security policies.
Choose difficult passwords	Passwords are more difficult to guess if they consist of a combination of lowercase and uppercase letters, numbers, and special characters.
Maintain strict account policies	Keep track of what types of access are given to important user accounts and groups. This includes knowing who has the ability to change security policies.
Limit the membership of the Administrators group	This group typically has full access to the computer.
Assign a password to the Administrator account	By default the password used for the Administrator account is blank. To improve security, set a difficult password for this account as discussed previously.

Services and Other Issues

You can use the tasks listed in the following table to make your services more secure and to address other security issues.

Task	Reason
Run minimal services	Run only the services that are absolutely necessary for your purposes. Each additional service that you run presents an entry point for malicious attacks. For more information about services and security, see the *Microsoft Windows 2000 Server Resource Kit.*
Do not use PDC as a server	The primary domain controller (PDC) is constantly processing authentication requests. Running a Web service on the PDC decreases performance. It could also expose your PDC to attacks that could render your entire network non-secure.
Enable auditing	Auditing is a very valuable tool for tracking access to secure or critical files. You can also use auditing for tracking server events, such as a change in your security policy. You can archive audit logs for later use.
Use encryption if administering your computer remotely	Typically, remote administration involves the exchange of sensitive information, such as the password for the Administrator account. To protect this information over open networks, use Secure Sockets Layer (SSL) encryption.
Use a low–level account to browse the Internet	Using the Administrator, Power User, or another highly privileged account to browse the Internet can potentially open entry points on your computer for attack. Likewise, never browse the Internet from the PDC.
Back up vital files and the registry often	No security effort can guarantee data safety. For more information, see the *Microsoft Windows 2000 Server Resource Kit.*
Run virus checks regularly	Any computer on an open network is susceptible to computer viruses. Regular checkups can help avoid unnecessary data loss.
Unbind unnecessary services from your Internet adapter cards	**Caution** Be sure to check with your system administrator before unbinding services, because this could have unwanted effects on other users of your system.

IIS Security

IIS provides frontline security for your Web site, including authentication and Web permissions. The following tables describe tasks you can perform for authentication and Web permissions.

Authentication

You can use the tasks listed in the following table to make your IIS authentication more secure.

Task	Reason
Use the most secure form of authentication possible	Use the most secure form of authentication that your clients support. For example, Integrated Windows authentication (NTLM) and Digest authentication are more secure than Basic authentication. You can also use client certificates for highly secure authentication.
One-to-one mapping versus many-to-one mapping	You can use either or both of these methods to map client certificates to Windows user accounts. One-to-one mapping offers a higher level of certainty, but requires a copy of the client certificate to be stored on the server. Many-to-one mapping is easier to implement and does not require a copy of the certificate to be stored on the server.

Web Permissions

You can use the tasks listed in the following table to make your IIS Web permissions more secure.

Task	Reason
Synchronize Web and NTFS permissions	If Web permissions and NTFS permissions are not synchronized, the more restrictive of the two is used. You can synchronize these permissions manually or use the Permissions Wizard.
Use IP address restriction if you are administering IIS remotely	For more information, see "Granting and Denying Access to Computers" in the IIS 5.0 online documentation.
Use the most restrictive permission possible	For example, if your Web site is used only for viewing information assign only Read permissions. If a directory or site contains Active Server Pages (ASP) applications, assign Scripts Only permissions instead of Scripts and Executables permissions. For more information, see "Setting Web Server Permissions" in the IIS 5.0 online documentation.
Write and Scripts and Executables permissions	Use this combination with extreme caution. It can allow someone t upload potentially dangerous executable files to your server and ru them. For more information, see "Setting Web Server Permissions" in the IIS 5.0 online documentation.

Physical Security

You can use the tasks listed in the following table to implement physical security for your site.

Task	Reason
Lock the computer when you are away	When you are not at the computer, lock the desktop by pressing CTRL+ALT+DELETE, and selecting Lock Computer.
Use a password-protected screen saver	The time delay should be short so that no one can use the computer after you leave. The screen saver should be blank; animated screen savers can decrease server performance.
Lock up the computer	Keep the computer locked in a secure room in order to reduce the chance of access by malicious individuals.

Personnel Security

You can use the tasks listed in the following table to secure the appropriate levels of access for your site development and management personnel.

Task	Reason
Use different Administrator accounts	Each individual who has administrative privileges should be given a distinct user account and password. Using distinct user accounts and passwords will make it easier to track any changes that are made.
Use non-disclosure agreements	Using non-disclosure agreements can enforce further accountability by your personnel.
Periodically reassign accounts	To lower the risk of user account information being compromised, assign new user accounts to personnel with Administrator or other high-level privileges.
Quickly delete unused accounts	This will lower the risk of a disgruntled former employee or vendor gaining access to your network.

Commerce Server Security Checklist

Before you deploy your site, make sure you have planned and implemented your site security.

Use the following guidelines when setting up security for your site:

- Whenever possible, install IIS 5.0 and SQL Server on separate computers. Having users connect to the computers that store your databases presents security risks to your data. You should keep Web applications and databases on separate computers.

- Always keep sensitive data secure behind a firewall.

Use the following deployment guidelines to protect your site from internal attacks:

- Restrict physical access to all computers.

- Restrict the number of users logged on to all computers; give users only the minimum necessary privileges needed to get their work done.

- Change passwords frequently, especially after someone leaves your organization.

- Keep logs of all system activity and review them frequently.

- Keep all backups in a secure place.

- Use the Commerce Server CS Authentication resource to establish or change the authentication and identification method for your Commerce Server site.

Implementing Your Contingency Plan

A contingency (or *risk management*) plan describes preparations for events that could interrupt e-business services. An interruption could be caused by an event that ranges in severity from an application, system, or network failure to a complete loss of a business location.

The possible disasters that your contingency plan should cover include:

- Fire, sabotage, and theft

- Flood, natural disaster, pest damage, and building damage

- Industrial action and accidental damage

- Equipment loss or failure—computing, network, or environmental controls

- Software failure

- Data loss or corruption

Contingency planning uses risk management principles to identify threats to service, such as equipment failure or fire. Introducing countermeasures, such as an alternative network link, can eliminate vulnerable areas of the service design to limit the impact of a threat to your site. In the event of a major threat, the contingency plans for service continuity must provide the facilities, information, and procedures for a full recovery of service.

Technical Solutions for Risk Reduction

When you develop the technical solutions required for contingency planning, you must spend time reviewing your existing infrastructure to assess the risk of its failure. Where possible, make changes to the production environment to reduce risk. An e-commerce solution should not include any systems that are vulnerable to a single point of failure. Also, applications developed for e-commerce service should be designed to use technologies that allow for component failure or damage.

The design solutions considered here can help reduce risk and improve service availability. Because it is impossible to eliminate all risk, a contingency plan is an essential part of the overall risk management solution.

This section explains how you can use the following technologies in an e-commerce installation to reduce risk:

- Network Load Balancing

- Application Center COM+ Load Balancing (CLB)

- Windows Clustering

Network Load Balancing

Windows 2000 Network Load Balancing enhances the availability and scalability of Commerce Server applications. By combining the resources of two or more Web servers into a single load-balancing cluster, you can deliver a more reliable Web site.

Each server runs separate copies of your Commerce Server applications. Network Load Balancing balances the workload among servers by allowing the group of them to be addressed by the same set of cluster IP addresses.

You can use any of the following programs to install Network Load Balancing:

- Application Center

- Windows 2000 Advanced Server

- Windows 2000 Datacenter Server

Network Load Balancing provides a good solution to scale and mitigate the risk of a single failure in a front-end system that does not hold changing data. Network Load Balancing offers a good solution for front-end Web servers and front-end reverse proxy servers.

For information about installing Network Load Balancing, including hardware requirements, see the documentation for the product you will use for the installation.

Application Load Balancing

Application Center is designed to increase the scale, size, and availability of Web-based applications. Application Center builds onto the functionality of Network Load Balancing to increase the availability of application components.

Application Center ties the application components together in an application cluster. COM+ Load Balancing (CLB) distributes the workload across multiple servers running a site's business logic. It complements both Network Load Balancing and the Cluster service by acting on the middle tier of a multi-tiered clustered network, as discussed here, separating COM+ components into a middle tier.

Because the applications are tied together, the front-end server gets equal response from the back-end components. If any one of the application component servers were to fail, the other servers would share the load of the failed server. The application, not the computer, is being clustered.

This architecture splits the content servers (the front-end servers) from the application components and the data engines. It also separates the application components from the data engines.

Windows Clustering

While Network Load Balancing and Application Center mitigate risk for the Web server and Commerce Server layer, the failover clustering features in Windows Clustering mitigates the risk of using back-end services, such as SQL Server.

Failover clustering increases server availability. When a server fails, clustering allows the system to automatically switch the processing for a service to a working server. (Failover handles failed processors, motherboards, power supplies, and memory, but does not take failed disk arrays into account.) For example, an instance of SQL Server can quickly restore database services to a Web site or enterprise network even if the server running the instance fails.

Cluster Topology

Windows Clustering supports two-node failover clusters in Windows 2000 Advanced Server and four-node clusters in Windows 2000 Datacenter Server. The following three connections connect the servers together:

- Small computer system interface (SCSI) connection (each computer shares the same clustered disk array)

- Heartbeat network, second local area network (LAN) connection

- Standard LAN connection

The system is set up so that each application does not share resources with any other application, but takes over the resources of a failed processor unit.

Only one server can access a shared disk drive at any one time. If, for example, processor Unit One should fail, processor Unit Two takes over that role and the application.

For more information about Windows Clustering, see the Microsoft Windows NT Server, Windows 2000 Server, Windows 2000 Advanced Server, or Windows 2000 Datacenter Server documentation.

SQL Server Failover Clustering

The type of Windows Clustering failover cluster used by SQL Server 2000 consists of multiple server computers (up to four on Windows 2000 Datacenter Server) that share a common set of cluster resources, such as disk drives. Each server in the cluster is called a node. Each server, or node, is connected to the network, and each node can communicate with each other node. Each node runs the same version of Windows Clustering.

The shared resources in the failover cluster are collected into cluster groups. For example, if a failover cluster has four clustered disk drives, two of the drives can be collected in one cluster group and the other two in a second cluster group. Each cluster group is owned by one of the nodes in the failover cluster, although the ownership can be transferred between nodes.

Applications can be installed on the nodes in the failover cluster. These applications are typically server applications or distributed Component Object Model (DCOM) objects that users access through network connections. The application executables and other resources are typically stored in one or more of the cluster groups owned by the node. Each node can have multiple applications installed on it.

The failover cluster nodes periodically send each other network messages called *heartbeat* messages. If Windows Clustering detects the loss of a heartbeat signal from one of the nodes in the cluster, it treats the server as a failed server. Windows Clustering then automatically transfers the cluster groups and application resources of that node to the other nodes in the network. The cluster administrator specifies the alternate nodes to which cluster groups are transferred when any given node fails. The other nodes then continue processing user network requests for the applications transferred from the failed server.

Deploying Your Commerce Server Site

This section describes how to deploy the following aspects of your site:

- Site architecture
- Site platform software
- Commerce Server software
- Commerce Server features

Deploying Your Site Architecture

The site architecture specifies:

- The hardware you are using.
- The software that is installed on each computer and in which order.
- How the computers are connected together and which ports are open.
- How your hardware and software is secured.

During the Planning phase, you determine your hardware, software, and networking requirements, and document them in a site architecture diagram. During the Deployment phase, you deploy and test the site architecture.

When you deploy your site architecture, it is important that you document any changes that you make to the hardware or software configuration. This information must be accurate and immediately available at all times in order for your team to efficiently troubleshoot problems. In addition, this information will be helpful to new system administrators, testers, and developers who work on your site.

Figure 14.2 shows the hardware and software architecture for a small-to-medium size site.

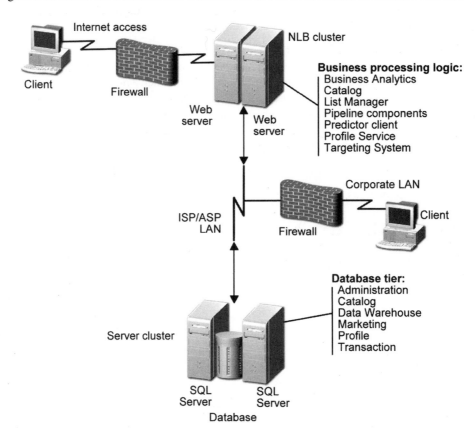

Figure 14.2 Small-to-medium site hardware and software architecture

This architecture diagram shows a basic Web service available to the Internet. The failover clusters take into account contingency planning requirements. The firewalls provide basic security; however, it is recommended that you create a separate network security architecture.

Installing Hardware and Software

First, you install the hardware and software you need to run the Web site, and also install the hardware you need to administer the site, such as computers for monitoring performance and network sniffers.

You install and configure the hardware and software as specified in your site architecture diagrams. Document all software, service packs, and hotfixes you install on each computer. If you need to make changes, be sure to update the site architecture document so you have a record of your current configuration. This information will be critical during the testing stage and when you are troubleshooting your site.

For instructions for installing Commerce Server and prerequisite software, see http://support.microsoft.com/support/commerceserver/2000/install/default.asp.

For detailed examples of installing Commerce Server in a multi-computer deployment, see the following topics in "Installing Your Site" in the "Deploying Your Site" section of Commerce Server 2000 Help:

- "Example A: Installing on a Four-Computer Clustered Configuration"

  This topic explains how to install Commerce Server and unpack applications on a four-computer configuration consisting of:

  - Two Web servers in a Network Load Balancing cluster. These servers also contain the Commerce Server administration tools.

  - Two SQL Server servers configured as a single server cluster. These servers are referred to by their shared cluster name.

- "Example B: Installing on a Three-Computer Non-clustered Configuration"

  This topic explains how to install Commerce Server and unpack applications on a three-computer configuration consisting of:

  - One SQL Server server (used for the Commerce Server Administration database).

  - One SQL Server server used for the Commerce Server databases.

  - One Web server that hosts your applications.

Deploying Site Platform Software

This section contains information about deploying Application Center and Active Directory in your site platform environment.

Application Center

To make Application Center aware of the Commerce Server applications, including Business Desk, you must access each Commerce Server application (Web site) manually on each Web server (by computer name) with the browser.

Active Directory

You can use the following deployment information when you include Active Directory in your site.

Commerce Server Does Not Extend Active Directory Schema

If you are using Active Directory for user profiles, note that Commerce Server does not extend the underlying Active Directory schema because changes to the Active Directory schema are irreversible.

To review the mapping of profile definition properties to Active Directory attributes, see the ProfileAD_SQL.xml file that is installed with Commerce Server.

Limit User Names to 20 Characters

A Windows logon_name must be used to create a user in Active Directory; the maximum length of that name is 20 characters. This enables backward compatibility with Windows NT 4.0.

If your site does not allow e-mail names longer than 20 characters, then you can permit users to use their e-mail name as their logon name.

Deploying Commerce Server Software

This section contains information about installing, packaging, and unpacking your Commerce Server application.

Installing Commerce Server

You can use the following deployment information when you install Commerce Server.

Commerce Server Requires SQL Server

Commerce Server requires SQL Server 7.0 or SQL Server 2000. You can use an Oracle database in addition to SQL Server, but you cannot use Oracle in place of SQL Server.

You must store design-time information (for example, the profile definition store and the catalog design-time tables) in a SQL Server database. For the Profiling System only, you can store run-time information exclusively in an Oracle database. For all other Commerce Server components, you must store run-time information in a SQL Server database.

The Product Catalog System requires the full-text search feature of SQL Server. The Administration and Commerce Server Direct Mailer databases use SQL Server, and the Business Analytics System uses the data warehousing capabilities of SQL Server.

The Commerce Server 2000 OLE DB provider supports any data source that either conforms to LDAP-v3 protocol or has an OLE DB provider with support for specified interfaces and ANSI SQL support.

SQL Server Servers in a Different Domain than Web Servers

If your SQL Server server is in a different domain than your Web server (for example, they are separated by a firewall), you must open a security context between the Web servers and SQL Server servers in the two domains. Use the **Net use** command on a resource on the SQL Server server from the Web server.

For example, type **Net use** * <*<computer name>**<share name>* /U:*<domain name>**<user name>*. You will then be prompted for a password.

To use the **Net use** command over a secure channel, use **ipc$**. For example, type **net use** * <\\*computer1 name*\ipc$> /U:*<domain1 name>*\joeuser.

Host Names

Commerce Server by default uses the computer name of the first computer installed in an Administration database as the host name in Uniform Resource Locators (URLs) generated in sites. Typically, you will want to change the host name so that Commerce Server uses a Domain Name System (DNS) host name, for example, www.microsoft.com.

For information about setting the non-secure and secure host names, see "Renaming an Application" in the "Managing Commerce Server Applications and Web Servers" section of Commerce Server 2000 Help.

Packaging Your Application

When the development team is finished developing and testing the application, they package it into a Commerce Server Site Packager file (with a .pup extension). You can then unpack and deploy the application in a multi-computer environment. This section contains information about what data and settings are included when an application is packaged.

Resources and Data

The following table lists the resources and the data packaged in a Site Packager file.

Resource	Data packaged
App Default Config	All property values.
Campaigns	The following tables in the Campaigns database: IndustryCode, Customer, EventType, Campaign, CreativeType, CreativeSize, Creative, CreativeProperty, Creative_PropertyValue, CampaignItemTypes, CampaignItem, OrderDiscount, DmItem, AdItem, CreativeTypeXref, PageGroup, PageGroupXref, TargetGroup, Target, TargetGroupXref, OrderDiscountExpression, OrderDiscountMisc.
CS Authentication	Settings in the AuthSetup.ini file. When you unpack a site, you can create a new resource or point to an existing one.
Commerce Server Data Warehouse	None. When you unpack a site, you can create a new Data Warehouse resource or point to an existing one.
Direct Mailer	None. Confirms the existence of Direct Mailer in the site. Which Direct Mailer global resource to use is specified during unpacking. When you unpack a site, you can point to a Direct Mailer resource. You must use Commerce Server Setup to create a new one.
Predictor	None. Confirms the existence of a Predictor resource in the site. Which Predictor global resource to use is specified during unpacking. When you unpack a site, you can point to a Predictor resource. You must use Commerce Server Setup to create a new one.
Product Catalog	The following tables in the Catalogs database: CatalogAttributes, CatalogDefinitions, CatalogDefinitionProperties, CatalogGlobal, CatalogUsedDefinitions, CatalogEnumValues, CatalogStatus, CatalogCustomCatalogs, CatalogCustomPrices, CatalogSet_Info, CatalogSet_Catalogs, CatalogToVendorAssociation, x_ProductsComplete, x_Relationships, x_Hierarchy.
Profiles	Schema script and data script. Defaults are <*commerce_server_root*>\Profilesql.sql and <*commerce_server_root*>\PopulateProfileSql.sql, respectively. Existing databases are not packaged. When you unpack a site, you can create a new resource or point to an existing one.
Transactions	The following tables in the Transactions database: TransDimension, TransCategory.
Transactions Config	The following tables in the Transactions Config database: Decode, Region, RegionalTax, ShippingConfig, TableShippingRates.

IIS Settings

When you package a site, Site Packager includes many of your IIS settings. It does not package an IIS Web Site (such as Default Web Site), but it does package the files in the physical root folder of the application and all of its physical child folders and files.

To view IIS settings for an application, folder, or file

1. Click **Start**, point to **Programs**, point to **Microsoft Commerce Server 2000**, and then click **Commerce Server Manager**.

2. In the **Commerce Server Manager** window, expand **Internet Information Services**, expand the name of the Web server containing an application, expand the name of the IIS Web site in which the application resides, right-click the name of an application, folder, or file, and then click **Properties**.

The **Properties** dialog box for the application appears.

The following tables list the settings for the **Virtual Directory** and **Directory Security** tabs in the **Properties** dialog box, and indicate which ones are packaged when you use Site Packager.

Virtual Directory Tab

Field	Whether it is packaged
Script source access	Packaged
Read	Packaged
Write	Packaged
Directory browsing	Packaged
Log visits	Packaged
Index this resource	Packaged
Application name	Not packaged
Starting point	Not packaged
Execute permissions	Packaged
Application protection	This is always set to Medium when unpacking
Application Configuration settings (shown after Configuration is clicked)	Not packaged

Directory Security Tab

Field	Whether it is packaged
Anonymous access	Packaged
Anonymous access account	Not packaged
Basic authentication	Packaged
Basic authentication domain	Not packaged
Digest authentication	Packaged
Integrated Windows authentication	Packaged
IP addresses and domain name restrictions	Not packaged
Secure communications (SSL certificates)	Not packaged

Note Nothing in the **Documents**, **HTTP Headers**, and **Custom Errors** tabs is packaged. The Unpack.vbs script file for Business Desk adds custom errors for Business Desk after unpacking.

IIS Virtual Directories

If you have virtual directories located within the application, the virtual directory object and the folders and files in the path it points to will not be packaged. If you want to package these folders and files, copy them to a folder in the physical path of the application before packaging them.

NTFS Permissions

NTFS permissions and access control lists (ACLs) on folders and files are not packaged. You can use the Unpack.vbs script (or create a Post<*package name*>.vbs script) to apply NTFS permissions automatically after unpacking.

Unpacking Your Application

After your hardware and software are installed, you deploy your Commerce Server application on the test computers. To move the Commerce Server application from the development environment to your test and production environments, you use Site Packager. The site developer packages the Commerce Server application on the development environment, including IIS 5.0 settings (metabase), file system, resources from the Administration database, and SQL Server databases.

When you unpack the application, you unpack the Commerce Server site (or portions of it) onto other computers.

Two global resources—Predictor and Direct Mailer—are installed by using Commerce Server Setup; all other global resources are installed using Site Packager. Before you unpack a site that requires the global resources Predictor or Direct Mailer, you must use Commerce Server Setup to install them.

In most cases, you use Site Packager for the initial deployment of your site. For future deployments, incremental updates, and rollbacks, use other tools, such as Application Center or other content management products. For information about deploying content, see Chapter 15, "Deploying Content."

Site Packager

You can refer to the following deployment information when you use Site Packager.

Install Resources Before Unpacking

You must install resources before you can unpack them. For example, if you have installed the Predictor resource, you can unpack it when it is part of a package. If you do not install the resource, it will unpack, but it will not work.

Do Not Unpack to Remote Servers

Site Packager does not unpack application data to remote servers. However, you can unpack resources to remote servers.

For example, if you have the Retail Solution Site on one computer and the Business Desk application on another computer, you must package each of these separately, creating two packages, and unpack them separately.

Packaging Extended Profile Schemas

Site Packager doesn't automatically package extended profile schemas. You must create an SQL script before packaging your site, and then supply your script when prompted during the packaging process.

When you package an application, the **IPuP** object for Profiles copies data into the package in the following order:

1. Profile definition schema (from the profile definition store of the site) in the form of Extensible Markup Language (XML).

2. CatalogSchema.sql from the Commerce Server root.

3. If the data store is SQL Server, it prompts you for the user data and data store schema script files.

4. If the data store is Active Directory, it prompts you for the data population script file.

5. Site terms definition schema in the form of XML.

In Steps 3 and 4, if you don't supply any file names, you will receive a warning message. If you dismiss the warning message, the corresponding files are not copied into the Site Packager package.

The same **IPuP** object also copies the following expression store files into the Site Packager package:

- The expressions defined, streamed out in the form of XML

- The Es_create.sql and Es_stored_procs.sql files from the Commerce Server root directory

Deploying Commerce Server Features

This section contains information about deploying the following Commerce Server features:

- Product Catalog System

- Direct Mailer

- Profiling System

- Data Warehouse

Product Catalog System

You can use the following deployment information when you use the Product Catalog System.

Create CommerceCatalogs Shared Folder

To enable business managers to import and export catalogs using Business Desk, it is recommended that you create the CommerceCatalogs shared folder on the server. If business managers use the CommerceCatalogs share, they will not have to specify the complete path and file name to perform a catalog import or export.

Maximum Number of Product Catalogs

SQL Server 2000 (or SQL Server 7.0, depending on your implementation) determines the maximum number of product catalogs you can create. Commerce Server uses one SQL Server full-text catalog for each Commerce Server product catalog.

There is a SQL Server limitation of 256 full-text catalogs per server. However, you can have multiple tables in one SQL Server full-text catalog, and the tables are full-text searchable.

There is no limit to the number of category hierarchies you can create in a catalog.

No Sharing Product Data Across Catalogs

To have a product appear in multiple catalogs, you must manually add the product data to each catalog. You cannot share product data across catalogs.

Sharing Catalogs Across Sites

To share a product catalog with more than one Commerce Server site, you can create and manage the catalog in one site. Then on other sites, you can set the connection string for the Product Catalog resource to point to the Catalogs database.

Note   You cannot make the Product Catalog resource a global resource.

Name Restrictions for Catalogs

In Commerce Server product catalogs, at the application level (Business Desk), note the character restrictions for the following properties:

- **Property Definition Name**. Do not use the characters /, <, >, &, (, and). Also, a numeral is not allowed in the first position. Do not use characters that are not accepted in an XML tag name.

- **Product Definition Name**. No restrictions.

- **Category Definition Name**. No restrictions.

- **Category Name**. Do not use the characters <, >.

- **Catalog Name**. Do not use the characters <, >, [,], and apostrophe (').

- **Custom Catalog Name**. Do not use the characters <, >, [, and].

In the Catalog application programming interface (API), note the character restrictions for the following properties:

- **Property Definition Name**. Do not use the characters [,], comma (,), and double quotation mark (").

- **Product Definition Name**. No restrictions.

- **Category Definition Name**. No restrictions.

- **Category Name**. No restrictions.

- **Product Name**. No restrictions.

- **Catalog Name**. Do not use the characters [,], comma (,), double quotation mark ("), and apostrophe ('). Also, a Catalog Name should not begin with the number sign (#).

- **Custom Catalog Name**. Do not use the characters [,], comma (,), double quotation mark ("), and apostrophe ('). Also, a Custom Catalog Name should not begin with the number sign (#).

Importing Product Variants

When you import a catalog with product variants, you must use XML to preserve your variants. Comma-separated value (CSV) files do not support product variants.

Creating Categories with the Same Name

To create categories with the same display name, first create a property definition called **Display Name**. Then add the property definition to the category definition.

Implementing Order Fulfillment

If multiple vendors supply the products on your site, you can use the Splitter component in Commerce Server to divide an order among the appropriate vendors. When a user selects a product, it will be sent to the correct vendor for fulfillment.

The **Splitter** component divides an order into groups based on a list of item keys. For example, in the Accept stage, the **Splitter** component can be used to divide orders by catalog and vendor; in the Shipping stage it can be used to divide an order into shipments by shipping methods and addresses.

Direct Mailer

Refer to the following deployment notes when you use Direct Mailer:

- Direct Mailer cannot be installed on a SQL Server cluster.

- Direct Mailer requires SQL Server to be installed locally.

- Direct Mailer can process one million mails per day, 5 KB in size, personalized. It can process up to one million personalized messages in 24 hours.

- Direct Mailer can process one million mails per day, 5 KB in size, non-personalized. It can process up to two million non-personalized messages in 24 hours.

Profiling System

You can refer to the following deployment information when you use the Profiling System.

Multivalued Properties

Multivalued properties are able to store more than one value. However, you cannot search on multivalued properties.

The way the underlying store handles multivalued properties depends on whether the store is Lightweight Directory Access Protocol (LDAP) or ANSI SQL. Consider the following:

- LDAP stores such as Active Directory support multivalued properties; Commerce Server provides no special processing.

- ANSI SQL stores such as SQL Server 2000 do not natively support multivalued properties. In this case, the provider handles multivalued properties by appending all values together separated by semicolons and stores them in a single column. This is transparent to the user.

Note the following requirements for storing multivalued properties in ANSI SQL stores:

- Only string properties can be multivalued; multivalued numbers are not supported.

- The total length of all strings appended together cannot exceed the maximum size of the underlying column.

- The individual values cannot contain semicolons.

- The delimiter between values is a semicolon (;).

Profile Definition Properties Must Be Keys

The Profiling System only supports profile definition properties marked as keys (for example, join key and primary key) to be mapped to a string type or an integer column. Support for other data types (such as **uniqueidentifier**) does not exist.

The user ID in the UserObject table is a globally unique identifier (GUID) stored in an **nVarchar** field. The impact on index size and performance is insignificant.

Multiple Baskets and One User Profile

You can associate multiple baskets with a single user profile. This may be helpful if you have a site where account managers manage multiple baskets for each customer and want to be able to preserve baskets across sessions.

To do this, use the OrderGroup template feature to save each customer's basket as a template. You can then use the **OrderGroupManager** object to get a list of all templates that belong to a particular dealer/account manager. This is easy to implement, and the Commerce Server Order Management API directly supports it.

Multiple Addresses for Users

If you use SQL Server to store user profiles, by default, the addresses are stored in a separate SQL table and referenced by the user ID (GUID) as one column in the Address table. There is, by design, no limit to the number of addresses a user profile can have. However, you can configure your site to work differently.

Extracting the Profile Catalog from Profile Definition

To extract the profile catalog from a site, you can package the site that contains the catalog, and then unpack only the Profiles resource on the new site.

Data Warehouse

You can refer to the following deployment information when you use the Data Warehouse:

- You must install the online analytical processing (OLAP) client on the same computer as the one on which the Data Warehouse resource is unpacked.

- The logged on user must be an OLAP administrator to unpack the OLAP resource.

- If you are using SQL Server 7.0, you must install the Runtime Objects option "Analysis and Data Warehouse" (available when performing a Custom installation) on the same computer as your Web server.

Securing Your Site

It is critically important that you completely secure your Commerce Server site. This section addresses the following topics:

- General security elements
- Platform security
- Network security
- Database security
- Web server security
- Commerce Server security
- Security and authentication scenarios
- Site security deployment notes

General Security Elements

This section describes the main security elements that you can use to secure an e-commerce site:

- Authentication
- Access control
- Certificates
- Encryption
- Auditing

Authentication

Commerce Server supports seven authentication methods: three authentication methods provided by Commerce Server (Windows Authentication, Custom Authentication, and Autocookie), and four authentication methods provided by IIS (Anonymous, Basic, Integrated Windows, and Certificates). For more information about Commerce Server authentication methods, see "Commerce Server Security" later in this chapter.

Commerce Server cannot detect which of the IIS authentication methods is in use. When you use any of these authentication methods, except Anonymous, Commerce Server can access the ASP environment and programmatically request the name of the user (currently logged on) using server request variables.

The security features that IIS provides are fully integrated with Windows. Commerce Server supports the following four IIS authentication methods that you can use to confirm the identity of anyone requesting access to your Web sites:

- **Anonymous authentication**. Allows anyone access without asking for a user name or password.

- **Basic authentication**. Prompts the user for a user name and password, which are sent unencrypted over the network.

- **Integrated Windows authentication**. Uses hashing technology to identify the user without actually sending the password over the network.

- **Certificates**. Employ digital credentials that can be used to establish an SSL connection. They can also be used for authentication.

You can use these methods to grant access to public areas of your site, while preventing unauthorized access to your private files and directories.

Access Control

Using NTFS access permissions as the foundation of the security for your Web server, you can define the level of file and directory access granted to Windows users and groups. For example, if a business decided to publish its catalog on your Web server, you would need to create a Windows user account for that business and then configure permissions for the specific Web site, directory, or file. The permissions would enable only the server administrator and the owner of the business to update the content for the Web site. Public users would be allowed to view the Web site, but could not alter its contents. For more details about setting NTFS permissions, see "Setting NTFS Permissions for a Directory or File" in the IIS 5.0 online documentation.

Web Distributed Authoring and Versioning (WebDAV) is an extension of the Hypertext Transfer Protocol (HTTP) version 1.1 that facilitates file and directory manipulation over an HTTP connection. Through the use of WebDAV "verbs," or commands, properties can be added to and read from files and directories. Files and directories can also be remotely created, deleted, moved, or copied. Additional access control can be configured through both

Web server permissions and NTFS. For more information, see "About Access Control" and "WebDAV Publishing" in the IIS 5.0 online documentation.

Certificates

Certificates are digital identification documents that allow both servers and clients to authenticate each other. They are required for both the server and the browser belonging to the client to set up an SSL connection over which encrypted information can be sent. The certificate-based SSL features in IIS consist of a server certificate, a client certificate, and various digital keys. You can create these certificates with Microsoft Certificate Services or get them from a mutually trusted, third-party organization called a certification authority (CA). For more information about setting up certificates and keys, see "Setting Up SSL on Your Server" in the IIS 5.0 online documentation.

Server Certificates

Server certificates provide a way for users to confirm the identity of your Web site. A server certificate contains detailed identification information, such as the name of the organization affiliated with the server content, the name of the organization that issued the certificate, and a public key used in establishing an encrypted connection. This information helps to assure users of the authenticity of Web server content and the integrity of the secure HTTP connection.

Client Certificates

With SSL, your Web server also has the option of authenticating users by checking the contents of their client certificates. A typical client certificate contains detailed identification information about a user, the organization that issued the certificate, and a public key. You can use client certificate authentication, along with SSL encryption, to implement a highly secure method for verifying the identity of your users.

Encryption

You can enable users to exchange private information with your server, such as credit card numbers or phone numbers, in a secure way by using encryption. Encryption "scrambles" the information before it is sent, and decryption "unscrambles" it after it is received. The foundation for this encryption in IIS is the SSL 3.0 protocol, which provides a secure way of establishing an encrypted communication link with users. SSL confirms the authenticity of your Web site and, optionally, the identity of users accessing restricted Web sites.

Certificates include keys used in establishing an SSL secure connection. A key is a unique value used to authenticate the server and the client in establishing an SSL connection. A public key and a private key form an SSL key pair. Your Web server uses the key pair to negotiate a secure connection with the Web browser to determine the level of encryption required for securing communications.

For this type of connection, both your Web server and the Web browser must be equipped with compatible encryption and decryption capabilities. During the exchange an encryption, or session, key is created. Both your server and the Web browser use the session key to encrypt and decrypt transmitted information. The degree of encryption, or strength, of a session key is measured in bits. The greater the number of bits comprising the session key, the greater the level of encryption and security. Although these greater encryption key strengths offer greater security, they also require more server resources to implement. The session key of your Web server is typically 40 bits long, but can be 128 bits long depending upon the level of security you require.

You can use Commerce Server to generate new encryption keys. For information, see "Generating a New Encryption Key" in Commerce Server 2000 Help.

Auditing

You can use security auditing techniques to monitor a broad range of user and Web server security activity. You should routinely audit your server configuration to detect areas where resources might be susceptible to unauthorized access and tampering. You can use the integrated Windows utilities, the logging features built into IIS 5.0, or ASP applications to create your own auditing logs.

For highly sensitive information, you should seek the assistance of a professional security consulting firm. A consulting firm can help you establish proper security policies and procedures.

Platform Security

This section discusses some issues to consider when you secure the platform for your e-commerce site.

Separating Users from Internal Domains

If you use Active Directory for your site and for your internal organization, you should use separate domains. Administering user data outside of your corporate network might require more administrative time and effort, but the security improvement is usually worth the cost. If you share a domain for internal and external use, it is possible for external user data to wind up in your internal Active Directory global catalog. If you have a reason to use your internal Active Directory in your site, it is a good idea to put your Business Desk server on the same side of the firewall as your Active Directory domain controller. The risks of sharing internal and external Active Directory information include site defacement, fraudulent purchases, account changes, denial of service, and virus placement.

Securing Cookies

By default, cookies travel in clear text. It is possible for intruders to intercept information contained in cookies and use that information to impersonate users. However, cookies can be encrypted. Commerce Server employs authentication and anonymous cookies that are encrypted to enhance security. To help secure cookies, use encryption, and embed the IP address of the client in them. This allows the target server to verify that the correct user actually sent the cookies.

Using Scripts to Set Permissions on Folders

Site Packager does not package or unpack any NTFS folder or file permissions (ACLs). Make sure you secure the files and folders that contain your site after you unpack it. A good way to do this is to use the scripting hooks of Site Packager to change folder permissions while or after you run Site Packager.

Limiting Access to Your Site

Site Packager does not affect Windows access control lists (ACLs). After you unpack a site, you should lock down some of the files and folders on your Commerce Server site by changing permissions on them. You can also limit access to files by setting Web server permissions.

When you limit access to the files and folders on your site, you should consider the following:

- Business Desk users must have access to the log file in the Profiles folder before they can save changes to a profile definition. A business manager must also have access to the log file in the Profiles folder to be able to save any changes made in the Profile Designer module. The IIS Web server permissions have read access turned off by default when you use the Commerce Server Solution Sites, but you can increase security by also denying read access on this folder's NTFS permissions.

- If you use pipeline logging to debug a pipeline, be aware that sensitive information appears in clear text in the log files. Make sure you secure against read access the Pipelines\Logfiles folder, which contains these pipeline log files.

- If, when you unpack a non-Business Desk application, you use an Unpack.vbs script file that you created, make sure you delete or secure the file immediately after unpacking. The file exists in the root directory and can be accessed by anonymous users. Unauthorized use of this script could lead to denial of service or the breaking of site settings. This file does need to be present, however, if you repackage the site.

  In the Commerce Server Solution Sites, the Unpack.vbs file is secured by default.

- You can set file and folder permissions only on drives formatted to use NTFS.

- To change permissions, you must be the system administrator or have been granted permission to do so by the system administrator.

- Groups or users given Full Control permissions for a folder can delete files and subfolders within that folder regardless of the permissions protecting the files and subfolders.

- If the check boxes under the **Permissions** box are shaded, or if the **Remove** button is unavailable, then the file or folder has inherited permissions from the parent folder.

Web Farms Using Proxy Accounts

Consider the case of a user, with a valid ticket that contains a proxy account ID, who visits a new site on a Web farm. AuthFilter uses the proxy account ID to retrieve the profile of the user. Because the proxy account ID does not have a profile associated with it, the ticket is considered invalid. The user is denied access and is redirected to the login page.

To avoid this, add the custom **guid** property to the ticket using the **AuthManager** object. After the **guid** property has been set, AuthFilter uses it to access the password cache instead of the proxy account ID. When the GUID is not found in the password cache, AuthFilter uses the user ID from the MSCSAuth ticket, instead of the proxy account ID, to look up the profile. In this case, the profile should exist, and the user is redirected to the originally requested URL.

Using Windows Authentication with Active Directory in a Web Farm

If you are using Active Directory, you cannot get clear text passwords from Active Directory, so you must enable *sticky sessions*. Active Directory support in a Web farm requires sticky sessions.

If you are using Active Directory and SQL Server aggregation, you can capture a password from the Login.asp page and store it in the user's profile store in SQL Server. The password is then accessible from another server and the custom code in Login.asp can log the user in transparently. This authentication process does not require sticky sessions.

You do not need to maintain two passwords. The password from Active Directory is cached only in SQL Server. Users must explicitly change their passwords in SQL Server.

> **Note**   The proxy client works in a Web farm, because it requires keeping an SQL store of the password and allows credentials to be re-submitted to Active Directory. This issue relates to the fact that IIS and Active Directory require both a user ID and password to authenticate a user and load it into the token cache.

You can also use Application Center to implement a workaround to an Active Directory implementation without sticky sessions. Application Center has the Request Forwarder that starts before Integrated Windows (NTLM) authentication. This enables Network Load Balancing without sticky sessions, although the actual request is "stuck" to one physical Web server. This solves issues with proxied client access (for example, as used with AOL).

Note that this Application Center feature works only if cookies are supported on the client side. Cookieless browsing requires sticky sessions.

Securing an Intranet (Supplier) Site

When you secure an intranet site, you must use Standard Authentication to SQL Server 2000. You cannot use Windows NT Authentication to SQL Server. Because Windows NT Authentication is not supported, all connections to the SQL Servers are under the same account.

All Business Desk users have the same access to the SQL Server databases. You cannot differentiate SQL Server access among Business Desk users by creating multiple SQL Server accounts, each with different access rights.

Hosting Sites for External Customers

If you are an Application Service Provider (ASP) hosting sites for external customers, you must ensure a secure environment if you host multiple sites on a single computer. Any environment where multiple sites are hosted on the same computer (or in a Web farm) introduces additional risk. Any scripts or code uploaded to the Web farm must be carefully inspected to ensure there is no unexpected or potentially malicious corruption of the Administration database. Users from one site might be able to read data from other sites because the Administration database is shared.

Network Security

To implement network protection in an e-commerce site, you use the following security elements:

- DMZ
- Firewalls
- Network segregation
- Data encryption using SSL
- Credit card information security
- Intrusion detection

DMZ

A DMZ (derived from the military term *demilitarized zone*) consists of front-end servers, back-end servers, and firewalls. The firewalls protect the front-end servers from the public network and filter traffic between the corporate network and back-end servers. A DMZ provides a multilayer protection system between the Internet and the internal network of an organization.

To provide protection, the DMZ contains:

- A firewall that protects the front-end servers from Internet traffic.

- A set of "security hardened" servers that support the services provided by the application. These servers are set up so that dangerous Internet services, such as file sharing and telnet, are disabled.

- A firewall that separates the back-end servers from the corporate networks and enables communication between the back-end servers and a few servers within the corporate network.

A DMZ is an important element for securing a site. However, you need to take additional security measures to protect data stored by the back-end servers. You can also store extremely sensitive data or data that's needed elsewhere in your enterprise outside the DMZ, although doing so has negative performance implications and runs a risk, however small, of opening your corporate network to hacking.

Firewalls

Firewalls are often implemented at the network protocol layer and used to filter incoming network traffic. You can configure a firewall to pass or block packets from specific IP addresses and ports. To implement a firewall, you can use a network router and configure it or you can buy dedicated firewall hardware with enhanced capabilities. More sophisticated firewalls can detect denial-of-service attacks and provide network address translation (NAT) to hide the addresses of the resources behind the firewall.

For a Microsoft Windows.NET site, you configure both Internet-facing and internal firewalls. The Internet-facing firewall must provide access to services such as HTTP, LDAP, File Transfer Protocol (FTP), and Simple Mail Transfer Protocol (SMTP) mail. To secure the firewall further, you can close all ports except port 80 (for HTTP) and port 443 (for Hypertext Transfer Protocol Secure (HTTPS) and SSL) and block access to all IP addresses except the IP address of your Web cluster. You might also need to support a virtual private network (VPN) for a business-to-business site.

You need to restrict access to services that can potentially damage the system, if a Web user can access them. For example, you must remove access to the telnet service. For a business-to-business site, it is possible to set up your firewall so your site will respond only to requests that come from one of the known list of IP addresses your customers and vendors use.

Internal firewalls restrict traffic between back-end servers and the internal network and protect the resources in the internal network from destructive attacks. You must configure these firewalls to support only those services and protocols that are required for managing the DMZ components.

If the Web server hosting the Commerce Server application and the SQL Server computer are separated by a firewall, you should open the following ports in the firewall:

- **Port 135**. Remote procedure call (RPC) End Point Mapper (EPM) Transfer Control Protocol (TCP)/User Datagram Protocol (UDP)

- **Port 1433**. TDS (for SQL Server traffic)

- **Port 5100-5200**. Microsoft Distributed Transaction Coordinator (MSDTC) (The EPM dynamically assigns it a port.) 1024->65,535

For more information, see the following Microsoft Knowledge Base articles:

- Q191168 - INFO: Failed to Enlist on Calling Object's Transaction, located at http://support.microsoft.com/support/kb/articles/Q191/1/68.ASP.

- Q248403 - Event ID 12293: Transacted Commerce Server Pipeline Failure, located at http://support.microsoft.com/support/kb/articles/Q248/4/03.ASP.

- "Using Distributed COM with Firewalls" – a white paper by Michael Nelson, located at http://www.microsoft.com/com/wpaper/dcomfw.asp.

Network Segregation

You can segregate the network within a DMZ using two or more network interface cards (NICs) in each computer. Network segregation allows you to:

- Separate different types of Internet traffic and route them to different Web servers. For example, HTTP requests can be routed to one set of Web servers and FTP requests can be routed to another cluster. This doesn't necessarily help with security, but it can help with load balancing.

- Separate Internet traffic from the back-end traffic and prevent direct access to the internal network. The NICs can be configured to allow only packets appropriate for the server.

- Avoid IP forwarding between the front-end servers. The only publicly accessible IP address is the virtual IP address used by the load-balanced front-end server cluster. Disabling IP forwarding is crucially important to the security of your site.

You can also use network segregation to separate network traffic from management traffic, thus preventing management traffic from passing through firewalls.

Data Encryption Using SSL

In an e-commerce site, you process sensitive information, such as customer credit card numbers. This data must be encrypted and transmitted over a secure channel. For implementing secure data transfer, you use Secure Sockets Layer (SSL).

To implement this functionality, you need to acquire a digital certificate and install it on your server(s). You can apply to one of the certification authorities for a digital certificate. Some of the commonly known commercial certification authorities are VeriSign, CyberTrust, and GTE.

SSL is a scheme for protocols such as HTTP (named HTTPS when secure), FTP, and Network News Transfer Protocol (NNTP). When you use SSL to transmit data:

- The data is encrypted.

- A secure connection is established between the source and destination servers.

- Server authentication is enabled.

Credit Card Information Security

You should store credit card information only in encrypted format. When a customer uses a credit card to pay for a product on your site, the credit card information must be transmitted over a secure channel. To do so, you should put the ordering form or page on a secure server. The customer can identify a secure form by looking at its URL; Web pages that require SSL for data transmission have URLs beginning with "https" instead of "http." Also, a lock icon is displayed in the status bar of the browser. The browser checks for the digital certificate and verifies it. It then uses the public key within the certificate to encrypt the information. After the customer submits the information, it is transmitted over a secure channel to the server.

Using SSL is processing-intensive because data must be encrypted and decrypted. Also, SSL servers must maintain their state between requests because a secure channel is needed for a specific user—the same key pair is used to decrypt the information sent back as was used to encrypt it. This can cause problems in a load-balanced site that routes client requests based on the availability of a server and does not maintain state on the servers. To avoid these problems, you need to set up Network Load Balancing so that it has client affinity for HTTPS (port 443).

Because HTTPS can slow the processing of other Web pages on the same server, you might also want to segregate HTTPS pages on a few Web servers in the cluster that are dedicated to processing requests associated with sensitive data. This will prevent the degradation of performance on the site as a whole. You can also use hardware accelerators to avoid affecting the performance of a site without compromising site security.

Intrusion Detection

An intrusion detection system (IDS) can identify attack signatures or patterns, generate alarms to alert the operations staff, and cause the routers to terminate connections with hostile sources. These systems can also prevent denial–of-service attacks. A denial-of-service attack occurs when a hacker sends fragments of TCP requests masked as legitimate TCP requests or sends requests from a bad IP source. The server cannot handle so many requests and displays a denial-of-service message to legitimate site users. An IDS provides real-time monitoring of network traffic and implements the "prevent, detect, and react" approach to security.

You should implement an IDS in front of a firewall in every security domain. Although IDSs are necessary for security, you should consider the following issues associated with their use:

- They are processing-intensive; an IDS can affect the performance of your site.

- They are expensive.

- An IDS can sometimes mistake normal network traffic for a hostile attack and cause unnecessary alarms.

There are a number of third-party tools available for intrusion detection. For example, you can use Cisco's NetRanger or ISS's RealSecure for real-time network traffic monitoring. Enhancing and developing IDS technology is an ongoing process within the computer industry.

Database Security

This section describes the deployment of security features in Active Directory and SQL Server.

Active Directory Security

Active Directory provides protected storage of user account and group information by using access control on objects and user credentials. Because Active Directory stores not only user credentials but also access control information, users who log on to the network obtain both authentication and authorization to access system resources.

For example, when a user logs on to the network, the Windows 2000 security system authenticates the user with information stored in the Active Directory. Then, when the user attempts to access a service on the network, the system checks the properties defined in the discretionary access control list (DACL) for that service.

Because Active Directory allows administrators to create group accounts, administrators can manage system security more efficiently. For example, by adjusting a file's properties, an administrator can permit all users in a group to read that file. In this way, access to objects in Active Directory is based on group membership.

In Commerce Server, user information, including passwords, credit card numbers, and phone numbers are stored in clear text in the Profiles database. SQL Server secures this information against unauthorized access; however, to improve its security, consider using Active Directory to store this sensitive user data.

When determining whether to use Active Directory or SQL Server, consider the following questions:

- Applications such as Microsoft Exchange Server require an operating system security context. Do you need a security context for users?

- Do you need to authenticate site visitors with their Windows 2000 security context?

- Do you need to protect file system content? Will some of the file system content be WAV files or other blobs?

- Do you have complex group membership requirements?

If you answer yes to any of these questions, then you should consider using Active Directory.

For information about using Active Directory and SQL Server together, see "Using Active Directory and SQL Server" later in this chapter.

SQL Server Security

A user passes through two stages of security when accessing SQL Server: *authentication* and *authorization* (permissions validation). The authentication stage identifies the user using a login account and verifies only the ability to connect to an instance of SQL Server. If authentication is successful, the user connects to an instance of SQL Server. The user then needs permissions to access databases on the server, which is done by granting access to an account in each database, mapped to the user login. The permissions validation stage controls the activities the user is allowed to perform in the SQL Server database.

SQL Server can operate in one of two security (authentication) modes:

- **Mixed mode (Windows Authentication and SQL Server Authentication).** This is the required configuration for using Commerce Server.

  Mixed mode allows users to connect to an instance of SQL Server using either Windows Authentication or SQL Server Authentication. Users who connect through a Windows NT 4.0 or Windows 2000 user account can make use of trusted connections in either Windows Authentication mode or mixed mode.

  SQL Server Authentication is provided for backward compatibility. For example, if you create a single Windows 2000 group and add all necessary users to that group, you must also grant the Windows 2000 group login rights to SQL Server and access to any necessary databases.

- **Windows Authentication mode (Windows Authentication).** Windows Authentication mode allows a user to connect through a Windows 2000 user account.

Using Active Directory and SQL Server

If your site requires both the access control provided by Active Directory and the performance of SQL Server, you should use both Active Directory and SQL Server together to store user profile information. In this scenario, you store data that is associated with user credentials and data that is static in an Active Directory data store. You would store the remaining data (such as dynamic data) in SQL Server.

For example, you might want to divide the attributes as shown in the following list:

- User profile data stored in Active Directory:
  - User name
  - Password
- User profile data stored in SQL Server:
  - Credit card
  - Home address, city, state, postal code
  - Home phone number
  - Date/time of last visit
  - Favorite color
  - Last page visited
  - Year-to-date total spent on site

For detailed instructions for setting up your site to use Active Directory and SQL Server, see "Configuring a Sample Supplier Solution Site" in Chapter 3, "A Supplier Scenario."

Web Server Security

IIS Web server permissions can be set up to limit the access of anonymous users to your applications, and can also be used to limit the viewing of source code over the Internet, even for users with Windows permissions (or access control entries (ACEs)).

It is important to understand the distinction between Web server permissions and NTFS permissions. Unlike NTFS, Web server permissions apply to all users accessing your Web sites. NTFS permissions apply only to a specific user or group of users with a valid Windows account. NTFS controls access to physical directories on your server, whereas Web server permissions control access to virtual directories on your Web site.

When you use Site Packager to package a site, it will pick up the Web server permissions as set in the source site. For example, if you have the Execute Permissions setting set to "Scripts and Executables" in the root folder of the application on the source computer, the virtual root folder on the destination computer will have the same setting.

For example, the following table describes how the IIS permissions are set in the Commerce Server Solution Sites.

Folder	Permissions
Root	Set Execute permission to "Scripts and Executables."
Pipeline, Include, Template	Deny permission to "Read", "Write," and "Execute."

Commerce Server Security

In a Commerce Server installation, one of the ways in which you implement security is by authenticating users. In this section the following topics are addressed:

- Using AuthFilter and the **AuthManager** object

- Authenticating users in a Web farm

- Using Commerce Server authentication modes

- Using Commerce Server authentication features

- Securing Business Desk

- Securing Commerce Server databases

- Limiting access to Commerce Server services

- Providing access to Commerce Server resources

- Commerce Server and Microsoft Outlook Web Access (OWA) integration

- Active Directory and anonymous users on the Supplier site

- Adding products to a basket without an account

Using AuthFilter and AuthManager

Commerce Server provides two tools to implement user authentication and identification: the **AuthManager** object and AuthFilter.

- **AuthManager** is a COM object that exposes methods for identifying users and controlling access to dynamically generated content. For example, a site developer could invoke the **GetUserID** method of the **AuthManager** object to identify a user based on a cookie or a query string.

- **AuthFilter** is an Internet Server API (ISAPI) filter that is used at the IIS Commerce Server application level. It can be applied to all users visiting the application. You configure properties used by AuthFilter at the global CS Authentication level. You configure the authentication mode at the application level. You can choose the following authentication modes: Windows Authentication, Custom Authentication, and Autocookie.

When you configure the **AuthManager** object and AuthFilter, the authentication properties are stored in the Administration database. The CS Authentication resource interacts with the **Config** objects to store and retrieve the properties from the Administration database.

The Solution Sites do not use AuthFilter because they are designed to support cookieless shopping.

The following table summarizes the differences between the features supported by AuthFilter, the **AuthManager** object, and the Solution Sites.

Feature	AuthFilter	AuthManager	Solution Sites
Checks whether session cookies (non-persistent cookies) are supported	Yes	No	Yes
Supports cookieless shopping	No	Yes	Yes
Provides granular access control using ACLs	Yes	No	No
Supports custom login pages for retrieving Windows credentials	Yes	Yes	No
Provides URL case correction	Yes	No	Yes

Commerce Server extends the authentication methods supported by IIS 5.0 in two ways. First, it adds granular access control for dynamic content through AuthFilter. Second, it provides a way to use Windows Authentication or Custom Authentication in an Internet environment where you need to address a wide range of browsers. Commerce Server provides this support for Windows and Custom Authentication.

Authentication Using AuthFilter

For authentication using AuthFilter, if a profile is stored in SQL Server, you can retrieve the password in clear text through a profile object (with the **user_security_password** property) and compare it with the one input by the user.

If the profile is stored in Active Directory and you want to perform authentication using Active Directory Service Interfaces (ADSI), you must perform the following steps to retrieve the password:

1. Use Business Desk to extend the default schema.

2. Use SQL Server Enterprise Manager to add new a column (such as u_Pref1).

3. Use the Profiles resource in Commerce Server Manager to map the password property to the new column.

You will be able to retrieve the password for all the subsequently created profile instances.

Authenticating Users in a Web Farm

Commerce Server supports the single authentication of a user in a Web server farm. For example, if a user is authenticated on one Web server, and then is redirected or load-balanced to another Web server, the second Web server does not prompt the user to log in again.

When the user is redirected to the second Web server, AuthFilter reads the user cookie and identifies that the cookie contains the user ID and that it is valid. If you are using Custom Authentication mode, no other steps are performed. If you are using Windows Authentication mode, Commerce Server performs the following steps:

1. It redirects the request for the secured page to the Login.asp file. This redirect is transparent to the user.

2. In the Login.asp file, using the user ID, it queries the Profiles data store for the user profile. This returns the user login ID and password in clear text.

3. It appends the login ID and password to the URL, and then redirects the request for the secured page.

4. The filter intercepts the request for the secured page, removes the user ID and password from the URL, and stores the login ID and password in the ISAPI filter cache.

5. The filter then displays the secured page to the user. The user ID and password are not transmitted to the user.

If the request is sent with the **Post** method using non-sticky load balancing, any information contained in the header body is lost during the required redirection. Only use the **Post** method with sticky load balancing. If you use non-sticky load balancing, always use the **Get** method and HTTPS for additional security.

When you use AuthFilter, follow these deployment scenarios:

- Have all sites in the same directory, for example, www.microsoft.com/bookstore and www.microsoft.com/msdn. Do not have one site in the subdirectory of another site, for example, www.microsoft.com and www.microsoft.com/bookstore.

- Use dissimilar names for sites in the same directory. A site name should not be a subset of another site name, for example, www.microsoft.com/retail and www.microsoft.com/retail2.

These requirements are due to the dependence of AuthFilter on cookies. If AuthFilter is not used and the ticket is placed in a URL query string, then a site can be in a subdirectory of another site.

Using Commerce Server Authentication Modes

When a user logs in to your site, Commerce Server authenticates the user by verifying the login and password against the login and password stored in the Profiles database. After Commerce Server verifies the user information, it creates a non-persistent cookie and stores it in the ISAPI filter cache for the application. The cookie specifies that the user is authenticated and is allowed to see secured pages on your site.

When you use AuthFilter, you can choose the following authentication modes:
- Windows Authentication mode
- Custom Authentication mode
- Autocookie mode
- Windows Authentication with Autocookie mode
- Custom Authentication with Autocookie mode

Windows Authentication Mode

In Windows Authentication mode, AuthFilter uses Windows Authentication—through ACLs—to control access to the site. Anonymous and registered users can access the site, depending on the ACLs. Registered users are tracked; anonymous users are not tracked.

When you select the Windows Authentication mode, AuthFilter looks up the access rights for users in Active Directory. When a user logs in to a site running in this mode, AuthFilter retrieves the user name and password from the HTTP request and stores it in a cache. It also sets a cookie that is valid only for the duration of the user session. Other pages that the user visits during the session can then check the cookie. In Windows Authentication mode, ACLs determine access to any resource on the Web site.

A user is validated by setting a session cookie that contains an MSCSAuth ticket. An MSCSAuth ticket contains a user ID, the last login time, and a time window specifying how long the ticket is valid after the last login time. No expiration date is specified for the cookie and the cookie is deleted after the session expires. A validated user does not automatically have access to a requested URL. The credentials of the user, once validated, are checked against the access rights of the URL that are maintained through ACLs.

Windows Authentication supports a Web farm scenario with a single login, and it supports using proxy accounts. When you use Windows Authentication mode, you should note the following:

- When Windows Authentication mode is enabled, the security of the site is automatically set to IIS Basic authentication. This must not be changed, because it allows IIS to notify AuthFilter of events.

- After unpacking a Solution Site for use with Commerce Server, the files contained in the *<site name>*\AuthFiles folder have anonymous access enabled. If these files are not used, you should delete them.

Custom Authentication Mode

In Custom Authentication mode, you can use AuthFilter to provide a custom authentication process to control access to the site while still using the base services (URL correctness, cookie support, and ticket validation) of AuthFilter.

If you need to implement Custom Authentication, you can still use AuthFilter to integrate it into your site. If you select Custom Authentication, AuthFilter will check for a valid MSCSAuth ticket. If the valid MSCSAuth ticket is not found, the user is redirected to a login page, where you can do your own custom authentication by validating credentials and setting MSCSAuth ticket upon success.

For example, you could use the Profiling System to retrieve access rights from the user profile when a user logs in. The Profiling System retrieves user information from a data source. This data source could be a SQL Server database, the Windows 2000 Active Directory, another OLE DB-compliant data source, or a valid LDAP-v3 store.

In the Custom Authentication mode, AuthFilter performs the following steps after being notified that an SF_NOTIFY_PREPROC_HEADERS event has occurred:

1. It checks for site configuration properties in the local site cache and, if not found, it reads the site configuration properties from the Administration database using a **SiteConfig** object and stores them in the site cache.

2. It detects whether the requested URL is correct and automatically corrects for case sensitivity in the URL.

3. It checks for session-cookie support and, if unavailable, AuthFilter redirects the user to the ASP page specified in the **s_NoCookie_Form** ("No-Cookie form" in the Commerce Server Manager UI) property of the CS Authentication resource. Usually this page notifies the user that cookies are required and that the user should resubmit the request after cookies are enabled.

4. It checks whether the cookie contains an MSCSAuth ticket, and if it does not, AuthFilter redirects the user to a login page.

5. If the cookie contains an MSCSAuth ticket, AuthFilter checks the current time against the last login time on the ticket to see if it is within the time window specified in the ticket.

6. If the current time is past the time window specified in the ticket, the user is redirected to the login page as a non-validated user.

7. If the current time is within the time window, the ticket is considered valid, and the user is redirected to the login page as a validated user. If the current time is within five minutes of the last login time plus the time window, the last login time on the ticket is changed to the current time so an active user can continue browsing.

Autocookie Mode

In Autocookie mode, you can use AuthFilter to permit anonymous users to access the site. AuthFilter automatically generates a persistent cookie (MSCSProfile ticket) so a user can be tracked.

When you choose Autocookie mode, AuthFilter always checks to see whether the browser has this anonymous cookie. If the anonymous cookie is not in the browser, then the filter redirects the user to the AutoCookie Form.

Autocookie mode enables Commerce Server to keep track of anonymous users between pages and across sessions. A unique ID is generated to identify the user and, if required, a profile is created to store information about the user.

When a user sends a request to access a site, AuthFilter performs the following steps after being notified by IIS that an SF_NOTIFY_PREPROC_HEADERS event has occurred:

1. It checks for site configuration properties in the local site cache and, if not found, AuthFilter reads the site configuration properties from the Administration database using a **SiteConfig** object and stores them in the site cache.

2. It checks whether the URL is correct and automatically corrects for case sensitivity in the URL.

3. It checks for cookie support on the browser.

4. If cookies are not supported, the user is redirected to the ASP page specified in the **s_NoCookie_Form** ("No-Cookie form" in the Commerce Server Manager UI) property of the CS Authentication resource. Usually this page notifies the user that cookies are required and that the user should resubmit the request after cookies are enabled. By default, an ASP page named Nocookie.asp is supplied for this purpose. This file is located in the AuthFiles folder in the Commerce Server installation directory.

5. If a cookie is returned, AuthFilter checks whether it contains an MSCSProfile ticket.

6. If the MSCSProfile ticket exists, AuthFilter uses a valid Windows user account to impersonate the user in IIS.

7. If the requested URL has anonymous access rights, the URL is returned.

8. If the ticket does not exist, the user is redirected to the ASP page specified in the **s_AutoCookie_Form** ("AutoCookie Form" in the Commerce Server Manager UI) property of the CS Authentication resource.

Windows Authentication with Autocookie Mode

The mixed authentication mode of Windows Authentication with Autocookie accepts both anonymous and registered users and enables you to track both types. This mode is useful for sites where part of the content is available to everyone and the rest is available only to registered users.

The primary differences between this mixed mode and Windows Authentication mode are as follows:

- The mixed mode allows tracking of anonymous users.

- In mixed mode, an anonymous user must have a valid MSCSProfile ticket to access any URLs regardless of the ACL settings. In Windows Authentication mode, an anonymous user does not need a ticket and can access any URL with anonymous access rights.

Custom Authentication with Autocookie Mode

The mixed authentication mode of Custom Authentication with Autocookie allows both registered and anonymous users access to the site, and allows tracking of the anonymous users through persistent cookies. Instead of controlling access using Windows ACLs, the site developer can supply a custom authentication process.

Using Commerce Server Authentication Features

This section describes the following authentication features that Commerce Server supports:

- Multi-domain, single login capability
- Cookie sharing across domains and applications
- Anonymous users who register
- Single sign-on support
- Clear text password in Active Directory
- Proxy accounts
- Prevention of distributed denial-of-service attacks
- Enabling only the most secure version of Integrated Windows authentication

Multi-Domain, Single Login Capability

Commerce Server provides multi-domain, single login capability. In this scenario, cookies are shared between domains with their domain property. The domains must have a common sub-domain name. For example, premier.microsoft.com and msn.microsoft.com can share cookies with the microsoft.com domain name.

However, two domains such as microsoft.com and microsoft.uk cannot support single-login capability; they cannot share cookies because the subdomain name is not common. In this scenario, users are required to log in again each time they switch domains. For more information about Passport integration, see "Integrating with Passport" in Commerce Server 2000 Help.

To use multi-domain single login, you set two authentication properties at the site level: "Set cookie path to application" and "Number of shared domain levels." You must set "Number of shared domain levels" to at least two, and use domains that share the same top-level name, for example, msn.microsoft.com and premier.microsoft.com.

Cookie Sharing Across Domains and Applications

You can share cookies across domains, which enables you to track users across multiple domains and applications. For multiple domains to share cookies, the domains must have a common sub-domain name. For example, msdn.microsoft.com and premier.microsoft.com can share cookies with the domain property set to ".microsoft.com." You cannot set the domain to ".com."

If you do not want to share cookies across domains, you can instead share them across applications. To do this, you set the **path** property on the cookie to the application. For example, you would set the property to "/retail" to share the cookie across all applications in a retail site. To share cookies between applications that do not have the same virtual directory, you must set the **path** property to the root (/).

When a cookie is shared among multiple domains, two properties are set on the cookie, **domain** and **path**. This resembles the following:

```
";domain=DomainName;path=Path"
```

The **domain** property is used to specify the domains for which the cookie is valid. The **path** property is used to specify the subset of URLs in the domain for which the cookie is valid.

Before sending a request, the client browser checks to see if a cookie is available that contains a **domain** property that matches the last part of the fully qualified domain name of the host specified in the requested URL. If such a cookie exists, the **path** property of the cookie is compared to the path name component of the requested URL. If they match, the cookie is sent with the request.

On the server side, while setting the property, if the value of the **domain** property is not specified, it defaults to the host name of the server that generated the cookie. Only hosts within the specified domain can set the **domain** property on the cookie. The most general **path** property is "/". If the **path** property is not specified, it defaults to the path of the virtual root of the IIS application that generated the cookie.

In Commerce Server, each site has its own cookies by default; however, the AuthFilter allows these cookies to be shared.

To share cookies between sites in the same domain, set the **b_CookiePath_ApplicationScope** property (clear the "Set cookie path to application" check box in the Commerce Server Manager UI) to **False**. This causes the host to set the **path** property to "/". If the **b_CookiePath_ApplicationScope** property is **True**, the **path** property is set to the current application path.

To share cookies between domains, set the **u_CookieDomain_Scope** property ("Number of shared domain levels" in the Commerce Server Manager UI) to the required number.

Anonymous Users Who Register

A user who visits a site anonymously receives an MSCSProfile ticket. If the user decides to register, the user receives an MSCSAuth ticket. The user now has two cookies in the HTTP header containing different tickets. The order of the tickets is unknown and can vary between requests. AuthFilter recognizes this and automatically searches all cookies for an MSCSAuth ticket before searching for an MSCSProfile ticket.

Both cookies get logged in the Web log file in the order they appear in the HTTP request header. The Web server log import DTS task imports the first cookie it finds. That one user can appear to be two users to the DTS task if it finds hits in the log file with the cookies in different orders. This compromises the ability to track the user and might produce erroneous visit and user calculations.

The solution is to map the user IDs from both the MSCSAuth ticket and the MSCSProfile ticket to the same user ID. Then set the MSCSProfile ticket to an empty string, which causes the MSCSProfile ticket to be deleted.

Single Sign-On Support

Single Sign-On (SSO) support allows a user who successfully logs on to one site or server access to other sites and servers without having to log on again. AuthFilter in Windows Authentication mode provides support for the following, using cookies:

- SSO between domains.
- SSO in a Web farm scenario. For more information, see "Authenticating Users in a Web Farm" earlier in this chapter. Support for SSO in a Web farm is also included in Custom Authentication mode using cookie sharing.

Clear Text Password in Active Directory

User passwords in Active Directory are stored in an encrypted format. To access this password in clear text, the following two options are available when the password is initially retrieved in the login page:

- Extend the profile schema by adding a new property to store the clear text password. Extending the schema must be performed through the Profile Designer module in Business Desk.
- Create a custom cache to store the clear text password.

Proxy Accounts

When a user accesses a site using a proxy account, the process for the login page is the same as with the **Post** method. However, the user ID is used to retrieve a proxy account ID and password, and these credentials are set into the URL query string and stored in the password cache instead of the user ID and password. On subsequent visits to the site, the proxy account ID, instead of the user ID, is used to access the password cache.

The proxy account credentials can be stored in an extended property of the default profile schema or by some other means. You extend the profile schema using the Profile Designer module in Business Desk.

To track individual users when using proxy accounts, add the custom **guid** property to the ticket using the **AuthManager** object. After it is set, AuthFilter uses the **guid** property to access the password cache instead of the proxy account ID.

Prevention of Distributed Denial-of-Service Attacks

A distributed denial-of-service (DDOS) attack is an attempt to shut down a server by repeatedly logging on with a known valid user ID and an incorrect password. By default, AuthFilter does not associate each password cache entry with one, and only one, client session. When a user logs in with a valid user ID, the password cache is updated with the submitted password. A malicious user can use this technique to disrupt service. The malicious user does not gain entry to the site, but forces a registered user who is active when the password is changed to log in again.

To avoid the attack, AuthFilter can store an additional property in the cache in addition to the user ID and password. This property is generally a globally unique identifier (GUID) and is used to distinguish between different client sessions using the same user ID and possibly different passwords.

On the login page, the GUID is placed on the ticket of the user as a custom property, **guid**, by the **SetProperty** method of the **AuthManager** object. Additionally, the property is appended to the query string for the redirected URL.

After the **guid** property has been set, AuthFilter uses it to access the password cache instead of the user ID. When a user logs on with the same user ID but with a different password, AuthFilter identifies this as a different user and a new entry is made in the password cache instead of overwriting the original password. AuthFilter then follows the same steps as for a new user.

Enabling Only the Most Secure Version of Integrated Windows Authentication

If you use Integrated Windows authentication and the client computers connecting to your Web server use Windows 2000 or Windows NT 4.0 Service Pack 3 or later, you can configure your Web server to use only the strongest version of Integrated Windows authentication, NTLMv2.

You can set a Windows policy to specify that only the latest version of NTLM is used. In the Local Security Policy of your Web servers, set the **LAN Manger Authentication Level** policy to "Send NTLMv2 response only\refuse LM & NTLM" to use the most secure setting.

Securing Business Desk

This section provides the following information about securing your Business Desk application:

- Securing Business Desk sessions
- Securing Bdrefresh.asp and RefreshApp.asp scripts
- Limiting access to Business Desk modules
- Securing Business Desk user access to Catalogs

Securing Business Desk Sessions

When Site Packager unpacks a Commerce Server Business Desk application, it is configured to use Integrated Windows authentication. Although this secures client authentication, the Business Desk session itself passes data in clear text. To provide security for Business Desk sessions, consider allowing only Business Desk clients inside your Internet firewall. To provide additional security, you can use SSL for Business Desk connections. For more information about SSL, see "Setting Up SSL on Your Server" in the IIS 5.0 online documentation.

Securing Bdrefresh.asp and RefreshApp.asp

You should use IP address access restrictions to limit permissions on Bdrefresh.asp and RefreshApp.asp so that unauthorized users cannot run these scripts. By default, Bdrefresh.asp and RefreshApp.asp are set to anonymous access, which is required in order for Business Desk users to publish changes to the Web site. To secure these files, grant access to specific Business Desk users by using IP address access restrictions in IIS.

The Bdrefresh.asp script clears the Business Desk cache. The RefreshApp.asp script clears the Profiles cache. Clearing either of these caches repeatedly could lead to a denial of service for users. These files are located in the root folder of an unpacked Solution Site.

There are other files similar to Bdrefresh.asp and RefreshApp.asp included with the Commerce Server Solution Sites. You should also secure these files.

Limiting Access to Business Desk Modules

You can prevent specific users from accessing particular Business Desk modules. You do this by setting ACEs on Business Desk ASP files. Each Business Desk module has a main ASP file that is checked for ACEs before it is added to the Business Desk navigation pane. If the logged-in user running Business Desk does not have Read permission on the main ASP file for that module, the module will not be exposed in the navigation pane for that user.

The following table shows the files on which you can set ACEs for each Business Desk module.

To control access to this category and module	Set an ACE on this ASP file
Analysis/Reports	Analysis\Analysis_reports.asp
Analysis/Completed Reports	Analysis\Analysis_report_viewer.asp
Analysis/Segment Viewer	Segviewer\Modellist.asp
Campaigns/Campaign Manager	Marketing\Cmanager.asp
Campaigns/List Manager	Marketing\Listmanager.asp
Campaigns/Campaign Expressions	Marketing\Targetexpr.asp
Campaigns/Target Group	Marketing\Target_group.asp
Campaigns/Reference Tables	Marketing\Reftable.asp
Campaigns/Publish Campaigns	Productionrefresh\refresh.asp
Catalogs/Catalog Designer	Catalogs\Designer\List_categorydefinitions.asp
Catalogs/Catalog Editor	Catalogs\Editor\List_catalogs.asp
Catalogs/Catalog Sets	Catalogsets\Catalogsets_list.asp
Orders/Basket Manager	Orders\Basket_list.asp
Orders/Data Codes	Application\Datacodes_list.asp
Orders/Order Status	Orders\Orderstatus_list.asp
Orders/Publish Transactions	Productionrefresh\refresh.asp
Orders/Shipping Methods	Shipping\Shipping_list.asp
Orders/Tax Rates	Tax\Regionaltax.asp
Users/Users	Users\Registered.asp
Users/Organizations	Organizations\Orgs.asp
Users/Profile Designer	Profiles\Profileselector.asp
Users/Site Terms Editor	Profiles\Profileeditor.asp
Users/Publish Profiles	Profiles\Refreshprofilesvcall.asp

If an individual user and the Authenticated Users group have access to a Business Desk module, and you take permission away from the individual user, restart the client computer in order to redraw the navigation pane, so that the modules the user has permissions to use are refreshed in the navigation pane.

If you include an ACE for the Administrator account, you must also grant permissions to the Everyone group. The exact set of permissions is not significant, but the Everyone group must be present in the list of users and groups. If the Everyone group does not have permissions to a Business Desk module, an administrator will not be able to access that module.

If you secure one of the following modules, all three of them are secured by default: Publish Profiles, Publish Campaigns, and Publish Transactions.

Securing Business Desk User Access to Catalogs

You cannot use Authfilter to authenticate users that are accessing the Business Desk to, for example, set access control on the administration tasks.

If you have one site with multiple customers, each of whom needs to update only their own catalog on that same site, you can customize the Catalog Editor module and restrict users to their own catalogs (that is, application level security) by not allowing them to select any other catalog. You do this by creating a filter that displays only their catalogs.

Securing Commerce Server Databases

This section provides the following information about securing your Commerce Server databases:

- Protecting SQL Server passwords
- Setting up Data Warehouse permissions
- Limiting access to the Administration database
- Securing log files
- Using the "sa" login name for SQL Server administrative login
- Differentiating access to resources
- Changing the Data Warehouse password

Protecting SQL Server Passwords

When a Web server connects to a SQL Server, the SQL password travels in clear text. To protect a SQL Server connection from intruders, use the multi-protocol network driver in SQL Server, which allows encryption of session connections. If you use Windows NT Authentication, this password will be protected, except in Commerce Server Setup or if you choose the Quick Unpack option in Site Packager.

Setting Up Data Warehouse Permissions

One way to give Business Desk users the ability to read and modify objects in the Data Warehouse is to give them a Windows Administrator account. However, you may want some Business Desk users to be able only to read reports. You can do this by assigning specific

SQL Server database roles to different users. The **db_datareader** role allows users to see all data from all tables in a database. The **db_datawriter** role allows users to add, change, or delete data from tables in the database.

Limiting Access to the Administration Database

It is important to lock down the server that hosts the Administration database for your site. When you run Commerce Server Setup, you give users of that computer full control of the Administration database. Although the SQL password for the Administration database login is encrypted in the Windows registry, it is possible for users to gain access to it by using a script that accesses one of these programming objects: **SiteConfigReadOnly**, **SiteConfig**, or **GlobalConfig**. Make sure users cannot gain access to the computer or run scripts on it after you complete Setup. Disable the Guest account and disallow access to everyone without administrative privileges.

You can restrict use of the **SiteConfig** and **GlobalConfig** objects by modifying the ACLs on the registry keys for these object classes. To restrict access to these objects, change the permissions on these objects through the Windows Registry Editor.

The **SiteConfigReadOnly** object must be accessible by all user accounts that will access Commerce Server applications. If you want to allow anonymous access, the object must be available to the anonymous account, named IUSR_*<computer name>*. The key for the **SiteConfigReadOnly** object is D1AA04A4-B00D-4D30-88AA-E3070DAE8040.

Securing Log Files

It is a good idea to move your log files from your Web servers to a more secure location. When you move these files, do it in a secure way. One way to achieve security is to use separate network lines that run directly from your staging environment to your production environment. This separate line is a good way to update content and to move log files to secure servers. Another way to safely move log files is through SSL over HTTP or FTP.

If you use pipeline logging to debug a pipeline, be aware that sensitive information may appear in clear text in the log files. Make sure you secure the folder that contains these pipeline log files (by default, the \Pipeline\Logfiles folder in the application).

Using the "sa" Login Name for SQL Server Administrative Login

It is recommended that you do not use the "sa" login name that SQL Server creates by default. You should specify a different administrative login name for your database servers. If you do use the "sa" login name, do not use a blank password for it. Doing so increases security risks for your site.

Differentiating Access to Resources

Commerce Server resources have single connection strings to each database. Therefore, you cannot specify different access privileges for different Commerce Server site users.

Changing the Data Warehouse Password

If you change the password for your SQL Server computer, you must also change the password in the Data Warehouse and the connection strings for all resources.

Limiting Access to Commerce Server Services

During Commerce Server Setup, in the Services Account dialog box, you specify the Windows user name and password for the following Commerce Server services: List Manager, Direct Mailer, and Predictor. Setup automatically grants these Windows accounts the "Log On as a Service" permission.

Also in the Services Account dialog box, you specify an account under which Event Logging will be performed. This last account is used in the Commerce Event Logging COM+ package that is created by Setup.

Make sure you specify the proper account for each service. For List Manager, your Business Desk users must be able to read folders from which they import lists and write to folders onto which they export lists. The List Manager service account must have appropriate NTFS permissions on the folders from which users will import and export lists.

Setup does not permit you to set up these services to use the Local System account. Although it is possible to do this manually after Setup, it is not a good idea because doing so might give the services more permissions than they require.

Providing Access to Commerce Server Resources

Business Desk users and administrators must have sufficient permissions to access the SQL Server database that corresponds to the resource in order to access those resources, such as the Product Catalog. A user should have a SQL Server login name that is linked to a SQL Server user that has the **db_owner** database role. Or, to allocate more specific roles, you can assign the user to the **db_ddladmin**, **db_datareader**, and **db_datawriter** roles.

Commerce Server and Outlook Web Access (OWA) Integration

Outlook Web Access (OWA) for Microsoft Exchange Server 2000 secures access to its site by leveraging the IIS Basic Authentication mechanism. As part of this authentication method, a server variable accessible from within ASP pages named AUTH_USER is populated with the user name. OWA uses the AUTH_USER variable to determine which Exchange 2000 mailbox to open for the session.

AuthFilter intercepts the normal mechanism of IIS authentication by trapping an access-denied event. AuthFilter provides an HTML Forms login page instead of the usual Web browser login dialog box, and allows the session to proceed with the same security context as provided by normal IIS Basic Authentication.

Active Directory and Anonymous Users on the Supplier Site

The Supplier Solution Site, which uses Active Directory, does not allow anonymous users. The Supplier site is designed for a business-to-business scenario, which typically requires that all users are registered.

If you want to use Active Directory in this scenario, you can create a separate SQL Server profile store for your anonymous users, and then use Windows Authentication mode. Windows Authentication is ACL-driven, so your resources must be enabled for anonymous users. For more information, see "Enabling AuthFilter for the Supplier Solution Site" in the "Managing the CS Authentication Resource" section of Commerce Server 2000 Help.

Adding Products to a Basket Without an Account

You can enable users who do not have an account to add products to a basket. However, the cookie that identifies the anonymous basket and profile should expire when the user closes the browser. You do not want other users to be able to view the contents of the anonymous basket (for example, in a school or an Internet cafe setting).

To have Commerce Server distribute the MSCSProfile ticket as a non-persistent cookie, simply turn ASP buffering on (default) and at the end of the page (or after you've called the **SetProfileTicket** method) modify the expiration date of the MSCSProfile ticket.

ASP buffering allows you to modify HTTP headers (for example, changing the cookie) even after you've written other information to the buffer already. If you reach the maximum buffer size limit and then try to write headers, the modification will not work.

Security and Authentication Scenarios

This section provides information about implementing security and authentication for static and dynamic content.

Protecting Static Content

You can use Authfilter to protect static content on a Web site. The following two modes of AuthFilter do this:

- Windows Authentication uses Active Directory. You set permissions on static files.

- Custom Authentication uses SQL Server. It protects all content at the virtual directory level of the site. This means that you can't implement discretionary access: it's "all or nothing" from the virtual directory level.

Protecting Dynamic Content

In Site Server 3.0, Personalization & Membership, you were able to secure content on a file system using Windows NT Groups. You might want to secure content the same way in Commerce Server, using Custom Authentication instead of Windows Authentication, especially if your site content is predominantly dynamic content.

To protect dynamic content, use AuthFilter with proxy accounts (add the proxy accounts to security groups). Use AuthFilter in Windows Authentication mode, but validate credentials against a SQL store (that is, store your users in a SQL profile store) and protect your static files with ACLs.

During login, AuthFilter traps access denied to files protected with ACLs and redirects to a login page, where you accept the user ID and password, validating the user against the profile data in the SQL Server database. If the information is validated, then it chooses an Active Directory account to use as a proxy and provides the Active Directory user ID and password as credentials on the redirect from the Login.asp file to the original request page.

Site Security Deployment Notes

The following deployment notes pertain to site security.

Auditing Site Deletions

You can identify the account that was used to delete a site from Commerce Server Manager (not the service account used to remove the entries, but the account that was used to start the delete process). Check to see which accounts have access to modify data in the Administration database. After Commerce Server is installed, the ID used for Commerce Server doesn't require privileges to create tables, databases, and so on.

Put a trigger on the site table that creates a record when another record is deleted. While there are other tables in use on the site, you cannot delete them from the site table if these tables contain data.

A record is created if the Administration database is edited manually or the **SiteAdmin** or the **GlobalConfig** component is modified.

Using Windows Authentication against Windows NT 4.0 Domain Accounts

In an intranet, you can use Windows Authentication to authenticate users against their Windows NT 4.0 domain accounts. To do this, you must create an Active Directory domain and set it to trust the Windows NT Server 4.0 domain.

For information about configuring Windows Authentication for this scenario, see the *Microsoft Windows 2000 Server Resource Kit*.

Testing Your Environment

After you deploy your site, perform the following tests:

- Measure recovery time on the hardware. Take your hardware offline and measure how long it takes the hardware to recover. Is the time acceptable to you? If your target is 99.9 percent uptime, you can calculate how many minutes of downtime you can allow.

- Test your ASP availability code. Just as you test for functionality, test that the code you have to handle downtime or system failure works. If you have code to handle certain scenarios, implement the scenarios to make sure the code works.

- Verify that your backup services are running.

- Pull the plug on the network cards to test whether the failover configuration works.

- Test the distribution of the load on each computer to determine whether every computer is being used equally.

- Take down a server preemptively to test what happens. Are the appropriate people notified?

In addition, you should hire third parties to perform security analysis, and capacity and reliability analysis. For more information about testing your site, see Chapter 16, "Testing Your Site."

Implementing Initial Operational Procedures

When your site is ready to go live, there are several operations to perform on your site before you deploy it. Some of these procedures you perform only once before the site goes into production. Others, like backing up your site, you perform for the first time at this stage and many times afterward, during the Management phase of your site.

Final Steps Before Production

After you test your deployment, you are ready to put it in production. Consider the following production issues:

- If you have extra logging to track intermediate phases for debugging purposes, remove it now. Consult with the development team to determine whether some of it should be on for the first two weeks.

- A week before going live, set the **MSCSEnv** variable in the Global.asa file to the PRODUCTION server-side constant.

- Perform a final audit of the hardware to verify it is calibrated as specified. Update your hardware configuration documents.

- Perform a final audit of the software to verify it is calibrated as specified. Update your software configuration documents.

- Set up the performance monitoring and event monitoring service on your production computers.

- Determine which reports you need to monitor after the site is in production.

- Determine the process for resolving problems and assign members of your team to monitor for specific problems.

After Your Site Is in Production

During the first month that your new site is in production, you should perform the following steps:

- Keep the development and test teams available for at least the first two weeks.

- Hold daily meetings with the development, test, and deployment teams to make sure the site is behaving as expected.

- Track administrator logins for security purposes.

- Revisit the usage profile. How are people actually using your site?

- Review the size of your Web log files to verify they don't become too large for the disk, and that your strategy for Web log management will keep up with the rate of growth.

- Observe the growth of your databases to ensure they are in line with expectations. Make sure the rate of growth of the Data Warehouse, Transactions database, and Web log files is the rate you were planning.

  If, for example, the rate at which your database is growing outpaces the number of users visiting your site, you might have a bug in your system.

- Analyze the site to make sure there are no bottlenecks in the hardware architecture.

- Verify that third-party components are working in the production environment. Are you getting the right types of confirmation?

- Verify that the business processes are working.

As you modify your system to resolve these issues, you must update your site architecture and configuration documents. For additional ongoing maintenance tasks, see Chapter 17, "Managing Your Site."

Backing Up Your Site

To ensure recovery from a disaster, you must back up all the information needed to recreate your production environment. You should use a backup service that can back up the following:

- Server configuration

- System state

- File system

- Application data and open files

- Network configuration

Gathering Server Configuration Data

Always keep a current record of your configuration data. If you have to reconfigure any part of your system due to a disaster, this record will be a critical resource.

At a minimum, you must back up the following data:

- A list of the data that is stored on each computer

- Hardware configuration

- Disk size/configuration

- Operating system and service patches

- Key software installations

- Identification

- Server name

- Network configuration/addressing

- System role

- Services running

- Other configuration information

- Wide area network (WAN) diagram

- Local area network (LAN) diagram

- Service description

There are many automated methods of gathering this type of information, including technologies offered by Microsoft. Most of this information can be detected using Windows Management Instrumentation (WMI), a management technology within Windows 2000.

System State Backup

As part of any backup and recovery application for Windows 2000, the backup service should back up the Windows 2000 system state.

The system state consists of:

- Boot files, including the system files and all the files protected by Windows File Protection (WFP)

- Active Directory (on a domain controller only)

- Sysvol (on a domain controller only)

- Certificate Services (on certification authority only)

- Cluster database (on a cluster node only)

- The registry

- Performance counter configuration information

- Component Services Class registration database

All Windows 2000 backup applications back up this data as part of the backup process. To ensure full recovery of the system, the backup service you use must include backing up the system state.

File System Backup

A file system backup must include a back up of the file data and file attributes. If the file system is NTFS, the attributes consist of normal attributes and file permissions. If you backed up files without their attributes and permissions in an e-business environment, you would have to set them manually when you restored the data.

In Windows 2000, NTFS file permissions, share permissions, and file attributes limit access to NTFS files. To back up or restore NTFS files to which you do not have access rights, you must:

- Belong to the permissions group of administrators, backup operators, or restore operators.

- Have user rights to back up files and directories (if you are backing up) and restore files and directories (if you are restoring).

Neither the FAT16 nor the FAT32 file systems provide file permissions.

After the data file side of the file system backup service has been designed, the next decision concerns the type of backup the service will use. There are three types:

- **Normal backup**. Copies all selected files and marks each as having been backed up. With normal backups, you need only the most recent copy of the backup file to restore all of the files.

- **Incremental backup**. Backs up only those files created or changed since the last normal or incremental backup. It marks files as having been backed up. If you use a combination of normal and incremental backups, you need the last normal backup set as well as all of the incremental backups to restore your data.

- **Differential backup**. Backs up files created or changed since the last normal backup. It does not mark files as having been backed up. If you are doing normal and differential backups, you must have the last normal and last differential backup sets to restore your data.

Consider the following factors when you decide what type of backup to use:

- The normal backup type provides a baseline for the other backup types. It is best to use when a large amount of data changes between backups.

- The incremental backup type works well to record the progression of frequently changed data.

- The differential backup type simplifies the process for restoring files.

To provide for long-term storage with fewer media, you can use a combination of a normal backup plus either incremental or differential backups.

Some backup types use *backup markers*, also known as archive attributes, to track when a file has been backed up. When the file changes, Windows 2000 marks the file to be backed up again. Files or directories that have been moved to a new location are not marked for backup.

An incremental backup allows you to choose to back up only files with this marker set, and to choose whether or not to mark files as having been backed up.

Application Data Backup

If your Commerce Server site is small, the easiest way to back it up is to repackage it using Site Packager. The new package will save many of the configuration settings specific to your current site. However, Site Packager does not package properties that are specific to the computer you are on. For example, Web server properties and some application properties that are set in Commerce Server Manager are not packaged. For a list of the data that is packaged for each resource, see "Site Packager Reference Information" in the "Deploying Your Site" section of Commerce Server 2000 Help.

If your site is large, creating a package file for it may not be practical. In this case, you need to back up each component (each application and database, for example) using the appropriate method for that component.

The following table lists appropriate backup tools for each Commerce Server component type.

To back up this component type	Use this
Application files, Windows registry, and IIS 5.0 metabase	Windows 2000 Backup Wizard or Application Center
Commerce Server site	Site Packager
SQL Server databases	SQL Server Enterprise Manager
Domain information	Active Directory replication between multiple domain controllers

Network Configuration Backup

The configuration of routers or firewalls in the modern e-business environment can be complex. As part of any contingency plan, the network equipment configuration should be backed up periodically. This information then becomes part of the offsite backup data.

Deploying Content

This chapter describes how to deploy content on a Microsoft Commerce Server 2000 site. If you are deploying content on a new site, be sure to read "Deploying Your Site" in Commerce Server 2000 Help, particularly the "Using Site Packager" section. Also, read the "Application Center 2000" section later in this chapter, which describes how you can deploy your site using Microsoft Application Center 2000.

This chapter also describes how to migrate from the Site Server Content Replication System (CRS) to Commerce Server using Application Center. For more information about migrating from Site Server to Commerce Server, see Chapter 11, "Migrating from Site Server to Commerce Server 2000."

The following are some examples of site content:

- Web pages and page elements, including:

  - Static content (Hypertext Markup Language (HTML), graphics, digital media, advertisements, and so on)

  - Dynamic content (such as Active Server Pages (ASP) and scripts)

- Applications, middle-tier components (such as COM+), database procedures, and other programming logic

- Data that supports the creation of dynamic Web pages or enables customers to make transactions (such as the product catalog, campaigns and ads, and user profiles)

- Reports

- Files of all types that users can download or view online (including Microsoft Word documents, Portable Document Format (PDF) files, compressed file archives, graphics)

- Content on related support sites, in addition to the primary public site

This chapter describes content deployment for the following three scenarios:

- **Small-to-medium site**. Usually contains development, test/staging, and production environments, with 1 to 20 servers in each of the three environments. This type of site contains a small-to-medium volume of content (approximately 1 to 2 GB), with a low amount of content turnover.

- **Medium-to-large site**. Usually contains development, test/staging, Enterprise Resource Planning (ERP) systems, and production environments, with 20 or more servers in the production environment and 10 to 20 servers in each of the other environments. This type of site contains a medium volume of content (more than 2 GB), with a medium amount of content turnover. When you deploy content to a medium-to-large site, you should consider deploying in stages, rather than trying to deploy all of the content at once. You should also consider compressing content during replication.

- **Global site**. Usually consists of several large, geographically separated sites connected by a dedicated wide area network (WAN). This type of site contains a large volume of content, with a medium amount of content turnover. When you deploy content to a global site, you should consider deploying in stages, rather than trying to deploy all of the content at once. You should also consider compressing content during replication, and make provisions for recovering from errors due to failures in the WAN link.

Although each of these scenarios varies in complexity and approach, they all share a common development life cycle. Figure 15.1 shows how content moves from the development environment to the test/staging environment, and then to the production environment.

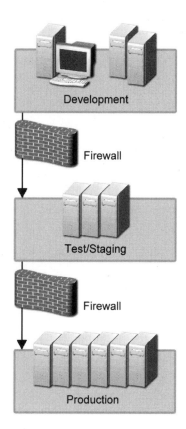

Figure 15.1 Content development and deployment

In the content development and deployment model shown in Figure 15.1, you do the following:

1. Develop new content within the confines of the corporate network, using tools such as Microsoft Visual Studio (C++, Microsoft Visual Basic, Microsoft Visual InterDev), Microsoft Visual SourceSafe, and Microsoft PhotoDraw.

2. Unit-test changes in the development environment.

3. When content is ready for integration and regression testing, you move it from the development environment to the test/staging environment. The test/staging environment should be similar in network topology to the production environment, at smaller scale (fewer processors or Web servers, and so on). It might be located within the corporate network, if you are developing and administering applications in-house; or it can be located offsite at the Internet Service Provider (ISP)/Application Service Provider (ASP) if your site is being administered externally.

4. When you have successfully completed regression testing, you can move the content from the test/staging environment to the production environment.

You create content in the development environment and administer it in the production environment. Business managers and system administrators use Commerce Server Business Desk and Commerce Server Manager to create and administer various types of content. The following is a list of the organizational roles that are usually involved with creating, administering, and deploying content:

- **Business managers**. Add, change, and delete content, using Business Desk in the development environment. Business managers work with the following types of content:
  - Catalogs (products, prices)
  - Campaigns (discounts, advertising, direct mail, expressions)
  - Reports
  - Orders
  - User profiles
  - Site terms
  - Shipping methods and tax rates
- **Site developers**. Add, change, or delete content, using Visual Studio or another tool, in the development environment. Site developers work with the following types of content:
  - Pipelines
  - COM+ components
  - Internet Server Application Programming Interface (SAPI) filters and extensions
  - Dynamic content (ASP pages, Visual Basic scripts, and so on)
  - Static content (HTML, Graphics Interchange Format (GIF), Joint Photographic Experts Group (JPEG), streaming media, and so on)
  - Database schema changes
  - Data (catalogs, campaigns, user profiles, site terms, and so on)
- **Testers**. Test and approve newly developed content in the test/staging environment, prior to deployment in the production environment.

- **System administrators**. Administer change requests from both business managers and site developers, using Commerce Server Manager resources or Business Desk modules. System administrators are responsible for:

  - Deploying new Business Desk modules.

  - Managing Internet Information Services (IIS) 5.0 metabase changes.

  - Timely and accurate deployment of new site content in all environments (development, test/staging, and production).

Typically, business managers add new campaigns, manage catalog changes, and make other related system changes within the development environment. These changes are tested in the test/staging environment and, when approved, moved to the production environment.

Developers also work in the development environment. Their changes are also tested in the test/staging environment and, when approved, moved to the production environment. System administrators adjust the supporting infrastructure (software, hardware, and network) within the development environment. You need to duplicate these changes in the test/staging environment for testing and, when approved, duplicate them in the production environment.

The content management process usually contains the activities listed in the following table.

Activity	Description
Design	Define the content that authors should publish on the Web site.
Author	Develop and produce the content. Graphic artists, videotape production crews, photographers, technical writers, advertising writers, application developers, Web page developers, lawyers, human resource personnel, marketers, or anyone else who produces original material for the Web site create this content. You usually use a source code management system, such as Visual SourceSafe, to track the authored content.
Review	Review content. You should make sure that reviewer responsibilities are well-defined and technical reviewers identified before content is created and deployed.
Approve	Approve content for deployment. The cross-functional nature of Web content makes it important to have a well-defined content-approval process in place and approvers named, beginning with the earliest stages of content creation through final deployment.
Convert	Transform content from the format in which an author created it to the format in which you can display it on your site. For example, word processor documents must be converted to formatted HTML text, bitmapped images must be modified so that they load faster on the Web, and image formats might have to be changed. Site developers use templates, layouts, themes, and other methods to convert text into uniformly formatted Web pages.
Store	Place content in file systems, version-control systems, or other types of repositories. Integrated application development systems store varied Web content in a file system that replicates the hierarchical structure of the Web site.
Stage	If you have a separate staging environment, you should use it to assemble all content after the content has been thoroughly tested and before you move it to the production environment.
Test	Test the finished content. For example, testing should include identifying broken or missing links, identifying pages that load slowly, load testing, component testing, database access testing, script testing, and performance testing. Comprehensive, final integration testing should be done in a test/staging environment that exactly mirrors the production environment. Developers need to make sure that database connections are valid for the test/staging environment and the production environment. For more information about testing a Commerce Server site, see Chapter 16, "Testing Your Site."
Deploy and replicate content	Place new content into production. You must be sure that all content gets moved to the live system, including middle-tier components and transactional packages.
Monitor and update	Monitor your production site and update the content when necessary. The content management process does not end when you install content in the production environment. You must continuously monitor and update content, in order to keep the site current and working properly.
Remove and archive	Remove stale or out-of-date content from the production environment and archive it for a pre-determined length of time.
Analyze	Analyze the site and user traffic on an ongoing basis.

Deployment Tools

Today, no single tool appears to be sufficient for deploying all types of content or for fulfilling the needs of everyone involved (business managers, site developers, or system administrators). You should evaluate and choose a deployment tool based on its core capabilities, supportability, and ease of use. This section describes the following tools for deploying Commerce Server content:

- Application Center 2000

- Content Replication Service (CRS)

- Custom SQL Server Data Transformation Services (DTS) tasks and packages

- Custom scripts (Visual Basic, Visual Basic Script)

- Third-party deployment tools

For an explanation of how to use Commerce Server Site Packager to unpack your Web site and settings, see "Using Site Packager" in Commerce Server 2000 Help.

In addition to the tools described in this section, you can also use Visual Studio or Visual InterDev to publish a Web site by copying the files in the Web site to a destination such as a Web server. For more information about Visual Studio, see http://msdn.microsoft.com/vstudio. For more information about Visual InterDev, see http://msdn.microsoft.com/vinterdev.

Application Center

Application Center is a deployment and management tool that consists of a suite of monitoring and diagnostic tools for Web applications. You can use Application Center to manually define the composition of a Web application. This composition, called the *application image* or *resource set,* contains the following content and components:

- System data source names (DSNs)

- File system paths (pipelines)

- COM+ applications and ISAPI filters

- Dynamic content (ASP pages, Visual Basic scripts, and so on)

- Static content (HTML, GIFs, JPEGs, video, and so on)

- Registry keys

- Web sites (default and administration) and virtual directories

Application Center automatically synchronizes online content and server configuration settings when they are updated. You can also manually synchronize the settings at any time from the cluster controller. In addition, you can deploy COM+ applications across an

Application Center cluster or outside the cluster. Application Center supports the following functionalities:

- Administration of IIS 5.0 metabase changes and related content, effectively replicating the metabase from the cluster controller to all members of the cluster (or outside the cluster) and overwriting metabase settings for each member of the cluster.

- Replication of Microsoft Windows NT and Microsoft Windows 2000 access control lists (ACLs).

Application Center does not support the following functionalities:

- Deployment of changes to the database or database schema. This includes nearly all of the functionality required to replicate the tasks that business managers perform using Business Desk.

- Content replication over a WAN link.

- Distribution of application installation packages like new Business Desk modules, Commerce Server, or Windows 2000.

- A native roll-back feature.

For more information about Application Center, see http://www.microsoft.com/applicationcenter/.

Content Replication Service

Content Replication Service (CRS), which was a feature of Site Server 3.0, is now available on the Application Center 2000 CD. With CRS, you can easily replicate file-based content, such as files, directories, metadata, and ACLs from directory to directory, between local servers, or across the Internet or a corporate intranet. You can also use CRS to replicate and install server applications, including Microsoft ActiveX Server Components and Java applets. You can use CRS to replicate the following types of content:

- File system paths (pipelines)

- COM+ components

- Dynamic content (ASP pages, Visual Basic scripts, and so on)

- Static content (HTML, GIFs, JPEGs, video, and so on)

CRS supports the following functionalities:

- Deployment over WAN links, through firewalls on TCP port 507

- Pre- and post-replication script execution

- User-defined rollback

- Transaction-based processing of replicated content

- Transaction logging

- Command line-based administration

- Replication of Windows NT and Windows 2000 ACLs

CRS does not support the following functionalities:

- Deployment of database or database schema changes. This includes nearly all of the functionality required to replicate the tasks that business managers perform using Business Desk.

- Distribution of application installation packages like new Business Desk modules, Commerce Server, or Windows 2000.

- Administration of IIS 5.0 metabase changes, unless manually scripted.

Custom SQL Server DTS Tasks and Packages

You can't use Application Center or the CRS tool to deploy database or database schema changes throughout a three-tier environment. However, you can use Microsoft SQL Server 7.0 or SQL Server 2000 to create DTS packages that move both schema and data changes between two servers running SQL Server. Each of the tasks that business managers perform when they add, change, or delete content should have an associated DTS task.

You can create DTS tasks and packages to support the following functionalities:

- Deployment over WAN links, through firewalls on TCP port 1433

- Pre- and post-replication script execution, as part of the DTS package, or scheduled after using another mechanism like Windows Task Scheduler

- User-defined rollback (such as database backup prior to DTS execution)

- Transaction logging

- E-mail notification (such as SQL Mail or a Collaboration Data Objects (CDO) message)

- Deployment of database or database schema changes

DTS tasks and packages do not support the following functionalities:

- Command line-based administration (only SQL Server graphical user interface (GUI) or Executive Scheduled Task are supported)

- Distribution of application installation packages like new Business Desk modules, Commerce Server, or Windows 2000

- Administration of IIS 5.0 metabase changes

Custom Scripts

Although it is possible to write custom Windows Scripting Host (WSH) scripts to automate the entire content deployment process, it is much easier to use other tools (such as Visual Basic or Visual Basic Script). You should create WSH scripts only to enhance the capabilities of the other tools you're using or to integrate their processes. For example, you can define pre- or post-processing of scripts in a deployment project managed with tools such as CRS, Application Center, or OpenDeploy. (OpenDeploy is discussed in the following "Third-Party Deployment Tools" section.)

The object model in Commerce Server also provides the ability to script certain tasks, such as updating prices for all of the items in a catalog. For more information about using Commerce Server to create custom scripts, see "Programming with Commerce Server Objects" in Commerce Server 2000 Help.

Third-Party Deployment Tools

Interwoven OpenDeploy 4.2 is content replication software for the Web that provides a secure, flexible, and scalable solution for transferring transactional content between servers.

OpenDeploy 4.2 supports the following functionalities:

- Comparison of content in the development and production environments

- Deployment of Web content over WAN links through firewalls

- Transfer of data by list, delta, and package

- Automatic site rollback

- Transactional rollback

- Retries and retry intervals for locked files on production servers

- Encrypted deployment (48-bit symmetric key encryption and 128-bit asymmetric key support) to ensure transfer of content only between approved sources

- Command line-based administration

- Configuration files with multiple "named deployment" configurations.

For more information about Interwoven OpenDeploy, DataDeploy, and TeamSite, as well as other software developed especially to work with Commerce Server 2000, see: http://www.microsoft.com/commerceserver.

Deployment Scenarios

This section describes how to apply the tools discussed previously in this chapter to the following types of sites:

- Small-to-medium

- Medium-to-large

- Global

Small-to-Medium Site

A small-to-medium site typically has from 1 to 20 servers per environment. This type of site usually contains a small-to-medium volume of content (approximately 1 to 2 GB), with a low amount of content turnover. Figure 15.2 shows an example of a small-to-medium site.

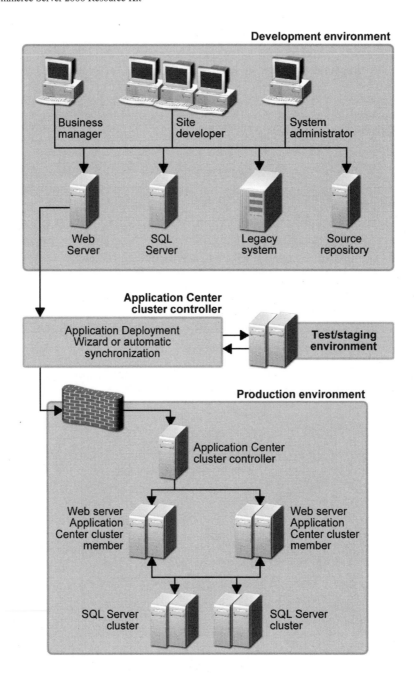

Figure 15.2 Small-to-medium site

In a small-to-medium site, the business manager adds new ad campaigns, discounts, and so on to the development environment. Developers develop new versions of applications, make enhancements, and debug production issues within the development environment. The system administrator supports the site and makes administrative changes to the development environment.

New content is deployed to the test/staging environment using Site Packager, Application Center, CRS, or OpenDeploy. Figure 15.2 shows a deployment done with Application Center. Database transfers are created and run using SQL Server DTS packages or DataDeploy. Content is deployed either from the development SQL Server or the Web server to a stand-alone Application Center cluster controller.

You use the Application Center Microsoft Management Console (MMC) to make the necessary changes to the application manifest and start the Application Center Application Deployment Wizard to deploy the application to the Application Center cluster controller. The Application Deployment Wizard helps you deploy content and configure one or more applications to selected Application Center clusters or members.

When new content has been sent to the test/staging environment, the test team can begin to test it. If changes are necessary, the entire content deployment process begins again.

You deploy content from the test/staging environment to the production environment using the Application Deployment Wizard. The Application Center stand-alone cluster controller deploys the application to each Application Center cluster controller in production, thus effectively distributing the new or updated content throughout the production environment.

Medium-to-Large Site

A medium-to-large site usually contains development, test/staging, ERP systems, and production environments, with 20 or more servers in the production environment and 10 to 20 servers in each of the other environments. This type of site generally contains a medium volume of content (more than 2 GB), with a medium amount of content turnover. When you deploy content to a medium-to-large site, you should consider deploying in stages, rather than trying to deploy all the content at once. You should also consider compressing content during replication. Figure 15.3 shows an example of a medium-to-large site.

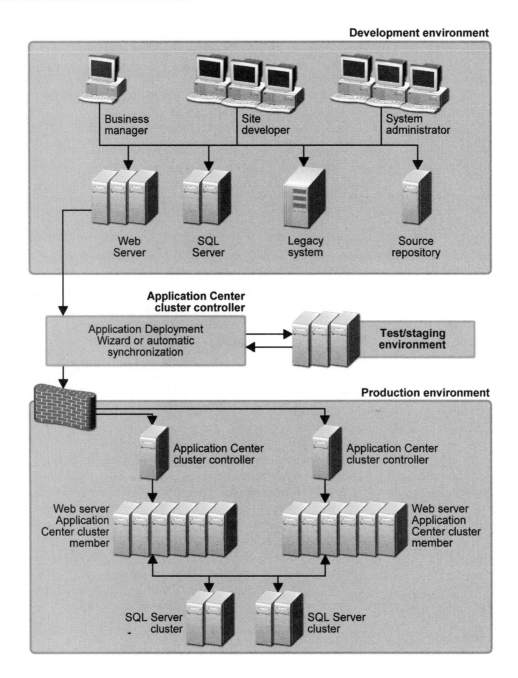

Figure 15.3 Medium-to-large site

In a medium-to-large site, the business manager adds new ad campaigns, discounts, and so on, to the development environment. Developers develop new versions of applications, make enhancements, and debug production issues in the development environment. The system administrator supports the site and makes administrative changes to the development environment.

In Figure 15.3, Application Center is used to deploy updated content to a load-balanced Application Center cluster in the development environment. The system administrator can then build an environment in which business managers and site developers can add, change, or delete content. The system administrator can also change the application manifest and test application deployment inside the development environment before deploying the completed application to the test/staging environment.

You can deploy new content over a WAN link to the test/staging environment using CRS or OpenDeploy. You use SQL Server DTS packages or OpenDeploy to create and run database transfers.

You deploy content either from the development SQL Server or the Web server with the Application Center cluster controller to the Web server in the test/staging environment, acting as a stand-alone Application Center cluster controller. The system administrator then uses the Application Center MMC console to make the necessary changes to the application manifest and starts the Application Deployment Wizard to deploy the application to the Application Center cluster controller.

When new content has been sent to the test/staging environment, the test team can begin to test it. If changes are necessary, the entire content deployment process begins again.

You deploy new content using the Application Deployment Wizard. The Application Center stand-alone cluster controller deploys the application to each Application Center cluster controller in the production environment, thus effectively distributing the new or updated content throughout the production environment.

Global Site

A global site usually consists of several large, geographically separated sites connected by a dedicated WAN or an ISP/ASP-provided WAN. A global site might even be hosted by multiple ISPs/ASPs. This type of site contains a large volume of content, with a medium amount of content turnover. When you deploy content to a global site, you should consider deploying in stages, rather than trying to deploy all the content at once. You should also consider compressing content during replication, and make provisions for recovering from errors due to failures in the WAN link.

The development environment for a global site is usually centralized, and looks very much like the medium-to-large site development environment shown previously in Figure 15.3. However, it is not uncommon in a global site to have local development satellite locations devoted to localizing content, adapting content for a local market, or just participating in the general development effort.

You can typically consolidate content from satellite development sites by transferring it over dedicated WAN links to the primary development location using CRS or OpenDeploy. You can create and run database transfers using SQL Server DTS packages or DataDeploy. At the primary development location, you integrate the transferred content into the centralized development effort and redeploy it to each of the distributed test/staging environments.

Testing in each location is done in a similar fashion to the testing done in small-to-medium and medium-to-large sites. Figure 15.4 shows how a global site might be structured.

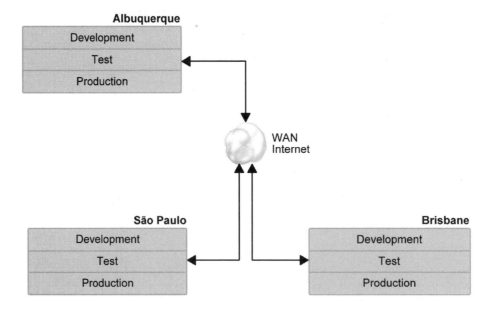

Figure 15.4 Global site

You deploy new or updated content using the Application Center Application Deployment Wizard. The Application Center cluster controller in the test/staging environment deploys the application to each Application Center cluster controller in production, effectively distributing the new or updated content throughout the production environment.

Deployment Examples

This section contains deployment examples for the following types of content:

- Campaigns, campaign items, expressions
- COM+ applications
- Databases

Campaigns, Campaign Items, and Expressions

This section describes a scenario that you might use to deploy new campaigns, campaign items, or expressions, using CRS over a WAN link to an Application Center cluster controller. You then use Application Center to deploy your content to the cluster and its members. Figure 15.5 shows how the new ad campaign is deployed in this scenario.

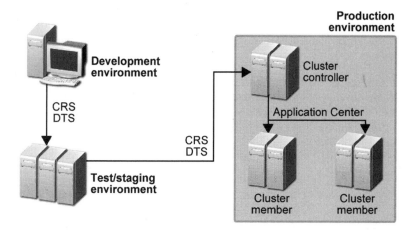

Figure 15.5 Deploying a new ad campaign

When you design a new Commerce Server site, you must estimate the number of campaigns, campaign items, and expressions that might be created and archived over the life of the site. In most Commerce Server sites and under most circumstances, a dedicated SQL Server cluster will handle requests for these items. For this reason, you should create your site so that related campaign tables are stored in a separate database. It will then be a relatively simple task to move those tables and related sets of records through the entire development life cycle as a unit.

> **Important**   When you update campaigns, ads, and discounts, move only tables containing these records. Do not overwrite the Performance table.

In this scenario, business managers solicit a new advertising campaign, payment for which is based on the number of ad requests. The campaign is designed in conjunction with some static HTML content. The business managers, using Business Desk, then place the required ad campaign content into the development environment.

Content developers prepare the static content to which the ad campaign will link and add it to the development environment. The business managers and developers unit-test the new ad campaign within the development environment.

The system administrator then moves a copy of the database tables and the new static HTML content to the test/staging environment. Using CRS, the system administrator first creates a project to deploy the static HTML content to the Application Center cluster controller. Next, the database administrator creates a SQL Server DTS package to transfer the required database tables.

After running the DTS package, testers can test the campaign on the Application Center cluster controller, which has its own dedicated SQL Server server. The system administrator next uses Application Center to deploy the static HTML content to each member of the cluster. Finally, the system administrator uses a similar DTS package to deploy the campaign tables to the SQL Server cluster serving ad campaigns for other members of the Application Center cluster. For more information about DTS tasks, see "Running the Data Warehouse" in Commerce Server 2000 Help.

If the ad campaign does not successfully pass the tests, you repeat this campaign deployment process until it does. When the ad campaign has successfully passed all the tests in the test/staging environment, you use the same process to move the ad campaign from the test/staging environment to the production environment.

COM+ Applications

This scenario describes how to deploy a new COM+ application, using CRS over a WAN link to deploy any related static or dynamic content, and to install the COM+ application on the remote Application Center cluster controller. This scenario also explains how to deploy a COM+ application and related content to its members. Figure 15.6 shows how to deploy a COM+ application.

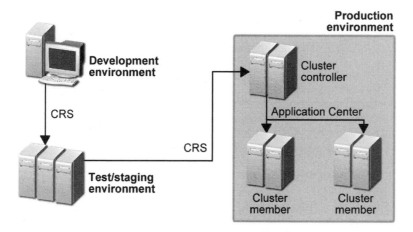

Figure 15.6 Deploying a COM+ application

When you design a Commerce Server COM+ application, you must consider the related business logic components. You must install Commerce Server on the same server as the COM+ component. You can't reference Commerce Server components from COM+ components unless they are installed on the same server. COM+ components can reference both local Commerce Server components and remote COM+ components. However, you should only have a COM+ component access a remote COM+ component when it's absolutely necessary (for example, to access secure data), because remote access impacts performance.

The following steps explain how to move the COM+ object and the ASP pages to the test/staging environment and then to the production environment:

1. Create a COM+ application with the Component Service snap-in and add the COM+ object.

2. Export the resulting COM+ application to a Microsoft Windows Installer file.

3. Create a batch file to install the COM+ application and the ASP pages, such as the following:

```
net stop "World Wide Web Publishing Service"
xcopy Templates\menu.bak c:\Inetpub\wwwroot\b2csite\template\ /E /R /Y
xcopy Templates\menu.asp c:\Inetpub\wwwroot\b2csite\template\ /E /R /Y
xcopy sitemap.asp c:\Inetpub\wwwroot\site\ /E /R /Y
xcopy team.xml c:\Inetpub\wwwroot\site\ /E /R /Y
xcopy images\*.png c:\Inetpub\wwwroot\site\images\ /E /R /Y
msiexec -i htmlhelper.msi
net start "World Wide Web Publishing Service"
```

4. Using CRS, create a project to deploy the files, and then run a batch file (such as the batch file, `msiexec -i htmlhelper.msi`, in Step 3) to install the COM+ application.

Running the CRS project copies the ASP pages and runs the batch file as a post-replication script. The Application Center cluster controller must not be serving active HTML/ASP requests from any other test team member when you run the CRS project. The pages can be tested on the Application Center cluster controller.

5. Create an Application Center application image containing the following:

   - COM+ application

   - Virtual root

   - Files (ASP and other resource files, such as HTML, images, and so on)

6. Deploy the Application Center application image (manually synchronized) to the members of the cluster.

If the pages don't pass the tests, repeat this COM+ application deployment process until the tests complete successfully. When the pages have been approved, you use the same process to move them from the test/staging environment to the production environment.

Databases

To ensure availability and scalability for large Commerce Server sites, you might want to replicate your Catalogs database. Use SQL Server to do this. For more information about how to use SQL Server to replicate Commerce Server databases, see SQL Server Books Online. Also see "Using SQL Server to Replicate Databases" in Commerce Server 2000 Help.

Use the Profiles Schema Mover utility to move profile schemas. For information about the Profiles Schema Mover utility, see Chapter 9, "Developer Notes."

Whether you use snapshot replication, transactional replication, or merge replication, the tasks described in the following table should be helpful.

Stage	Tasks
Configuring replication	• Identify the publisher, distributor, and subscribers in your topology. • Use SQL Server Enterprise Manager, SQL-DMO, or Transact-SQL system stored procedures and scripts to configure the publisher, create a distribution database, and enable subscribers.
Publishing data and database objects	• Create the publication. • Define the data and database object articles in the publication. • Apply any necessary filters to data that is to be published.
Subscribing to publications	• Create push, pull, or anonymous subscriptions to indicate what publications should be propagated to individual subscribers and when.
Generating the initial snapshot	• Identify where to save files. • Specify whether or not the files should be compressed. • Identify scripts that should be run before and after applying the initial snapshot.
Applying the initial snapshot	• Apply the snapshot automatically by synchronizing the subscription, using the Distribution Agent or the Merge Agent. You can apply the snapshot from the default snapshot folder or from removable media that can be transported manually to the subscriber before the snapshot is applied.
Synchronizing data	• Run the Snapshot Agent, Distribution Agent, or Merge Agent to synchronize data and propagate updates between publisher and subscribers. • For snapshot replication, a snapshot will be taken and propagated to subscribers. • For transactional replication, the Log Reader Agent will store updates in the Distribution database and the Distribution Agent will propagate updates to subscribers. • If you use subscriptions that can be updated with either snapshot replication or transactional replication, data will be propagated from the subscriber to the publisher and to the other subscribers. • For merge replication, data is synchronized during the merge process. Conflicts, if any, are detected and resolved at that point.

Testing Your Site

This chapter provides a general methodology for testing software, and then provides more specific information about how to test your Microsoft Commerce Server 2000 site. Testing is essential for any Commerce Server implementation to ensure software reliability and system performance and capacity.

Testing Methodology

Testing is a key part of the software development process. This section describes the types of testing you should do and the documents you must create to define your testing process.

Types of Tests

The following table lists the five types of tests you should use in your testing process.

Test type	Tests
Build Verification Testing (BVT)	Stability of the software build.
Function	Program functions. A program can have several levels of functionality, depending on its complexity.
Ad hoc ("guerilla")	Various site components. This is unstructured, random testing by casual users.
Integration	Interaction between modules or program components and the ways in which the program works with other products or platforms (both hardware and software).
Stress (also known as load or performance testing)	Number of transactions or levels of use that an application can consistently sustain.

Tests can be manual, scripted, or automated. The types of testing you do can vary, but should always include BVT, functionality, and ad hoc tests. Performance testing is especially important for an e-commerce application. The following table lists the two types of test methods that you can apply to each type of test.

Method	Tests
Black box	Standard user interface. Test cases should be constructed so that they test the same standard interfaces that customers are expected to use.
White box	Application code. Test cases use batch files, SQL queries, and similar methods to interact directly with program code.

Types of Test Documents

There are three types of documents to create before you begin testing your site:

- **Test plan**: Strategy and schedule for testing your Commerce Server site.

- **Test cases**: Detailed, step-by-step descriptions of each test.

- **Test error reports**: Reports that describe errors encountered during testing.

Test Plan

Developing a good test plan is key to successful testing. In fact, it can help define the application. To create an effective test plan, you must first understand your company's strategic vision for the site, and then define your test strategy accordingly.

A test plan includes the strategy and scheduling information for the entire project—everything except descriptions of the test cases. The test plan lists the features that need testing, the required resources, the risks you need to consider, and the testing schedule. The results of your test-planning process should be a stable specification, an accurate schedule, and a test plan containing an effective test strategy.

The test plan should reiterate the goals of the site and divide the site into testing areas. In addition, the plan should include inter-group procedure information, such as how bugs will be tracked and resolved, how test releases will be handled, how shared components will be tested, and criteria for determining whether a build is accepted or rejected for testing. Finally, the test plan must identify which testing tasks will be automated and which testing tasks will be done manually.

Test plans should describe in detail everything that the test team, the program management team, and the development team need to know about the testing to be done.

The following table lists the sections of a test plan.

Section	Describes
Introduction/purpose	The site and its features, followed by the test methodology and approach.
Scope	<ul><li>What will be tested and what won't be tested.</li><li>The types of tests to be conducted, such as:<ul><li>Black box and/or white box</li><li>Manual, scripted, and/or automated</li><li>BVT, functionality, integration, stress, and so on</li></ul></li><li>Deliverables, including a list of reports to describe test results and bugs to be tracked.</li></ul>
Feature/function	Functionality to be tested, on a feature-by-feature basis.
Test environment	Platform (operating system) and platform dependencies.
Test criteria	Acceptance criteria, pass criteria, and suspension of test criteria.
Bug tracking	Location of the bug database and the bug data format.
Test case management	How to manage test cases and where they will be located.
Test team	Members of the test team and each tester's responsibilities; escalation path for resolving issues.
Test platform (hardware)	The computers, networks, and other hardware required to perform the tests, both for office-based test hardware and lab-based test hardware. If you are setting up a test lab, it should be described in this section.
Test schedule	The beginning and ending dates for the project, the release date for the site, and the key dates for all milestones.
Assumptions and risks	Conditions that must be met for testing to be successful and the probable outcome if the necessary conditions aren't met.
Appendix	The following information (as appropriate):<ul><li>High-level test specification matrix</li><li>Test error report template</li><li>Sign-off page</li></ul>

Test Cases

A test case is a detailed, step-by-step description of a test. The following table lists four basic types of test cases.

Type of test case	Tests
Functionality	What the site is supposed to do
Boundary	Defined values and defaults
Positive (or Valid)	That the site does what it should do
Negative (or Invalid)	That the site doesn't do what it shouldn't do

You can organize test cases in a variety of ways, depending on the size, type, and complexity of the site you are testing. For example, you can organize test cases by type of test, by site feature, or by a combination of the two.

You can organize test cases by test type, such as the following:

- BVT tests
- Functional tests
- Integration tests
- Stress tests

Alternatively, you can organize test cases by product feature, such as the following:

- Primary-level features or functions
- Secondary-level features or functions
- Tertiary-level features or functions

Depending on the complexity of the site, you might organize test cases using a combination of methods, such as the following:

- Primary level:
  - BVT tests
  - Functional tests
  - Integration tests
- Secondary level:
  - BVT tests
  - Functional tests
  - Integration tests
- Tertiary level:
  - BVT tests
  - Functional tests
  - Integration tests
  - Stress tests

The following table lists the sections of a test case.

Section	Describes
Title	The test. The title should be a one-line description of what is being tested (ideally implying the expected result).
Steps	How to do the test, including a list of the discrete tasks required to complete the test. You should specifically identify the form names, menu items, field names, and input data in each step.
Expected results	What should happen (system behavior and/or output) after each step of the test.
Assumptions	Any special platform requirements, key functionality, and the steps needed to set up the test case.

Test Error Reports

A test error report is a report that describes errors encountered during testing. An error, or bug, occurs when the site doesn't perform the way it was designed to perform. For example, if you attempt to add an item to your shopping basket, but the application doesn't add the item, an error has occurred. The following table lists the information that a test error report should contain.

Section	Describes
Description	The operation that did not work correctly. This section should describe in detail what the error is and where it is located.
Reproduction steps	Detailed steps for reproducing the error. This might include platform or installation details, if necessary.
Tracking data	The person who found the error, the person who is responsible for fixing it, and any other pertinent data.

Testing a Commerce Server Site

Before you begin testing, you must set up your test environment.

Important Create a separate test environment in which to do your testing. Do not install new content or software in your production environment before it has been thoroughly tested.

For best results, you should create a test environment that exactly duplicates your production environment. Testing each tier of the architecture separately, as shown in the following list, also helps to reduce the complexity of the testing task. You must also test the security of each tier. The following is a sample tiered architecture:

- User interface layer (top tier)
    - Visual appearance and usability
    - Links
    - Browser compatibility
- Business logic layer (middle tier)
    - Software performance testing (business logic, tax, shipping calculations)
    - Server load
    - Stress
    - Gateways
- Database layer (bottom tier)
    - Search results
    - Query response time
    - Data integrity
    - Data validity
    - Recovery

User Interface Layer (Top Tier)

To be sure that your site is attractive and user-friendly, you should test the following elements in the user interface layer (top tier):

- Visual appearance and usability
- Links
- Browser compatibility

Visual Appearance and Usability

The visual appearance and usability of a Web site, including its catalog pages, is important because a visually pleasing and easy-to-use site enhances the customer experience and encourages repeat visits. The following table lists the elements that you should test in the user interface layer.

Element	Test for
Text font style	Compatibility with different browsers. Many available fonts don't display well on all browsers, especially older browser versions. In some cases, fonts can even be displayed as unreadable characters.
Font size consistency	Consistency of font size throughout the Web site. A body text font size of 10 to 14 points, and a heading font size of 18 to 24 points are generally acceptable sizes.
Use of colors	User-friendly combinations of foreground and background colors throughout the site. Avoid combinations that make the site difficult to use. For example, it is difficult to read yellow text on a white background. You also should not use red and green in close proximity, because many people are red/green colorblind.
Images	Speed of download. Balance the use of images to get a reasonable download speed. The fewer images you use, the faster your site can download. To increase download speed, for example, consider replacing full-size images with thumbnails.
Spelling and grammar	Correct spelling and grammar. Use the spelling checker to check the spelling throughout the site, and then proofread the site for errors the spelling checker didn't catch, such as the different uses for "there" and "their."
	Proofread the entire site for correct grammar.
	Note Be sure to give your home page special attention, because it is the first page that a visitor to your site sees.
Reliable and consistent information	Information accuracy. Verify all facts and figures that relate to products and services with the legal, marketing, and business teams.

The following list describes some other tests you should perform. Test to be sure that:

- Each toolbar and menu item can be used to navigate correctly using either the mouse or the keyboard.

- It's possible to navigate correctly through all pages using either the mouse or the keyboard.

- You have used proper format masks. For example, all drop-down lists should be sorted alphabetically. The date entry should also be properly formatted.

- Colors, fonts, and font widths are standard for the field prompts and displayed text.

- Vertical scroll bars or horizontal scroll bars do not appear unless needed.

- The window can be resized.

- All of the text displayed in each window is spelled correctly, including the window caption, status bar options, field prompts, pop-up text, and error messages.

- All character or alphanumeric fields are left-aligned (depending on the language).

- All numeric fields are right-aligned.

- Defaults are displayed, if there are any.

- All windows have the same look and feel.

- The tab order is from top left to bottom right, avoiding read-only or unavailable fields in the tab sequence.

- The cursor is positioned on the first input field when a window is opened.

- Each control behaves correctly, including push buttons, radio buttons, list boxes, and so on.

- The command buttons appear dimmed when not in use.

Links

Hyperlinks in Web sites can be broken, missing, or improperly assigned, making it impossible for a site visitor to navigate to the appropriate Web page. Make sure that all links work properly. You can use third-party software to search for broken and incorrect links; however, you must search for missing links manually.

The following table describes the types of links you should test.

Type of link	Test for
Broken links	A break in a link between the current page and a linked page or graphic. For example, if a developer changes the name of a products page from "Product.htm" to "Products.htm," the link between the home page and the Products page will no longer work. When users click this type of link, they go to an error page instead of to the correct page.
Missing links	Links that have not yet been created. For example, a developer might forget to create a link between the **Products** button on the home page and the Products page. If this happens, site visitors can't use the **Products** button to go to the Products page from the home page.
Incorrect links	Links that take a site visitor to the wrong page.

The following Web sites offer online testing for broken and incorrect links at a nominal fee:

- http://netmechanic.com/
- http://www.linkalarm.com/index.html
- http://www.Websitegarage.com

Browser Compatibility

Text, graphics, or colors can appear differently, depending on the browser used to look at them. To ensure that your site appears the way you want it to look on all major browsers, you should use development software that is compatible with most of the popular browsers, such as Microsoft Internet Explorer, Netscape Navigator, America Online (AOL), and Microsoft WebTV.

The following table compares the compatibility of browsers with common Web site components.

Web site components	Internet Explorer 4.0 and later	Internet Explorer 3.0	Netscape Navigator 4.0 and later
Microsoft ActiveX controls	Enabled	Enabled	Disabled
Microsoft Visual Basic Scripting Edition (VBScript)	Enabled	Enabled	Disabled
JavaScript	Enabled	Enabled	Enabled
Java applets	Enabled	Disabled	Enabled
Dynamic HTML	Enabled	Enabled	Enabled
Frames	Enabled	Enabled	Enabled

Business Logic Layer (Middle Tier)

Middle-tier testing primarily tests software performance and load. You test software performance to ensure that the software performs in accordance with operational specifications for response time, processing costs, storage use, and printed output, regardless of the volume of traffic on your site.

If your servers are overloaded during peak traffic volumes, you might have to invest in additional Web servers to prevent downtime and to enable you to offload traffic from an overloaded server during peak times. The ability of a Web server to handle a heavy load at peak hours depends on network speed and the server's processing power, memory, and storage space.

You should gather data on software performance during:

- Current and expected normal transaction volumes

- Current and expected peak transaction volumes

- Minimal transaction volumes

You should test all components fully, including facilities and equipment, and make sure that your local area networks (LANs) and wide area networks (WANs) are performing satisfactorily.

The following table lists the elements you should test in the middle tier.

Element	Test that
Server load	Servers continue to function during heavy traffic volume. Identify the optimum number of simultaneous users that the server can handle before performance begins to degrade (capacity). Then, use the results of load tests to decide whether or not to add additional servers to manage peak traffic loads.
	Most load-testing software simulates multiple logons, after which it calculates the optimum load factor for the server. Software is then configured using this test data so that the server will stop accepting further requests from online users if the traffic increases beyond its load capacity.
	The Microsoft Web Application Stress (WAS) tool simulates multiple browsers requesting pages from a Web site. This tool can realistically simulate many requests with relatively few client computers. For more information about Web server load testing, see http://www.Webperfcenter.com.
Stress	The server can process the expected load. For example, a bank transaction processing system might be designed to process up to 100 transactions per second and an operating system might be designed to handle up to 200 separate terminals.
	Stress tests steadily increase the load on the system beyond the maximum design load until the system fails. This type of testing has the following functions:
	• To test the failure behavior of the system so that if system load should exceed the maximum-anticipated load, you can see whether you lose data or services.
	• To discover system defects that would not be detectable under normal circumstances.
Payment gateways	Payment gateways are reliable and compatible. The payment gateway is software that facilitates payment transactions by taking credit card details from customers, and then validating them with a transaction clearinghouse.

Database Layer (Bottom Tier)

The database for a Commerce Server site typically contains data for catalogs, shopping baskets, user profiles, and orders. For this reason, it's extremely important to test the database layer to ensure the integrity of your data. Database testing is an ongoing process because no database is static. When you create a database, you should also create a copy and store it either on the same computer or on another computer. Run your tests on the copy of the database, not the original. When your tests are successful, you can install the necessary changes in the original database.

The database does not have to be, and usually isn't, located on the same server that hosts your Web site's storefront. The database server should be separated from the Web server by a firewall, which adds complexity to the testing processes.

The following table lists the elements that you should test in the database layer.

Element	Test that
Search results	Search results are relevant, provide direct links to the requested pages, and do not result in "wild goose chases." The Search option is one of the most frequently used functions of online databases.
	Testers can assume the role of the online user and try out random Search options with different keywords. Search results should be recorded by the percentage of relevance to the keyword.
Query response time	The turnaround time for responding to database queries is within specifications. These test results can help identify problems such as bottlenecks in the network, problems with specific types of queries, problems with database structure, or problems with the hardware.
Data integrity	Important data, including catalog, pricing, shipping table, tax table, order, and customer data are correct. Testing should be repeated on a regular basis, because data changes over time.
Data validity	Data is valid. Errors caused by incorrect data entry are probably the most common data-related errors, and also the most difficult to detect. For example, $67 can be entered mistakenly as $76.
	To find this type of error, you can sometimes use queries to validate data fields. For example, you can write a query that compares the sum of the numbers in the database data field to the sum of the numbers from the data source. A difference between the sums indicates an error in at least one data element.
	Another way to reduce data validity errors is to use data validation rules in data fields. For example, if the date field uses the MM/DD/YYYY format, you can incorporate a data validation rule, such that MM does not exceed 12, DD does not exceed 31, and so on.
Recovery	• The system can recover from faults and resume processing within a predefined period of time.
	• The system is fault-tolerant; processing faults don't halt system functioning.
	• Data recovery and restart are correct (in case of auto-recovery). If recovery requires manual intervention, then the mean time to repair the database should be within predefined, acceptable limits.
	Recovery testing forces the system to fail in a variety of ways to ensure that you can recover from system failures.

The following list describes some tests you should do to ensure data integrity. Make sure that:

- Data creation, modification, and deletion in data tables work as specified.
- Sets of radio buttons represent a fixed set of values. Test what happens when a blank value is retrieved from the database.
- Each value is saved fully when a particular set of data is saved to the database. Strings should not be truncated and numbers should not be rounded off.
- Default values are saved in the database if a user doesn't enter other values.
- New data is compatible with existing data, hardware, versions of the operating system, and interfaces with other software.

Security

You must test security on all parts of your site because ensuring the security of transactions over the Internet is important to gaining customer confidence. Gaining and keeping the confidence of online customers is extremely important to the success of your site.

The main technique for testing security is to attempt to violate built-in security controls. You must make sure that system protection mechanisms can prevent unauthorized access. You should then attempt to overwhelm the system by continuous requests, thereby denying service to others. You might purposely cause system errors during recovery or browse through unsecured data to find any possible keys to system entry.

The following table lists types of security breaches that you should test for.

Security breach	Description
Secrecy	There are two types of secrecy breaches: the ability to read a file to which you have not been granted access, and the ability to read data while in transit between two computers.
	Secrecy breaches differ from authentication and spoofing security breaches in that the perpetrators access the information directly rather than by having to imitate a legitimate user.
	Spoofing a user's identity means breaching the user's authentication information. In this case, a hacker obtains a user's personal information or the necessary information to replay the authentication procedure.
Authentication	Sending a network ID and password copied from an authorized user. An authentication breach is often caused by spoofing.
Non-repudiation	An unknown user, who cannot be traced, performing an illegal operation.
Integrity control (data tampering)	• Modifying system or user data with or without detection, such as an unauthorized change to stored or in-transit data • Formatting a hard disk • Introducing an undetectable network packet in a communication • Making an undetectable change to a sensitive file

For more information about best practices for setting up security on your site, see *Designing Secure Web-Based Applications for Microsoft Windows 2000* by Michael Howard (published by Microsoft Press). There are two primary areas of concern in e-commerce security: network security and payment transaction security.

Networks

Unauthorized users, or hackers, can wreak havoc on your Web site by accessing confidential information or by damaging data. To prevent unauthorized access, you can configure the network operating system and the firewall to manage network security.

You must configure the network operating system to allow only authentic users to access the network. You must also install and configure firewalls to ensure that data transfer is restricted to only one point on the network. This effectively prevents hackers from accessing data.

For example, if hackers access an unsecured FTP port (such as Port 25) on a Web server, they could use it as an entry point to the network and access data on the server. The hackers might also be able to access any computer connected to this server. You should design your security tests to reveal vulnerable areas and highlight the network settings that need to be reconfigured to enhance security.

You can use third-party programs to test for the following:

- User rights
- Removable disk locations
- Strong password policies
- Use of logon scripts and password expiration dates
- Passwords stored in clear text or encrypted form

For more information about testing network security, see http://www.intrusion.com.

Payment Transactions

When customers purchase goods and services over the Internet, they can be apprehensive about providing their credit card information. To make your site secure for your customers, you must ensure that the following two conditions are met:

- Credit card information is transmitted and stored securely.
- Strong encryption software is used to store credit card information, and only limited, authorized access to this information is allowed .

For more information about secure electronic transactions, see the following third-party sites:

- http://www.verisign.com
- http://www.cylink.com
- http://www.terisa.com
- http://www.cybercash.com
- http://www.checkfree.com

Part Five: Managing

Microsoft
**Commerce
Server** 2000

Managing Your Site

During the Management phase, you continue to monitor, test, and resolve problems in the hardware, software, and content of your site. You analyze the data you collect by monitoring site activity, and then use that data to improve site performance from both a technological and a marketing perspective. Finally, you create and perform operational procedures such as backup, recovery, and log capture, for administering the day-to-day operation of your site. Figure 17.1 shows a high-level view of the management process.

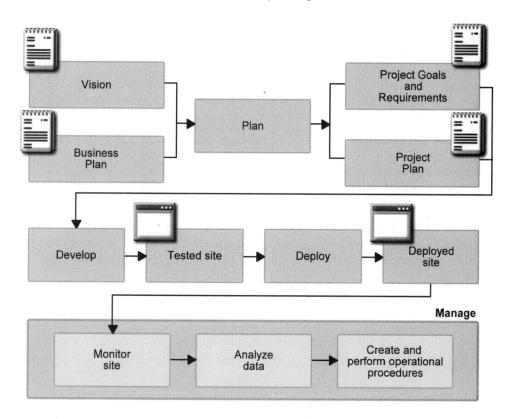

Figure 17.1 High-level view of the site management process

This chapter describes how to:

- Perform a site checkup

- Monitor and analyze log data

- Set up and perform the operational procedures necessary to manage your site

In addition, the Management section of this book contains the chapters listed in the following table.

Chapter	Title	Description
18	Problem Management	Best practices for managing problems and troubleshooting your Microsoft Commerce Server 2000 site
19	Maximizing Performance	Methods for creating site usage profiles, and analyzing and managing site performance

Performing a Site Checkup

E-commerce sites are dynamic and the requirements for a successful site can change dramatically over time. For example, your product line might change, site visitor usage profiles change, and from time to time you need to introduce new software, new catalogs, and other new content. Over time, the impact of the changes can affect the stability of your site.

It is a good idea to periodically conduct a site "checkup" to make sure that everything is working properly. A good time to conduct the checkup is prior to gearing up for the holiday shopping season, to give you time to correct any problems that might have crept into your site during the previous year, and to be sure that your customers have the best possible shopping experience.

Your site checkup should be a collaborative process, involving your system administrators, development staff, and business management. If other companies are developing or managing your site, you should include them, as well. The questions in the following table can provide guidelines for the types of questions you need to ask during the checkup. You might also have additional questions specific to your site.

Category	Questions	Comments
Backup and maintenance	• What procedures do we have for rebuilding services? • What are our database maintenance procedures? • When was the last time we rebuilt the site from scratch? • Do we have off-site storage for critical databases?	Regular backup and maintenance procedures ensure that you can identify and access all parts of your site, if necessary. Reconstructing a site is an effective way to make sure all the parts are available.
Event logs	• What warnings and errors have been occurring in our system and application event logs? • How do current warnings and errors compare to those reported in previous periods?	Event logs provide a useful gauge for the health of your system.

Load	• What is our current site load for the following:
	  • Transactions per day
	  • Peak concurrent shoppers
	  • CPU utilization on Web servers
	
	• How has our site load changed over the past year?
	
	• What have we done to accommodate load changes?
	
	• What incremental load do we anticipate during the holiday season and during the coming year?
	
	• What changes do we have to make to accommodate increases in load in the following areas:
	  • Hardware
	  • Network
	  • Monitoring tools
		Carefully managing site load is an effective means of improving site stability. Many sites experience large increases in traffic during the holiday season or as a result of advertising campaigns. Simulating the projected load is an effective way to make sure your site can handle the increased load.

Security	• When was our most recent security audit? • Have we applied the most recent security patches?	Security requires constant vigilance.

Category	Questions	Comments
Software changes	<ul><li>When was the last version or service pack applied?</li><li>When was the last platform upgrade?</li><li>Are we planning any platform or application changes? If so:<ul><li>What validation procedures are in place?</li><li>What are our procedures for backing out changes?</li></ul></li><li>Have we reviewed our application code against the latest software best practices?</li><li>When was our last software audit of the production servers?</li></ul>	Software upgrades, no matter how simple, introduce change and threaten system stability. Over time, software can drift from the specified configuration, making it difficult to identify problems and impossible to rebuild a server for debugging purposes.
Software problems	<ul><li>How many software problems have been reported since the last version or service pack was installed?</li><li>How has the "find rate" for problems changed over the past year?</li></ul>	Problem counts are an effective way to track site quality. Although there will always be problems, a stable site should show a decreasing problem find rate.
Stability and availability	<ul><li>How stable is our site, on a scale of 1 to 5?</li><li>How often do we reboot our Web servers, and why? Has the frequency increased within the past three months?</li><li>How are we eliminating single points of failure in the following:<ul><li>Web servers</li><li>Database servers</li><li>Power supplies</li><li>Network access</li></ul></li><li>What is our disaster recovery plan?</li></ul>	Eliminating single points of failure can dramatically increase site availability. For suggestions for eliminating single points of failure, see Chapter 6, "Planning for Reliability and High Availability."
Support	<ul><li>Is our staffing and problem escalation planning adequate for our availability requirements?</li><li>Do we have current support contracts and contacts for any third-party software that we are using?</li><li>Do we have a separate test environment?</li></ul>	The ability to efficiently report and escalate problems to knowledgeable sources is important for ensuring a healthy site.

Monitoring and Analyzing Log Data

For very serious errors and events, you should install an automated alarm system that continuously monitors your log files and sends notification (for example, an e-mail or pager message) when a particular type of error or event occurs. Your contingency plans should include notification and action scenarios. For more information about developing a contingency plan, see Chapter 14, "Deploying Your Site."

An alarm system scans for predefined errors and events by continuously monitoring the data written to any log files that you specify. In addition to errors and events, alarm systems can check for highs and lows in performance counters. You can configure an alarm system by setting priorities and responses for error, event, and failure information.

Your alarm system should respond to:

- Backups that fail
- System resources that become dangerously low
- Services that stop unexpectedly
- Events or system states that can affect site functionality

In addition to sending e-mail and pager messages, your alarm system might log the event or notification in a special file, run a script or program to correct the problem (for example, restarting a service), or log ancillary data to help you troubleshoot the error. For more information about system monitoring, see Chapter 19, "Maximizing Performance."

Analyzing Log Data

The log files created by your software applications record site usage, operational events, and performance data, as well as errors and warnings. Log files store the history of events within a system, and are often the only way to detect and trace an intrusion by a hacker. You can use the data in log files to diagnose server problems, to track the number of users who visit your site so that you can plan for expansion, and to know which pages of your site are the most popular. You should capture and analyze log data on a regular basis to evaluate the health of your system.

Logs can contain vast amounts of data, so it is important to identify which information is valuable and configure the log files to record only that information. Some applications create a new log file at the beginning of each day. Other applications begin to delete older data or start a new log file when the logs reach a specified size.

It is also important to keep track of which log files contain what data, and where each log file is located, to facilitate analysis. Configure your system to maintain the log files that provide the information you need. Be sure to consider the size of the log files, and archive or delete them often enough to prevent the files from becoming too large. You should design a methodology for analyzing log file data that includes the following:

- A list of the log files to be analyzed

- The frequency of analysis

- The data to be analyzed

- A distribution list for the resulting reports

- A schedule for archiving report data and removing it from your site databases

Start by identifying which applications are necessary to site operation, and then gather the available log files from those applications and analyze their contents. Answers to the following questions will help you design your analysis methodology:

- What information do we want to analyze?

- Which log files contain that information?

- How large are the log files we want to analyze?

- How many log files does each server have?

- How many servers do we have?

- Where are the log files stored on each server?

- What reporting application can produce log file storage information?

- What input does the reporting application require to produce that information?

- What application should we use to transform the raw log file data into input for the reporting application?

- How often should we capture and analyze each log file?

You must decide whether you want to manage access to the data by having a central team create requested reports, or by having each interested team access the data and create their own reports. You must also decide how often to capture the log files, based on the nature and the volume of the data they contain.

For example, some log files contain data such as error messages and event notifications that is critical to preventing system failures. Analyzing this data after the system fails can provide clues to the reason for the failure. Access to this data at the time of the event or error might even help you prevent the system from failing.

You can use Commerce Server to import the contents of the Web log files into the Commerce Server Data Warehouse. Then you can use the Analysis modules in Commerce Server Business Desk to run reports. For more information, see "Business Desk Analysis" in Commerce Server 2000 Help.

In addition to your server log files, Commerce Server creates the following log files:

- Pup.log (created by Commerce Server Site Packager)

- Setup.log (created by Commerce Server Setup)

- Debug.log (records all actions for the Profile Designer module in Business Desk)

- Basket.log, Total.log, and Checkout.log (created each time a pipeline is used)

  Important You should use the pipeline log files (Basket.log, Total.log, and Checkout.log) only for debugging purposes. You should not use them in your production environment because they can significantly slow pipeline execution. In addition, they might log and expose sensitive information, such as credit card numbers. Because they are intended only for debugging purposes, they are not thread-safe.

E-mail messages sent out by Commerce Server Direct Mailer are logged in a file in the folder you specify in the Direct Mail Properties dialog box. Direct Mailer creates a new log file every day to log direct mail activities (service starts and stops, jobs processed, and so on). The default location for the Direct Mailer log files is c:\winnt\system32\logfiles\, but you can change that location, if necessary, using Commerce Server Manager.

You can use the advanced features of the Web log file import process to modify log file data to provide the information you want to analyze. To do this, you can set the following properties for the imported data:

- **Default files**. Identify different versions of the path into your Web site so that the hit counts for unique visitors to your site are accurate. For example, visitors entering your site using http://www.contoso.tld and http://www.contoso.tld/index.htm, should be counted as hits on the same page.

- **Excludes**. Prevent the following data from being imported into the Data Warehouse: hits from specific hosts, requests for specific file types or expressions, and hits by crawlers. For example, exclude hits on your Web site by users within your corporation from being counted.

- **Inferences**. Customize the assumptions made during import about users and visits.

- **Log Files**. Customize the response to time overlaps in log files.

- **Query strings**. Import Web site query strings, so that you can analyze the data associated with them.

For more information about setting these properties, see "Running the Data Warehouse" in Commerce Server 2000 Help.

Reports

After you import the Web log files into the Data Warehouse, you use the Analysis reports from Business Desk to analyze the data. When you design your analysis strategy, you need to know who will use the data and how they will use it. The following table lists the different ways in which team members might use log file data.

Group	Statistics analyzed	Purpose
Application developers	Application errors and warnings	• Monitor the health of the application • Identify and anticipate system failures
Marketing	Usage statistics	• Identify customer demographics • Determine how the site is used • Identify popular pages or content
Site architects	• Usage statistics • Performance statistics	Plan for expansion, better performance, and increased availability
Web designers	Usage statistics	Improve the user interface (UI) and site functionality

Commerce Server provides a variety of reports that show log file and Web site data in useful formats. For information about the reports shipped with Commerce Server, see "Business Desk Analysis" in the "Working with Business Desk" section in Commerce Server 2000 Help. For information about creating custom Commerce Server reports, see "Creating Custom Reports" in the "Extending Commerce Server" section in Commerce Server 2000 Help.

In general, you should create and use two types of reports:

- **Analytical reports**. To analyze the performance of your site and evaluate the success of marketing and content.

- **Error/warning reports**. To identify errors and failures occurring in the system.

When you create your reports strategy, you should use a tool to convert the data from your log files into useful information. The Data Warehouse performs the conversion as part of the log file import process. The process of converting the data is often referred to as *performing aggregations and summations*. This process changes raw data collected in the log files into useful information and provides some interpretation of the results.

For example, a Web server log file containing 1,000 separate hits for a page is imported into the Data Warehouse. In the Data Warehouse, the hits are totaled and the results are reported so that you know the page had a total of 1,000 hits.

Setting Up and Performing Operational Procedures

Site management includes the following:

- Continuous monitoring and routine administrative maintenance, including log file analysis and site backup

- Periodic administration, including upgrading hardware and software to improve performance, log archiving, and planning for expansion

- Contingency planning and management, including preparing for calamities such as power outages, earthquakes, fire damage, security breaches, hardware and software failures, and the loss of key personnel

If your goal is to have your Commerce Server site continuously available, you must monitor your site constantly for system failure and for events that necessitate immediate intervention. For more information about setting up operational procedures, see the chapters listed in the following table.

Chapter	Title	Description
5	Planning for Scalability	Various ways of scaling your site to increase site capacity
6	Planning for Reliability and High Availability	Various techniques for protecting your site from outages
14	Deploying Your Site	How to do contingency planning for your site
19	Maximizing Performance	How to monitor the performance of your system

Creating a Site Administration Plan

You should set up an administration plan in which you assign monitoring, analysis, and administrative responsibilities. For example, you might decide to form a technology team to respond to system errors and to improve site performance. Or, you might decide to form a marketing team to respond to customers and analyze site usage to improve the commercial success of your site.

Your site administration plan is based on your site development, testing, and contingency planning efforts, and should contain the sections listed in the following table.

Title	Contains procedures for
Site Administration	• Performing routine site maintenance and backups
	• Capturing and analyzing log files
	• Site monitoring and event notification
	• Data archiving and database management
Problem Management	Mitigating system hardware and software problems. For information about creating a problem management plan, see Chapter 18, "Problem Management."
System Monitoring	Monitoring the health of your system to alert you to system failures. For information about system monitoring, see "Monitoring System Health" in Chapter 18.
Site Documentation	Maintaining complete documentation for your site hardware, software, and content. For information about site documentation, see "Documenting Your Site" in Chapter 19, "Maximizing Performance."
Traffic Analysis	Analyzing site traffic, to get key information such as the number of users visiting your site concurrently. For information about analyzing site traffic, see "Analyzing Traffic" in Chapter 19.
Performance Measuring	Measuring site performance, to identify bottlenecks that indicate the need to increase the capacity of the software or hardware running your site. For information about measuring site performance, see "Measuring Performance" in Chapter 19.

Your site administration plan should answer the following questions:

- How should we respond when we receive an alert?

- Who is responsible for performing site backups and where should we store the media?

- What should we do if hardware fails?

- How can we ensure that site upgrades do not interrupt functionality?

- Are we hosting our site internally? If not, what does our hosting provider take care of?

- Which teams are responsible for what tasks?

- Where are the handover points between teams?

- How are we tracking changes?

- Who is updating site documentation and what should be documented?

- What is our procedure for documenting events and subsequent actions?

- What tools should we use to monitor, notify, track, and report events?

- What site data should we plan to analyze? How should we use the data?

- Do we have a plan for manual backup in case of system problems? (For example, if a server malfunctions while a customer is placing an order, do we provide a telephone number on the Web page so that the customer can call and speak to customer service to complete the order?)

You also need to consider whether to administer your site locally or remotely. If you are using a hosting provider, it is especially important to understand what administrative services the hosting provider will perform.

Your administration plan should also include growth and upgrade scenarios, maintenance schedules and procedures, and a schedule of daily, weekly, monthly, and as-needed activities for administering your site.

Creating and Performing Operational Procedures

You should create a schedule of daily, weekly, monthly, and as-needed activities for operating your site.

Daily activities might include the following:

- Check logs (server event logs, router logs, and firewall logs) and fix problems, as necessary

- Maintain accounts, directories, shares, and security groups

- Monitor Web traffic for indications of attacks and plug security holes

- Perform and verify backups

- Visually inspect indicator lights on servers and hubs

- Check available space on all servers

- Verify that all services on all servers are running

- Ensure that anti-virus software is up-to-date

- Monitor replication

- Monitor performance

- Monitor network traffic

- Check print queues

- Keep a maintenance log

- Monitor the load on the database server

Weekly activities might include the following:

- Clean servers

- Produce reports on the week's activity

- Update software, as necessary

- Audit the network for unauthorized changes

Monthly activities might include the following:

- Rebuild databases, if needed

- Produce reports on activity for the month

- Change passwords

- Manage off-site storage of backup media

- Perform a system vulnerability analysis

Initial or as-needed activities might include the following:

- Practice recovering from disaster

- Document the full network

- Rebuild corrupt servers

- Test the recovery procedure

- Get a performance baseline

The actions listed are just a starting point. There are many more actions you can add to these lists to ensure that your site operates at an optimal level.

Managing Security

Managing security includes activities designed to maintain, improve, and restore (when necessary) the security of your site. Security plays a critical role in the success of an online e-commerce site. You must be able to protect the interests and confidential information of both your business and your customers.

As part of managing security, you should:

- Monitor your site for security breaches and holes.

- Maintain the most current anti-virus protection.

- Constantly research industry security issues, product reviews, and threats.

In addition to monitoring for external threats, you must also guard against internal threats by controlling and monitoring the number of individuals inside your organization who have administrative permissions to your Web site servers. For more information about how to manage security, see *Designing Secure Web-Based Applications for Microsoft Windows 2000* by Michael Howard, located at http://mspress.microsoft.com/prod/books/4293.htm.

Managing Changes

You must create procedures for implementing requested features and changes on your site. You should always implement changes in a test environment and thoroughly test any changes you make before moving them to your production site. You should also update your site documentation with information about any changes you make. For more information about setting up a process for managing changes, see "Managing Change" in Chapter 8, "Developing Your Site."

Backing Up and Restoring Site Data

Your requirements for the availability of site data determine the content of your site backups. Performing a daily backup of your site is critical. For maximum security, store backups offsite in a secure fire- and water-proof environment. Your backup strategy should specify the following:

- Type and frequency of backups

- Hardware and software to use to perform backups

- Type of media to use for backups

- The frequency with which you should recycle the media

- Secure location (onsite and offsite) in which to store the backups

- A method for managing the security of the backup location

To ensure reliable recovery of your site in case of disaster, you must thoroughly test your backup and recovery procedures. Test different failure scenarios to be sure that you can recover quickly from different types and severities of failures.

To develop a successful backup and recovery plan, you must identify the data that is critical to your business and know the frequency with which it changes. Many of your decisions should be driven by data availability, the financial cost of your site being inaccessible, whether or not you can recreate lost data, the size and type of the data to be backed up, and the complexity of your site.

You also need to determine whether to perform full site backups or to back up site components individually. Assuming that you can re-create the architecture of your site, you should back up the following:

- Commerce Server databases, including the Administration database and the Data Warehouse

- All content, including Active Server Pages (ASP), dynamic-link library (DLL), Graphics Interchange Format (GIF), and Hypertext Markup Language (HTML) files

- Web site log files, especially if you are actively analyzing site traffic data

You should also back up metadata and registry information, and other site architecture and implementation information. The following practices can help you reduce the time it takes to recover your data after a disaster:

- Use archiving to reduce the size of your Commerce Server databases. Archiving enables you to retain historical data, yet clear space in your site databases.

- Use multiple backup devices simultaneously.

- Use a combination of full-database, differential-database, and transaction-log backups to minimize the number of backups that must be applied at the point of failure.

- Use file and file-group backups and transaction log backups. Back up only those files that contain relevant data.

- Use snapshot backups to minimize or eliminate the use of server resources in the backup process. (Snapshot backups require third-party hardware and software.)

For more information about these practices, see "Backing Up and Restoring Databases" and "Archiving and Restoring Databases" in SQL Server Books Online.

For more information about tools and techniques for backing up and restoring Commerce Server, see "Backing Up and Restoring Commerce Server" and "Backing Up and Restoring a SQL Server Database" in Commerce Server 2000 Help. Also, see "Backing Up Your Site" in Chapter 14, "Deploying Your Site."

Problem Management

This chapter describes how to manage problems with your Microsoft Commerce Server 2000 site. Problem management is the process of reducing business losses resulting from a service outage. It is also the process you use to deal with a situation that causes or threatens to cause a break in service. You should design your problem management process to minimize the impact of incidents and problems, as well as to collect information that can help correct the underlying causes.

The following terms are key to understanding the components of problem management:

- **Incident**. An event that is not part of the normal operation of a system.

- **Problem**. A significant incident or group of incidents that exhibit common symptoms for which the cause is unknown.

- **Known error**. A known fault in a configuration item (CI). For more information about CIs, see Chapter 8, "Developing Your Site."

Technical problems are a part of every site, so it is important to allocate sufficient resources to handle them efficiently. An effective problem management process will save you both time and money.

Problem management focuses on the following:

- Incident control

- Problem control

- System health

Incident Control

Incident control is the process of identifying, recording, classifying, and tracking incidents until the affected services are corrected and return to normal operation. The incident management team, which should include the help desk or product support personnel and the initial response team, owns the incident control process. Incidents should be escalated to bring in additional expertise when team members can't restore normal service rapidly or when they can't identify the cause of the problem. Figure 18.1 shows a typical incident control process.

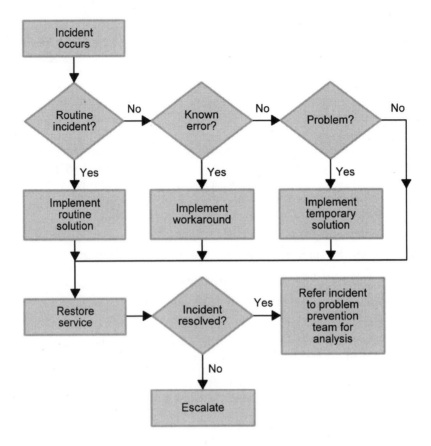

Figure 18.1 Incident control process

The incident management team resolves issues identified by user requests to the help desk, issues raised by event logs, and issues discovered through other internal processes. The incident management team should record all incidents in an incident database, which should contain information about incidents, changes, configuration management, and problem management. If you use different databases for managing site configuration, tracking changes, and tracking problems, be sure that the records for each incident are linked to the other databases so you can easily track the different aspects of an incident. Ideally, you should store incident information in the Configuration Management database, in which you also store information about requests for changes, and so on. For more information about the Configuration Management database, see Chapter 8, "Developing Your Site."

You should classify incidents by severity and priority. Figure 18.2 shows a sample classification grid, in which 1 is the highest priority and 7 is the lowest.

Severity

	Critical	Urgent	Important	Monitor
Monitor	4	5	6	7
Important	3	4	5	6
Urgent	2	3	4	5
Critical	1	2	3	4

Priority

Figure 18.2 Sample incident-classification grid

A classification grid can help you to set priorities and expectations, and to facilitate cooperation between technical teams. Classification systems do not need to be complex. The following table shows a typical classification system.

Classification	Impact	Commitment level
Critical	Server down, loss of business	24 hours and seven days a week – total resource and commitment level to problem resolution
Urgent	Production severely impaired, but system still operational	High resource and commitment level to problem resolution
Important	Important problem	Commitment to resolution
Monitor	Under surveillance	No action items

When you have set up a classification system, technical and operational teams can use it to agree on action paths, response times, and the ways in which each type of issue can take priority in their schedules.

Classification systems promote cooperation between teams because each team understands the potential impact and expected commitment level. Classification also creates a metric that can be used to track the potential impact of problems, and that can be useful for future planning and quality control.

Problem Control

Problem control is the process of identifying, recording, classifying, investigating, and tracking problems until a problem is solved or until it is assigned a "known error" status. The problem management team's mission is to identify the cause of problems and to help restore normal service as quickly as possible. After the cause of a problem is identified, the problem can be classified as a known error. The problem management team then works with the change management team to coordinate fixes for known errors. For more information about the change management process, see Chapter 8, "Developing Your Site."

The problem management team identifies problems in two ways:

- Through immediate investigation of a significant first incident

- Through incident logs for multiple incidents with similar symptoms

When a problem is identified, the problem management team should create a record in the Problem Management database that contains a list of incidents relating to the problem, as well as updates. The problem management team should then refer the problem to the appropriate technical specialists for analysis. After the specialists determine the cause of the problem, they can reclassify it as a known error.

Isolating the Problem

The first step in solving a problem is to create a reproducible scenario to isolate the problem. Few problems are difficult to solve once you know exactly what is going wrong. The difficulty with isolating a problem is that isolation is more of an art than a science. The approach you use to identify a problem can largely depend on the specifics of your system or application.

When you try to isolate a problem, you might have to stress your system or alter configuration settings to duplicate the conditions that caused the problem. You should do this in your test environment, not in your production environment. If a problem occurs only in your production environment, however, there are techniques and tools that you can use to make troubleshooting easier.

One of the most common approaches to troubleshooting a problem in a production environment is to use load balancing. In a typical load-balanced system, a number of servers are placed online and accessed through software that evenly distributes client requests across the server farm. In a load-balanced environment, you can usually take a failing server offline without affecting the other servers in the server farm. The remaining servers can then absorb the production load so that there is no interruption in service. After a server is offline, you can troubleshoot and fix it without impacting the other servers.

The following table lists some effective troubleshooting approaches.

Troubleshooting approach	Description
Simplify	The simpler your application, the less it will cost to support and maintain it.
	If a complex system is failing and you don't have enough diagnostic information to isolate the problem, try eliminating areas until you end up with a small, reproducible failure. Use the process of elimination to rule out as many technologies and dependencies as possible.
Add troubleshooting flags	If a failure is occurring somewhere in your code, add troubleshooting flags to trace and record successes, failures, starts, finishes, and so on.
Be systematic	Successful troubleshooting is mostly a systematic process of elimination. Create a list of the most probable causes of a problem, and then systematically eliminate each one until you find the cause of the problem. Keep lists of theories, isolation steps, and results so that you can share what you have already done with others working on the problem.
Use action plans	Use a written action plan to define the problem, detail the problem status, and designate action items.
Keep a clear perspective	If you seem to hit a dead end, take a break. Sometimes it's helpful to bring in someone new to get a fresh perspective on the problem.
Use a consistent development methodology	The best way to minimize the need for troubleshooting and increase support efficiency is to develop consistent practices as part of your development cycle. Time and effort spent improving your testing process, architectural design, monitoring, and diagnostic systems will help minimize troubleshooting efforts.

Using Historical Performance Data

Records of historical performance that you capture in event logs can help you troubleshoot some types of problems. It is also useful to have the baseline logs from any quality control or stress tests. You should archive System Monitor and event logs on a regular basis. If a production server starts having problems, you can then study the previous performance and event data of the server for possible clues to the cause of the problems. The cumulative production data that this type of regular archive provides is also useful for identifying growth trends that might indicate the need for additional hardware or resources.

System Health

There are a number of software products that you can use to monitor server performance to be sure that your system is performing as expected. These products perform many tasks, from measuring the total response time of a Web page request to monitoring user-defined performance counters for alert thresholds. Most of these products can be configured to notify administrators by pager or e-mail when a failure occurs.

When you have monitoring processes in place and decide which counters to use to track system performance, you should set performance goals for each operation so that you have benchmarks of satisfactory system performance to use as a basis for comparison. For information about setting and tracking performance goals for your Commerce Server site, see Chapter 19, "Maximizing Performance."

There are a number of different types of system failures:

- Response failures
- Errors and access violations
- Memory and resource leaks
- Security failures
- Queuing
- CPU saturation
- Corruption

Response Failures

When the program fails to respond, it is often because the CPU is at 100 percent utilization or because a process has become unresponsive. If the CPU is at maximum utilization (100 percent) for any length of time, a process is often executing what is known as a *spinning thread*, an endless loop in the code that leaves a thread executing and consuming CPU cycles. If a process becomes unresponsive, a thread has usually entered a state in which it is waiting for a resource that never becomes available.

In both cases, you should focus on isolating the path of code execution leading up to the failure. If this path points to an obvious section of code, you can identify and fix the problem. If no code path is apparent or the failure occurs in third-party components, you can use a tool like UserDump (contained in the Microsoft Windows 2000 Driver Development Kit) to create a process snapshot of all executing threads. You can use UserDump with the appropriate symbols and performance monitor log to identify what each thread was executing when it failed.

Errors and Access Violations

One characteristic of errors and access violations is that the executing process often just stops. The type of notification you receive when an error occurs depends on how errors are handled within the application. You might see a very detailed "Access Violation" message with addresses and numbers, or you might not see anything. When access violations occur inside COM+ server packages, the system restarts the process and logs an event in the event log. If an error or access violation occurs in Internet Information Services (IIS) 5.0, then the system often stops serving Active Server Pages (ASP) and reports various ASP failures.

You should focus on change control and process isolation to correct errors and access violations. These types of failures often occur after system updates when unreliable components have been introduced. You might separate process components into individual COM+ packages to isolate them. You can also use tools like IIS Exception Monitor and UserDump to monitor for and detect both of these types of failures.

Memory and Resource Leaks

You can often identify memory and resource leaks through standard System Monitor counters, such as Private Bytes. If necessary, you can also use COM+ packages to separate components, to help you identify which component is leaking resources. There are also numerous development and troubleshooting tools that can help you track and identify memory and resource leaks. For more information, see the "Additional Resources" section at the end of the book.

Security Failures

You can usually identify a security failure if an operation consistently fails for a specific user but works for other users who are logged on with Administrative rights. Keep in mind that some environments will access resources under different security contexts, depending on the configuration. This is especially true for IIS and COM+. You can configure operations to run under a static user account or under the account of the active user. You can change how IIS accesses resources, depending on how a client is authenticated. Take the time to understand security implications for these environments and always test a consistently failing operation as a system administrator to rule out a security configuration issue.

Queuing

Queuing is commonly associated with IIS, but the concept applies to many different environments. Most high-transaction systems employ some kind of thread pool that services client requests. When all threads are busy serving clients, requests are typically queued until a free thread becomes available or requests are serialized on a single thread. The most common characteristic of a problem with a queue is a slow or unresponsive server. For ASP, you might see a "Server Too Busy" message if there is a problem, but for an Internet Server Application

Programming Interface (ISAPI), the server might fail to respond with any error message. However, in both cases, the system will recover if you remove client load from the server.

You can easily identify issues with IIS queuing through System Monitor counters (such as Active Server Pages, Requests Queued, and Requests Executing counters). Keep in mind that the ASP default thread queue is 25 threads per processor on IIS 5.0. When all 25 threads become busy, requests start queuing and IIS sends the "Server Too Busy" message. ISAPI does not use the ASP thread pool directly and, unless you implement a custom pool, it will reach its maximum number of requests at 256 concurrent requests.

Protect your thread pool by writing efficient code for common requests. It takes only one slow page to exhaust your thread queue in a high-traffic environment.

CPU Saturation

You typically identify CPU saturation through System Monitor or Task Manager. You can use either tool to find out when a system is under high CPU stress. When CPU levels consistently exceed 80 percent, you should increase the number of CPUs or the amount of processing power. When you troubleshoot CPU utilization, you should focus on the process that is consuming the most CPU time. On a well-optimized multiprocessor system, CPU load should be evenly distributed.

Watch for processes that are using excessive CPU time or that have a high number of threads, which could cause excessive context switching. One common misconception is that more processors and more threads mean better performance. In some situations, more CPUs and threads can actually decrease performance. Also remember that threads can become blocked on shared resources (shared data, default heap allocations, and so on) and that this type of software bottleneck limits the effectiveness of additional hardware. Stress testing, effective architecture, and code optimization are the best approaches to keeping CPU utilization down.

Corruption

Corruption is an extremely difficult problem to isolate. Corruption typically occurs from a boundary overwrite in memory. In many cases, it is the process heap that becomes contaminated. This type of problem often occurs without warning. As a result, you can end up chasing the effect of the problem, rather than the problem itself. The characteristics of corruption are generally random access violations or corrupt data.

If your memory is corrupted, you should focus on isolating components through COM+ or, in some cases, the use of a boundary-checking tool, heap checking API functions, or a small reproducible scenario that you can examine in a test environment.

Troubleshooting Your Commerce Server System

You should monitor your system logs on a regular basis to help avoid catastrophic failures and to enable you to respond to unexpected increases in server activity on a timely basis. Use a separate server that is not part of the run-time services to monitor your production servers. You don't want the process of monitoring to affect the performance or operation of your production server. Also, if you use a separate server, you will get a more accurate measurement of the true performance of your production servers.

The following list provides some tips for effectively monitoring and troubleshooting your Commerce Server system:

- At least twice a day, you should use Event Viewer to review event activity and then inform the appropriate personnel about any anomalies.

- At least once a week, you should analyze your IIS logs for changes in user-access trends and to be sure that site traffic is within your system specifications. You might also want to reconfigure your Web pages or product offerings, based on the trend analysis.

- Back up and truncate your database logs on a regular schedule. You should copy database logs to an external backup device, such as a tape drive, before deleting them. Retain logs over extended periods of time.

- Enlist help from an external analysis agent to monitor the page latency of your site from many remote locations.

- Configure Performance Logs and Alerts to report data for the recommended counters at regular intervals, such as every 10 to 15 minutes.

When a problem occurs in your production environment, it is important to get as much diagnostic information as possible during the failure. At a minimum, always capture the following information:

- Complete System Monitor logs (all counters)

- UserDump snapshot or Exception Monitor log of the failing process

- IIS log files

- Event logs

- Any custom diagnostic output from your application components

Note that for a UserDump snapshot to provide useful information about your custom components, matching program database files (source debugging information) must be available. They do not have to be on the failing server, but they should be accessible to anyone who is analyzing the resulting UserDump logs. In order to obtain meaningful results from Exception Monitor, you must have Exception Monitor symbols installed on the production server prior to the failure.

The following table lists tools that are available with Windows 2000 Server to help you monitor and troubleshoot your system.

Tool	Description
ClusterSentinel	Integrates with Network Load Balancing (NLB) clustering technology to monitor the health of servers and determine whether the server is available.
HTTP Monitoring tool	Gathers large amounts of data about a Web site, enabling immediate monitoring of Web server(s).
Microsoft Cluster Tool	Backs up and restores a cluster configuration, and moves resources to a cluster.
Web Application Stress (WAS) tool	Simulates Web activity to enable you to evaluate the performance of your Web application, server, or network. With this tool, you can simulate a wide variety of workload scenarios to help determine the optimal configuration for your server.
Web Capacity Analysis Tool (WCAT)	Evaluates how Internet servers running Windows 2000 Server and IIS respond to various client workload simulations.
WinRep Deployment Software Development Kit	Collects information about client computers that you can use to diagnose and troubleshoot problems.

Maximizing Performance

No company wants its customers to have poor experiences when they visit its Web site. Customers can become frustrated by slow response times, timeouts, and errors or broken links, prompting them to go to other sites to find what they're looking for. To keep customers interested, you must build an infrastructure that can handle not only average levels of demand but peak levels as well.

The success of your site depends heavily on how well you plan for capacity and manage site performance. To ensure adequate capacity, you must calculate how much computing hardware you need to handle the load that thousands or hundreds of thousands of users can put on your site. These calculations can help you find weak areas that can cause performance degradation. You can resolve weak areas by adding hardware or by redesigning dynamic pages or other CPU-intensive tools.

Good capacity planning can also help you decide how widely to advertise your site to attract more customers, as well as help you plan future infrastructure improvements to adequately handle growth. Realizing your site's full potential depends largely on satisfying the demands of your customers, which means providing:

- Quality of service

- Quality of content

- Speedy access

Capacity planning is the process of measuring a Web site's ability to serve content to its visitors at an acceptable speed. You determine capacity by measuring the number of visitors to your site, determining how much demand each visitor places on the server, and then calculating the computing resources (CPU, RAM, disk space, and network bandwidth) necessary to support current and future usage levels.

The following table lists three factors that determine site capacity.

Factor	Description
Number of visitors	As your site attracts more visitors, you must increase capacity or performance will degrade.
Server capacity and configuration of hardware and software	Upgrading your computing infrastructure can increase site capacity, thereby allowing more visitors, more complex content, or a combination of the two.
Site content	As the content becomes more complex, the servers have to do more work per visitor, thereby lowering site capacity. Sometimes you can increase capacity by simplifying content, minimizing database use and dynamic content, and using simpler HTML pages.

Capacity planning should be an ongoing concern for any Web site. Whenever any one of the three factors changes significantly, you must recalculate site capacity. Capacity can be expressed as the following equation:

```
Number of concurrent users = Hardware capacity / Load on hardware per user
```

(In this equation, `hardware capacity` refers to both server and network capacity.)

This capacity equation suggests two corollaries:

- Decreasing the load that each user puts on the hardware by planning, programming, and configuring site content to make more efficient use of computing resources can enable you to increase the number of concurrent users.

- Configuring the site infrastructure to increase hardware capacity can enable you to increase the number of concurrent users. You can increase hardware capacity by scaling the hardware horizontally (adding more servers) or vertically (upgrading existing servers).

When you study capacity, you should address the following areas:

- Number of concurrent users supported by the current hardware

- Scalability options if the number of concurrent users increases

- Scalability options if site content becomes more complex

- Potential bottlenecks in the system

- Performance guidelines for programmers and other content developers

- Site performance predictions

Logically, managing site performance correlates very closely with planning site capacity. You manage site performance to tune your site so that you can support more visitors. To properly manage performance, you must continuously evaluate your site to see whether or not it is delivering the level of performance you want, and then if it does not, tune it until it does. To tune your site, you need to evaluate its architecture and the code in the Active Server

Pages (ASP), and then investigate available technologies to see what you can use to enhance performance. You must also make sure that the infrastructure of your site (hardware and software) can support the number of concurrent users to your site with an acceptable response time. Maximizing performance is especially important to e-commerce sites because the number of visitors, as well as the content of the site, can change over a short period of time.

Transaction Cost Analysis

One method of measuring site capacity is called transaction cost analysis (TCA). TCA is a method of measuring the performance cost of a transaction. TCA helps you compare server transactions with one another to determine which ones are putting the greatest demands on your system.

The term *transaction* (also called *operation*) refers to work done by a server or servers (Web servers, middle-tier servers, and Microsoft SQL Server servers) to fulfill a user request. For example, a request for a product description page stored in a database is a transaction, as is a request to add an item to a shopping basket. This term does not refer to e-commerce transactions in which money is exchanged.

Dynamic sites that involve database transactions tend to be more complex and place heavier demands on Web servers than static sites that usually serve only static HTML pages. Customers of dynamic sites typically use the sites not only to look up information already stored at the site, but also to add new information of their own.

TCA can help you answer the following questions:

- What hardware do we need?

- How many concurrent users can our site serve?

- When do we need to add servers?

- Can our site handle peak traffic (such as Back-to-School, holidays, and so on)?

- Where are the bottlenecks in our site?

Documenting Your Site

The first step in performing TCA is to document your site hardware, software, and content. These diagrams can help highlight data center issues, and are very helpful for visualizing traffic flow through your system.

Figure 19.1 shows the type of hardware diagram you should create.

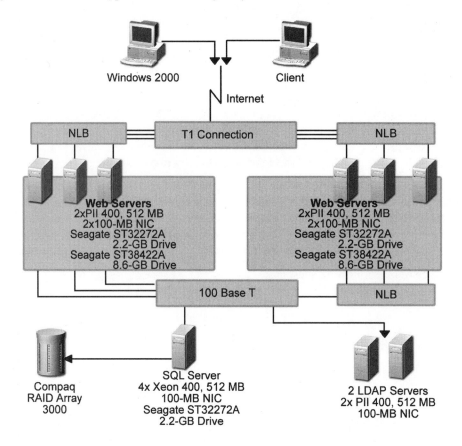

Figure 19.1 Sample hardware diagram

Figure 19.2 shows the type of software diagram you should create to help you understand any site software issues and to see how the software is interrelated.

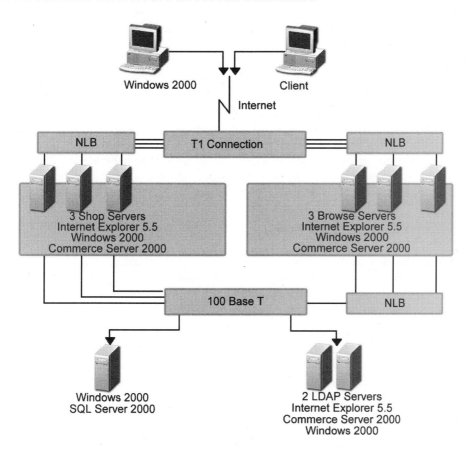

Figure 19.2 Sample software diagram

To document site content, record the following information for each server:

- Server type (Web, database, and so on)
- Description of the content on the server
- Directory structure
- File permissions

Analyzing Traffic

Next, you must determine how many users typically visit the site concurrently. This data usually comes from:

- **Market analysis**. Analysis of a new site. You have probably commissioned a market analysis report to predict how much traffic your site can expect to receive at the time it is deployed and afterward. Use this report as the basis for your TCA.

- **Site usage analysis**. Analysis of an existing site. Analyze your Web server log files to see how many hits your site receives at any given time, as well as usage trends that might indicate whether parts of the site have become more or less popular over time. When calculating how many concurrent users your site currently supports, remember to base your calculations on peak usage, rather than on average usage. Commerce Server provides Web usage and diagnostic reports for analyzing Web site usage.

Creating a Site Usage Profile

After you know how many customers are visiting your site, you must then determine how they use it so that you can estimate how much demand a typical customer places on the system. A usage profile describes the way in which customers use a site by determining site traffic patterns, such as how many customers browse a certain page and how many add an item to their basket and then remove it.

To create a usage profile, you need to analyze your site's usage log files. If you have them, use logs gathered over a long period of time (at least a week) to get accurate averages. First, identify operations that customers can do (browse, search, and so on). Next, gather the following data:

- Number of customers visiting the site

- Number of hits each page receives (which pages have been visited)

- Time spent on each page

- Session length

- Peak periods of activity

You can use the number of visits to each page to profile typical shopper operations for the site. The following table shows a usage profile with typical shopper operations for an e-commerce retailer.

Shopper operation	Operations per session	Operations per second (transaction frequency)	Percentage of total
Add Item	0.24	0.00033	2.00
Add Item + Checkout	0.02	0.00003	0.17
Add Item + Delete	0.04	0.00006	0.33
Basket	0.75	0.00104	6.25
Default (home page)	1.00	0.00139	8.33
Listing	2.50	0.00347	20.83
Lookup	0.75	0.00104	6.25
New	0.25	0.00035	2.08
Product	4.20	0.00583	35.00
Search	1.25	0.00174	10.42
Welcome	1.00	0.00139	8.33

This table shows the shopper operations that account for 90 percent of the hits received by the site in this example. As a rule, you should generate a usage profile that lists the pages or operations responsible for 90 percent of the total hit count of your site. Note that files such as images are not included in this table, for simplicity; if image and static HTML file requests contribute to the top 90 percent of the hits received by your site, be sure to include them in your usage profile.

Defining Acceptable Operating Parameters

The primary benchmark for determining whether a Web site is operating at an acceptable level is *latency*, or how long a user must wait for a page to load after a request has been made. Note that although some servers can handle every request they receive, the load might create unacceptable response times, requiring a better solution if the site is to operate efficiently and at an acceptable level of service. In general, static content like HTML pages and graphics do not contribute to server latency as much as dynamic content like ASPs or other content that requires database lookups. Even when a Web server can deliver a large number of ASPs per second, the turnaround time per ASP can be unacceptable.

In general, reasonable user latency is as follows:

- Home page: 1 second

- Catalog page: 3 to 7 seconds

- Credit card verification: 15 to 30 seconds

Figure 19.3 illustrates the latency experienced by users of a four-processor Web server as the number of users and ASP requests increases.

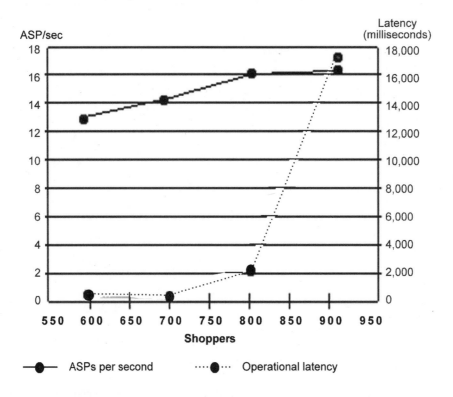

Figure 19.3 ASP requests per second versus latency

The capacity of the site in this example is between 700 and 800 concurrent users per second. The latency rises to unacceptable levels when the number of users exceeds 800. This server's performance peaks at just over 16 ASP requests per second. At that point, users are waiting approximately 16 seconds for their pages, due to extensive context switching.

When you compile a list of shopper operations by viewing Internet Information Services (IIS) 5.0 logs or usage analysis reports, it is important to recognize that one shopper operation can be composed of multiple ASP requests, which the log lists as separate entries. For example, the log might list five separate shopper operations needed to complete a purchase, as shown in Figure 19.4.

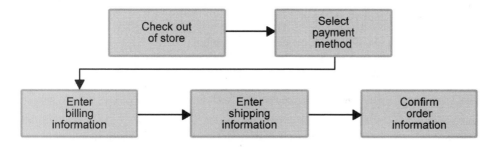

Figure 19.4 Shopper operations needed to complete a purchase

A shopper operation can also generate more than one ASP request. Figure 19.5 shows that adding a product to the shopping basket generates two ASP requests. The first ASP processes the add request, and the second ASP displays the contents of the shopping basket. The first ASP calls the second ASP, using a **Server.Transfer** command.

Figure 19.5 ASP requests for adding a product to the shopping basket

If you want to convert a list of the most commonly performed ASP requests into a list of the most commonly performed shopper operations, you need to do some investigation. ASP requests are recorded in IIS log files and can be used to identify shopper operations. By looking at the log files after completing an operation, you can find the related requests.

Calculating Cost per User

You can use TCA to calculate the processing cost for each concurrent user. You measure cost by creating a load-monitoring script to calculate each of the identified shopper operations. You can then measure the resource utilization level at that specific load level. Or, instead of creating your own script, you can use the Microsoft Web Application Stress (WAS) tool to monitor load. (For more information about creating scripts and using WAS, see http://webtool.rte.microsoft.com/.)

The objective of running a script exclusively for an individual operation is to load the IIS/ASP server with as many requests as possible, in order to achieve optimal ASP throughput per second. Optimal ASP throughput occurs when you measure a drop in ASP throughput with a higher shopper load or when you measure a sudden increase in operation latency or ASP requests queued.

WAS can be integrated with System Monitor to simplify test data collection by simply adding the following counters:

- Active Server Pages: Requests per second

- System: % Processor Time

The following table provides a list of important counters to monitor.

Counter	Measures
Active Server Pages: Request wait time	Length of time that requests wait to be processed. This should be very close to zero.
Active Server Pages: Requests executing	Number of requests executing simultaneously. There should be only one request executing at a time.
Active Server Pages: Requests per second	Rate at which the ASPs are processing requests.
Active Server Pages: Requests queued	Number of requests waiting for service from the queue. If the number fluctuates considerably during stress and processor utilization remains relatively low, this could be an indication that the script is calling a Component Object Model (COM) object that is receiving more calls than it can handle.
CS2000: AuthManager: AuthMgr Objects/sec	Number of Authentication Manager objects created per second. It is useful to track this number because object creations are costly in terms of performance.
CS2000: Catalog: Catalog Queries per second	Number of queries made to the catalog system per second. The catalog query rate is the uncached rate. If this rate is high, you should change the application code to take advantage of a local caching mechanism, such as the **LRUCache** object.
CS2000: UPM: No. of Cache Purges	Number of times the foreground thread purged entries from the profile object cache to search for a free block of memory. If this rate is greater than zero, you should increase the amount of space allocated in the Global.asa file.
Memory: Available bytes	Total physical memory available to the operating system. This amount of available memory is compared with the memory required to run all of the processes and applications on your server.
	Try to keep at least 10 percent of memory available for peak use. Keep in mind that, by default, IIS 5.0 uses up to 50 percent of available memory for its file cache, leaving the rest of the memory available for other applications running on the server.

Counter	Measures
Memory: Page faults per second	Memory bottleneck due to page faults. If a process requests a page in memory and the system cannot find it at the requested location, this constitutes a page fault. If the page is elsewhere in memory, it is called a soft page fault. If the page must be retrieved from disk, it is called a hard page fault.
	Most processors can handle large numbers of soft page faults without consequence, but hard page faults can cause significant delays. If the number of hard page faults is high, you might have dedicated too much memory to the caches, not leaving enough memory for the rest of the system.
	Sustained hard page fault rates of over five per second are a key indicator of not having enough RAM. Try increasing the amount of RAM on your server or lowering cache sizes. Other counters that can indicate a memory bottleneck are Memory:Pages input/sec, Memory:Page Reads/sec, and Memory:Pages per second.
Memory: Pages per second	Number of pages retrieved per second. The number should be less than one per second.
Network Segment: Bytes received per second	Number of bytes received per second in a network segment. If a network card approaches its maximum capacity, add another.
Physical Disk: Avg. Disk Queue Length	Average disk queue length. If the disk is not fast enough to keep up with read and write requests, requests will queue up. Acceptable queue length is a function of the number of spindles in the array.
	Other counters that can be used to observe disk traffic include Physical Disk: Disk Reads/second and Physical Disk: Disk Writes/second. If necessary, consider adding more physical drives, such as a Redundant Array of Inexpensive Disks (RAID) system, to increase the number of spindles that can read and write, as well as to increase data transfer rates.
Physical Disk: Disk Reads/second Physical Disk: Disk Writes/second	Number of disk reads and writes per second on the physical disk. Combined, these two counters should be well under the maximum capacity for the disk device. To enable this counter, run **diskperf –y** from the command shell and reboot the computer.
Physical Disk: % Disk Time	Percentage of elapsed time that the selected disk drive is busy servicing read or write requests. Together with the Physical Disk: Avg. Disk Queue Length counter, this is a key indicator of a disk drive bottleneck. Note that the percentages for this counter can vary, depending on which storage solution you use. See the documentation for your storage solution for more information.
Process: Inetinfo: Private bytes	Current number of bytes this process has allocated that cannot be shared with other processes. If system performance is degrading over time, this counter can be a good indicator of memory leaks.

Counter	Measures
Process: Thread Count: dllhost	Number of threads created by the pooled out-of-process application (the most recent value).
Process: Thread Count: dllhost#1, #2, U, #N	Number of threads created by the isolated out-of-process application (the most recent value).
Process: Thread Count: Inetinfo	Number of threads created by the process you're monitoring (the most recent value).
SQL Server: Cache Hit Ratio	Percentage of time that SQL Server finds data in its cache, rather than having to go to disk. To give SQL Server more RAM, use the **sp_configure** stored procedure or the SQL Server Enterprise Manager (Sqlew.exe).
SQL Server: I/O transactions/sec	Amount of activity the SQL Server actually performs.
SQL Server - Locks: Total Blocking Locks	Number of blocking locks. A high blocking lock count can indicate a database problem.
System: Context Switches/sec	Context switches per second. If this number is too high, add another system.
System: % Processor Time	Percentage of time that processors are working. When this counter is running consistently between 80 and 100 percent, it is a key indicator of a CPU bottleneck.
System: Processor Queue Length	Instantaneous count (not an average) of the number of threads waiting in the queue shared by all processors in the system. A sustained value of two or more threads indicates a processor bottleneck.
Thread: Context Switches: sec: Inetinfo =>Thread#	Maximum number of threads per processor, or thread pool. Monitor this counter to make sure you are not creating so many context switches that the memory you are losing negates the benefit of added threads. At that point, your performance will decrease rather than improve. Anything over 5,000 context switches per second per server is probably excessive.
Thread: % Processor Time: Inetinfo =>Thread #	Amount of processor time each thread of the Inetinfo process uses.
Web: Total connections	Number of users.

Calculating Cost per User for CPUs

You must measure hardware capacity on all types of servers in your system if you want an accurate picture of your cost per user. To calculate the performance cost per user for a CPU, use a tool like WAS to simulate a load on the server. Increasing the number of simulated users increases the load. In turn, increasing the number of threads increases the number of simulated users. These threads will be spread among the client servers configured in WAS.

If the number of threads becomes too much for the clients to handle (for example, if you specify 200 threads, but have only five client computers), change the number of sockets per thread. For example, 40 threads at five sockets per thread have the same effect as 200 threads. This will simulate 200 concurrent users.

ASP requests per second and CPU use grow with the number of users. However, when CPU use reaches 100 percent, adding more users results in lower ASP requests per second. Therefore, the number of ASP requests processed per second at the point at which CPU use reaches 100 percent is the maximum number of ASP requests your site can handle.

Before you can calculate the cost of a shopper operation, you must know the number of ASP pages used in the operation. For example, checkout operations typically involve several ASP pages, such as a shopper information page, credit card page, shipping page, confirmation page, and so on. Remember to account for ASP pages that users never see, such as action pages, because they are usually posted to and redirected to a continuing page. Make sure to include these "hidden" pages in the WAS script for that operation, or simply use RECORD mode in WAS to record these pages.

You calculate the cost of a shopper operation by multiplying the number of ASP pages by the cost per ASP page. This calculation is based on megacycles (Mcycles). The Mcycle is a unit of processor work. One Mcycle is equal to one million CPU cycles. As a unit of measure, the Mcycle is useful for comparing performance between processors because it is hardware-independent.

Note The following examples illustrate tests run on a dual-processor server. Adding processors changes the way threading and context switching is handled. For this reason, the results of these equations, such as 0.5624 for the *CPU Cost per User* equation and the *Upper CPU Boundary* equation can change if you add processors.

Do not extrapolate the numbers in these examples to predict how a quad-processor system would perform. Different applications scale differently across multiple processors, so these numbers cannot be re-used for other applications and/or other system configurations.

For example, a dual-processor 400 MHz Xeon Pentium II has a total capacity of 800 Mcycles. Using the maximum number of ASP requests per second, you can calculate the cost per ASP request (operation), as follows:

```
C = U × N × S / A × B
```

Where:

```
C = Cost per operation (cost for all files in the WAS script)
U = CPU utilization (by percentage)
N = Number of CPUs
S = Speed of CPU (in MHz)
A = ASP requests per second
B = ASP requests per operation
```

For example, if you have a server with two CPUs, and if the browse operation results in 11.50 ASP requests per second with CPU utilization of 84.10 percent, the cost per ASP page is then 84.10% × 2 × 400 / 11.50 = 58.50 Mcycles.

The result of TCA measurement is a set of CPU costs for each shopper operation, as shown in the following table.

Shopper operation	Optimum ASP throughput (ASP requests per second)	Percentage of CPU (at optimum ASP throughput)	CPU cost per ASP (Mcycles)	ASP requests per operation	CPU cost per operation (Mcycles)
Add Item	23.31	96.98	33.29	2	66.57
Add Item + Checkout	18.48	94.31	40.82	7	285.74
Add Item + Delete	22.29	95.86	34.40	4	137.61
Basket	16.81	91.73	43.64	1	43.64
Default (home page)	102.22	98.01	7.67	1	7.67
Listing	21.49	91.87	34.21	1	34.21
Lookup	75.40	99.52	10.56	2	21.12
New	65.78	96.61	11.75	2	23.50
Product	18.23	94.81	41.61	1	41.61
Search	37.95	95.11	20.05	2	40.10
Welcome	148.93	96.97	5.21	1	5.21

After you have the CPU cost for each operation, you must calculate how often these operations are performed. You can derive this from a typical usage profile to get the CPU cost per user.

You can calculate CPU usage for each shopper operation by multiplying the CPU cost per operation by transaction frequency in operations per second. The result is the CPU usage (in MHz) for each shopper operation:

```
CPU usage = (CPU cost per operation) X (operations per second)
```

The following table shows sample results from this calculation.

Shopper operation	CPU cost per operation (Mcycles)	Operations per second	CPU usage (Mcycles)
Add Item	66.57	0.00033	0.0222
Add Item + Checkout	285.74	0.00003	0.0079
Add Item + Delete	137.61	0.00006	0.0076
Basket	43.64	0.00104	0.0455
Default (home page)	7.67	0.00139	0.0107
Listing	34.21	0.00347	0.1188
Lookup	21.12	0.00104	0.0220
New	23.50	0.00035	0.0082
Product	41.61	0.00583	0.2427
Search	40.10	0.00174	0.0696
Welcome	5.21	0.00139	0.0072
Average CPU usage per shopper (Mcycles)			0.5624

The total (0.5624 Mcycles per user) is the performance cost of an average user performing the shopper operations described in the usage profile. You can use this number to estimate the capacity of your site, based on the assumed usage profile. For example, the cost of 100 concurrent users is $100 \times 0.5624 = 56.24$ Mcycles.

The Product operation has a relatively high cost, at 41.61 Mcycles. The frequency of the Product operation is very high, at 0.00583, so the Product operation places a large load on the site. The cost of the Product operation per shopper operation shows a high number of 0.2427 Mcycles out of 0.5624 Mcycles (approximately 43 percent of the cost of the entire usage profile).

The Listing operation shows a moderate cost, at 34.21 Mcycles.

The Add Item + Checkout operation shows a heavy cost, at 285.74 Mcycles. However, because its frequency is so low (0.00003), it places a small load (0.0079 Mcycles) on the site. This is only approximately 1 percent of the cost of the entire usage profile. Therefore, although classified as a "heavy" operation, the Add Item + Checkout operation places a relatively light load on the server.

Thus, the numbers for this example suggest that it would be best to start optimizing performance with the Product and Listing operations to improve capacity.

The sum of the CPU usage for each shopper operation in a single session is equal to the average CPU usage per user. This makes it possible to calculate CPU usage for any given number of users using the following equation:

```
C = Min [(N × K), M]
```

Where:

```
C   = CPU usage (in MHz)
Min = Minimum value taken from within the brackets
N   = Number of users
K   = CPU usage per user (in MHz)
M   = Upper CPU boundary (maximum CPU usage)
```

You calculate the upper CPU boundary to anticipate the ceiling for CPU utilization and user capacity at a value below 100 percent (2×400 MHz CPU, or 800 MHz). Ideally, the CPUs are fully utilized when you reach user capacity. However, usually you reach user capacity even though CPU usage is below maximum, so you have to calculate the upper CPU boundary.

For example, if the CPU usage per user is 0.5624 MHz and the upper CPU boundary is 526 MHz, then the CPU usage for 100 users is 56.24 MHz:

```
C = Min [(100 shoppers × 0.5624 MHz), 526 MHz]
C = Min [56.24 MHz, 526 MHz]
C = 56.24 MHz
```

CPU usage for 935 shoppers would be 500 MHz, which also happens to be the upper CPU boundary:

```
C = Min [500 MHz, 526 MHz]
C = 500 MHz
```

Shopper loads higher than 935 exceed the upper CPU boundary. This means that at that point, demand exceeds user capacity.

You can calculate the upper CPU boundary from the weighted average of the percentage of the CPU utilization for each shopper operation, as shown in the following table. In this calculation, CPU measurements for each shopper operation are weighted, based on the distribution of shopper operations in the usage profile. The table shows that the upper CPU boundary (M) is 94.86 percent, or 759 MHz. The equation is as follows:

```
Weighted % CPU = % CPU at optimum ASP throughput × % of Total (from usage profile)
```

The following table shows the upper CPU boundary (2x400 MHz server) for the shopper operations.

Shopper operation	Percentage CPU at optimum ASP throughput	Percentage of total (from usage profile)	Weighted percentage CPU
Add Item	96.98	2.00	1.94
Add Item + Checkout	94.31	0.17	0.32
Add Item + Delete	95.86	0.33	5.73
Basket	91.73	6.25	0.16
Default (home page)	98.01	8.33	8.17
Listing	91.87	20.83	19.14
Lookup	99.52	6.25	6.22
New	96.61	2.08	2.01
Product	94.81	35.00	33.18
Search	95.11	10.42	9.91
Welcome	96.97	8.33	8.08
Upper CPU boundary (weighted average)			94.86

Plugging in values for CPU usage per shopper operation and upper CPU boundary yields the following equation:

```
Min [(N × 0.5624), 759]
```

Figure 19.6 illustrates the values for the previous equation.

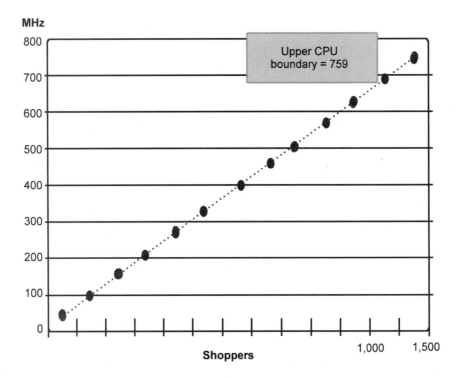

Figure 19.6 Projected CPU usage (2x400 MHz server)

Calculate the capacity as follows:

```
Concurrent users = CPU capacity / CPU cost per user
```

(However, the upper boundary of the CPU is at 94.86 percent of CPU capacity, so
```
True capacity = Max capacity × 94.86%)
```

```
Concurrent users = (800 Mcycles × 94.86%) / 0.5624 Mcycles per user
Concurrent users = 759 Mcycles / 0.5624 Mcycles per user
Concurrent users = 1,350
```

These figures are the calculated or projected user capacity in relation to CPU power.

In tests, WAS scripts were run on one operation at a time, in order to weigh each operation separately. In a production environment, all operations are called together, creating a much more complex environment, and one in which caching and context switching can make a difference. For this reason, you must perform verification tests, in which all operations are stress-tested together, based on each usage profile.

Using WAS, a sample script was created to simulate shopper load levels in increments of 250 until usage exceeded capacity. Resource utilization and ASP performance monitored with System Monitor produced the results shown in the following table.

Shopper load	Percentage CPU utilization	Context switches per second	ASP requests per second	ASP request execution time (ms)	ASP request wait time (ms)
250	17.42	4,763	4.918	87.32	0.16
500	37.83	5,426	9.548	111.33	0.47
750	54.45	7,017	15.021	117.44	0.16
1,000	72.89	8,190	19.659	130.46	0.63
1,500	98.37	9,470	26.607	1619.63	4636.00

At 1,000 users, the ASP request wait time starts to reach one second.

Figure 19.7 shows the same results in a graph. Note that CPU usage increases in a linear fashion until maximum CPU usage (800 MHz) is reached.

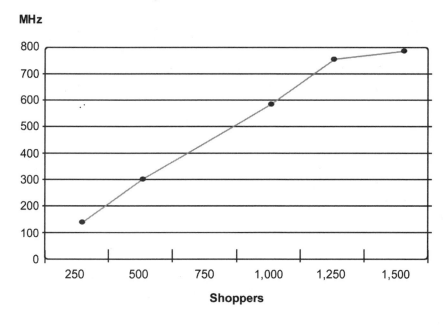

Figure 19.7 CPU usage and shopper load (2x400 MHz server)

If you cannot upgrade or add processors, there are two other steps you can take to improve CPU efficiency:

- **Add network adapters**. If you have a multiprocessor system that does *not* distribute interrupts symmetrically, you can improve the distribution of the processor workload by adding one network adapter for every processor. Generally, you add adapters only when you need to improve the throughput of your system. Network adapters, like any additional hardware, have some intrinsic overhead. However, if one of the processors is nearly always active (that is, if the % Processor Time counter equals 100 percent CPU) and more than half of its time is spent servicing deferred procedure calls (DPCs) (if the % DPC Time counter is greater than 50 percent CPU), then adding a network adapter is likely to improve system performance. Adding a network adapter is a viable option, as long as the available network bandwidth is not already saturated.

- **Limit connections**. Consider reducing the maximum number of connections that each IIS 5.0 service accepts. Limiting connections can result in blocked or rejected connections, but it helps ensure that accepted connections are processed promptly.

Calculating Memory Cost per User

Because memory usage relates directly to the content of the site (caching, out-of-process dynamic-link libraries (DLLs), and so on), instead of to the number of concurrent users, you must calculate costs carefully. To calculate memory costs, you should monitor the following:

- Amount of Inetinfo that is paged out to disk (if any)

- Memory usage during site operation

- Efficiency of cache utilization

- Number of times the cache is flushed

- Number of page faults that occur

- User Profile Management cache

- Cache manager for discounts and advertisements

You can specify whether the **CacheManager** object should be a **Dictionary** object or an **LRUCache** object. The Gobal.asa file in the Retail Solution Site, available for download from http://www.microsoft.com/commerceserver/solutionsites, contains sample code for the **CacheManager** object.

Internet Information Services (IIS) 5.0 runs in a pageable user-mode process called Inetinfo.exe. When a process is pageable, the system can remove part of or all of it from RAM and write it to disk if there isn't enough free memory.

If part of the Inetinfo process is paged to disk, the performance of IIS 5.0 suffers. It's very important to make sure that your server or servers have enough RAM to keep the entire Inetinfo process in memory at all times because the Web, File Transfer Protocol (FTP), and Simple Mail Transfer Protocol (SMTP) services run in the Inetinfo process. Each current connection is also given about 10 KB of memory in the Inetinfo working set. The working set of the Inetinfo process should be large enough to contain the IIS object cache, data buffers for IIS 5.0 logging, and the data structures that the Web service uses to track its active connections.

You can use System Monitor to monitor the working set of Inetinfo.exe. In addition to the performance counters listed in the previous "Calculating Cost per User" section, you should also monitor the Inetinfo counters listed in the following table.

Counter	Measures
Memory: Page Reads/sec	Hard page faults. This counter displays the number of times the disk is read to satisfy page faults. It displays the number of read operations, regardless of the number of pages read in each operation. A sustained rate of five read operations per second or more can indicate a memory shortage.
Memory: Pages input/sec	Cost of hard page faults. This counter displays the number of pages read to satisfy page faults. One page is faulted at a time, but the system can read multiple pages ahead to prevent further hard faults.
Process: Inetinfo: Page faults/sec	Hard and soft faults in the working set of the Inetinfo process.
Process: Inetinfo: Working set	Size of the working set of the process, in bytes. This counter displays the last observed value, not an average.

You should log this data for several days. You can use performance logs and alerts in System Monitor to identify times of unusually high and low server activity.

If the system has sufficient memory, it can maintain enough space in the Inetinfo working set so that IIS 5.0 rarely has to perform disk operations. One indicator of memory sufficiency is the amount the size of the Inetinfo process working set varies in response to general memory availability on the server.

You can use the Memory:Available bytes counter as an indicator of memory availability and the Process:Inetinfo:Working set counter as an indicator of the size of the IIS 5.0 working set. Make sure to examine data collected over time, because these counters display the last value observed, rather than an average.

When you look at page faults, compare your data on the size of the Inetinfo working set to the rate of page faults attributed to the working set. You can use the Process: Inetinfo:Working set counter as an indicator of the size of the working set, and the Process: Inetinfo:Page faults/sec counter to indicate the rate of page faults for the IIS 5.0 process. When you have reviewed data on the varying size of the Inetinfo working set, you can use its page fault rate to determine whether the system has enough memory to operate efficiently. If the system cannot lower the page fault rate to an acceptable level, you should add memory to improve performance.

IIS 5.0 relies on the operating system to store and retrieve frequently used Web pages and other files from the file system cache. The file system cache is particularly useful for servers of static Web pages, because Web pages tend to be used in repeated, predictable patterns.

If cache performance is poor when the cache is small, use the data you have collected to deduce the reason that the system reduced the cache size. Note the available memory on the server and the processes and services running on the server, including the number of simultaneous connections supported.

When you add physical memory to your server, the system allocates more space to the file system cache. A larger cache is almost always more efficient, but each additional megabyte of memory becomes increasingly less efficient than the previous one. You must decide at what point adding more memory produces so little improvement in performance that it ceases to be worthwhile.

Calculating Cost per User for Disks

IIS 5.0 writes its logs to disk, so there is usually some disk activity, even when clients are hitting the cache 100 percent of the time. Under ordinary circumstances, disk activity (other than that generated by logging) serves as an indicator of issues in other areas. For example, if your server needs more RAM, you'll see a lot of disk activity because there are many hard page faults. There will also be a lot of disk activity if your server houses a database or your users request many different pages.

Because IIS caches most pages in memory, the disk system is rarely a bottleneck as long as the Web servers have enough installed memory. However, SQL Server reads and writes to the disk frequently. SQL Server also caches data, but uses the disk a lot more than IIS. You should test disk activity on all servers if disk activity could become a bottleneck.

To measure the disk activity of a site, use System Monitor to record the Physical Disk: Disk Reads/second and % Disk Time counters while a WAS script is running for each shopper operation, such as when calculating the cost per user for the CPU. (The WAS tool cannot report the activity on the SQL Server server if it is running on a different server. If that is the case, use System Monitor instead.)

In our example in this chapter, the percent of disk utilization is based on a calibration of a maximum of 280 random seeks per second. For example, if the Web server generates 2.168 Add Item operations, then the SQL Server server performs 9.530 disk seeks per second (for a disk utilization of 3.404 percent). Calculate disk cost per user by dividing disk seeks per second by operations per second (which you will have determined as part of the usage profile). The equations are as follows:

```
Disk read cost per operation = disk reads per second / operations per second
Disk write cost per operation = disk writes per second / operations per second
```

The following table lists the results of calculating disk *reads* on the site in our example. (Remember that you must also measure disk *writes*.)

Shopper operation	Operations per second	Disk seeks per second	Percentage of disk	Disk cost
Add Item	2.168	9.530	3.404	4.395
Add Item + Checkout	0.903	19.688	7.031	7.266
Add Item + Delete	9.384	8.956	3.199	0.954
Basket	8.728	7.050	2.518	0.808
Browse	6.033	0.103	0.037	0.017
Default (home page)	28.330	0.248	0.089	0.009
Listing	5.533	0.148	0.053	0.027
Lookup	12.781	0.063	0.023	0.005
New	12.196	9.275	3.313	0.760
Search	8.205	0.100	0.036	0.012
Welcome	31.878	0.080	0.029	0.003

Note   This table reflects a busy server with a higher frequency of operations than in some of the other tables in these examples. The disk cost is still the same.

After you calculate the cost, the next step is to calculate the average load per user per second, as shown in the following table.

Shopper operation	Ratio of hits (percent)	Usage profile operations (over 11 minutes, 660 seconds)	Usage profile operations per second (usage profile operations / 660 seconds)	Cost per operation per second (read + write)
Add Item	1.76	0.2	0.000293	4.395
Add Item + Checkout	1.10	0.1	0.000183	7.266
Add Item + Delete	1.07	0.1	0.000178	1.274
Browse	36.61	4.0	0.006102	0.017
Default (home page)	22.82	2.5	0.003804	0.009
Login	1.73	0.2	0.000288	0.012
Register	1.06	0.1	0.000176	3.295
Search (Good)	14.35	1.6	0.002391	0.012
Search (Bad)	1.02	0.1	0.000170	0.012
View Cart	2.53	0.3	0.000421	0.027
Total		11.0		16.319 KBps

These calculations yield a load per user per second of 16.319 kilobytes per second (KBps). You can use this number to determine the capacity of the disk system.

Figure 19.8 shows disk seeks climbing to 4.38 seeks per second for a projected peak load of 400 users. Given that disk performance for the SQL Server server was calibrated at 280 random seeks per second, this translates to a disk utilization of 1.56 percent.

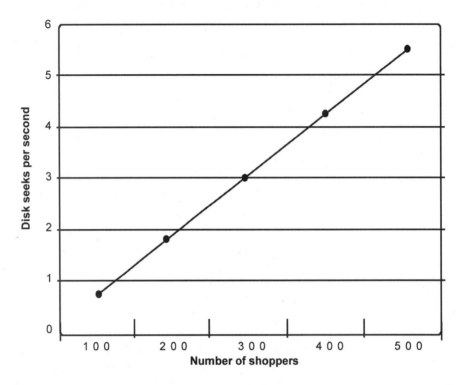

Figure 19.8 Projected disk costs versus shopper load

You can draw the following conclusions from the calculation results in the previous tables:

- You can use the results with the following equation to determine how many disk spindles are required for your system:

  ```
  Disk spindles required = (disk cost per user per second / disk maximum reads per second)
  (disk write cost per operation / disk maximum writes per second)
  ```

- On multiple disk RAID arrays, the average disk queue length per array should not exceed the number of physical disks per array. If it does, this indicates a bottleneck.

Adding disk spindles usually means adding another disk to the RAID system. This ensures that there are enough disks to distribute the load between them efficiently.

You must calibrate the disk subsystem to determine the maximum number of reads and writes per second for an individual disk. The disk calibration process performs a large number of uncached reads and writes to the disk to determine the maximum number of reads and writes that the disk array can support. The maximum numbers of reads and writes are functions of disk seek time and rotational latency.

Ultimately, these calculations reveal that the cost per user for a disk in our sample is 0.00360763 KB per user per second, and the site capacity for a disk is 25,600 concurrent users per SQL Server server, based on the test platform's single hard drive.

Calculating Cost per User for Networks

Network bandwidth is another important resource that can become a bottleneck. You can calculate total network cost from the sum of the costs of the individual shopper operations. However, two network costs are associated with each shopper operation—the connection between the Web client and the Web server, and the connection between the SQL Server server and the Web server.

> **Note** On a switched Ethernet LAN, traffic is isolated, so network costs are not added together. On an unswitched Ethernet LAN, network traffic is cumulative, so network costs are added together.

When a shopper performs an operation, the action generates network traffic between the Web server and the Web client, as well as between the Web server and the SQL Server server (if the SQL Server database needs to be accessed).

The Add Item operation, for example, shows that optimal throughput is 2.168 operations per second. The network cost of Add Item is 5.627 KBps per operation between the Web client and the Web server and 129.601 KBps between the Web server and the SQL Server server. Most of the traffic generated by the Add Item operation is between the Web server and the SQL Server database. The following table shows the combined net Web cost and net SQL Server cost as the net total cost of each operation.

Shopper operation	Net Web cost	Net SQL Server cost	Net total cost
Add Item	5.627	129.601	135.23
Add Item+Checkout	24.489	55.215	79.70
Add Item+Delete	10.763	5.392	16.16
Basket	2.750	4.010	6.76
Default (home page)	1.941	0.000	1.94
Listing	25.664	23.134	48.80
Login	17.881	1.380	19.26
Lookup	14.475	0.861	15.34
Main	24.437	9.503	33.94
New	18.859	0.492	19.35
Product	21.548	21.051	42.60
Search	20.719	10.725	31.44

Net Web cost represents the bytes transmitted per operation between the Web client and the Web server.

Net SQL Server cost represents the bytes transmitted per operation between the SQL Server server and the Web server.

Net total cost represents the total bytes transmitted per operation on an unswitched Ethernet LAN, where costs are added together. On a switched Ethernet LAN network, costs are separate because the segments are isolated.

The following table shows the total bytes transmitted per operation (total network cost per user per second) on an unswitched Ethernet LAN.

Shopper operation	Ratio of hits (percent)	Usage profile operations per second	Net Web cost	Net SQL Server cost	Cost per user per second (Web server)	Cost per user per second (SQL Server)	Total cost per user per second (added together, unswitched LAN)
Add Item	1.76	0.000293	5.627	129.601	0.001649	0.037973	0.039622
Add Item + Checkout	1.10	0.000183	24.489	55.215	0.004481	0.010104	0.014586
Default (home page)	22.82	0.003804	1.941	0.000	0.007384	0	0.007384
Listing	2.53	0.000421	25.664	23.134	0.010805	0.009739	0.020544
Login	1.73	0.000288	17.881	1.380	0.00515	0.000397	0.005547
Product	36.61	0.006102	21.548	21.051	0.131486	0.128453	0.259939
Register	1.06	0.000176	5.627	129.601	0.00099	0.02281	0.0238
Search (Bad)	1.02	0.000170	20.719	10.725	0.003522	0.001823	0.005345
Search (Good)	14.35	0.002391	20.719	10.725	0.049539	0.025643	0.075183

The following table illustrates an unswitched network, at 0.459729 KBps per user (total network traffic escalation).

Number of users	Total cost per user per second	Total network traffic (KBps)
100	0.459729	45.9729
200	0.459729	91.9458
300	0.459729	137.9187
400	0.459729	183.8916
500	0.459729	229.8645
600	0.459729	275.8374
700	0.459729	321.8103
800	0.459729	367.7832
1,000	0.459729	459.729
1,200	0.459729	551.6748
10,000	0.459729	4,597.29
20,000	0.459729	9,194.58
100,000	0.459729	45,972.9

Even in an unswitched network, the traffic on the network is low. However, this can still cause a potential bottleneck, because it is possible to have many servers on the same network hosting the site.

If the network is a Carrier Sense Multiple Access with Collision Detection (CSMA/CD) Ethernet network running at 100 megabits per second (Mbps), or 12.5 megabytes per second (MBps) (100 megabits / 8 bytes per bit), then collisions will cause network congestion. For this reason, you should not push network utilization over 36 percent, which means no more than 4.5 MBps on the network. The network illustrated in the previous table reached the 4.5 MBps threshold at about 10,000 users, which is the site's capacity. At 20,000 users, the network will become congested due to excessive collisions, and will therefore cause a bottleneck. To add capacity, you can move to a switched network, or at least separate the Web network traffic from the network traffic on the SQL Server server.

Note   Remember to measure network traffic for the entire site and not just for individual servers.

There are two primary flows of network traffic to consider in a typical site: Web client to Web server and Web server to SQL Server server. Sites that are more complex can have more flows, depending on the number of servers and the architecture of the site.

Network capacity can become a bottleneck to your site as it grows, especially on sites where the ASP content is relatively simple (low CPU load) and the content (like static HTML or pictures) is relatively large. A few servers can easily serve the content to thousands of users, but the network might not be equipped to handle it. Most of the traffic on the network flows between the Web server and the SQL Server server.

Finally, these examples reveal that the cost per user for the network in the site in this example is 0.459729 KB per user per second, and the site capacity for the network is 10,000 concurrent users, based on a 100 Mbps unswitched network.

Managing Performance

Managing the performance of your Commerce Server 2000 site largely consists of finding and removing bottlenecks. A bottleneck is hardware or software that is operating at maximum capacity. As the load approaches maximum capacity, the bottleneck begins to restrict the flow of work through the system. Performance tools can help you determine what hardware or software has reached its limit. You can then improve the hardware, change the configuration, or tune the software to improve overall performance.

Performance is only one factor in developing your Commerce Server site. Other important factors include ease of development and maintenance, time to market, availability of good programming tools, and in-house site developer expertise. Optimizing for performance can affect any of these other factors.

Web development is driven by a business case that determines priorities. For example, project goals might specify a particular programming language or data-access technology, and such decisions always affect performance to some degree. It is very important to determine the *necessary* level of performance appropriate to your Web site, then develop the site and manage it to that level of performance.

Web sites often run on multiple physical tiers, each of which has its own hardware, system software, and application software. As a result, Web applications can have many types of performance problems: hardware (client computer, Web server, database server, the network), system software (operating systems, networking software, system services), client applications, browsers, logical database, physical database, data access, and so on.

You can use the following questions to help determine your performance tuning goals:

- Will the performance of this site meet our goals today and in the future?

- What hardware and software configuration do we need to meet our performance goals?

- Will the site run on our existing hardware and software configuration?

- Can we expect our current configuration to become a bottleneck?

- How many users can our site support?

- What will it cost to develop this site (hardware, software, and development)?

Monitoring performance regularly is the only way to be sure that the site is meeting its specified performance goals. Regular performance monitoring can also provide an early warning when a change degrades performance. You can collect performance data using existing system tools, having the site monitor report on its own performance, or by building special client applications to drive the system.

When you tune performance, you should measure system performance first to see if it meets your goals. If performance doesn't meet your goals, find the bottleneck, remove it, and then repeat the process. Remember to stop when you reach your performance goal. You can always increase performance further, but when site performance meets your goals, additional tuning is generally not cost-effective.

This section describes a performance tuning methodology that you can use repeatedly. You should manage and document your performance tuning process carefully by working systematically and according to your plan.

Identifying Site Constraints

Management uses a business case to determine priorities for developing your Commerce Server site. Often there are higher priorities than just the maximum-possible performance. These constraints cannot be altered in search of higher performance. For example, one business requirement might be that no changes should impact maintainability or time to market, even if those changes might improve performance. As a result, performance work must focus on factors that are not constrained.

Hardware is one factor that can often be changed to improve performance. Buying bigger and faster servers or using more servers and partitioning the load can be cost-effective ways to improve performance. If you plan to add more servers, you need to design the site accordingly.

Another alternative is to tune other parts of the system. The database is a critical factor in overall system performance. Designing an efficient, logical database and tuning the physical database are crucial to achieving good performance.

If site performance still falls short of your goal, ask yourself the following questions:

- Should we use a different programming language or a different data-access technology?

- Can the database be housed on a separate server?

- Can more stateless components be used?

Defining Load

You can analyze usage log files to determine the load factors in the following table.

Load factor	Description
Number of concurrent users	Number of users visiting your site at the same time.
Time between operation calls (or *think time*)	Average delay between the time when a user receives one reply and submits another request. For example, if the operation is called only once every two seconds, the operation only has to be faster than two seconds in order to perform as needed.
Number of ASP requests per operation	Number of ASP requests in an operation. Performance must be measured in operations per second, but System Monitor measures only ASP requests per second. To know how many ASP requests are in an operation, either review the ASP code or analyze a Network Monitor capture file of a single operation.
Number of static pages versus number of dynamic pages	Number of static and dynamic pages in your application.
Number of secure pages versus number of non-secure pages	Number of secure pages and pages containing no security in your application.
Variation in load over time	Difference between the average load and peak load.

Setting Performance Goals

After you define site constraints, services the site provides, and demand for those services, you can set specific performance goals for your site.

First, you should choose metrics for evaluating the performance of your site. One common metric is *total system throughput*. Throughput is often expressed as ASP requests per second. You should measure throughput per operation, because each operation has its own inherent value.

Another common metric is *required response time*. *Response time* is the time between the submission of a request and the receipt of the reply. Response time requirements are often expressed by specifying the ninety-fifth percentile. For example, a required response time of one second means that 95 percent of client calls must return in less than one second.

Next, you must choose required values for your metrics. Setting explicit performance goals is the key step in tuning system performance. The result of this step is to determine how many operations or transactions your site must support per second. After you have chosen required values and set specific goals, you iterate through a series of controlled performance tests until you reach your goals. Use the procedures in the following table to tune system performance.

Procedure	Description
Measure application performance on the target platform	If performance equals your goal, you are done. When you reach your goal, stop tuning performance. (You should, however, continue to monitor performance to be sure that it continues at a satisfactory level.) If performance does not equal your goal, go on to the next procedure.
Find the bottleneck	If performance does not equal your goal, use performance monitoring tools to find the bottleneck. You don't have to find all of the bottlenecks at once. After you identify a few bottlenecks, determine which one will yield the biggest performance increase when fixed. Keep the cost of fixing the bottleneck in mind (hardware, software, and extra development) when determining which bottleneck to fix.
Fix the bottleneck	Form a hypothesis as to what is causing the bottleneck. Devise a fix for the problem. Apply the fix. This step is not always easy, of course. Sometimes performance tools do not clearly identify the problem. When that happens, you have to experiment with one factor at a time. The more you know about the site and the system, and the more experience you have managing performance, the better you will be at finding performance problems and determining the best solutions for them.
Repeat the tuning process	Make sure that the changes you made did not introduce new errors, and then repeat the tuning process. The only way to know if the change actually improved performance is to measure performance again. Sometimes you must undo a change because it had no effect or even made performance worse.

Measuring Performance

Measuring performance accurately can be extremely challenging due to the complex nature of systems. This section describes how to measure the performance aspects of:

- Memory
- Processor capacity
- Network
- Disk access
- Database
- Security
- Bottlenecks
- Optimization

For most sites, you can simply gather performance data using WAS to run scripts that constantly request the ASP pages for a specified operation. While the WAS scripts run, you can use System Monitor to monitor selected counters. (WAS can also capture these counters, but it displays them in text format, not graphically.) The best way to get an overview of system performance is to chart a set of System Monitor counters for every performance test. Choose counters that can indicate common bottlenecks, such as those listed previously in this chapter.

WAS is designed to simulate multiple browsers requesting pages from a Web site. This tool can realistically simulate many requests with relatively few client servers. However, you must be sure that you have an adequate number of client servers. Beyond a certain point, the overhead of context switching on a client server can influence the effectiveness of simulating a number of virtual users, giving skewed results.

Sometimes the only way to measure performance is to program hooks into the system to log performance metrics. (A hook is a location in a routine or program in which other routines can be inserted, in this case to log metrics.) Although these hooks can impact application performance, they can be helpful if it is critical for you to know a particular performance measurement.

It is hard to accurately identify bottlenecks from performance data, but there are some telltale signs that indicate bottlenecks. For example, if available memory falls below 4 MB, the system is probably accessing the disk too often. To solve this, add more memory.

Another indication of a bottleneck is fluctuations in the Active Server Pages: Requests queued performance counter, which indicates the number of requests waiting for service from the queue. If the requests queued fluctuate considerably during a stress test and processor utilization remains relatively low, this is an indication that the script is calling a server COM component that is receiving more calls than it can handle. In this case, the server COM component is probably the bottleneck.

The following table lists ways in which you might measure the performance of each element of the site.

Element	Description
Client	Use WAS to load or generate scripts that request an ASP page and measure the response time.
SQL Server	Use either Query Analyzer (analyzes individual query time) or SQL Profiler to measure response time for SQL Server.
	If SQL Server is the bottleneck, first try to optimize SQL Server itself, making sure it has enough memory, the configuration is optimized, you have the best indexes where they matter the most, and so forth. Sometimes, however, the only way to substantially improve performance is to optimize the design of the database, redesign queries, convert queries to stored procedures, and so forth.
Data access method (ActiveX Data Objects (ADO))	If ADO is the bottleneck, make sure that your application is using it correctly. If optimizing ADO still doesn't produce the performance improvements you're looking for, consider using the **LRUCache** object, instead.
COM	Use tools such as COM+ to measure the performance of COM objects.

Memory

Performance bottlenecks caused by memory shortages can often appear to be problems in other parts of the system, so you should monitor memory first to verify that your server has enough, then move on to other components. A dedicated Web server needs at least 128 MB of RAM to run Microsoft Windows 2000, IIS 5.0, and Commerce Server, but 256 MB to 1 GB is usually better. Since the IIS file cache is set to use up to half of available memory by default, the more memory you have, the larger the IIS file cache can be.

Note Microsoft Windows 2000 Advanced Server can support up to 8 GB of RAM, but the IIS file cache will not use more than 4 GB.

To determine whether you have enough memory on your server, use System Monitor to graphically display counter readings as they change over time. Also, monitor your cache settings. Adding memory alone won't necessarily solve performance problems. You need to be aware of IIS cache settings and how they affect server performance. If these settings are not appropriate for the loads placed on your server, the cache settings, rather than a lack of memory, can cause performance bottlenecks.

Processor Capacity

Processor bottlenecks occur when one or more processes consume most of the processor time, forcing other process threads to wait in a queue. IIS 5.0 scales effectively across two to four processors, providing more processor time. Consider the business needs of your Web site if you're thinking about adding more processors.

If you primarily host static content on your server, a two-processor computer is likely to be sufficient to prevent bottlenecks. If you host dynamically generated content, a four-processor setup might be sufficient. However, if the workload on your site is highly CPU-intensive, no single computer can keep up with requests. If this is the case, you should scale your site across multiple servers, using Network Load Balancing (NLB) or a hardware load balancer. If you already run your site on multiple servers, and you are still experiencing performance bottlenecks, consider adding more servers.

Networks

The network is the line through which clients send requests to your server. The time it takes for those requests and responses to travel back and forth is one of the largest limiting factors in user-perceived server performance. This latency is almost completely out of your control. There is little you can do about a slow router on the Internet or the physical distance between a client and your server, except possibly setting up geographically distributed Web servers.

On a site consisting primarily of static content, network bandwidth is the most likely source of a performance bottleneck. Even a fairly modest server can completely saturate a T3 connection (45 Mbps) or a Fast Ethernet connection (100 Mbps). You can mitigate the problem somewhat by tuning your network connection and maximizing your effective bandwidth.

The simplest way to measure effective bandwidth is to determine the rate at which your server sends and receives data. There are a number of performance counters that measure data transmission in many components of your server. These include counters on the Web, FTP, and SMTP services, the **TCP** object, the **IP** object, and the **Network Interface** object. Each of these counters reflects different Open Systems Interconnection (OSI) layers. The following table lists two of the main counters you should monitor to measure network bandwidth performance.

Counter	Measures
Network Segment: Bytes received per second	Bytes received per second on a segment of the network. Compare this counter to the total bandwidth of your network adapter card to determine whether your network connection is creating a bottleneck. To allow room for spikes in traffic, you should usually use no more than 50 percent of capacity. If this number is very close to the capacity of the connection, and processor and memory use are moderate, then the connection might be a problem.
Web: Maximum connections Web: Total connections	Maximum connections on the Web; total number of connections. Monitor these two counters to see whether your Web server is able to use as much of the connection as it needs, if you are running other services on the computer that also uses the network connection. Compare these numbers to memory and processor usage figures so that you can be sure that the connection is the problem, not one of the other components.

Disk Access

Disk access is another common performance bottleneck, especially for database-intensive applications. Both Microsoft Distributed Transaction Coordinator (MSDTC) and SQL Server keep durable logs, and they must write their log entries to disk before they commit each transaction. When transaction rates are high, writing to these logs generates a lot of disk activity. It is often a good idea to provide dedicated disk drives for both logs.

Since IIS 5.0 also writes logs to disk, there is regular disk activity even with 100 percent client cache hits. Generally speaking, if there is high disk read activity other than logging, other areas of your system need to be tuned. For example, hard page faults cause large amounts of disk activity, but are indicative of insufficient RAM, not insufficient disk space.

Accessing memory is faster than accessing disks by a factor of roughly one million; so clearly, searching the hard disk to fill requests degrades performance. The type of site you host can have a significant impact on the frequency of disk seeks. If your site has a very large file set that is accessed randomly, if the files on your site tend to be very large, or if you have a very small amount of RAM, then IIS is unable to maintain copies of the files in RAM for faster access.

Typically, you should use the Physical Disk counters to watch for spikes in the number of disk reads when your server is busy. If you have enough RAM, most connections will result in cache hits, unless you have a database stored on the same server and clients are making dissimilar queries, which precludes caching. Be aware that logging can also cause disk bottlenecks. If there are no obvious disk-intensive issues on your server, but you see a lot of disk activity anyway, you should check the amount of RAM on your server immediately to make sure you have enough memory.

Database

To enhance database-driven performance in a production environment, use SQL Server. Both IIS and SQL Server perform best with plenty of memory, so try storing the database on a separate server from the Web service. Communication across computer boundaries is frequently faster than communication on a single computer. Also be sure to create and maintain good indexes to minimize input/output (I/O) on your database queries. Take advantage of stored procedures, which take much less time to execute and are easier to write than an ASP script designed to do the same task.

Hot spots in the database can become bottlenecks in the system. A hot spot occurs when many transactions are trying to access the same resource, such as an index, a data page, or a row at the same time. When that happens, many transactions get blocked, which reduces concurrency, and which in turn decreases system throughput. SQL Server prevents concurrency anomalies by using locks to protect data accessed in a transaction. The locks block other transactions that try to access the locked data area until the first transaction completes.

Security

Balancing performance with users' concerns about the security of your Web applications is one of the most important issues you will face, particularly if you have an e-commerce Web site. Since secure Web communication requires more resources than non-secure Web communications, it is important that you know when to use various security techniques, such as the Secure Sockets Layer (SSL) protocol or Internet Protocol (IP) address checking, and when not to use them. For example, your home page or a Search results page probably doesn't need to be accessed through SSL. However, a Checkout or Purchase page needs to be secure.

If you use SSL, remember that establishing the initial connection is five times as expensive as reconnecting using security information in the SSL session cache. The default timeout for the SSL session cache is five minutes in Windows 2000. After the cache is flushed, the client and server must establish a completely new connection. Make sure that you enable HTTP keep-alive connections (that is, persistent connections) because SSL sessions don't expire when used in conjunction with HTTP keep-alive connections unless the browser explicitly closes the connection.

The most common way to measure security overhead is to run tests comparing server performance with and without a security feature. You should run the tests with fixed workloads and a fixed server configuration, so that the security feature is the only variable. During the tests, you should measure the elements in the following table.

Element	Description
Processor activity and the processor queue	Authentication, IP address checking, SSL protocol, and encryption schemes are security features that require significant processing. If there are performance bottlenecks, you will probably see increased processor activity, both in privileged and user modes, and an increase in the rate of context switches and interrupts. If the processors are not sufficient to handle the increased load, queues will develop. Custom hardware, such as cryptographic accelerators address this problem.
Physical memory used	Security requires that the system store and retrieve more user information. Also, the SSL protocol uses long keys for encrypting and decrypting the messages (40 bits to 1,024 bits long).
Network traffic	Performance bottlenecks will probably result in an increase in traffic between the IIS 5.0 server and the domain controller used to authenticate logon passwords and verify IP addresses.
Latency and delays	The most obvious performance degradation resulting from complex security features like SSL is the time and effort involved in encryption and decryption, both of which use many processor cycles. Downloading files from servers using the SSL protocol can be 10 to 100 times slower than from servers that are not using SSL.

If a server is used both for running IIS 5.0 and as a domain controller, the proportion of processor use, memory, and network and disk activity consumed by domain services is likely to increase the load on these resources significantly. As a result, you should not run IIS 5.0 on a domain controller.

Bottlenecks

Finding bottlenecks or hot spots is sometimes more of an art than a science. The trick is to find a true bottleneck, and not just the symptom of a bottleneck. The suggestions in the following table can help you set up and track your performance testing.

Suggestion	Description
Check the functional correctness and performance of your application	You can get definitive performance results only when the application is functionally correct. Although you should consider performance implications during design and implementation, your application must work before you can start tuning performance. Keep in mind that you might have to redesign parts of the application to meet performance goals. Of course, any change can introduce errors, so test the correctness of the application whenever you make any changes.
Make the tests repeatable	Run the same tests both before and after any change, to measure the impact of the change. Use the same transaction mix, the same clients generating the same load, and so on. Keep the same hardware and the same software configurations. Run the same system services. Don't run applications, such as e-mail, because behavior might differ between test runs. If network traffic is a factor, you might have to test on a private network.
Take careful notes	Record the results of each test and any changes from previous tests. Successful performance tuning depends on working systematically. Keep a performance log and take written notes on each test run. Describe the configuration, especially any changes from the previous test. Record performance and the data gathered from performance monitoring tools.
Change only one factor at a time	If you change more than one factor in a single test, and performance changes, you won't be sure which factor impacted performance. Whenever possible, change only one factor each time you run a test.

Bottlenecks are unavoidable. There is always something preventing a system from operating at optimum performance levels. The trick is to find and remove the biggest bottlenecks that are also the easiest and least expensive to fix. For example, it might be simple to rewrite an ASP page, but it might not be as simple to rewrite a Microsoft Visual Basic COM object in Microsoft Visual C++. You must evaluate the potential performance gain against the cost of the work and the time necessary to do the optimization.

For example, if an operation is currently processing about 7 operations per second, but the goal is 10 operations per second, time must be decreased by 40 milliseconds per operation. Rewriting a Visual Basic COM object to a Visual C++ object is estimated to save 17 milliseconds; rewriting the ASP code is estimated to save 35 milliseconds; installing more memory on the SQL Server server is estimated to save 7 milliseconds. To save 40 milliseconds per operation, you can optimize the ASP code and put more memory on the SQL Server server. Both options are inexpensive compared to rewriting the COM object, even though that would give you even better performance. However, your priority should be to reach your performance goals, which you can do without rewriting the COM object.

Optimizations

The following table lists some elements you should consider optimizing for your site.

Optimization	Description
Optimize your code	Try to conserve memory, use objects for as short a time as possible, avoid expensive loops, and so forth. Remember that there is a difference between optimizing and rewriting code. Rewrite code only when optimization techniques don't give you the performance you need.
Optimize components	Make sure you call the components in the correct and most efficient manner, as late as possible, and release them as early as possible. Try to take advantage of connection pooling and/or component pooling (COM+) as much as possible.
Minimize or eliminate steps that cause bottlenecks	Try making dynamic pages static, refreshing the content on a scheduled basis. Many sites contain steps that are repeated often, such as retrieving headlines from SQL Server. Although such steps might be relatively cheap in processing cost, calling them frequently can make them bottlenecks.
	A popular way of solving this type of problem is to schedule a custom program to retrieve the headlines from SQL Server every 10 minutes and write the headlines into an HTML file, which can then be used by the site. This is a less expensive way of performing this operation, since SQL Server is now queried only every 10 minutes for the headlines, instead of hundreds of times per minute.
Convert slow-running ASP pages with ISAPI extensions	Internet Server Application Programming Interface (ISAPI) can be an extremely fast and efficient way to handle Web server requests. A code example for a basic checkout process is provided on the Commerce Server 2000 Resource Kit CD.
Optimize design and architecture	Good design can increase performance better than most other optimizations.
	Carefully consider how you could optimize the design and architecture of the following areas: • Site (Web servers, SQL Server servers, and other servers) • Database (partition the database and optimize the database schema) • Site logic (flow of users and data) • Content distribution (in a server farm environment) • Load distribution • Asynchronous Message Queuing or e-mail (for updating systems) • Commerce Server pipelines

Optimization	Description
Consider new bottlenecks	It is important to examine any proposed optimization in context before you do any work. Remember to consider the entire system as a whole, not just one ASP page or even one Web server.
	For example, creating a SQL Server index might result in a great performance gain for one operation (retrieving data), but could create a new bottleneck for a different operation (inserting data).
Consider new errors	Note all areas affected by changes in architecture, components, or code (directly and indirectly).
	It is not unusual to introduce a new error into a system when you make changes. All changes should be reviewed carefully to ensure that the system works the way you intended after the changes are made. Be sure to test the entire system, not just the part that changed.
Upgrade to larger L2 caches	If you add or upgrade processors, choose processors with a large secondary (L2) cache. Server applications need a large processor cache because their instruction paths involve many different components and they need to access a lot of data. A large processor cache (2 MB or more if it is external, up to the maximum available if it is on the CPU chip) will improve performance.
Upgrade to faster CPUs	Web applications particularly benefit from faster processors.
Use Expires headers	Set Expires headers on both static and dynamic content so that both types of content can be stored in the client's cache. This results in faster response times, less load on the server, and less traffic on the network.
	For example, you could create a header that won't download your company's logo file if the user has already visited your site. To set Expires headers for static content, use the HTTP Headers property sheet. To set Expires headers for dynamic content, use the **Response.AddHeader** method.
Enable ASP buffering	ASP buffering is on by default after a clean install of Windows 2000. However, if you have upgraded from Microsoft Windows NT 4.0, you might need to turn it on. ASP buffering collects all output from the application in the buffer before sending it across the network to the client browser. This reduces network traffic and response times.
	Although buffering reduces response times, users might have the perception that the page is slower and less interactive, because they see no data until the page has finished executing. Judicious use of the **Response.Flush** method can increase the perception of interactivity.

Optimization	Description
Reduce file sizes	You can increase the performance of your Web server by reducing file sizes. Image files should be stored in an appropriate compressed format. Limit the number of images and other large files whenever possible. You can also reduce file size by "tightening up" HTML and ASP code.
Store log files on separate disks and remove nonessential information	If your server hosts multiple sites, a separate log file is created for each site, which can cause a bottleneck. Avoid logging non-vital information and try storing logs on a separate partition or disk from your Web server.
Use RAID and striping	To improve disk access, use RAID and striped disk sets. Consider using a drive controller with a large RAM cache. If your site relies on frequent database access, move the database to a separate computer.

Case Study: MSNBC

MSNBC is the 24-hour cable and Internet joint venture of Microsoft and NBC News. MSNBC.com is the number one news site with the fastest growth in frequency of downloads for all of 1999. It was voted "best Web site and most interactive" by *PC Magazine* and rated "best news portal" by *Yahoo! Internet Life*. MSNBC.com delivers the best of NBC News, MSNBC Cable, CNBC, and NBC Sports. Expanded news and feature reporting is provided to MSNBC.com users through strategic partnerships with Ziff Davis, The Wall Street Journal, MSN Money Central, The Sporting News, Expedia, E! Online, PencilNews, FEED magazine, Oncology.com, and APB News. MSNBC.com is a provider of broadband content for Road Runner, Sprint High Speed DSL, and Excite@Home, and programs interactive television with MSNBC Cable and NBC News.

The MSNBC.com Web site is hosted on 48 Web servers, each of which contains 1 GB of RAM running Windows 2000 Server. Newer servers have four 500 MHz Pentium III processors and older servers have two 400 MHz Pentium II processors.

Each of the eight IP addresses in the Domain Name System (DNS) entry of the site is a virtual IP address that represents six identical Web servers (Figure 19.9). When a user makes a request of the MSNBC.com site, the site uses NLB to direct the request to one of the eight virtual IP addresses, which then redirects it to one of the six servers in the cluster. If a page contains a number of different elements, such as graphics or inline frames, it is possible that each element could come from a different server. Figure 19.9 shows the hardware infrastructure for MSNBC.com.

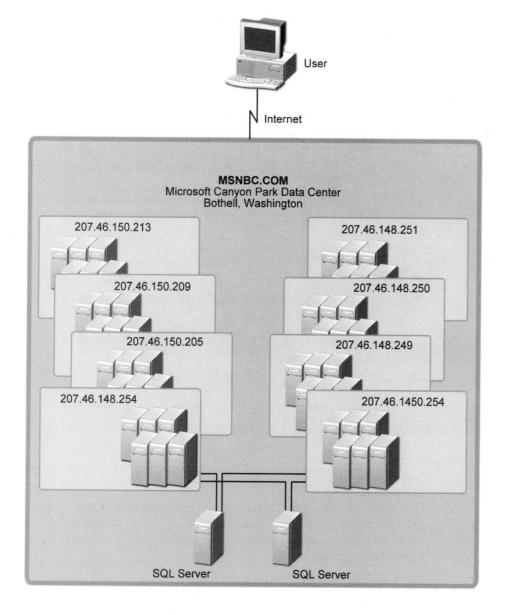

Figure 19.9 MSNBC.com hardware infrastructure

Site administrators use NLB when they need to take down servers for repairs or upgrades without affecting traffic to the site. Because the site typically runs at about 50 percent of capacity, it can withstand the loss of several servers before users will notice performance degradation.

The Web pages on MSNBC.com contain a great deal of dynamic content. Servers assemble almost every page on the site from various databases each time a user makes a request. Figure 19.10 shows the MSNBC.com home page.

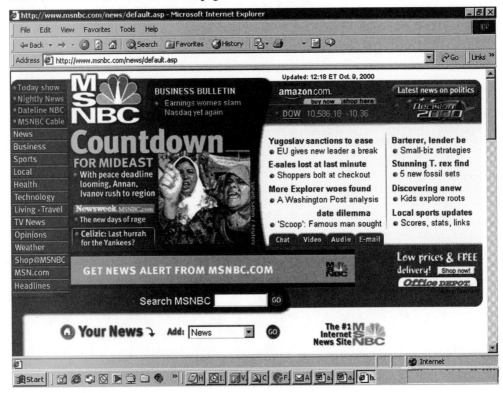

Figure 19.10 MSNBC.com home page

This home page contains the following dynamic elements:

- An ActiveX control that supplies the site's navigation menu on the left side of the page. First, a user clicks a link on the home page to go to a section of the site. Then, when the user points to a menu item on a subject page, a submenu appears, offering access to the stories and subsections within that section.

- The latest Dow Jones Industrial Average figures, updated throughout the business day.

- Several advertisements, retrieved from databases.

- Local news and weather content tailored to the user.

A dynamic Web site like MSNBC.com puts a great deal of demand on its network and computing hardware and software. MSNBC uses ASP technology to serve stories and graphics. The Web servers communicate with four SQL Server servers on the back end that store data.

As a news site with a reputation for bringing news to readers quickly, MSNBC.com regularly experiences usage spikes during periods of significant, breaking news. Sometimes, site operators can anticipate these spikes, but at other times spikes are completely unexpected. Site operators must ensure that the site has enough capacity to handle sudden, unanticipated demand.

On a typical day, MSNBC.com runs at about 50 percent of total capacity. During times of high demand, it sometimes nears or exceeds capacity. When this happens, site operators have to take additional steps to handle the demand, such as decreasing the amount of dynamic content on the site.

Load Monitoring Tools

MSNBC uses performance monitoring tools (such as System Monitor) in Windows 2000 to monitor load and performance, including the number of concurrent users accessing the site. If any of the System Monitor counters routinely exceed the recommended baseline, site operators consider upgrading server hardware. The Active Server Pages: Requests queued counter is especially important, due to the high level of ASP content on MSNBC.com. If the number of requests in the ASP queue reaches approximately 300, site developers simplify or reduce ASP content or add more hardware.

Planning for the Future

As a rule, the production team performs growth planning every three months or so by looking at historical trends and upcoming events. By comparing page views for the current month with figures from the previous year, and taking into account such things as big news stories, they can spot growth trends. Sometimes site operators can make educated guesses about upcoming major growth periods and plan accordingly. For example, two events in the late summer and fall of 2000—the Olympic Games in Sydney, Australia and the U.S. presidential election—caused long periods of heavy, sustained use. MSNBC added capacity through the spring and summer to handle the increase. Adding partnerships and linking arrangements can also result in increased demand.

Although MSNBC is positioned to adequately handle current typical and peak levels of traffic, proper capacity planning requires attention to the future as well. MSNBC is considering several options to handle expected levels of growth.

Currently, MSNBC serves all Web traffic from its Canyon Park data center in Bothell, Washington. However, in the future, MSNBC plans to open a satellite data center in Santa Clara, California, to take advantage of the high-capacity Internet infrastructure and peering arrangements available in and around Silicon Valley. Over the long term, site operators plan to serve Web traffic from data centers on the East Coast as well, to better serve users in the eastern half of the United States.

Future plans might also include a caching scheme, such as a separate set of servers for graphics or a reverse proxy setup. A proxy server or servers might then be able to intercept all page requests from the Internet, and serve static content from their own disks or RAM, passing ASP requests on to existing server clusters. This approach could be used in combination with a distribution scheme, a central server that distributes requests to several reverse proxies around the United States.

A similar approach might be to use a caching service. MSNBC could contract with such a service to serve static content, such as graphics, from its own geographically dispersed network of servers.

Best Practices

MSNBC.com uses the following best practices to address capacity planning:

- **Page weight standards**. Content developers for MSNBC try to stay between 150 and 200 KB per page, including all content and graphics. Graphics are responsible for most of the page size and loading time.

- **Tuning content**. During periods of high demand, MSNBC takes steps to reduce the amount of dynamic content in order to increase the capacity of its servers. This is usually done by moving to a "light" version of the site in which many of the ASP pages are replaced by static HTML pages.

Tools

Microsoft offers a numbers of tools for performance tuning and testing. Some of these tools are included with Windows 2000 and IIS 5.0, others are offered on the Windows 2000 Resource Kit CD, and still others are available on the Microsoft Web site (www.microsoft.com). For example, System Monitor (formerly called Performance Monitor) is built in to Windows 2000 and is essential to monitoring nearly every aspect of server performance.

This section briefly describes the following tools:

- Microsoft Web Application Stress (WAS) tool
- Network Monitor
- SQL Profiler
- System Monitor
- Visual Studio Analyzer

In addition to these tools, you might also consider using the tools listed in the following table.

Tool	Description
Process and Thread Status (Pstat.exe)	Shows the status of all running processes and threads. Pstat.exe is available on the Windows 2000 Server Resource Kit companion CD.
Process Tree (Ptree.exe)	Queries the process inheritance tree and shuts down processes on local or remote computers. Ptree.exe is available on the Windows 2000 Server Resource Kit companion CD.
HTTP Monitoring	Monitors HTTP activity on your servers and can notify you if there are changes in the amount of activity. HTTP Monitoring is available on the Windows 2000 Resource Kit companion CD.
NBTStat	Detects information about your server's current network connections. For more information about NBTStat, see http://www.microsoft.com/WINDOWS2000/library/resources/reskit/samplechapters/pref/pref_tts_omfx.asp.

Microsoft Web Application Stress Tool

The Microsoft Web Application Stress (WAS) tool is a simulation tool developed by Web testers to realistically reproduce multiple browsers requesting pages from a Web application. Microsoft has made the tool easy to use by masking some of the complexities of Web server testing. This makes the WAS tool useful for anyone interested in gathering performance data on a Web site.

The WAS tool is a consolidation of many of the best features developed over the years, as well as a few new features. In addition, this version covers the most needed features for stress testing three-tiered, personalized, ASP page sites running on Windows 2000. To download WAS, see http://webtool.rte.microsoft.com/.

Microsoft Network Monitor

Network Monitor (Netmon.exe) is a Windows 2000 administrative tool you can use to monitor network traffic. It is not installed by default, but you can install it by using the **Add/Remove Programs** option in the **Control Panel**.

Network Monitor captures network traffic for display and analysis. You can use it to perform tasks such as analyzing previously captured data in user-defined methods, extracting data from defined protocol parsers, and analyzing real-time traffic on your network.

Network Monitor is useful for capturing packets between browsers, Web servers, and SQL Server. It provides valuable timing information as well as packet size, network utilization, and many other statistics that can be valuable for managing system performance. For more information about Network Monitor, see Microsoft Windows 2000 Help.

SQL Profiler

SQL Profiler is a tool that captures Microsoft SQL Server events from a server. The events are saved in a trace file that you can analyze later or use to replay a specific series of steps when you are trying to diagnose a problem. You can use SQL Profiler to:

- Step through problem queries to find the cause of the problem.

- Find and diagnose slow-running queries.

- Capture the series of SQL statements that lead to a problem. The saved trace can then be used to replicate the problem on a test server where the problem can be diagnosed.

- Monitor the performance of SQL Server to tune database performance.

For more information about SQL Profiler, see http://www.microsoft.com/sql/techinfo/perftuninguide.htm.

System Monitor

With System Monitor, you can collect and view extensive data about the ways in which hardware resources are used and the activities of system services on your site. You can use System Monitor to:

- Collect and view real-time performance data on a local computer or from several remote computers.

- View data in a counter log that is either being collected currently or was collected previously.

- Present data in a printable graph, histogram, or report view.

- Incorporate System Monitor functionality into Microsoft Word or other applications in the Microsoft Office suite by means of automation.

- Create HTML pages from performance views.

- Create reusable monitoring configurations that can be installed on other computers using the Microsoft Management Console (MMC).

For more information about System Monitor, see
http://support.microsoft.com/support/kb/articles/Q248/3/45.ASP.

Visual Studio Analyzer

You can use Visual Studio Analyzer, a tool in Microsoft Visual Studio 6.0 Enterprise Edition, to analyze performance, isolate page faults, and understand the structure of your distributed applications. You can use Visual Studio Analyzer with applications and systems built with any of the Visual Studio tools.

Several Microsoft technologies, such as COM, ADO, and COM+, are shipped with the ability to provide information to Visual Studio Analyzer. If your applications use any of these technologies, you can get detailed information about this use in Visual Studio Analyzer. In addition, you can customize your own applications to provide information to Visual Studio Analyzer.

For more information about Video Studio Analyzer, see
http://msdn.microsoft.com/library/periodic/period99/analyzer.htm.

Part Six: Appendices

Microsoft®
**Commerce
Server** 2000

Commerce Server 2000 Resource Kit CD Contents

The compact disc (CD) included with the *Microsoft Commerce Server 2000 Resource Kit* contains tool and code examples that you can use in conjunction with this book.

Make sure to read the Readme.txt at the root of the CD because it contains the latest information about the Commerce Server 2000 Resource Kit CD. You will also find the End-User License Agreement in the root of the CD.

The Commerce Server 2000 Resource Kit CD includes the following folders:

- Checkout_Process_ISAPI
- Comti_Bridge
- Documentation (contains an electronic copy of the book)
- DW_Delete
- IE_XML_Schema_Validation_Tool
- JDE_Code_Samples
- Migrate_Catalog
- Prediction_Viewer
- Predictor_Tutorial
- Profiles_Schema
- Sample_SQL_Reports
- SAP_Code_Samples
- Site_Terms_Viewer
- Static_Export
- Template_Creator
- Transaction_Migration_Tool
- VCTurbo_CS2K

Checkout_Process_ISAPI

When you properly implement an Internet Server Application Programming Interface (ISAPI), it can be an extremely fast and efficient way to handle Web server requests. The CS2KCheckout ISAPI extension provides an example of how you might integrate ISAPI into a Commerce Server 2000 Solution Site. ISAPI is slightly more complex to build and debug than an Active Server Pages (ASP) solution. ASP pages are the right solution for most sites, but if raw performance is the primary goal, then you should consider ISAPI.

This sample implements a basic check out process (CS2KCheckout) for a Commerce Server Web site. It integrates with various Commerce Server Component Object Model (COM) objects and the Order Processing pipeline (OPP) to handle order calculations and payment processing. You can expand this sample to implement much more in the way of functionality—multiple ship methods, multiple addresses, and so on. This sample is designed to get you started using ISAPI.

Comti_Bridge

The ComtiBridge Pipeline Component helps you integrate mainframe applications with a Commerce Server pipeline. You can have your Order Processing pipeline (OPP) call out to the mainframe to check whether or not a given customer is a valid customer or you can call out to the mainframe to manipulate the order in some manner.

Documentation

You will find an electronic copy of the *Commerce Server 2000 Resource Kit* in the Csreskit.chm file. This fully-searchable online version of the book is installed in the \Documentation folder.

DW_Delete

You can use the DW_Delete tool to delete data using the All option in the Select Delete Type list box in the dialog box that opens during the creation of a package for the Delete Data Transformation Services (DTS) task. The same dialog box opens on an existing package when you choose properties in the Delete DTS task and removes all the data from the Data Warehouse. The deletion of data using the All option in the drop-down box deletes all the data in the Data Warehouse that you chose.

IE_XML_Schema_Validation_Tool

You can use the IE_XML_Schema_Validation_Tool to validate Extensible Markup Language (XML) documents. When you browse XML files using Microsoft Internet Explorer, the XML documents are not validated. In addition, when you view the source of the document, only the XML is returned and there is no way of viewing the output from the XSL or XSLT stylesheet that may have been used to transform that XML document.

You can use the Internet Explorer Tools for Validating XML and Viewing XSLT Output to invoke a shell option when you view XML files to see the processed XSL output. In addition, you can also validate XML against an embedded schema when you load XML through the Internet Explorer MIME viewer. This capability to validate the XML can be very useful when you are trying to debug XSL formatting problems in Internet Explorer or are doing quick schema validation.

JDE_Code_Samples

The code samples for integrating J.D. Edwards OneWorld with Microsoft Commerce Server 2000 are located in the folder \JDE_Code_Samples on the Commerce Server 2000 Resource Kit CD. These code samples are discussed in Chapter 10, "Integrating Third-Party ERP Systems with Commerce Server Applications." You can also find Chapter 10 in the \Documentation folder on the Resource Kit CD.

Migrate_Catalog

The MigrateCatalog.vbs tool is discussed in Chapter 11, "Migrating from Site Server to Commerce Server 2000." You can also find Chapter 11 in the \Documentation folder on the Resource Kit CD.

Prediction_Viewer

You can use the Prediction Viewer tool to get sample recommendations from a Prediction model. The viewer is useful for understanding and debugging models, and for tuning the parameters that govern prediction -- especially the Popularity Penalty.

Predictor_Tutorial

The Predictor Tutorial consists of a demonstration or "demo" site, found in PredictorDemoSite.pup, as well as other supporting files. Full instructions for using the Predictor Tutorial can be found in the Predictor Tutorial.doc file found in the \Predictor_Tutorial folder.

Note that the Predictor Tutorial requires that you have a complete installation of Commerce Server (including the Predictor resource) on your computer, including SQL Server 2000 in the platform.

Profiles_Schema_Mover

The Profiles Schema Mover tool is a compiled Microsoft Visual Basic application that enables you to define and configure the profile schema in one Commerce Server environment (such as your development environment), then migrate it to another (such as your test or production environment). You can also use this tool to change the data source connection strings for the target environment when you migrate the schema.

This tool is discussed in Chapter 9, "Developer Notes." You can also find Chapter 9 in the \Documentation folder on the Resource Kit CD.

Sample_SQL_Reports

You can use the sample scripts located in Sample_SQL_Reports to create custom reports.

SAP_Code_Samples

The code samples for integrating SAP with Commerce Server are located in the folder SAP_Code_Samples on the Commerce Server 2000 Resource Kit CD. These code samples are discussed in Chapter 10, "Integrating Third-Party ERP Systems with Commerce Server Applications." You can also find Chapter 10 in the \Documentation folder on the Resource Kit CD.

Site_Terms_Viewer

The Site Terms Viewer tool is a Visual Basic script that shows how to access site terms programmatically. This tool is discussed in Chapter 9, "Developer Notes." You can also find Chapter 9 in the \Documentation folder on the Resource Kit CD.

Static_Export

You can use the StaticExport.vbs script located on the Commerce Server 2000 Resource Kit CD as a prototype for creating comma-separated value (CSV) files for import into the Commerce Server Direct Mailer database. This script is discussed in Chapter 11, "Migrating from Site Server to Commerce Server 2000." You can also find Chapter 11 in the \Documentation folder on the Resource Kit CD.

Template_Creator

The Template Creator tool is useful for creating new content templates that the Content Selection Framework (CSF) can use. You might want to use this tool if your site requires customization to the CSF templates that are provided with the out-of-the-box Solution Sites, if you want to add new templates for your campaigns, or if you want to manage your site's content templates after you have created them.

You must use the Template Creator tool on a computer that has a Commerce Server installation.

Transaction_Migration_Tool

You can use the Transaction Migration tool to migrate transaction data from Web sites running Site Server 3.0 Commerce Edition (SSCE) to Web sites running Commerce Server 2000.

VCTurbo_CS2K

The VCTurbo tool, which contains the files MigrateUser.vbs and VCTurboCS2K.pup, is discussed in Chapter 11, "Migrating from Site Server to Commerce Server 2000." You can also find Chapter 11 in the \Documentation folder on the Resource Kit CD. The MigrateUser.vbs file is discussed in the Anatomy_of_Volcano_Coffee_migration.doc file, which contains additional information. The VCTurboCS2K.pup file contains the Volcano Coffee (VC) Turbo site after migration from SSCE to Commerce Server 2000.

Additional Resources

The following entries list resources that you might find helpful when you plan, develop, deploy, and manage your Microsoft Commerce Server 2000 Web site.

To "cut-and-paste" these links into your browser, view the online version of the book text, available in the \Documentation folder of the Commerce Server 2000 Resource Kit CD-ROM.

Microsoft Products and Tools

For information about Microsoft Windows 2000 Index Server, see http://www.microsoft.com/ntserver/web/techdetails/overview/IndxServ.asp.

For information about the *Microsoft Windows 2000 Server Resource Kit*, see http://mspress.microsoft.com/books/1394.htm.

For information about the *Windows 2000 Server Operations Guide*, located in the *Microsoft Windows 2000 Resource Kit*, see http://mspress.microsoft.com/books/1394.htm.

For information about *Microsoft Windows 2000 Server Resource Kit* support tools, see http://www.microsoft.com/windows2000/library/resources/reskit/default.asp.

For information about troubleshooting Extensible Markup Language (XML) schema validation and catalog import issues, see http://www.msdn.microsoft.com/downloads/webtechnology/xml/iexmltls.asp.

For the latest updates and information targeted at the system administrator, browse the Commerce Server section under "Navigate by Product" on http://www.microsoft.com/technet.

For information about Microsoft FrontPage, see http://www.microsoft.com/frontpage/.

For information about Microsoft Visual InterDev, see http://msdn.microsoft.com/vinterdev/.

For information about InetMonitor, see:

- http://www.microsoft.com/siteserver/ssrk/inet

- http://www.microsoft.com/SITESERVER/site/DeployAdmin/InetMonitor.htm

For information about the Microsoft Web Application Stress (WAS) tool, see http://webtool.rte.microsoft.com/.

For information about the Microsoft Complete Commerce Toolkit, see http://www.microsoft.com/isn/deployment/comtoolkit.asp.

For information about Microsoft BizTalk Server 2000, see http://www.microsoft.com/biztalkserver.

For information about Microsoft Servers, see http://www.microsoft.com/servers.

For information about Microsoft Business, see http://www.microsoft.com/business/ecommerce/default.asp.

For information about configuring Internet Information Services (IIS) 5.0, see http://www.microsoft.com/technet/iis/deploy.asp.

For information about configuring and using the international support of Windows 2000 and the Windows 2000 MultiLanguage Version, see http://www.microsoft.com/globaldev/win2k/setup/default.asp.

For information about Microsoft Scalable Web Cache (SWC) 2.0, see http://www.microsoft.com/TechNet/iis/swc2.asp.

You can download the Solution Sites from http://www.microsoft.com/commerceserver/solutionsites.

You can download Windows 2000 debugging symbols from http://msdn.microsoft.com/downloads/default.asp?URL=/code/sample.asp?url=/MSDN-FILES/027/000/189/MsdnCompositeDoc.xml.

You can download the Platform Software Development Kit (SDK) from http://msdn.microsoft.com/downloads/sdks/platform/platform.asp.

For information about the Microsoft Management Console (MMC) snap-in for Windows 2000, see http://www.microsoft.com/WINDOWS2000/library/howitworks/management/mmcover.asp.

For information about SQL Server, including SQL Profiler, see http://www.microsoft.com/SQL/productinfo/bizopsoverview.htm.

For information about SQL Profiler and performance tuning, see http://www.microsoft.com/sql/techinfo/perftuninguide.htm.

For information about System Monitor, see:

- http://support.microsoft.com/support/kb/articles/Q248/3/45.ASP .

- http://msdn.microsoft.com/library/default.asp?URL=/library/psdk/winbase/sysmonauto_3jqd.htm.

For information about Microsoft Visual Studio, see http://msdn.microsoft.com/vstudio.

For information about Visual Studio Analyzer, see http://msdn.microsoft.com/library/periodic/period99/analyzer.htm.

For information about the Microsoft Visual Studio Interoperability Center, see http://msdn.microsoft.com/vstudio/centers/interop.

For information about the Microsoft Reference Architecture for Commerce, see http://msdn.microsoft.com/library/techart/ractp.htm.

For information about Microsoft Systems Management Server (SMS), including the Network Monitor component, see:

- http://www.microsoft.com/smsmgmt/

- http://msdn.microsoft.com/library/psdk/netmon/portalnm_6ilu.htm

- http://microsoft.com/smsmgmt/default.asp

For information about Data Transformation Services (DTS), see http://microsoft.com/sql.

You can download tools from http://www.microsoft.com/.

For information about Microsoft Application Center 2000, see http://www.microsoft.com/applicationcenter/.

For information about how to use SQL Server to replicate Commerce Server databases, see SQL Server Books Online.

For information about the NBTStat tool, which detects information about your server's current network connections, see http://www.microsoft.com/WINDOWS2000/library/resources/reskit/samplechapters/pref/pref_tts_omfx.asp.

Design Tips and Code Samples

For information about design tips and code samples, see http://www.msdn.microsoft.com/workshop/.default.asp.

For information about real-world strategies and practical advice for building Web-based commerce applications with Microsoft tools, see *Microsoft Commerce Solutions*, by Micro Modeling Associates, Inc. (ISBN 0735605793), located at http://mspress.microsoft.com/prod/books/2486.htm.

For tips and sample code for accessing Microsoft SQL Server through ActiveX Data Objects (ADO) and Active Server Pages (ASP), read the article, "Top Ten Tips: Accessing SQL Through ADO and ASP," by J.D. Meier, located at http://www.microsoft.com/mind/1198/ado/ado.htm.

For suggestions and tips for globalizing software, see the Microsoft Professional Developer's Site for Software Globalization Information, located at http://www.microsoft.com/globaldev/default.asp.

For free daily articles on writing ASP code, see http://www.asptoday.com.

For more information about securing your Web site, read the book, *Designing Secure Web-Based Applications for Microsoft Windows 2000*, by Michael Howard, located at http://mspress.microsoft.com/prod/books/4293.htm.

White Papers, Case Studies, and Technical Information

For a series of white papers about e-commerce, see
http://www.microsoft.com/technet/ecommerce/ecseries.asp.

For a white paper about risk management for product development, see
http://www.microsoft.com/siteserver/ssrk/docs/genericriskprocess.doc.

For information about technical information and white papers written for system integrators
and system engineers, see http://www.microsoft.com/ISN/news.asp.

For information about case studies of electronic commerce sites, see
http://www.microsoft.com/dns/ecommerce/default.htm.

For the latest articles about FrontPage Server Extensions and using FrontPage in conjunction
with IIS, see http://support.microsoft.com/support/search/c.asp?spr=.

For an MSDN online article about globalizing code and localizing Web sites, see "Web
Workshop - The Localization Process: Globalizing Your Code and Localizing Your Site" by
Sjoert Ebben and Gwyneth Marshall, located at
http://msdn.microsoft.com/workshop/management/intl/locprocess.asp.

For information about designing a globalized and localizable Web site, see the MSDN Online
article "Web Workshop - Designing a Globalized and Localizable Web Site" by Sjoert Ebben
and Gwyneth Marshall, located at
http://msdn.microsoft.com/workshop/management/intl/designloc.asp.

From the Microsoft Web Workshop - International Active Server Pages, author Seth Pollack
offers tips on constructing your Web site to reach beyond the English-speaking community,
located at http://msdn.microsoft.com/workshop/server/nextgen/nextgen.asp.

For information and articles about multilingual issues, see http://www.multilingual.com.

For information about product training and updates to the *Active Directory Service Interfaces
(ADSI) Programmers' Guide*, see
http://msdn.microsoft.com/isapi/msdnlib.idc?theURL=/library/psdk/adsi/ds2intro_6asp.htm.

For information about Site Server 3.0 Commerce Edition (SSCE), see
http://www.microsoft.com/technet/commerce.

For information about Microsoft Operations Framework papers, see
http://www.microsoft.com/enterpriseservices/.

For suggestions and tips for adapting software for an international audience, see
http://www.microsoft.com/globaldev/default.asp.

For tips for constructing your Web site to reach beyond the English-speaking community, see
http://msdn.microsoft.com/workshop/server/nextgen/nextgen.asp.

For information about optimizing Web server performance, see
http://www.microsoft.com/BackStage/whitepaper.htm.

For detailed installation instructions and programming procedures and considerations, see the
article "SAP DCOM Connector: Expanding SAP Business Processes," by Homann, Rogers,
and Russo, in *SAP Technical Journal*, Vol. 1, No. 2. You can also find the article online at
http://www.mysap.com/solutions/technology/bapis/com/dcom_mag/dcom_mag.htm.

For information about migrating from Site Server 3.0 and SSCE and third-party vendors, see
http://www.microsoft.com/commerceserver.

For information about various applications that you need to migrate from a Site Server 3.0 or
SSCE site, and platform software documentation and best practices, see
http://www.microsoft.com/technet.

Third-Party References

For information about Keynote and Keynote Perspective, a custom, outsourced service that
shows you how your end users experience your Web site, see http://www.keynote.com.

For information about software packages designed to make it easier for all sizes of
organizations to deploy e-commerce solutions, see:

- Impressa, for small- and medium-sized businesses, located at http://www.impressa.com/.

- VisualCommerce, for medium-sized businesses with large-scale integration needs, located
  at http://www.visualcommerce.com/main/index.asp.

- OneSoft, for large-scale businesses, located at http://www.onesoft.com/.

For a list of tool vendors that offer generalized XML support, see
http://msdn.microsoft.com/xml/general/xmltools.asp.

For information about Tivoli, see http://www.tivoli.com/.

For information about Unicenter from Computer Associates, see
http://www.cai.com/unicenter/.

For information about HP OpenView, see http://www.openview.hp.com/.

For information about SilkPerformer, a Web stress tool from Seque Software, see
http://www.segue.com/html/s_solutions/s_performer/s_performer.htm.

For information about SiteScope, a custom service that offers tools designed for deep
monitoring, see http://www.freshtech.com/.

For information about OnePoint Directory and Resource Administrator, a tool that gives you
relational-like views of your organization through ActiveViews, see
http://www.missioncritical.com/.

For information about XBuilder, a tool that helps you analyze performance of an existing site,
see http://www.xbuilder.net/.home/default.htm.

For information about Rainbow technologies tools for improving secure Web server response time, see http://www.rainbow.com.

For information about Microsoft Solution Providers, see http://microsoft.com/commerce.

For the latest information about third-party software developed especially to work with Commerce Server, see http://www.microsoft.com/commerceserver.

For information about companies who provide capabilities for Internet browsing and migrating transactions and reports, see http://www.microsoft.com/commerceserver/thirdparty/partover.htm.

For information about Web sites that offer online testing for broken and incorrect links at a nominal fee, see:

- http://www.netmechanic.com/
- http://www.linkalarm.com/index.html
- http://www.websitegarage.com/

For information about Web server load testing, see http://www.webperfcenter.com/.

For more information about testing network security, see http://www.intrusion.com/.

For more information about secure electronic transactions, see the following sites:

- http://www.verisign.com
- http://www.cylink.com
- http://www.terisa.com
- http://www.cybercash.com
- http://www.checkfree.com

Miscellaneous

To join a discussion with other IT professionals on the TechNet Answer Forums, see http://www.microsoft.com/technet/discuss/default.asp.

For a list of Development Strategies and Initiatives Seminars, see http://msdn.microsoft.com/training/seminars/DevStrategies.asp.

For advanced utilities, technical information, and source code related to Windows 2000 internals, see http://www.sysinternals.com.

For information about J. D. Edwards, see http://www.jdedwards.com/index2.asp.

For information about SAP, see http://www.sap.com/.

The bridge between the Windows 2000 platform and the SAP business object framework is the SAP DCOM connector. You can download the DCOM connector from the SAP Web site: http://www.sap.com/solutions/technology/bapis/resource/software/dcom/rfcsdk.exe.

Glossary

A

Active Directory

The directory service for Microsoft Windows 2000 Server. Active Directory stores information about objects on the network and makes this information available for authorized system administrators and users. It gives network users access to permitted resources anywhere on the network using a single logon process. It also provides system administrators with an intuitive hierarchical view of the network and a single point of administration for all network objects.

Active Directory Service Interfaces (ADSI)

A Component Object Model-based (COM-based) directory service model that ADSI-compliant client applications use to access a wide variety of distinct directory protocols, including Windows Directory Services, Lightweight Directory Access Protocol (LDAP), and Novell Directory Services (NDS), while using a single, standard set of interfaces. ADSI shields the client application from the implementation and operational details of the underlying data store or protocol.

Active Server Pages (ASP)

A server-side scripting environment that can be used to create dynamic Web pages or to build Web applications. ASP pages are files that contain HTML tags, text, and script commands. ASP pages can call Component Object Model (COM) components to perform tasks, such as connecting to a database or performing a business calculation. With ASP, you can add interactive content to Web pages or build entire Web applications that use HTML pages as the interface to your customers.

Active User Object (AUO)

A framework that provides a single, unified access mechanism for all user-profile information, so there is no need to specify user identification and profile storage location. You can configure a computer to define a virtual namespace of profile information, specifying the configuration information needed to access profile data from a variety of sources.

AUO is technically a container of ADSI objects. You define the number of objects that the AUO will contain and provide the information for managing these objects. By writing or reusing ADSI providers, you can access profile information that exists in any store.

ActiveX Data Objects (ADO)

A high-level, language-independent set of object-based data access interfaces optimized for data application. ADO enables client applications to access and manipulate data from a database server through an OLE DB provider. See also ActiveX Data Objects (Multidimensional) (ADO MD).

ActiveX Data Objects (Multidimensional) (ADO MD)

A high-level, language-independent set of object-based data access interfaces optimized for multidimensional data application. Visual Basic and other automation languages use ADO MD as the data access interface to multidimensional data storage. ADO MD is a part of ADO version 2.0 and later. See also ActiveX Data Objects (ADO).

anonymous access

One of the authentication methods that you can set at the Web Site or Application levels in Internet Information Services (IIS) 5.0. Anonymous authentication is used to establish an anonymous Web (HTTP) connection without providing a user name or password. It is commonly used in the public areas of an Internet site. If you enable anonymous authentication for a site, an anonymous connection will be made even if authenticated access has also been enabled, unless more restrictive NTFS permissions exist on the individual file being requested. Also called anonymous authentication.

anonymous user

A user who accesses content on a Web site without providing a user login name and password.

application

From a Commerce Server 2000 administration standpoint, an application is an ASP application accessible through a single Uniform Resource Locator (URL). An application appears in both the Commerce Server and Internet Information Services (IIS) console trees. The application that appears in the Commerce Server Manager console tree is a logical representation of the application in IIS.

Application Center 2000

A Microsoft deployment and management tool for high-availability Web applications built on Microsoft Windows 2000.

auditing

Tracking the activities of users by recording selected types of events in a security log.

AUO

See Active User Object.

authenticated access

A user access option that you can set at the Default Web Site or Application levels in IIS. As opposed to anonymous access, authenticated access requires a user to have a valid account and password to access the site. The three types of authenticated access are Basic authentication, Digest authentication, and Integrated Windows authentication/NTLM.

authorization
A process that verifies that a user has the correct permissions to access a resource such as a Web page or database, or has the correct privileges to perform a task such as performing backups.

availability
A measure of fault tolerance for a computer, server cluster, or system and its programs. A highly available computer or system is one that is up and operating at an acceptable service level at least 99.9 percent of the time.

B

B2B site
See business-to-business site.

B2C site
See business-to-consumer site.

basket
The list of items a user selects to purchase from an e-commerce Web site.

BizTalk Server 2000
A Microsoft product that provides the tools and infrastructure companies need to exchange business documents among various platforms and operating systems regardless of the application being used to process a business document.

Business Desk
See Commerce Server Business Desk.

business-to-business site
An e-commerce Web site designed for the creation and transmission of purchase orders between businesses that have an established relationship. Also known as a supplier site or a B2B site.

business-to-consumer site
A commerce Web site designed for retail shopping by the public. Also known as a retail site or a B2C site.

C

cache
A special memory subsystem in which frequently used data values are duplicated for quick access. A cache stores the contents of frequently accessed RAM locations and the addresses where these data items are stored. When the processor references an address in memory, the cache checks to see whether it holds that address. If it does, the data is returned to the processor; if it does not, a regular memory access occurs.

campaign
A marketing program that uses many communication vehicles (for example, ads and direct mail) to accomplish a specific result, such as increasing marketing share, introducing new products, or retaining customers.

campaign item
A communication vehicle that contributes to the specified result of a campaign. You can create three types of campaign items in Commerce Server: ads, direct mail, and discounts. You can use third-party products to create additional types of campaign items.

capacity planning

Planning for application, hardware, and network requirements to support expected site traffic and to achieve site performance goals.

catalog

A collection of categories and products.

catalog properties

The basic properties that describe a catalog, such as name, start date, end date, currency, unit of weight measure, and product unique ID.

catalog schema

A description of a catalog that specifies the format of its category definitions, product definitions, and property definitions. Several catalogs can share one schema.

checkout

The process of finalizing a purchase on a Web site. For example, when customers shop on your Web site, they may select several items and save them in their shopping basket. When they have finished shopping, they click on a checkout link or graphical button that takes them to an online form where they enter their name, billing address, payment type, and shipping information.

click URL

The URL that users see when they click a piece of content on your Web site or in a direct mail message. See also Uniform Resource Locator (URL).

client

The program or user that makes a request in a client/server relationship. For example, someone who uses Commerce Server Business Desk makes client requests for information from the Business Desk server.

COM

See Component Object Model.

comma-separated value file (CSV)

A text file that uses the comma character to separate, or delimit, columns or database fields. Most databases and other programs can export and import a CSV file, so that database files can be created in one program and used by another program.

Commerce Server Business Desk

A Web-based site management tool available in Commerce Server 2000 that hosts business management modules you use to manage and analyze your e-commerce sites. For example, you can update pricing information in your catalog, target new ads to specific users, and then run reports to measure how these changes affect site productivity. Commerce Server Business Desk is accessible from any computer running Microsoft Internet Explorer 5.5 and because it is Web based, it can be accessed either locally or remotely.

By default, every Commerce Server Web site has a distinct instance of Business Desk associated with it. It is designed so that site developers can modify or extend the management functionality provided with Business Desk.

Commerce Server Direct Mailer

A global resource that is also a Microsoft Windows 2000 service. Direct Mailer runs direct mail campaigns. It processes lists of recipients, constructs personalized message bodies from either Web pages or static files, and sends the mail message to the recipient. Use Commerce Server Manager to configure and manage Direct Mailer, and to specify the database connection string to the Direct Mailer database.

Commerce Server Manager

A system administration tool that you use to manage and configure Commerce Server resources, sites, applications, and Web servers. The Microsoft Management Console (MMC) hosts Commerce Server Manager.

Commerce Server Site Packager

A deployment tool that you use to package your site, applications, and resources into a single file (that has a .pup extension), and then move that file to another computer. Using Site Packager, you can deploy your site on multiple computers in a distributed environment.

Component Object Model (COM)

The object-oriented programming model that defines how objects interact within a single application or between applications. In COM, client software accesses an object through a pointer to an interface, which is a related set of properties and methods.

connection string

A series of semicolon-delimited arguments that define the location of a database and how to connect to it.

content replication

A method of copying Web site content from one server node to another. You can copy files manually, or use replication software to copy content automatically. Replication is a necessary function of clustering to ensure fault tolerance.

Content Selection Framework (CSF)

A development framework for the targeted delivery of content. The Content Selection Framework (CSF) provides the components you use to build a business-specific messaging system. CSF provides a platform for making high-speed decisions to target content to users.

cookie

Information about a user, such as an identification number, a password, click history, or number of times the user visited a site, stored in a file. A cookie can also store ticket data. Commerce Server supports both persistent and non-persistent cookies. Persistent cookies are stored on the user computers. Non-persistent cookies are used to track the activity of authenticated users who visit your site. When the session ends, the non-persistent cookie is deleted.

CS Authentication resource

A Commerce Server resource with global-level properties, managed through Commerce Server Manager. Use CS Authentication to configure authentication options for a site.

CSF

See Content Selection Framework.

CSV

See comma-separated value file.

cube

A structure that contains a subset of the data in the Commerce Server Data Warehouse, defined by shared dimensions and measures. A cube in Commerce Server 2000 is created during the unpacking process, and is populated and processed for data retrieval when the Report preparation DTS task is run. Storing data in cubes increases the speed of data retrieval.

custom price

The specific pricing rules that apply to products in a custom catalog. There are three types of custom prices: percentage off, fixed amount off, and explicit price.

D

data store

A database containing data used by an e-commerce site, such as information about registered users, products, or ads. This also refers to the server that contains the data (the data-store server).

Data Transformation Services (DTS)

A SQL Server component used to import, export, and transform data from different data sources. Commerce Server provides a set of DTS tasks that you use to import data into the Commerce Server Data Warehouse.

Data Warehouse

In Commerce Server, a combination of a SQL Server database, an online analytical processing (OLAP) database, and a set of processes that a system administrator uses to import and maintain large amounts of data from multiple data sources.

denial-of-service attacks

A form of hacker attack characterized by a large number of connection requests that consume all memory on a server. In extreme cases, the server can crash in the face of such an attack; in other cases, normal processing returns when the attack ceases.

design-time control (DTC)

A special type of Microsoft ActiveX control used to generate text in an editing environment. Typically, a user is presented with several choices in the control, which alters the details of a section of scripting code or HTML that is placed on the page being edited.

Direct Mailer

See Commerce Server Direct Mailer.

Direct Mailer database

A SQL Server database that contains e-mail message, event data, and job data. Commerce Server Setup installs the Direct Mailer database when you install Commerce Server Direct Mailer. The database is installed on the same computer as Direct Mailer. See also Commerce Server Direct Mailer.

DTC

See design-time control.

DTS

See Data Transformation Services.

dynamic list

A list of user records that the List Manager service creates at run time, when the list is needed (such as when the list data is being exported). Each time the list is requested, List Manager gathers the most recent data in the Data Warehouse. The information needed to create the list is stored in the List Manager database. (This differs from a static list where the entire list of user records is stored in the List Manager database.) Dynamic lists are useful for direct mail campaigns that are run frequently, or for lists of recipients that are updated frequently. See also static list.

dynamic report

A report that is created at run time. Each time the report is run, it gathers the most recent data in the Data Warehouse. Only the report definition, which remains the same over time, is stored. (This differs from a static report, where the report is stored, with the data, in the Data Warehouse.) You can view dynamic reports in a Microsoft PivotTable or a Microsoft PivotChart. Use the Reports module to run dynamic reports. See also PivotChart report and PivotTable report.

E

e-commerce

The process of buying and selling products and services over the Internet.

Electronic Data Interchange (EDI)

The transfer of data between different companies using networks, such as the Internet. As more and more companies connect to the Internet, EDI is becoming increasingly important as an easy mechanism for companies to use when they buy, sell, and trade information.

envelope

A named set of properties that represents a specific business document. Envelope properties include an envelope format and may include a pointer to an envelope specification. Or, the header and footer information, or header information only, that encapsulates electronic business data for transport.

event

The occurrence of a specific action performed by a user. Typical events include pressing a keyboard key or clicking a mouse to choose a button. Events are recorded with the time at which they occur. Programmers write code to respond to these actions.

explicit profiling

An information-collecting process in which users visiting a Web site supply profile data about themselves. For example, users might provide their names, addresses, phone numbers, and so forth. See also implicit profiling.

expression

A condition that is evaluated against user profiles to determine whether to deliver content or to perform another action. For example, an expression might be "user.totalvisit > 100". If this expression evaluates to True, then a specific piece of content is displayed. Use the Campaign Expressions module to create expressions, and then combine the expressions with the action you want to perform after the expressions are evaluated.

Expression Builder

A tool you use to create an expression. The Expression Builder includes a list of common expressions from which you can select to define the properties you want to target. You access the Expression Builder when creating a new target expression or catalog expression from the Campaign Expressions module. See also expression.

Extensible Markup Language (XML)

A data format for structured document interchange on the Web. It is called the Extensible Markup Language because it is not a fixed format like HTML. XML is designed to enable the use of Standard Generalized Markup Language (SGML) on the World Wide Web. XML is not a single markup language. It is a metalanguage that is used to design a markup language. A regular markup language defines a way to describe information in a certain class of documents (for example, HTML). With XML, authors can define their own customized markup language for many classes of documents.

F

failover

The process of taking resources, either individually or in a group, offline on one server cluster node and bringing them back online on another node.

firewall

A security checkpoint that separates an intranet from the Internet (or Internet groups). Only specific data may pass through a firewall. Only authorized users can access data secured by a firewall.

free-text searchable

A search that locates exact matches and words that are inflectionally generated from the one(s) you specified. For example, the word "drive" would return matches for drives, drove, driving, and driven.

G

Global.asa

A file maintained on an Internet Information Services (IIS) 5.0 server for each application. The server automatically processes the Global.asa file when the IIS application starts and stops or when individual users start and stop browser sessions that access the Web pages of the application. This file typically contains scripts to initialize application or session variables, connect to databases, send cookies, and perform other operations that pertain to the application as a whole.

global resource

A resource that is available for use by all sites. Global resources expose an object at the global level in Commerce Server Manager, and at the site level of those sites that are using the global resource. Properties for a global resource are configured at the global level.

The following global resources are included with Commerce Server: Commerce Server Direct Mailer and Predictor (which are also Microsoft Windows 2000 services), CS Authentication, Profiles, and Data Warehouse. Third parties can develop custom global resources to work with Commerce Server. Use Commerce Server Manager to manage global resources.

H

horizontal scaling
Increasing capacity by adding more servers to a server cluster. See also scaling and vertical scaling.

HTML Component (HTC)
A control implemented using Internet Explorer Dynamic Hypertext Markup Language (DHTML) behaviors. HTCs are used in Commerce Server Business Desk modules for data display and manipulation.

Hypertext Transfer Protocol (HTTP)
The client/server protocol used to transmit and receive all data over the World Wide Web. When you type a URL into your browser, you are actually sending an HTTP request to a Web server for a page of information.

I

IIS
See Internet Information Services.

implicit profiling
An information collection process in which the actions and behaviors of a user visiting a Web site are recorded as the user traverses and interacts with the Web site. See also explicit profiling, Predictor resource.

Independent Software Vendor (ISV)
A vendor who develops software such as tax, shipping, or inventory software, that integrates with Commerce Server and extends its functionality. You can compare an ISV to a Solution Provider, who customizes Commerce Server for specific customers or vertical markets, and designs and deploys systems.

Internet
A set of distinct computer networks joined together with gateways that handle data transfer and the conversion of messages from the sending network to the protocols used by the receiving networks. These networks and gateways use the Transmission Control Protocol/Internet Protocol (TCP/IP) suite of protocols.

Internet domain name
The name used for a site hosted on the Internet. An Internet domain name is a combination of a second-level domain name (such as "Microsoft") and a top-level domain name (such as "com" or "net"), separated by a period. Before establishing a commerce site on the Internet, a business must first apply for and register a second-level domain name with an authorized Domain Name System (DNS) domain name registration authority. Also called an Internet address, domain name, and URL.

Internet Information Services (IIS) 5.0
The Microsoft Windows 2000 services that support Web site creation, configuration, and management, along with other Internet functions. You must install IIS on a server before you install Commerce Server.

Internet Service Provider (ISP)

A public provider of remote connections to the Internet. An ISP may host e-commerce sites for client companies, hosting several sites on a single server or server cluster. The ISP often might provide the infrastructure and perform administration tasks common to all sites; clients usually perform some site administration tasks from their remote computers.

intranet

A network designed for information processing within a company or organization. An intranet is so called because it usually employs applications associated with the Internet, such as Web pages, Web browsers, File Transfer Protocol (FTP) sites, e-mail, newsgroups, and mailing lists, in this case accessible only to those within the company or organization.

ISP

See Internet Service Provider.

ISV

See Independent Software Vendor.

L

latency

The length of time that a user must wait for a response to a request. Latency is the primary benchmark for determining whether a Web site is operating at an acceptable level.

load balancing

Distribution of processing across multiple servers within a cluster. If a server fails, the load is dynamically redistributed among the remaining servers. Network Load Balancing,

available on Microsoft Windows 2000 Advanced Server, is the load balancing solution that Windows Clustering uses.

load testing

See stress testing.

log file

A record of the transactions or the processing that takes place on a computer system. The log file can be either a text file or a database file. Commerce Server log files are imported into the Data Warehouse so you can analyze site activity using the Analysis modules in Commerce Server Business Desk.

logical schema

In the Data Warehouse, a conceptual model that maps to the data in the physical store, and provides an understandable view of the data. When a developer creates code to access or change data in the Data Warehouse, the developer interacts with the logical schema. Commerce Server processes access data in the Data Warehouse through the logical schema.

M

mean time between failures (MTBF)

The average time interval, usually expressed in thousands or tens of thousands of hours, that will elapse before a hardware component fails and requires service.

mean time to recovery (MTTR)

The average time interval, usually expressed in hours, that it takes to repair a failed component.

messaging port

A set of rules configured by using BizTalk Messaging Manager with which you can direct how documents are enveloped, secured, and transported to a designated destination organization.

metadata

The data used to describe other data. For example, data type describes data that makes up a profile.

Microsoft Management Console (MMC)

A framework for hosting administrative tools, called consoles. A console can contain tools, folders, other containers, Web pages, and other administrative items. These items are displayed in the left pane of the console, called a console tree. A console has one or more windows that can provide views of the console tree. The main MMC window provides commands and tools for authoring consoles.

MIME

See Multipurpose Internet Mail Extensions.

MMC

See Microsoft Management Console.

Multipurpose Internet Mail Extensions (MIME)

A standard that extends the Simple Mail Transfer Protocol (SMTP) to permit data, such as video, sound, and binary files to be transmitted by Internet e-mail without having to be translated into ASCII format first.

N

navigation pane

In Commerce Server Business Desk, the window on the left side of a list page that displays the hierarchy of categories and modules.

node

Each member of a server cluster. See also server cluster.

O

Order Processing pipeline (OPP)

Software infrastructure that links several components and runs them in sequence. Commerce Server 2000 includes three Order Processing pipelines: Product, Plan, and Purchase.

online analytical processing (OLAP)

A class of technologies designed for live, ad-hoc data access and analysis. OLAP data is stored in a multidimensional database, which considers each data attribute (such as product, geographic sales region, and time period) as a separate dimension. OLAP data is grouped and organized, by shared dimensions, in cubes. The Data Warehouse uses OLAP cubes to store imported data, which accelerates report and query processing. See also cube.

P

package

A file created by the Commerce Server Site Packager deployment tool that contains all the data necessary to deploy a site onto a different computer. This includes applications and resources, including resource property settings stored in the Administration database. A package does not contain those property settings that are specific to a computer (such as connection strings). Package files have a .pup extension.

personalization

A feature used to direct Web-based content or e-mail messages to users, based on their user profile data and their previous requests for content. See also Commerce Server Direct Mailer, Predictor resource.

pipeline

A software infrastructure that defines and links together one or more stages of a business process, running them in sequence to complete a specific task. Each stage of a pipeline contains one or more pipeline components (COM objects) that can be configured to work with the unique requirements of the site.

Pipeline Component

A COM server object that implements the required Pipeline Component interfaces. Each component performs operations on some part of an **OrderForm** object or **Dictionary** object before sending it to the next component or stage in the pipeline.

pipeline configuration file

A file containing the configuration data for a pipeline. The pipeline specified in the file is created and run by a pipeline object. The file contains stages and components that can be customized using the Pipeline Editor.

Pipeline Editor

An application used to create and edit Commerce Server pipeline configuration files. The Pipeline Editor displays a pipeline as a pipe graphic, showing the stages of the pipeline as segments of the pipe. The components used in a stage appear as valves.

pipeline object

An object that uses pipeline configuration files to execute a series of components. Commerce Server 2000 provides six objects to execute pipelines: **MtsPipeline**, **MtsTxPipeline**, **PooledPipeline**, **PooledTxPipeline**, **OrderGroup**, and **OrderPipeline**. The **MtsPipeline** and **PooledPipeline** objects do not support COM+ transactions.

PivotChart report

A report displayed in an interactive chart. You can use the chart to view and rearrange data graphically, in a similar manner to a PivotTable report. In Commerce Server, you can view dynamic reports as PivotChart reports.

PivotTable report

A report displayed in an interactive table. You can rotate the rows and columns of the table to see different summaries of the source data, filter the data, or display detailed data for different areas of interest. In Commerce Server, you can view dynamic reports as PivotTable reports. To view PivotTable reports, use the Reports module in Commerce Server Business Desk.

Predictor resource

A global resource that is also a Microsoft Windows 2000 service. The Predictor resource is managed through Commerce Server Manager, and consists of a powerful data-mining engine that enables you to provide predictive capabilities for your Web site based on the aggregate properties of the entire user population that visits your site. Use the Predictor resource to build analysis models that you then deploy to your Web site in order to analyze user information. See also implicit profiling, personalization.

profile

A set of characteristics that define any business-related item, such as a user, a company, or a business process.

Profiles resource

A Commerce Server resource with global-level properties, managed through Commerce Server Manager. You use the Profiles resource to specify the database connection string to the database containing user profile data. You also use the Profiles resource to create, edit, and delete profile properties and profiles. You can add and remove data sources, such as SQL Server databases or Active Directory data sources.

proxy server

A firewall component that manages Internet traffic to and from a local area network (LAN) and can provide other features, such as document caching and access control. A proxy server can improve performance by caching and directly supplying frequently requested data, such as a popular Web page, and can filter and discard requests that the owner does not consider appropriate, such as requests for unauthorized access to proprietary files.

R

reference currency

The currency unit used by a site, in conjunction with an exchange rate table, to calculate product prices in other currencies.

registered user

Someone who visits a Web site and provides personal information, such as name, address, and phone number.

reliability

A measure of the time between failures (mean time between failures), where failure is defined as a departure from acceptable service for an application, a computer system, or the network system. In contrast, availability involves reliability as well as the time required to bring a system back to normal operations after it goes offline (or is taken offline for planned maintenance or upgrade). When you plan for a Commerce Server installation, you plan your hardware, network, and operational procedures to achieve the level of reliability you require.

replication

The process of copying content and/or configuration settings from one server node to another. You can copy files manually or use replication software to copy them automatically. Replication is a necessary function of server clustering to ensure fault tolerance.

resource

An entity that provides functionality to the applications in a Commerce Server site. A resource has one or more COM objects. These are used on the Web pages of an application to access the functionality of the resource. A resource may have group-level properties or site-level properties, but not both. Resource properties are stored in the Administration database. A set of resources ships with Commerce Server; some of these resources are also Microsoft Windows 2000 services. Third parties can develop custom resources to work with Commerce Server. Use Commerce Server Manager to manage

resources. See also global resource, site resource.

retail site

See business-to-consumer site.

S

SAN

See system area network (SAN).

scaling

Expanding the capacity of a Web server or server cluster to accommodate increased site traffic and improve site performance.

server cluster

Two or more computers connected together for the purpose of sharing resources. Each member of a server cluster is called a node. Nodes in a server cluster can have their own storage devices or share a common device. Typically, server clustering involves support for load balancing, fault tolerance, and failover. See also node, Web farm.

server extensions

A set of programs on a Web server that support administering, authoring, and browsing a Microsoft FrontPage-extended Web site.

service

A program, routine, or process that performs a specific system function to support other programs, particularly at a low (close to the hardware) level. When services are provided over a network, they can be published in Active Directory, facilitating service-centric administration and usage. Services have a set of common administration functions. For example, a service can be started, stopped, paused, and resumed; its start parameters can be modified; and it can be administered using command line utilities and scripts. Commerce Server includes the following resources that are also services: Direct Mailer, Predictor, and List Manager. See also resource.

site

In Commerce Server Manager, a container for Commerce Server applications and site-level resources. For example, the Retail Solution Site contains two applications: the business-to-consumer Web site and the business-to-consumer Commerce Server Business Desk, and both share the same site-level resources.

Site Packager

See Commerce Server Site Packager.

site resource

A resource that is available for use by a specific site. All resources used by a site expose an object at the site level in Commerce Server Manager. For example, a global resource can also be a site resource: a global resource used by a site exposes an object at the site level; the only property that the object exposes is a pointer to the associated global resource at the global level.

A site resource can have all of its properties at the site level, or all of its properties at the global level, but it cannot have both. You configure the properties of a site resource at the site level. A set of site resources is included with Commerce Server, and third parties can develop custom site resources. Use Commerce Server Manager to manage site resources.

SKU

Stock keeping unit. A unique identifier used to track a product for inventory purposes. A SKU can be associated with any item that can be purchased. For example, a shirt in style number 3726, size 8 might have a SKU of 3726-8.

Solution Site

A set of Commerce Server features that is pre-configured for a specific site scenario and bundled into a package file. Commerce Server includes the Blank Solution Site in the box. The two other Solution Sites, Retail and Supplier, are available online at http://www.microsoft.com/commerceserver/solutionsites. Each Solution Site is designed to be unpacked and then customized.

spoofing

The practice of making a transmission appear to come from an authorized user to obtain access to a computer or network.

static report

A report that is run immediately upon request and then stored, with the data, in the Data Warehouse. (This differs from a dynamic report, in which only the information needed to create the report is stored in the Data Warehouse.) You can post static reports to your Web site, and you can export the data in a static report to the List Manager module in Commerce Server Business Desk. Use the Reports module to run static reports, and use the Complete Reports module to view them.

stress testing

Testing performed on a Commerce Server application to ensure that it can support the expected number of concurrent users and handle peak user loads while maintaining the required level of performance. Stress testing is performed with a stress tool that generates loads defined by the system administrator to approximate the expected usage patterns of the site. Also called load testing.

supplier

A trading partner in a business-to-business site. Use Microsoft BizTalk Server 2000 to add suppliers to a site. Also known as a vendor.

supplier site

See business-to-business site.

system administrator

The primary user of Commerce Server Manager. This person is responsible for installing, configuring, and managing Commerce Server.

system area network (SAN)

A network typically used to interconnect nodes within a distributed computer system, such as a cluster. These systems are members of a common administrative domain and are usually in close physical proximity. A SAN is physically secure. Microsoft Windows 2000 Datacenter Server supports SANs with certain hardware.

T

TCA

See transaction cost analysis.

target

One or more expressions that identify to whom, where, and when content should be displayed. You can target demographics, sections of a Web site, or both.

targeting

Delivering specific content to specific users.

three-tier architecture

An architecture that divides a networked application into three logical areas: the user interface layer (also called the top tier), the business logic layer (also called the middle tier), and the database layer (also called the bottom tier or back end). Layers may have one or more components. For example, there can be one or more user interfaces in the top tier. Also, each user interface may communicate with more than one application in the middle tier at the same time, and the applications in the middle tier may use more than one database at a time. Components in a tier may run on a computer that is separate from the other tiers, communicating with the other components over a network.

trading partner

An external organization with which your organization exchanges electronic data. The exchange of data among trading partners is governed by the agreements, pipelines, and distribution lists that are created between your organization and the trading partners. Microsoft BizTalk Server 2000 handles the exchange of data among trading partners.

transaction

An action that adds, changes, or deletes data from a database.

transaction cost analysis (TCA)

A method of estimating site capacity by measuring the performance cost of an e-commerce transaction. TCA helps you compare types of transactions with one another to determine which types put the greatest demands on your system.

U

Uniform Resource Identifier (URI)

Identifies points of content on the Internet. The content can be a page of text, a video or sound clip, an image, or a program. The most common form of URI is the Web page address, also known as the Uniform Resource Locator (URL). A URI usually includes the filename for the resource, the name of the computer the resource resides on, and the protocol used to access it. For example, http://www.microsoft.com/sql/techinfo/security/password.htm.

Uniform Resource Locator (URL)

The address of a file (resource) accessible on the Internet. The type of resource depends on the Internet application protocol. For example, for the Hypertext Transfer Protocol (HTTP) used on the World Wide Web, the resource can be an HTML page, an image file, a program such as a Common Gateway Interface (CGI) application or Java applet, or any other file supported by HTTP. The URL

contains the name of the protocol required to access the resource, a domain name that identifies a specific computer on the Internet, and a hierarchical description of a file location on the computer.

usage profile

A set of properties that describe the traffic patterns on a site. For example, a usage profile shows how many people browse a certain page, the average browse-to-buy ratio, and so on. System administrators use the usage profile to perform transaction cost analysis (TCA), to determine how many Web servers are needed, and to configure a site.

user profile

A set of predefined properties that describe a user. For example, name, address, and other properties can constitute a user profile.

V

vertical scaling

Increasing Web site capacity by upgrading hardware (for example adding RAM or processors), while maintaining the physical footprint and number of servers in the server cluster. See also horizontal scaling.

virtual server

Also called a Web Site (such as the Default Web Site). A virtual computer that resides on an HTTP server but appears to users as a separate HTTP server. Several virtual servers can reside on one computer, each one capable of running its own programs and each one with individualized access to input and peripheral devices.

Each virtual server has its own Internet domain name and Internet Protocol (IP) address and appears to users as an individual Web site. Some Internet Service Providers (ISPs) use virtual servers for those clients who want to use their own domain names. An ISP may want to create multiple Internet Information Services (IIS) 5.0 Web Sites and unpack Commerce applications for different clients into separate IIS Web Sites. Commerce applications under different IIS Web Sites can share global resources. See also Web site.

visit

A series of requests by a user. A visit begins in one of two ways: the user can be referred to the site through a link, or the user can type the site URL in his or her browser. A visit ends when a specified period of time (the default is 30 minutes) has passed without any additional requests from the user.

W

Web farm

Two or more Web servers connected together for the purpose of sharing resources. Typically, servers in a Web farm share resources through load balancing software, such as Network Load Balancing, to increase fault tolerance and permit redistribution of load in case of failure. These servers appear to the user as a single server with a single Internet Protocol (IP) address. Also called a server farm or server cluster.

Web server

In general use, a computer equipped with the server software that uses Internet Protocols (IPs) such as HTTP to respond to Web client requests on a Transmission Control Protocol/Internet Protocol (TCP/IP) network.

Web site

In general use, a collection of files and applications accessed through a Web address, covering a specific theme or subject, and managed by a particular person or organization. Web sites typically use HTML to format and present information and to provide navigational facilities that enable users to move within the site and around the Web. From an Internet Information Services (IIS) 5.0 administration standpoint, Web Site specifically means a virtual server (such as the Default Web Site). See also virtual server.

X

XML

See Extensible Markup Language.

Index

A

access control 409
ACM/ACS 304, 321
Active Directory 39, 92, 223, 299, 325
   authentication 144
   availability 145
   monitoring tools 148
   replication 146
Active Server Pages (ASP) 519
Ad Server Migration tool 318, 330
Ad Server 304, 330
Ad sitelet 186
address profile 226
Administration and Management Tools 14, 88
Administration database 132, 434
advertising
   campaign goals 228
   item goals 228
   scoring and selection 228
   scoring 229, 230
ALE (Application Link Enable) 263, 264, 268
Analysis Report Writer 304
Analysis 304, 319
anonymous users 428
App Default Config resource 29, 47
Application Center 2000 5, 451
Application Center 393
Application Integration Components (AIC) 358
architecture 4, 78, 395
   capacity 82
   checklist 385
   hardware 82
   minimum configuration 78
   optimizing 99, 102
   performance 82
   sample 103
   service-to-service 82
ASP (Active Server Pages) 519
ATL Pipe Wizard 187

Auction sitelet 186
authentication 38, 144, 323, 390, 409, 413, 422, 423, 424, 426, 427, 478
   certificates 410
AuthFilter 421
AuthManager 421
Autocookie mode 425, 426
availability 85, 111
   Active Directory 145
   Administration database 132
   back-end systems 85
   Business Process Pipelines 140
   checklist 111, 385
   Commerce Server 126, 131
   Data Warehouse 142
   data 120
   database 125
   Direct Mailer 138
   environmental 117
   front-end systems 85
   hardware 117, 121
   HTTP 112
   measurements 128
   middle tier 124
   network 112, 117, 121
   operating system 143
   process 117
   Product Catalog System 136
   Profiling System 132
   security 118, 121
   server 121
   software 118
   SQL Server 148
   system 112
   Targeting System 137

B

backup 147, 152, 440, 441, 442, 443, 495
batch download 235, 236, 259, 260, 262, 263, 266, 267, 268, 285
batch processing 109
batch upload 271
BDAO 205

BizDesk Installer 185
Biztalk Editor 351
BizTalk Mapper 351
BizTalk Server Messaging Services 346
    receive functions 346
    transport services 347
BizTalk Server 6, 40, 277, 297
    data parsers 347
    data validation services 347
    document delivery services 347
    Orchestration Services 348
    Order Routing Manager 358
    ShippingMethodRouter component 359
    Splitter pipeline component 359
Blank Solution Site 172, 188
bottlenecks 534, 537, 542, 544
Business Analytics System 15, 89, 319
business data model 68
Business Desk 88, 89, 188, 300
    security 430
business object profile schema 202
business process checklist 387
business process diagram 68
Business Process Pipelines System 17, 90
Business Process Pipelines 140
business requirements 69
business rules 249
    pricing 250

C

cache key 337
CacheManager object 108, 526
caching
    static content 107
    static lookup data 107
campaigns 200, 461
capacity 23, 42, 79, 80, 508
    planning 507
    study 508
Catalog Migration tool 318
Catalog search 321
Catalog sitelet 186
catalog 44, 304
    BizTalk Server configuration 366
    exchange management 349
    exchange 356, 357
    export 356, 357
    generating 355
    import 356
    importing 27
    management scenario 350
    mapping 351

certificates 410
    client 410
    gift 193
    server 410
change
    advisory board 181
    database 181
    management 180
    process 182, 183
    requests for 180
channel 352, 371
checklists
    architecture 385
    availability 385
    business process 387
    Commerce Server security 391
    development and testing 386
    platform security 387
    post-production 439
    pre-production 439
CI (configuration item) 174, 175, 178
CIP (Commerce Interchange Pipeline) 304, 332
clustering
    SQL Server 394
ClusterSentinel 506
code example
    JDE_create_order 294
    JDE_mirrored_update 288
    JDE_orderform.txt 297
    JDE_sales_order 292
    SAP_create_order 274
    SAP_mirrored_update 278
    SAP_realtime_integration 280
    SAP_sales_order 272
coding standards 159
COM object 199
COM+ applications 5, 462
Commerce Interchange Pipeline (CIP) 304, 332
Commerce Server Business Desk 88, 89, 188, 300
Commerce Server Direct Mailer 21, 94, 321
Commerce Server features 158
Commerce Server Manager 88, 188
Commerce Server Pipeline Component Wizard 188
Commerce Server Site Packager 88, 188, 300, 320, 451
Commerce.BusinessDataAdmin object (BDAO) 205
conceptual design 68
configuration
    control 174
    item identification 174, 178

configuration *(continued)*
    management database 174, 176, 177
    management tools 190
    management 174
    planning 174
    status accounting 174, 179
    verification and auditing 174, 179
configuration item (CI) 174, 175, 178
Content Analyzer 304, 319
content management process 450
Content Replication Service (CRS) 452
content replication 146, 150
Content Replication 304, 320
Content Selection Framework (CSF) 20, 93
content 445
contingency plan 392
Contoso, Ltd. 11, 193
cookie 338, 341
cookies 412
    sharing 427
cost per request 519
counters 516, 517, 518, 527, 540
    Active Server Pages 516
    Commerce Server 516
    memory 516, 517, 527
    network 517, 540
    physical disk 517
    process 517, 518, 527
    SQL Server 518
    system 518
    thread 518
    Web 518, 540
CPU
    upper boundary calculation 522
    usage calculation 520, 521
Create SchemaObject.vbs 185
cross sell 304
CRS (Content Replication Service) 452
CSF (Content Selection Framework) 20, 93
CSOLEDB handles 221
currency
    multiple 340
    reference 340

D

data encryption 416
data flow diagram 68
data tampering 478
Data Warehouse 89, 142, 319, 408, 433
database
    offline 236, 237
    online 236, 237

Dbscripts 186
DCOM connector 241, 256, 257, 272, 279
Debug 186
debugging 176
DefaultParentURL 223
dehydrated schedule 349
DeleteDetailedData.vbs 186
deployment
    Active Directory 398
    Application Center 398
    architecture 395
    campaigns 461
    checklists 384
    COM+ applications 462
    Commerce Server features 398
    databases 464
    hardware 397
    packaging 400
    phase 382
    software 397
    tasks 383
    unpacking 402
deployment tools 451
    Application Center 2000 451
    CRS 452
    OpenDeploy 454
    SQL Server DTS 453
    third-party 454
    Visual InterDev 451
    Visual Studio 451
    WSH 454
design goals 158
development
    checklist 169
    completion criteria 170
    methodology 172
    phase 168
development and testing checklist 386
Direct Mail 304, 321, 322
Direct Mailer 21, 94, 138, 321, 406
Directory Migration Toolbox 327
disaster recovery plan 147
Disconnect Detailed Data.vbs 186
Discount sitelet 186
disk cost calculation 529
distribution list
    dynamic 321
    static 321
DMZ 414
DTS 318
Dynamic Directory 304, 323, 324

E

encryption 410
environments
    development 79
    redundant operating 79
    staging 79
    test 79
event-sequence charts 82
explicit targeting 22
Expression Builder 95
Expression Evaluator 22, 95
expressions 95, 323, 329

F

failure
    probability of 122
    reduction techniques 119
fault tolerance 98
feature analysis 304
Ferguson and Bardell 37
firewalls 72, 74, 75, 415
functional specification 158
functoids 352

G

gap analysis 304
GenCom component wrapper 283
gift certificates 193
    Business Desk modifications 195
    campaigns 200
    Checkout pipeline modifications 199
    deployment 201
    profile modifications 199
    report modifications 200
    site page modifications 198
    site resource modifications 198
    site terms modifications 200

H

hardware diagram 510
Headlines 186
hooks 538
Host Integration Server 6
hosting 414
HTTP Monitoring 506, 551

I

IDOC 271
IIS 5.0 (Internet Information Services
    security 389
IIS 5.0 (Internet Information Services) 299
implicit targeting 22
incident 497
    classification grid 499
    control process 498
    control 497
integration
    credit card authorization 251
    inventory 266
    OneWorld 281
    orders 270, 290
    physical architecture 234, 252, 253, 255
    pricing 262, 285
    product catalog 251, 258, 285
    SAP 254, 255
    shipping 251
    taxation 251
integration technique
    batch download 235, 259, 260, 262, 263, 266, 267, 268, 285
    batch upload 271
    combined real-time and batch 244
    mirrored update 235, 247, 260, 261, 268, 275, 277, 287, 295, 297
    queued component 273
    queued connector 235, 244, 293
    real-time connector 235, 240, 264, 265, 272, 279, 289, 291
    replication 252
integrity control 478
internationalization 87, 161
Internet Information Services (IIS) 5.0 299
inventory 266

K

keep-alive connections 541
keys 216, 218
Knowledge Manager 305, 321
known error 497

L

languages
    multiple 335
latency 513, 514, 539
LDAP 323, 324, 325

load balancing 98
   application 393
   network 393
load 536
locking 98
log files 487, 489, 490
LRUCache object 108

M

Membership Directory 327
Membership Migration tool 187, 318, 327, 328
membership 323, 325
Message Queuing 109, 275, 295
MetaEdit 190
metrics 536
   response time 536
   total system throughput 536
Microsoft .NET Enterprise Servers 5
Microsoft Cluster Tool 506
Microsoft Management Console (MMC) 189
Microsoft Network Monitor 552
Microsoft Project 157
Microsoft Visio 2000 Enterprise Edition 190
Microsoft Visual InterDev 189
Migration Ad Server tool 187
migration tool 318
   Ad Server Migration 318, 330
   Catalog Migration 318
   Membership Migration 318, 327, 328
   SQL Server DTS 318
   Transaction Migration 318, 333
migration 96
   Membership Directory 327
   planning 302
MinMaxShip 186
mirrored update 247, 248, 260, 261, 268, 275, 277, 287, 295, 297
MMC (Microsoft Management Console) 189
multiple currencies 340
multiple languages 335

N

NBTStat 551
Network Load Balancing 143, 393
Network Monitor 189
network segregation 416
networks 539
non-repudiation 478

O

OneWorld COM object 287, 291, 292
OneWorld GenCom component wrapper 283
OneWorld 281
Online Store 330
OpenDeploy 454
operational procedures 116, 491, 493
OPP (Order Processing Pipeline) 305, 331
optimization 544, 545, 546
Options dictionary 173
order form integration 361
Order Processing Pipeline (OPP) 305, 331
Order sitelet 186
orders 270, 290
   management 358
   receiving from BizTalk Server 363
   sending to BizTalk Server 361
organization profiles 38

P

packaging 400
Parent URL 224
ParentDN 223
Partner Service 41
Passport sitelet 186
performance 23, 42, 79
   metrics 113
   targets 169
   testing 475
Personalization & Membership 305
personalization 323
personnel 157
   accounting 12
   business managers 86, 164, 448
   executives 62, 157
   interface designers 12
   marketing & sales 62, 157
   marketing and sales 12
   security 12
   site designers 12
   site developers 12, 62, 162, 381, 448
   system administrators 12, 62, 86, 163, 381, 449
   technical writers 12
   technical 157
   testers 12, 381, 448
physical architecture
   integration 234, 252, 253, 255
physical conceptual design picture 68
pipelines 27, 331
Posting Acceptor 305, 320

Predictor resource 22, 95, 332
Predictor 305
pricing 262, 285
problem 497
   control 500
   isolation 500
   management 497
process/location matrix 68
Product Catalog System 18, 27, 91, 136, 330, 404
product catalog 251, 258, 285, 330
product information 336
profile definition keys 216, 218
profile mappings 226
   address profile 226
   UserObject profile 227
profile object
   properties 221
profile schema 202
Profile sitelet 186
profile 19
profiles
   database 201
Profiles Schema Mover 202
Profiling System 19, 92, 132, 300, 323, 406
   Active Directory stores 223
   CSOLEDB handles 221
   data size validation 223
   data type mappings 219
   design considerations 218
   operational considerations 215
   run-time considerations 221
   transactions 221
   utilities 201
project
   schedule 164
   scope 65
   team 161
   vision 64
Project Goals and Requirements 61, 64
Project Plan 61, 157
promotions 305, 333
   cross sell 333
   discount 333
   up sell 333
proxy accounts 429
Pstat.exe 551
Ptree.exe 551
Publish Transactions module 108
Publishing Wizard 305, 320
PuP Resource 185

Q

queued component 273
queued connector 244, 245, 293
queuing 98

R

real-time connector 240, 264, 265, 272, 279, 289, 291
recovery 147
_Recvpo.asp file 46
reference currency 340
Registration tool 187
rehydrated schedule 349
replication 146, 150
Report Writer 319
reports 490
requirements 68
   business 69
   capacity 79, 80
   international 87
   performance 79
   security 70
   site architecture 78
   system administration 86
   system integration 69
ResourceConfig 185
response time 536
Retail Solution Site 15, 172, 188
retry code 154
risk 67
   assessment 72
   management 392
   reduction 392
   severity 71
rules 305, 323, 329

S

SAP DCOM connector 241, 256
SAP 254
scalability 84
scaling
   horizontally 84, 99, 101
   vertically 84, 99, 100
Schema Tool 185
search
   catalog 322
   Internet 322
   intranet 322
Search 305, 322
secrecy 478
Secure Sockets Layer (SSL) protocol 541

security 25, 33, 70, 118, 121, 159, 495
    Active Directory 418
    Administration database 434
    BizTalk Server 348
    breach 478
    Business Desk 430
    checklist 387
    Commerce Server services 435
    Commerce Server 391, 421
    credit card 417
    Data Warehouse 433
    database 418, 433
    dynamic content 437
    file system 388
    IIS settings 78
    IIS 389
    log files 434
    network 414
    personnel 391
    physical 391
    planning 77
    platform 411
    services 389
    SQL Server settings 78
    SQL Server 419
    static content 437
    Supplier Site 414
    testing 478
    user accounts 388
    Web server 420
    Windows 2000 settings 78
    Windows 2000 387
server configuration matrix 82
shopper capacity calculation 524
Single Sign-On (SSO) 429
site
    administration plan 492
    checkup 484
    content 445
    global 459
    information 336
    management 86
    medium-to-large 457
    profile 159, 169
    small-to-medium 455
    terms 321
    topology 83
Site Packager 88, 188, 300, 320, 400, 403, 451
Site Status sample 185
site terms
    Site Terms catalog 208
Site Terms Viewer 202, 213
Site Terms 200

Site Vocabulary 305, 321, 322
sitelet
    Ad 186
    Auction 186
    Catalog 186
    Discount 186
    Order 186
    Passport 186
    Profile 186
software diagram 511
Solution Site 6, 172, 173
    Blank 6, 172, 188
    Retail 7, 15, 172, 188
    Supplier 7, 44, 46, 172, 188, 436
spoofing 75, 478
SQL Profiler 189, 552
SQL Server DTS 318, 453
SQL Server 6, 148, 325
    clustering 148, 151
    replication 150
SSO (Single Sign-On Support) 429
Supplier Solution Site 44, 46, 172, 188, 436
    example configuration 50
system
    administration 86
    architecture 160
    integration 69
    monitoring 502, 505
    tuning process 537
System Monitor 189, 552
system thresholds 143

T

Tag Tool 305, 320
target group 230
Targeting System 20, 93, 137
targeting 230
TCA (transaction cost analysis) 80, 509
test cases 470
test error reports 471
test plan 468, 469
testing
    ad hoc 467
    authentication breach 478
    black box 468
    bottom tier 476
    browser compatibility 475
    build verification (BVT) 467
    data tampering 478
    deployment 438
    function 467
    integration 467

testing *(continued)*
    integrity control breach 478
    links 474
    middle tier 475
    network 479
    non-repudiation breach 478
    payment transactions 479
    performance 475
    secrecy breach 478
    security 478
    stress 467
    top tier 472
    usability 473
    visual appearance 473
    white box 468
think time 536
throttling 98
throughput 98, 536
transaction cost analysis (TCA) 80, 509
Transaction Migration tool 318, 333
transactions 305, 333, 509
troubleshooting 505
    approach 501

U

usage analysis 512
usage profile 42, 81, 169, 512
user capacity 83
user profile
    import DTS task 226
UserObject profile 227
UserProfile object 329

V

VB Pipe Wizard 187
VCTurbo 330
Visual InterDev 451
Visual Studio Analyzer 189, 553
Visual Studio 451

W

WAS (Web Application Stress tool) 189, 506,
    515, 518, 551
Web Application Stress tool (WAS) 189, 506,
    515, 518, 551
Web Capacity Analysis Tool (WCAT) 506
Widgets 185
Windows Clustering 394
Windows Management Instrumentation
    (WMI) 190

Windows Scripting Host (WSH) 454
WinRep Deployment Software Development
    Kit 506
WMI (Windows Management
    Instrumentation) 190
WSH (Windows Scripting Host) 454

X

XLANG
    language 348
    schedule 348
    Scheduler Engine 349

Z

Z-Table 291

Ready
solutions
for the
IT administrator

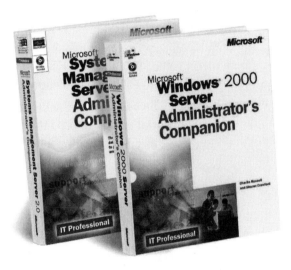

Keep your IT systems up and running with the ADMINISTRATOR'S COMPANION series from Microsoft. These expert guides serve as both tutorials and references for critical deployment and maintenance of Microsoft products and technologies. Packed with real-world expertise, hands-on numbered procedures, and handy workarounds, ADMINISTRATOR'S COMPANIONS deliver ready answers for on-the-job results.

Practical, *portable* guides for
IT administrators

For immediate answers that will help you administer Microsoft products efficiently, get ADMINISTRATOR'S POCKET CONSULTANTS. Ideal at the desk or on the go from workstation to workstation, these hands-on, fast-answers reference guides focus on what needs to be done in specific scenarios to support and manage mission-critical products.

Microsoft® Windows NT® Server 4.0
Administrator's Pocket Consultant

U.S.A.	$29.99
U.K.	£20.99
Canada	$44.99

ISBN 0-7356-0574-2

Microsoft SQL Server™ 7.0
Administrator's Pocket Consultant

U.S.A.	$29.99
U.K.	£20.99
Canada	$44.99

ISBN 0-7356-0596-3

Microsoft® Windows® 2000
Administrator's Pocket Consultant

U.S.A.	$29.99
U.K.	£20.99
Canada	$44.99

ISBN 0-7356-0831-8

Microsoft®
mspress.microsoft.com

Microsoft® Resource Kits— powerhouse resources to minimize costs while maximizing performance

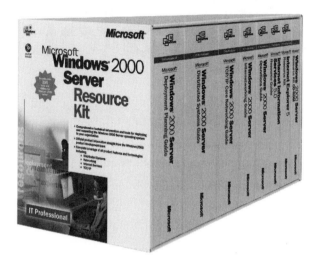

Deploy and support your enterprise business systems using the expertise and tools of those who know the technology best—the Microsoft product groups. Each RESOURCE KIT packs precise technical reference, installation and rollout tactics, planning guides, upgrade strategies, and essential utilities on CD-ROM. They're everything you need to help maximize system performance as you reduce ownership and support costs!

Microsoft® Windows® 2000 Server Resource Kit
ISBN   1-57231-805-8
U.S.A. $299.99
U.K.   £189.99 [V.A.T. included]
Canada $460.99

Microsoft Windows 2000 Professional Resource Kit
ISBN   1-57231-808-2
U.S.A. $69.99
U.K.   £45.99 [V.A.T. included]
Canada $107.99

Microsoft BackOffice® 4.5 Resource Kit
ISBN   0-7356-0583-1
U.S.A. $249.99
U.K.   £161.99 [V.A.T. included]
Canada $374.99

Microsoft Internet Explorer 5 Resource Kit
ISBN   0-7356-0587-4
U.S.A. $59.99
U.K.   £38.99 [V.A.T. included]
Canada $89.99

Microsoft Office 2000 Resource Kit
ISBN   0-7356-0555-6
U.S.A. $59.99
U.K.   £38.99 [V.A.T. included]
Canada $89.99

Microsoft Windows NT® Server 4.0 Resource Kit
ISBN   1-57231-344-7
U.S.A. $149.95
U.K.   £96.99 [V.A.T. included]
Canada $199.95

Microsoft Windows NT Workstation 4.0 Resource Kit
ISBN   1-57231-343-9
U.S.A. $69.95
U.K.   £45.99 [V.A.T. included]
Canada $94.95

***Microsoft*®**

mspress.microsoft.com

END-USER LICENSE AGREEMENT FOR MICROSOFT SOFTWARE

IMPORTANT—READ CAREFULLY: This Microsoft End-User License Agreement ("EULA") is a legal agreement between you (either an individual or a single entity) and Microsoft Corporation ("Microsoft") for the Microsoft software product identified below, which includes computer software and may include associated media, printed materials, and "online" or electronic documentation ("SOFTWARE PRODUCT"). By installing, copying, or otherwise using the SOFTWARE PRODUCT, you agree to be bound by the terms of this EULA. If you do not agree to the terms of this EULA, do not install, copy or use the SOFTWARE PRODUCT.

MICROSOFT COMMERCE SERVER 2000 RESOURCE KIT

The SOFTWARE PRODUCT is protected by copyright laws and international copyright treaties, as well as other intellectual property laws and treaties. The SOFTWARE PRODUCT is licensed, not sold.

1. GRANT OF LICENSE. This EULA grants you the following rights:

    a. Use and Copy. You may install and use copies of the SOFTWARE PRODUCT on an unlimited number of computers located at your premises for the sole purpose of installing, evaluating, configuring, deploying and maintaining Microsoft Commerce Server 2000. You may also make copies of the SOFTWARE PRODUCT for backup and archival purposes.

    b. Electronic Documents. Solely with respect to electronic documents included with the SOFTWARE PRODUCT, you may make an unlimited number of copies (either hardcopy or electronic form), provided that such copies shall be used for internal purposes and are not published or distributed to any third party.

    c. Sample Code. In addition to the rights granted above, Microsoft grants you the right to use and modify the source code version of those portions of the SOFTWARE PRODUCT that are identified as sample code in the appropriate documentation and/or listed in a samples directory located in the SOFTWARE PRODUCT, for the sole purposes of installing, evaluating, configuring, deploying and maintaining Microsoft Commerce Server 2000.

    d. No Other Rights. Microsoft and its suppliers retain title and all ownership rights to the SOFTWARE PRODUCT. All rights not expressly granted are reserved to Microsoft.

2. DESCRIPTION OF OTHER RIGHTS AND LIMITATIONS.

    a. Not For Resale, Rental or Transfer. You may not sell, resell, sublicense, assign or otherwise transfer the SOFTWARE PRODUCT (including all component parts, media, printed materials, and any updates). You may not rent, lease or lend the SOFTWARE PRODUCT.

    b. Limitations on Reverse Engineering, Decompilation, and Disassembly. You may not reverse engineer, decompile, or disassemble the SOFTWARE PRODUCT, except and only to the extent that such activity is expressly permitted by applicable law notwithstanding this limitation.

    c. Support Services. Microsoft may, but is not obligated to, provide you with support services related to the SOFTWARE PRODUCT ("Support Services"). Use of Support Services is governed by the Microsoft polices and programs described in the user manual, in "on line" documentation and/or other Microsoft-provided materials. Any supplemental software code provided to you as part of the Support Services shall be considered part of the SOFTWARE PRODUCT and subject to the terms and conditions of this EULA. With respect to technical information you provide to Microsoft as part of the Support Services, Microsoft may use such information for its business purposes, including for product support and development. Microsoft will not utilize such technical information in a form that personally identifies you.

    d. Termination. Without prejudice to any other rights, Microsoft may terminate this EULA if you fail to comply with the terms and conditions of this EULA. In such event, you must destroy all copies of the SOFTWARE PRODUCT and all of its component parts.

3. COPYRIGHT. All title and copyrights in and to the SOFTWARE PRODUCT (including but not limited to any images, photographs, animations, video, audio, music, text, and "applets" incorporated into the SOFTWARE PRODUCT), the accompanying printed materials, and any copies of the SOFTWARE PRODUCT are owned by Microsoft or its suppliers. The SOFTWARE PRODUCT is protected by copyright laws and international treaty provisions. You may not copy the printed materials, if any, accompanying the SOFTWARE PRODUCT.

4. U.S. GOVERNMENT RESTRICTED RIGHTS. All SOFTWARE PRODUCT and documentation provided to the U.S. Government pursuant to solicitations issued on or after December 1, 1995 is provided with the commercial rights and restrictions described elsewhere herein. All SOFTWARE PRODUCT provided to the U.S. Government pursuant to solicitations issued prior to December 1, 1995 is provided with RESTRICTED RIGHTS as provided for in FAR, 48 CFR 52.227-14 (JUNE 1987) or FAR, 48 CFR 252.227-7013 (OCT 1988), as applicable.

5. EXPORT RESTRICTIONS. You agree that you will not export or re-export the SOFTWARE PRODUCT to any country, person, entity or end user subject to U.S. export restrictions. You specifically agree not to export or re-export the SOFTWARE PRODUCT (i) to any country to which the U.S. has embargoed or restricted the export of goods or services, which currently include, but are not necessarily limited to Cuba, Iran, Iraq, Libya, North Korea, Sudan and Syria, or to any national of any such country, wherever located, who intends to transmit or transport the products back to such country; (ii) to any end-user who you know or have reason to know will utilize the SOFTWARE PRODUCT in the design, development or production of nuclear, chemical or biological weapons; or (iii) to any end-user who you know or have reason to know has been prohibited from participating in U.S. export transactions by any federal agency of the U.S. government.

MISCELLANEOUS

If you acquired this SOFTWARE PRODUCT in the United States, this EULA is governed by the laws of the State of Washington.

If you acquired this SOFTWARE PRODUCT in Canada, unless expressly prohibited by local law, this EULA is governed by the laws in force in the Province of Ontario, Canada; and, in respect of any dispute which may arise hereunder, you consent to the jurisdiction of the federal and provincial courts sitting in Toronto, Ontario.

If this product was acquired outside the United States, then local law may apply.

Should you have any questions concerning this EULA, or if you desire to contact Microsoft for any reason, please contact the Microsoft subsidiary serving your country, or write: Microsoft Sales Information Center/One Microsoft Way/Redmond, WA 98052-6399.

NO WARRANTY. MICROSOFT EXPRESSLY DISCLAIMS ANY WARRANTY FOR THE SOFTWARE PRODUCT OR RELATED SUPPORT SERVICES (IF ANY). TO THE MAXIMUM EXTENT PERMITTED BY APPLICABLE LAW, THE SOFTWARE PRODUCT AND ANY RELATED SUPPORT SERVICES AND DOCUMENTATION ARE PROVIDED "AS IS" WITHOUT WARRANTIES OR CONDITIONS OF ANY KIND, EITHER EXPRESS OR IMPLIED, INCLUDING, WITHOUT LIMITATION, THE IMPLIED WARRANTIES OR CONDITIONS OF MERCHANTABILITY, FITNESS FOR A PARTICULAR PURPOSE, OR NONINFRINGEMENT. THE ENTIRE RISK ARISING OUT OF USE OR PERFORMANCE OF THE SOFTWARE PRODUCT REMAINS WITH YOU.

LIMITATION OF LIABILITY. TO THE MAXIMUM EXTENT PERMITTED BY APPLICABLE LAW, IN NO EVENT SHALL MICROSOFT OR ITS SUPPLIERS BE LIABLE FOR ANY SPECIAL, INCIDENTAL, INDIRECT, OR CONSEQUENTIAL DAMAGES WHATSOEVER (INCLUDING, WITHOUT LIMITATION, DAMAGES FOR LOSS OF BUSINESS PROFITS, BUSINESS INTERRUPTION, LOSS OF BUSINESS INFORMATION, OR ANY OTHER PECUNIARY LOSS) ARISING OUT OF THE USE OF OR INABILITY TO USE THE SOFTWARE PRODUCT OR THE PROVISION OF OR FAILURE TO PROVIDE SUPPORT SERVICES, EVEN IF MICROSOFT HAS BEEN ADVISED OF THE POSSIBILITY OF SUCH DAMAGES. IN ANY CASE, MICROSOFT'S ENTIRE LIABILITY UNDER ANY PROVISION OF THIS EULA SHALL BE LIMITED TO THE GREATER OF THE AMOUNT ACTUALLY PAID BY YOU FOR THE SOFTWARE PRODUCT OR US$5.00; PROVIDED HOWEVER, IF YOU HAVE ENTERED INTO A MICROSOFT SUPPORT SERVICES AGREEMENT, MICROSOFT'S ENTIRE LIABILITY REGARDING SUPPORT SERVICES SHALL BE GOVERNED BY THE TERMS OF THAT AGREEMENT. BECAUSE SOME STATES AND JURISDICTIONS DO NOT ALLOW THE EXCLUSION OR LIMITATION OF LIABILITY, THE ABOVE LIMITATION MAY NOT APPLY TO YOU.

SI VOUS AVEZ ACQUIS VOTRE PRODUIT MICROSOFT AU CANADA, LA GARANTIE LIMITÉE SUIVANTE VOUS CONCERNE:

EXCLUSION DE GARANTIE. MICROSOFT EXCLUT EXPRESSÉMENT TOUTE GARANTIE RELATIVEMENT AU PRODUIT LOGICIEL OU À TOUT SERVICE D'ASSISTANCE S'Y RAPPORTANT (SELON LE CAS). DANS TOUTE LA MESURE PERMISE PAR LA LÉGISLATION APPLICABLE, LE PRODUIT LOGICIEL ET TOUS SERVICE D'ASSISTANCE OU AUTRE DOCUMENTATION S'Y RAPPORTANT SONT FOURNIS « TELS QUELS » SANS AUCUNE GARANTIE OU CONDITION QUELLE QU'ELLE QU'ELLE SOIT, EXPRESSE OU IMPLICITE, LÉGALE OU CONVENTIONNELLE, ÉCRITE OU VERBALE, Y COMPRIS, SANS LIMITATION, LES GARANTIES LÉGALES OU CONDITIONS DE QUALITÉ MARCHANDE, D'APTITUDE À UN USAGE PARTICULIER, OU D'ABSENCE DE CONTREFAÇON. VOUS ASSUMEZ TOUS LES RISQUES DÉCOULANT DE L'UTILISATION ET DE LA PERFORMANCE DU PRODUIT LOGICIEL.

LIMITATION DE RESPONSABILITÉ. DANS TOUTE LA MESURE PERMISE PAR LA LÉGISLATION APPLICABLE, MICROSOFT OU SES FOURNISSEURS NE SONT EN AUCUN CAS RESPONSABLES DES DOMMAGES SPÉCIAUX, INDIRECTS, ACCESSOIRES OU MORAUX QUELS QU'ILS SOIENT (Y COMPRIS, SANS LIMITATION, LES DOMMAGES RÉSULTANT DE LA PERTE DE PROFITS, DE L'INTERRUPTION DES AFFAIRES, DE LA PERTE D'INFORMATIONS COMMERCIALES OU DE TOUTE AUTRE PERTE PÉCUNIAIRE) DÉCOULANT DE L'UTILISATION OU DE L'IMPOSSIBILITÉ D'UTILISER LE PRODUIT LOGICIEL OU DÉCOULANT DES SERVICES D'ASSISTANCE FOURNIS OU DU DÉFAUT D'AVOIR FOURNI DES SERVICES D'ASSISTANCE, ET CE, MÊME SI MICROSOFT A ÉTÉ AVISÉE DE LA POSSIBILITÉ DE TELS DOMMAGES. EN TOUT ÉTAT DE CAUSE, LA RESPONSABILITÉ DE MICROSOFT EN VERTU DE TOUTE DISPOSITION DE CETTE CON-VENTION NE POURRA EN AUCUN TEMPS EXCÉDER LE PLUS ÉLEVÉ DES DEUX MONTANTS SUIVANTS: (I) LE MONTANT QUE VOUS AVEZ RÉELLEMENT PAYÉ POUR LE PRODUIT LOGICIEL, OU (II) $5.00 U.S. DANS L'ÉVENTUALITÉ OÙ VOUS AVEZ CONCLU UNE ENTENTE DISTINCTE AVEC MICROSOFT RELATIVEMENT À DES SERVICES D'ASSISTANCE, LA RESPONSABILITÉ DE MICROSOFT RELATIVEMENT AUX SERVICES D'ASSISTANCE SERA ENTIÈREMENT RÉGIE PAR CETTE ENTENTE POUR SERVICES D'ASSISTANCE. PUISQUE CERTAINS ÉTATS OU JURIDICTIONS NE PERMETTENT PAS L'EXCLUSION OU LA LIMITATION DE RESPONSABILITÉ, IL EST POSSIBLE QUE LA LIMITATION CI-DESSUS NE VOUS CONCERNE PAS.

SI VOUS AVEZ ACQUIS CE PRODUIT LOGICIEL AU CANADA, SAUF LORSQU'EXPRESSÉMENT PROHIBÉ PAR LA LOI LOCALE, CETTE CONVENTION EST RÉGIE PAR LES LOIS EN VIGUEUR DANS LA PROVINCE D'ONTARIO, CANADA. POUR TOUT DIFFÉREND QUI POURRAIT DÉCOULER DES PRÉSENTES, VOUS RECONNAISSEZ LA COMPÉTENCE DES TRIBUNAUX FÉDÉRAUX ET PROVINCIAUX SIÉGEANT À TORONTO, ONTARIO.

SI VOUS AVEZ DES QUESTIONS CONCERNANT CETTE LICENCE OU SI VOUS DÉSIREZ COMMUNIQUER AVEC MICROSOFT POUR QUELQUE RAISON QUE CE SOIT, VEUILLEZ CONTACTER LA SUCCURSALE MICROSOFT DESSERVANT VOTRE PAYS, DONT L'ADRESSE EST FOURNIE DANS CE PRODUIT, OU ÉCRIVEZ À: MICROSOFT SALES INFORMATION CENTER, ONE MICROSOFT WAY, REDMOND, WASHINGTON 98052-6399.

System Requirements

To use the Microsoft Commerce Server Resource Kit CD-ROM, you need a computer equipped with the following minimum configuration:

- PC with a Pentium-compatible 233-MHz or higher processor

- Microsoft Me (Millennium Edition), Microsoft Windows 2000 Professional, Windows 2000 Server, or Windows 2000 Advanced Server with Service Pack 1 or later

- Microsoft Word

- WinZip or equivalent decompression and archiving utility

- 32 to 128 MB of RAM, depending on operating system requirements

- 30 MB of available hard-disk space

- Microsoft Internet Explorer 5.5 or later

- Windows 2000-compatible video graphics adapter with 800x600 minimum resolution

- Microsoft Mouse or compatible pointing device

Actual requirements will vary based on your system configuration and the applications and features you choose to install.

OWNER REGISTRATION CARD   *Register Today!*   0-7356-1128-9

Return the bottom portion of this card to register today.

Microsoft® Commerce Server 2000 Resource Kit

FIRST NAME   MIDDLE INITIAL   LAST NAME

INSTITUTION OR COMPANY NAME

ADDRESS

CITY   STATE   ZIP

(   )

E-MAIL ADDRESS   PHONE NUMBER

U.S. and Canada addresses only. Fill in information above and mail postage-free.
Please mail only the bottom half of this page.

start faster **go** farther

For information about Microsoft Press®
products, visit our Web site at
mspress.microsoft.com

Microsoft®